Armed Diplomacy:
Two Centuries of American Campaigning

5-7 August 2003
Frontier Conference Center
Fort Leavenworth, Kansas

Published by Books Express Publishing
Copyright © Books Express, 2012
ISBN 978-1-78039-681-1

Books Express publications are available from all good retail and online booksellers. For publishing proposals and direct ordering please contact us at: info@books-express.com

Contents

Page

Foreword v

Introduction vii

Occupation and Stability Dilemmas of the Mexican War:
Origins and Solutions by Irving W. Levinson 1

The Politics of War in the Department of the Missouri, 1861-1864 by Donald B. Connelly........17

The US Army in the South: Reconstruction as Nation Building by Joseph G. Dawson III 39

The Frontier Army and the Occupation of the West, 1865-1900 by Robert Wooster 65

The US Army and Nation Building and Pacification in the Philippines
by Brian McAllister Linn 77

Lost in the Snow: The US Intervention in Siberia During the Russian Civil War
by Major Jeff Stamp, US Air Force...91

State Department Soldiers: Warlords, Nationalists, and Intervention by Katherine K. Reist 105

There and Back Again: Constabulary Training and Organization, 1946-1950
by Robert Cameron 115

Reconstructing the Civil Administration of Bremen, US Enclave by Bianka J. Adams 137

Victors and Vanquished: Americans as Occupiers in Berlin, 1945-1949 by William Stivers 157

Ps, Gs, and UW—Korea Style by Richard L. Kiper 177

Special Forces in Afghanistan: Oct 01-Mar 02 by Richard W. Stewart.......................................189

To Succeed Where Others Have Failed: Forming and Training the Afghan National Army, 2003
by Lieutenant Colonel Kevin W. Farrell, US Army 247

Occupations: Then and Now by Richard W. Stewart...267

"The Small Change of Soldiering" and American Military Experience by Roger Spiller 281

About the Presenters..291

Appendix A. Program...295

Foreword

The first annual military history symposium sponsored by the US Army Training and Doctrine Command (TRADOC) and hosted by the Combat Studies Institute (CSI) at Fort Leavenworth, Kansas, took place in August 2003. It brought together an outstanding group of civilian historians and military officers for the purpose of discussing a variety of historical case studies and the ways in which they illuminate current military issues and operations. As the subtitle of the symposium indicates, the topics spanned two centuries of American campaigning, ranging from the Army's "nation-building" activities during the Reconstruction of the post-Civil War South and the trans-Mississippi West; through US counterguerrilla warfare in the American Civil War, the Philippines, Korea, and Latin America; to the US occupation of Germany after World War II and American interventions in Mexico, China, Russia, Panama, and Afghanistan. Without exception, the presentations were thought provoking and elicited lively discussion among the attendees.

This volume contains most of the presentations made at the symposium. The entire symposium program can be found at appendix A. The presentations can also be found at <http://cgsc.leavenworth.army.mil/CSI/research/Conferance-03/ConfAnnouncement.asp>, the CSI website for the conference. A few presentations do not appear in these pages, generally for one of two reasons. Either they were not designed for publication, or they were still awaiting clearance for publication when the time arrived to send the present volume to the printer. Concerning the latter category, once a presentation has received clearance for publication, it will be posted on the cited web site.

The first annual military history symposium was an enlightening experience, both intellectually and practically, for those who attended. We hope the readers of this volume will share in that experience, even as we begin finalizing arrangements for the second annual conference, "Turning Victory Into Success: Military Operations After the Campaign," to be held in September 2004. As we look forward to the upcoming symposium, we at Fort Leavenworth would like to thank what was in 2003 the Doctrine, Concepts, and Strategy Directorate at TRADOC, specifically Major General Michael Vane and Colonel Michael Starry, US Army, Retired, for providing the support that made the first annual conference possible.

Lawyn C. Edwards
Colonel, Aviation
Director, Combat Studies

Introduction

In August 2003, military history scholars gathered at Fort Leavenworth, Kansas, in the first of what we intend to be a series of symposia specifically addressing issues that are of vital importance to today's and tomorrow's Army. Specifically, the 2003 gathering examined the question of "Armed Diplomacy," that is, instances in our military past which provide insights into the challenges that face our Army today in Kosovo, Afghanistan, and Iraq, and which are likely to characterize many of the Army's future engagements.

The symposium originated with members of the TRADOC Headquarters staff who admired *America's First Battles* and believed that the command's military history assets could provide similar insights for the current operational environment. The Combat Studies Institute (CSI) at Fort Leavenworth, TRADOC's center for historical research since 1979, took on administration of the symposium, and reached out to military historians in sister services and in colleges and universities around the country. All agreed that the history of American campaigning and expeditionary warfare provided the most obvious application of the past to the present.

I believe you will be stimulated and engaged by the results. I encourage you to begin with Roger Spiller's thoughtful overview, which elegantly frames many of the questions posed by these presentations. Then tackle each of the essays. I hope you will take the time to join in the discussion by providing your comments, using the links provided. This process—a symposium followed by postings on the worldwide web—will result in a hard-copy publication which we believe will take its place alongside other important CSI historical studies. This publication will serve as an indispensable teaching tool in our schoolhouses *and* as a resource for our senior leadership. Please join us. Together, we will produce a worthwhile contribution to developing great leaders for the challenges of tomorrow's operations.

Kevin P. Byrnes
General, U.S. Army
Commanding

Occupation and Stability Dilemmas of the Mexican War: Origins and Solutions

Irving W. Levinson

Traditionally, historians categorize the war between the United States and Mexico as a series of conventional battles that began at Palo Alto and ended when General Winfield Scott captured Mexico City. From this perspective, the Treaty of Guadalupe Hidalgo represented the inevitable diplomatic consequence of those victories. That picture is incomplete. A powerful force of Mexican guerrillas, the US Army's response to the challenges of occupation, the resolution of a difficult stabilization dilemma, and the persistence of significant resistance by mobile forces of the Mexican army throughout 1847 all proved to be important factors.[1] In this new perspective, Mexico stands as a distinct society whose history and resulting characteristics defined the types of resistance and accommodation open to the Mexican government during the war. The most important of those realities remained the deep and violent divisions between Mexicans that resulted from both the colonial experience and the early years of the nation's independence.

The first and most important of these chasms lay along lines of ethnicity and race. Unlike the British North American colonies, colonial Mexico was a land in which the Indians and their offspring permanently outnumbered the European settlers and their descendants. Almost three centuries after European settlement began, the *criollos* [native-born whites) and the resident Spaniards comprised barely 20 percent of Mexico's population.[2] That minority offered limited opportunity to the rest of the population as the political, economic, and social levers of power in New Spain remained primarily under the control of Spanish officials and their acquisitive, resentful, *criollo* colonists. In this environment, an arrangement emerged in which Indians who sought to retain control some of their remaining preconquest lands received protection from the Spanish Crown. In turn, the royal government used the Indians as a counterweight to colonists who sought to expand their own political and economic power at the expense of the metropolitan regime in Madrid. Also, the colony remained culturally divided because differing concepts of land ownership and political power generated continual conflict. These factors, combined with the heritage of a cruel Spanish conquest and horrific conditions of forced labor, prevented the emergence of a unified colonial society.[3]

Mexico's War of Independence did not change this situation. That conflict ended in 1821 with the *criollos* firmly in control of the newly independent state. This minority divided into three factions. The Conservatives favored preserving the colonial social structure, a state religion, a very limited suffrage, and a centralized federal regime dominated by the landed and the wealthy. Their Liberal opponents opposed all of these objectives and sought a more open and egalitarian society. The Moderate faction occupied a middle ground between these positions. For much of 1821-1846, the traditionalists remained in control and emphatically rejected such contemporary Spanish concepts as universal male suffrage. During the 1820s, less than 1 percent of Mexico City's estimated population of 200,000 owned the property necessary to qualify them as voters.[4] Politics remained the preserve of a small elite, and legal equality remained a concept that many prominent Mexicans of the day held in contempt.[5] By and large, Mexicans of primarily European descent governed the nation.[6] One of the earliest US Ambassadors to Mexico, Waddy Thompson, concluded, "the aristocracy of color is quite as great in Mexico as it is in this country."[7] Also he wrote of the sharp distinctions of wealth: "The lands of the country belong to a few large proprietors, some of whom own tracts of eighty and one hundred leagues square, with herds of sixty and eighty thousand head of cattle grazing upon them, whilst the Indian laborers upon those farms rarely have enough meat to eat."[8]

During 1821-1846, politically and economically dominant groups of Mexicans began both legal and physical assaults on lands that Indian villages and other poor Mexicans still held in communal ownership. They wanted to convert this territory from subsistence farming to market-oriented production. Consequently, many of the communities faced the grim alternatives of becoming tenants on land that had once been their own or of abandoning their homes. The loss of self-determination and the economic degradation inherent in such a choice guaranteed a violent response. During this time, peasant rebellions took place in Oaxaca (1827), Veracruz (1836), and Guerrero (1842).[9]

The most massive such revolt was the Alvarez Rebellion of 1844. During that uprising, rebels committed many violent acts against the persons and properties of estate owners over 60,000 square miles.[10] Given the threat that this revolt posed to the established social order, Conservatives and Liberals put aside their bitter differences to oppose it. The Mexican army crushed this and many other revolts. To further complicate matters, both military officers and civilian politicians accepted the use of force as a legitimate means of changing regimes and policies. The army's conduct militarized the political process just as the politicians' conduct politicized and factionalized the military. Dozens of coups against the national government took place during this period, so when US forces entered Mexican territory, they crossed into a nation at war with itself as well as being at war with an invader. This duality remains essential in understanding subsequent courses of events that involved governments, armies, and civilians.

The critical phase of the conflict began when General Winfield Scott took the port of Veracruz. Before beginning his march inland toward Mexico City, Scott sought to minimize potential conflicts with civilians. For example, his 1 April 1847 General Order 87 stipulated harsh punishment for US soldiers who committed crimes such as assassination, murder, rape, and malicious assault. The first record of a death sentence imposed for violating one or more of these acts occurred barely one week later on 9 April 1847.[11] Following the implementation of that sentence and lashing of errant soldiers, "such offenses by American soldiers abated in central Mexico."[12]

Those American officers trained at the US Military Academy and other literate men of the age studied an example of civilian hostility to invaders by reading the works of the most famous military theorist of their day, Baron Antoine Henri Jomini of France. This scholar general's experience as one of Napoleon Bonaparte's most valued officers included a leading role in invading Spain and the subsequently disastrous efforts to pacify that nation. The brutality with which the French troops treated the civilian populace, the occupiers' zealousness in assaulting widely respected social practices, and their hostility toward the Catholic Church fanned the flames of resistance.

Given such conduct, as well as the brutal tactics that Bonaparte employed in his struggles against Spanish guerrillas, patriots and the clergy converted their struggle against the invader into a broadly based nationalist uprising. Jomini claimed a single siege—Saragossa—cost his forces slightly less than 5,000 casualties, with the Spaniards' losses being 15,000 soldiers and 30,000 civilians.[13] Because the army that Scott took with him to Veracruz totaled little more than 12,000, even one American victory would have been pyrrhic. The Americans could not afford to provoke Mexican civilians as Jomini had provoked the Spanish.

In fact, the US Army needed some degree of Mexican acquiescence. Scott explained to his troops that their thrust toward Mexico City could succeed only if the civilians residing along his line of march agreed to supply provisions. Consequently, he ordered them to pay for all items they took lest the Mexicans hide those commodities. Further, he ordered that "The people, moreover, must be conciliated, soothed, or well treated by every officer and man of this army, and by all its followers."[14] To avoid provoking any religious hostility, he instructed his soldiers "to keep out of the way or to pay to the Catholic religion and to its ceremonies every decent mark of respect and deference."[15]

Understandably, the Mexican government decided to both disrupt the convoys carrying ammunition, hospital supplies, and other necessities to Scott's forces and to limit the Americans' access to central Mexico's agricultural bounty. Only 10 days after the battle of Cerro Gordo, President Pedro Maria Anaya signed a decree calling for the establishment of a light corps to function as part of the National Guard.[16] Consisting exclusively of volunteer forces that might be raised "by any citizen having sufficient means and influence in the country in which he resides," the leaders of these groups could begin organizing as soon as they received the federal or state government's authorization [*patente*] to proceed.[17] As an additional incentive, the national government promised to reimburse any commanders who funded the operations of their own units.

In restricting the qualifications for seeking a *patente* to those with "means and influence," the regime in Mexico City provided a clear demonstration of its enduring desire to concentrate power within a tiny group. Since only a small minority of Mexicans possessed such wealth and influence, these requirements excluded all but a few from qualifying for such appointment.[18] Of the 72 Mexicans who received such authorization, 21 were serving military officers.[19] These units would focus on several targets: convoys, small parties of Americans detached from the main force for foraging, stragglers, and garrisons. Scott acknowledged his concerns about—

> The danger of having our [supply] trains cut and destroyed by the exasperated rancheros, whose houses are thinly scattered over a wide surface, and whom it is almost impossible, with our small cavalry force, to pursue and to punish and . . . the consequent necessity of escorting trains seventy odd miles up, and the same down, with a meager cavalry that must from day to day become, from that intolerable service, more and more meager.[20]

The danger of which Scott wrote in April 1847 materialized in less than two months. By May-June 1847, the partisan strength along the Veracruz-Mexico City corridor had grown to the point at which the task of escorting American Major General John Anthony Quitman required "1,200 to 1,500 men."[21] American records detail substantial light corps attacks on convoys during summer and fall 1847.

On 4 June 1847 a supply convoy under Lieutenant Colonel James S. McIntosh's command left Veracruz with 128 wagons and 688 men. The Mexicans attacked this convoy three times on 6 June. The following day, McIntosh halted the column at Paso de Ovejas and requested reinforcements after losing 24 wagons (12 percent of the total) and taking 25 casualties. When 500 reinforcements arrived on 11 June under Brigadier General George Cadwaladar's command, the Americans successfully attacked the National Bridge at a cost of 32 dead and wounded. The convoy then proceeded to La Hoya, where the guerrillas attacked them on 20-21 June with a force that Cadwaladar estimated to consist of 700 men.[22] The Americans fought their way through to Scott's main force.

Given this situation, the next convoy left with a far larger escort. In July 1847, General Franklin Pierce led a force that included 2,500 troops, 100 wagons, 700 mules, and $1 million in specie. Some 1,400 Mexicans attacked the convoy at the National Bridge, forcing Pierce to return Veracruz for artillery and additional troops. He then set out again for Puebla. American reports listed a loss of 30 men in this encounter. On 6 August 1847, an American force of 1,000 men under Major Folliott T. Lally's command set out from Veracruz and suffered 105 casualties before reaching its goal.[23] The three companies of reinforcements sent out to aid this convoy on 13 August 1847 turned back to Veracruz after losing every wagon except one to partisan forces at Puente Nacional. In September 1847, yet another convoy went eastward from Veracruz. By this time, the Americans' estimation of the light corps' fighting ability stood so high that Major William Booth Taliaferro observed: "The last command which left the seaboard was defeated and had to retreat . . . and we left with the full expectation of a bloody and severe fight every day until we succeeded in our enterprise, and no day broke over our heads on the march but was looked upon as the last by many of our numbers."[24]

Nightfall often brought no rest for the weary. Taliaferro noted, "indeed it is so common to hear the reports of *escopettes* [shotguns] that I hardly care to get up at night to go out and see where they are fired from, and sleep soundly although I may be called to a fierce conflict before morning."[25] Also, the light corps placed great importance on picking off stragglers and men who otherwise became separated from their units. During the advance from Veracruz to Mexico City, General Gideon Johnson Pillow admonished his troops to avoid straggling or straying or carousing outside of camp on the grounds that such actions cost his unit more casualties than battles did.[26] Perhaps the best measure of the Mexicans' effectiveness in this regard lay in the warning the commanding general issued to American soldiers as they moved eastward from Jalapa toward the capital on 30 April 1847: "To prevent straggling and marauding, the roll of every company of the army will be called at every halt, by, or under the eye of an officer. In camps and in quarters there must be at least three such roll calls daily. Besides, stragglers, on marches, will *certainly* [author's italics] be murdered or captured by rancheros."[27]

Small parties of Americans leaving the main body of troops on foot or on horseback often fared no better than individual stragglers. For example, on 14 August 1847, a party of dragoons led by Scott's aide de camp, Lieutenant Alexander Hamilton, set out to determine if a foundry near Chalco might be used to manufacture shot and shells. A force of approximately 200 Mexican lancers surprised the dragoons, killing Hamilton and an undetermined number of others. The Americans withdrew.[28]

Mexicans proved equally adept at launching brief yet deadly attacks on small American garrisons. Commodore Matthew C. Perry described the situation in Villahermosa:

> In the meantime, Mexican troops infiltrated the town every night to pick off Americans; this was the kind of fighting they liked and they were good at it. Commander Bigelow of *Scorpion* decided to clean up Echagaray's army at Tamulte and dispersed it; but dispersing Mexicans was no more effective than chasing hungry deer out of a vegetable garden. They always drifted back, to take pot shots at "gringos."[29]

Even those Americans ensconced in the formidable fortress of Perote found themselves under attack. According to Colonel Thomas Claiborne, "The guerrillas were swarming everywhere under vigorous leaders, so that for safety the drawbridge was drawn up every night."[30] In summary, from May through September 1847, the light corps repeatedly attacked convoys bringing reinforcements, munitions, money, and other supplies to the advancing US Army in central Mexico. Although the American supply line did not break, the efforts required to keep that route open resulted in steady casualties and a significant commitment of troops.

Soon after he took Mexico City on 14 September 1847, Scott formulated a more severe response to this continuing disruption of the occupation. By mid-October, he finalized a plan mandating the creation of three new posts of between 500 and 750 men each along his supply route and garrisoning Puebla with a force of between 1,200 and 2,000 soldiers.[31] By November 1847, the American posts at Perote, Puente Nacional, Rio Frio, and San Juan consisted of 750 troops each with an additional 2,200 soldiers stationed at Puebla.[32] He ordered these garrisons to send out extended patrols that were to seek out and engage the enemy. The 5,200 troops thus committed to such work constituted 21 percent of the 24,500 US soldiers in central Mexico as of November 1847.[33] If we add the 1,300+-man escorts for the supply trains to the previously cited number of soldiers stationed at these posts, the percentage of American forces involved in trying to secure supply lines during late 1847 rises from 21 percent to 26 percent of Scott's total force.

Also during October 1847, Secretary of War William Learned Marcy ordered that "Their [the light corps'] haunts and places of rendezvous should be broken up and destroyed."[34] This directive gradually evolved into a scorched-earth policy that led even that most vigorous defender of the American cause during the past century and a half, Justin H. Smith, to acknowledge: "The torch was applied with much liberality, on suspicion, and sometimes on general principles, to huts and villages; and in the end a black swath of destruction, leagues in width, marked the route."[35] Despite these measures, the light corps attacks continued. A harsher American response soon followed. On 12 December 1847, Scott declared,,"No *quarters* [his italics] will be given to known murderers or robbers whether called guerillos or rancheros and whether serving under Mexican commission or not. They are equally pests to unguarded Mexicans, foreigners, and small parties of Americans, and ought to be exterminated."[36] Records indicate that only a few such executions took place.

Despite these efforts, light corps attacks continued. On 5 January 1848, they struck a 1,300-soldier US military and civilian convoy at Paso de Ovejas. After noting that the

Mexicans had "cut up" a company of mounted riflemen and taken about 280 cargo mules, the commanding officer, Colonel Dixon H. Miles, requested 400 to 500 more troops and a section of artillery to fight his way through.[37] The Mexicans preceded the injury inflicted by that attack with a 4 January 1848 looting of the same target. According to General David Emanuel Twiggs, a force of 100 to 400 guerrillas attacked near Santa Fe, Veracruz, and escaped with 250 pack mules and goods valued at between $150,000 and $200,000.[38]

Although the light corps posed a threat to the US Army, it would be wrong to assert that they represented the leading edge of a national resistance movement; to the contrary. Millions of the Mexicans along Scott's line of march preferred to go about their lives with indifference. For example, consider the city of Xalapa, capital of the state of Veracruz. From the US Army's entrance into city on 19 April 1847 to the date of their evacuation on 2 July 1848, only one instance of lethal violence against any American soldier within the city was recorded in either Mexican or US records. The city council showed an apparent indifference to the occupation by informing the state government of its objections to an intensification of guerrilla activities in the community.[39]

Scott minimized his forces' involvement in the local government.[40] By respecting and strengthening acquiescent local officials, the Americans limited the extent to which their front-line personnel became ad hoc town managers and civil servants. The decision to leave Mexicans in control of Mexican communities also allowed citizens of the occupied nation to preserve a greater measure of autonomy and self-respect. Municipal authorities could exercise considerable autonomy as long as they offered no opposition to the United States. In the previously cited case of Xalapa, the city government raised its revenues, debated its priorities, allocated its funds, and tended to the usual myriad of local concerns with no US interference.[41] However, in communities in which local officials organized resistance, the Americans dismissed the officials. For example, in Tampico, Colonel William Henry Gates fired the local police force on the grounds that it had conspired against the US Army.[42]

In Mexico City, the Americans promptly acted to ensure that the municipal government continued to function. Scarcely a week after the fall of the capital, civil and military governor, General Quitman, announced that the city's authorities would retain both their regular sources of revenue and the internal customs taxes the national government formerly collected.[43] The new military governor proved so eager to ensure that the municipal police retained the respect of one and all that he ordered "Soldiers and followers of the army who shall be found ill treating said police in the lawful discharge of their duties will be regarded as serious offenders and severely punished."

Whenever possible, American officers implemented Marcy's directive to take advantage of the division among Mexicans.[44] For example, in the months preceding the capital's fall, Mexican Vice President Valentin Gomez Farias sought to confiscate and sell various forms of church assets to raise additional funding for the war. This action aroused a level of opposition so fierce that two states, Oaxaca and Jalisco, flatly refused to enforce the law. Subsequently, Scott decided to curry favor with religious Mexicans by extending the protection of his army to the church's property. On 13 November 1847, the Office of the Civil and Military Governor of Mexico City prohibited the sale of ecclesiastical property without the US Army's consent.[45] This blatant and significant act no doubt impressed Mexico's Conservatives.[46]

So although Scott might be faulted for failing to bring the Mexican army's light corps under control, he and his forces nonetheless avoided provoking the *levee en masse* that rendered so miserable Jomini's occupation of Spain.[47] However, by late 1847, a powerful new force entered the military and political equations of leaders on both sides. The Americans' destruction of most of Mexico's army meant that the nation's rulers had lost the ultimate means of force with which they had previously suppressed peasant rebellions. Villages across Mexico took advantage of this situation and used it to launch new rebellions or intensify old ones. As indicated by their targets, these partisans identified the owners of large estates and the national government as their primary enemies. Thirty-five separate peasant revolts occurred in various parts of Mexico during 1846-48.[48]

In all of these except for two, Mexican officials characterized the rebels as being either Indians or peasants. In the reports of both field officers and senior officials of the national government, the theme of ethnic conflict occurs repeatedly. For example, in describing rebellions in the states of Mexico, San Luis Potosi, and Veracruz during May 1848, federal Minister of the Interior and Exterior Luis de la Rosa wrote of: "the war of death and of extermination that the subversives have declared on the white class [*clase blanca*] and the well-to-do."[49] He argued that the rebellions in these areas had the potential to reach those occurring in the Yucatan and the Sierra Gorda.[50] Several rebel manifestos included a call for the redistribution of land.[51]

That brings us to the military significance of these revolts. The largest revolt occurred in the Yucatan where the rebel ranks included an estimated 30,000 Indians whom the state governor contended were waging a "war of extermination against the white race."[52] At the other extreme, the number of soldiers deemed necessary to restore order in the Pueblan community of Huachinango totaled only 50 men.[53] Perhaps the best indication of the overall severity of the problem is that by 13 December 1848, 21,278 Mexican soldiers fought against rebellions in Huasteca, in the northwest, and in the Yucatan.[54] That figure exceeded the number of troops the Mexican army massed to defend the national capital against Scott in September 1847.[55] In addition, the various National Guard units, whose strength totaled 24,973 men by February 1849, remained ready to suppress rebellions that occurred within the individual states."[56]

The Mexican regime urgently needed to crush these revolts. The rebels threatened the social order of the nation. However, the task of raising and maintaining a new army for that work required restoring the government's sovereignty, and that would come only with peace. A cessation of hostilities would bring advantages to the United States as well. Most obviously, a durable peace and a recognized international boundary required the cooperation of a compliant Mexican government. For the long term, President James K. Polk conceded that "Both politically and commercially, we have the deepest interest in her [Mexico's] regeneration and prosperity. Indeed, it is impossible that, with any just regard to our own safety, we can ever become indifferent to her fate."[57]

In the short term, the persistent problem of the light corps along the Veracruz-Mexico City corridor remained, and Scott plainly warned his superiors that the most likely result of continued military occupation would be the same as the likely result of annexation:

"that all Mexico, or rather the active part thereof, would again relapse into a permanent state of revolution, being with one against annexation."[58] Consequently, the 2 February 1848 Treaty of Guadalupe Hidalgo and the almost equally important truce agreement of 6 March 1848 included both declarations that hostilities between the two nations were concluded and a stabilization program. The most blatant part of that commitment was Article 16 of the 6 March 1848 truce agreement. It read:

> If any body of armed men be assembled in any part of the Mexican Republic with a view of committing hostilities not authorized by either government, it shall be the duty of either or both of the contracting parties to oppose and disperse such body; without considering those who compose it, as having forfeited the protection of nations, unless they have been guilty of robbery or murder.[59]

Thus, Mexico procured from the United States more than a guarantee of American military action against any group of antigovernment guerrillas unfortunate enough to cross the US Army's path. Since American troops held Acapulco, Camargo, Mexico City, Monterrey, Puebla, Perote, Rio Frio, Saltillo, Tampico, Veracruz, and a number of other important points throughout central and northern Mexico, the Mexican government thereby received a guarantee that the Americans would defend all points should the rebels try to seize them. Faced with this reality, the rebellious peasants tried to avoid the US Army. Major Folliot T. Lally described one such situation:

> The hostile Indians have set up a claim to the land in that section of the country based upon the right of being the original owners prior to the invasion of Cortes, but do not design to war with the United States. They are, however, lawless and barbarous, and have for several months been savage in their progress through this part of the country where the towns of Huejutla, Huasteca, and Osiliwama [sic] lay.[60]

Throughout Mexico, the rebellious Indians and peasants targeted other Mexicans rather than Americans for attack.

US stabilization efforts also included supplying weapons and ammunition to the Mexican government. The first such transaction took place on 7 June 1848, when the Americans sold the Mexican government 5,125 rifles and cartridge belts with 762,400 rifle cartridges, 208 carbines with 30,000 carbine cartridges, and 124 fulminating rifles with 87,500 cartridges.[61] The US Army sold this equipment at a deeply discounted price, charging only half of the market cost of rifles at the start of the war.[62] In July 1848, the Americans once again disposed of infantry equipment on generous terms. General Persifor Frazier Smith, the last US military governor of Mexico City, ordered his subordinates:

> . . . to deliver to the Mexican Government, Señor Don Francisco Arrangoiz, all muskets remaining on hand, at the ordnance depot; and two hundred thousand flint musket cartridges: together with muskets and accoutrements turned in by the 12th & 14th Regiments Infantry and 1st Regt. of Artillery. Previous to delivery you will agree with the agent on

the prices to be paid to the United States for Said Military Stores, by the Mexican Government; and furnish him, finally, with Invoices of the articles he received, with the prices offered, and take from the corresponding receipts.[63]

Also, the Mexicans could expect to receive an ample supply of artillery and other resources once both governments ratified the Treaty of Guadalupe Hidalgo. The applicable clause specified that Mexico would receive "all castles, forts . . . together with all the artillery, arms, apparatus of war, munitions, and other public property which were in said castles and forts and which shall remain there at the time when this treaty shall be duly ratified by the Mexican Republic."[64] Captain Robert E. Lee gave one indication of the amount of weaponry involved in the transaction. In a letter written from the National Palace in Mexico City, he estimated that as of late 1847, the United States had taken some 600 artillery pieces.[65]

A third component of the stabilization effort consisted of providing the level of physical safety necessary for internal commerce to function. Americans invited both Mexican and foreign-born merchants to join its Army convoys traveling the Veracruz-Mexico City route. This offer met with an enthusiastic response from traders and those customers who transacted business along this key commercial route. For example, in the 16 April 1848 Mexico City-Veracruz convoy, half of the 400 wagons belonged to Mexican merchants. The US Army offered escorts on another key route as well. Any Mexican reaching Mazipil [Zacatecas] or Parras [Nuevo Leon] with gold or silver for commercial sale received a military escort from those places to Saltillo. From there, a new group of American protectors escorted them onward toward the coast.[66] Merchants traveling on less important journeys occasionally received protection.[67] The American escorts provided adequate security from the bandits and looters who inevitably emerge in time of war.

Not surprisingly, the Mexican army's light corps ceased to be a major problem once the Treaty of Guadalupe Hidalgo and the subsequent armistice went into effect. After all, Mexican officers led this most effective of their nation's forces, and almost all of them obeyed the order to lay down their arms. Only three of the 72 federally sanctioned commanders did not comply with the order to cease hostilities. Instead, they turned against the government in Mexico City on the grounds that the regime had betrayed the nation.

The Mexican government sought even more aid. In August 1848, a senior Mexican diplomat, *Señor* Don Francisco Arrangoiz, met with Secretary of State James Buchanan to ask that the Americans—

> . . . furnish to Mexico three or four thousand troops, to be employed, in the first place, against the Indians of Yucatan, and if need be, against Indians in other portions of Mexico. In case of necessity, they would, also, be employed to sustain the present government against the revolutionists. He proposed that they should receive from Mexico the same pay and rations as troops of the United States, and in all other respects should be placed on the same footing, and is willing that the next installment of the Treaty due on the 30th May, 1849, should be applied to this purpose.[68]

Secretary of State Buchanan demurred. The last American soldier left Mexico on 6 September 1848, and the Mexican government subsequently brought the incipient civil war to a successful conclusion.

In conclusion, the Mexican War should be seen not only as a series of set-piece battles but also as a multiple-sided conflict that involved war between Mexicans as well as between Mexicans and Americans. More important, the events of this war demonstrate that the United States successfully confronted issues of occupation policy and stabilization programs as early as the middle of the 19th century.

This conflict also illustrates an eternal lesson: national unity remains the prerequisite for success in any war. Throughout the campaign, the United States profited from internal divisions within Mexico. Consider for a moment the fate of Scott's army. Initially, he led a force of less than a single modern division through more than 4 million Mexicans who lived in the states bordering his line of march.[69] Had he confronted a united population determined to use every foot of mountainous terrain to wage the type of resistance that the Spanish waged against Jomini, the results might have been different. But 1848 Mexico was not united. Indeed, Mexico's rulers' acute desire to reestablish their domestic dominance proved to be a crucial component in bringing the diplomatic process to a conclusion.

Third, each national army entered the war with distinctive advantages. The new family of US artillery pieces first produced in 1840 and the highly mobile tactics with which the US Army's flying artillery employed its weapons proved so substantial that every fixed position that came under the fire from American mortars and cannon fell to its forces.[70] That artillery played a crucial role in open field battles as well.[71] By contrast, Mexico's greatest strength lay in the skill of its cavalry officers. Despite all efforts to destroy them, the light corps along the Veracruz-Mexico corridor remained a menace until its own government ordered it to lay down its arms. In northern Mexico, General Zachary Taylor took Monterrey and held at Buena Vista, but he could not challenge the command of the countryside between Tampico and Saltillo that the cavalry of Generals Jose Vicente Minon and Jose Lopez Urrea exercised.[72] Neither side blunted the other's main advantage.

Fourth, the degree to which the American definition of stabilization changed from the mid-19th century to the current time strikes me as quite significant. In 1848, the United States sought only to ensure the existence of a stable, sovereign, and reasonably cooperative government in Mexico. By contrast, the objective of creating a democratic order in fallen foes emerged as a core component of our recent military campaigns in Bosnia and Iraq. The task of first destroying a nation's armed forces and then reconstructing its civil society remains a lengthier and more complex process than President Polk's more traditional approach of invasion and stabilization.

Finally, this war leaves us with a puzzle far older than the 19th century and as recent as the wars in Afghanistan and Iraq. By what means and with what precision can we determine the extent to which the civilian populace of a liberated (or invaded) state will stand aside and thereby refrain from tipping the scales of conflict? I do not know, but the answer remains a worthy, if perhaps interminable, quest.

Notes

1. All of the contentions in this presentation will be developed at considerably greater length in a forthcoming book titled *War Within Wars: Mexican Guerrillas, Domestic Elites, and the Americans, 1846-1848* (Fort Worth: Texas Christian University Press, 2004).

2. Timothy E. Anna, *The Fall of the Royal Government in Mexico City* (Lincoln: University of Nebraska Press, 1978), 6.

3. Enrique Florescano, *Memory, Myth, and Time in Mexico: From the Aztecs to Independence* (Austin: University of Texas Press, 1994), 184. Florescano, the preeminent modern historian of this period, characterized the colony as "a disintegrated mosaic of contrasting peoples, ethnic groups, languages, and cultures disseminated in an extensive territory with poor communication."

4. Michael P. Costeloe, *Hombres de bien in the Age of Santa Anna*, published in *Mexico in the Age of Democratic Revolutions, 1750-1850*, Jaime E. Rodriguez O, ed. (Boulder, CO: Lynne Reiner Publishers, Inc., 1994), 247.

5. Jose Maria Luis Mora, *Ensayos, Ideas, y Retratos*, (Mexico, D.F.), (Ediciones de la Universidad Nacional Autonoma de Mexico, 1941), 17. Mora, the leading Mexican historian writing during that period, set down the widely held belief of his fellow *criollos* (Mexicans of European descent): "The evil understanding that has produced the principle of legal equality almost always has been the source of innumerable grief and awful results among the peoples who have adopted the representative system."

6. Jose Maria Luis Mora, *Ensayos, Ideas y Retratos,* 159, "With much success, the white population is the dominant one of the day because of the number of their individuals, because of their learning and wealth, because of the exclusive influence they exercise in business, and because of the advantageous position they guard with respect to the others.

7. Waddy Thompson, *Recollections of Mexico* (New York: Wiley and Putnam, 1846), 12.

8. Ibid., 150. Since a league's traditional measure is 3 miles, Thompson's statement meant that the landowners' properties ranged in size from 720 to 900 square miles.

9. Brief essays about these rebellions and source documents are found in Leticia Reina, *Las Rebeliones Campesinas en Mexico (1819-1906)*, (Mexico City, D.F.), Siglo Veintiuno, 1980. For those interested in a history of these rebellions in one time and place, I highly recommend Peter F. Guardino, *Peasants, Politics, and the Formation of Mexico's National State: Guerrero, 1800-1857* (Stanford, CA: Stanford University Press, 1986).

10. Ibid., 267. Also see John Mason Hart's essay on the Alvarez Rebellion in Frederick Katz, *Riot, Rebellion, and Revolution: Rural Social Conflict in Mexico* (Princeton, NJ: Princeton University Press, 1988).

11. For an overview of this conflict in a multi-generational context, see General Order No. 87, Orders and Special Orders—Headquarters of the Army—War With Mexico 1847-1848, Entry Number 134, Records Group 94, Adjutant General's Office, National Archives and Records Administration, Washington, DC and General Order No. 101, Orders and Special Orders—Headquarters of the Army—War With Mexico 1847-1848, Entry Number 134, Records Group 94, Adjutant General's Office, National Archives and Record Administration, Washington, DC.

12. *Mexico Under Fire: Being the Diary of Samuel Ryan Curtis 3rd Ohio Volunteer Regiment During the American Military Occupation of Northern Mexico 1846-1847*, Joseph E. Chance, ed. (Fort Worth, TX: Texas Christian University Press, 1994), 20.

13. Antoine Henry Jomini, *Life of Napoleon—Volume I*, translated from the French with notes by H. W. Halleck, LL.D, (New York: D. Van Nostrand, 1864), 444-47.

14. Major General Winfield Scott, General Order No. 128 issued 30 April 1847 in Jalapa found in *General Scott's Orders (41 ½)*, Orders and Special Orders—Headquarters of the Army—War With Mexico, 1847-1848, Entry Number 134, Records Group 94, Adjutant General's Office, National Archives and Records Administration, Washington, DC.

15. Major General Winfield Scott, *General Order 285*, found in the First Division Papers, Army of Mexico Papers, Army History Research Collection, US Army Military History Insitute.

16. *Reglamento Para El Servicio De Secciones Ligera De La Guardia Nacional De Los Estados Y Territorios De La* Republica, *Archivo de la Defensa Nacional, pagina* 0060, *foja* 2586, *expediente* XI/481.3, *Archivo de la Defensa Nacional*, Mexico City, DF. The light corps is probably best categorized as a partisan unit as the US Army subsequently defined that term. According to General Orders 100 issued on 24 April 1863, "Partisans are soldiers armed and wearing the uniform of their army but belonging to a corps which acts detached from the main body for the purpose of making inroads into the territory occupied by the enemy. If captured they are entitled to all the privileges of prisoners of war." Except for the fact that some light corps members did not wear regular uniforms, they fit this definition.

17. Ibid., 60.

18. The initial cost to equip a mounted partisan force of 200 men roughly equaled four times the annual salary of a federal cabinet minister. A startup budget is found on *pagina* 0003, *foja* 2582, *expediente*, *Archivo de la Defensa Nacional*, Mexico City, DF, XI/481.3.

19. Applications and authorizations are found in *fojas* 2505, 2582, and 2586 of *expediente* XI/481.3, *Archivo de la Defensa Nacional*, Mexico City, DF. These 21 officers included five generals, seven colonels, four lieutenant colonels, and five captains. The extent to which the Mexican government adhered to the financial qualifications set forth in the original proclamation cannot be determined. However, the fact that two members of the lower clergy received such authority would indicate that the requirements could be waived.

20. Letter of General Winfield Scott to Brevet Colonel Henry Wilson dated 13 April 1847 in *Executive Document 56 of the House of Representatives—Messages From the President of the United States Transmitting Reports From the Secretary of State and the Secretary of War With Accompanying Documents in Compliance With the Resolution of the 7th February 1848* (Washington, DC, 20 March 1848), 136.

21. James K. Polk and others, *Executive Document 56*, 216-17.

22. Nathan Covington Brooks, *A Complete History of the Mexican War: Its Causes, Conduct, and Consequences*, (Philadelphia, PA: Grigg, Elliot, & Co., 1849), 444-52.

23. Ibid., 454.

24. 10 September 1847 journal entry of Major William Booth Taliaferro, *The Aztec Club Archives—Historical Papers* (Carlisle, PA: US Army Military Institute).

25. Ibid.

26. Jacob J. Oswandel, *Notes of the Mexican War, 1846-1847-1848*, (Philadelphia, PA, 1885), 153.

27. Major General Winfield Scott, General Order No. 128 issued 30 April 1847 in Jalapa found in *General Scott's Orders (41 ½)*, Orders and Special Orders—Headquarters of the Army—

War With Mexico, 1847-1848, Entry Number 134, Records Group 94, Adjutant General's Office, National Archives and Records Administration, Washington, DC.

28. Ethan Allen Hitchcock, *The Ethan Allen Hitchcock Diary, Volume 50* Tulsa, OK: Gilcrease Museum of Western History), 17-19,

29. Commodore Matthew C. Perry quoted by Samuel Eliot Morison in *Old Bruin Commodore Matthew Calbraith Perry, 1794-1858* (Boston, MA: Little, Brown, & Co., 1967), 238.

30. Colonel Thomas Claiborne, *Colonel Thomas Claiborne's Memoirs Written When He Was About Seventy Years of Age*, Volume XV-G220, *The Justin H. Smith Collection*, Benson Latin American Collection, (Austin, TX: University of Texas), 211.

31. Winfield Scott in a letter to Secretary of War William Learned Marcy of 13 October 1847 cited by James K. Polk in *Executive Document 56*, 219.

32. Jose Marie Roa Barcena, *Recuerdos de la Invasion Norteamericana 1846-1848, Tomos I-III,* Editorial Porrua, SA, Mexico City, DF, 1971. Tomo 3, 168.

33. Ibid, 168.

34. Secretary of War William Learned Marcy to General Winfield Scott in a 6 October 1847 order cited by John Reese Kenly, *Memoirs of a Maryland Volunteer* (Philadelphia, PA: J.B. Lippincott & Co., 1873), 309.

35. Justin H. Smith, *The War With Mexico, Volumes I and II*, (Gloucester, MA, 1919) and reprinted by Peter Smith, 1963, *Volume II*, 156.

36. Major General Winfield Scott, General Order No. 372, 12 December 1847, Orders and Special Orders—Headquarters of the Army—War With Mexico 1847-1848, Entry Number 134, Records Group 94, Adjutant General's Office, National Archives and Records Administration, Washington, DC. The previously referenced General Orders 100 of 24 April 1863 stated: "Men, or squads of men, who commit hostilities, whether by fighting, or inroads for destruction of plunder, or by raids of any kind, without commission, without being part of the organized hostile army, and without sharing continuously in the war, but who do so with intermitting returns to their homes and avocations, or with the occasional assumption of the semblance of peaceful pursuits, divesting themselves of the character or appearance of soldiers—such men, or squads of men, are not public enemies and therefore, if captured, are not entitled to the privileges of prisoners of war, but shall be summarily treated as highway robbers or pirates."

The question of whether a light corps member(s) not wearing a Mexican army uniform while attacking Americans ought to have been classified as a highwayman or a partisan can be disputed. At least one aspect of his conduct would have fallen into each category.

37. Letter of 5 January 1848 from Lieutenant Colonel Dixon H. Miles, cited by James K. Polk and others, *Executive Document Number 56*, 259.

38. Letter of 5 January 1848 from General David E. Twiggs to General Roger Jones, Document Number T-37 found in *Letters Received by the Adjutant General's Office*, Microcopy M-567, Roll 393, National Archives and Records Administration, Washington, DC.

39. *Paginas 104-110, Volumen 59, Actos del Cabildo, Archivo Historico del Municipio de Jalapa,* Jalapa, Veracruz, Mexico. The counselors feared that arming additional forces would lead to an increase in crime.

40. Proclamation of 6 October 1847 signed by Major General J.A. Quitman, *caja* 211, *legajo* 135, *Ramo de Gobernacion, Archivo General de la Nacion*, Mexico City, DF.

41. *Volumenes 59-60, Actos del Cabildo, Archivo Historico del Municipio de Jalapa.* The minutes of the *cabildo* (city council) taken during the US occupation contain no reference to the US civil and military governor countermanding any order of the city council in any of the above-cited areas of jurisdiction. However, on one occasion, the United States imposed an assessment on the community for maintaining the American garrison. Records do not indicate that the Americans ever received the money. The US commander promptly complied with one request the city council made during the occupation—that a structure with thick walls other than the principal church be used to store ammunition.

42. Unnumbered Order of Colonel William Gates, *Mexican War—Orders 1845-1848, Tampico, March 1847-June 1848* from *Mexican War Orders 1845-1848, Volume 7 of 25*, Entry 134, Records Group 94, Adjutant General's Office, National Archives and Records Administration, Washington, DC.

43. Proclamation of 22 September 1847 issued by Major General J.A. Quitman, *caja* 1, *foja* 2, *seccion sin classificacion* 1847, *Ramo de Gobernacion, Archivo General de la Nacion*, Mexico City, DF.

44. William Learned Marcy in a letter of 9 July 1846 to General Zachary Taylor cited in Thirtieth Congress, First Session, *Executive Document No. 60, Messages of the President of the United States* (Washington, DC, 1848), 157. "In a country so divided into races, classes, and parties as Mexico is, and with so many local divisions among departments, and personal divisions among individuals, there must be great room for operating on the minds and feelings of a large portion of the inhabitants, and including them to wish success to an invasion which has no desire to injure their country; and which, in overthrowing their oppressors, may benefit themselves."

45. *El Monitor Republicano* issue of 23 November 1847, *Hemeroteca Nacional de Mexico*.

46. George Ballantine, *The Mexican War by an English Soldier Comprising Incidents and Adventures in the United States and Mexico With the American Army* (New York: W.A. Townsend & Co., 1860), 272. As this soldier confirmed, the national capital by no means remained as safe and calm as Xalapa. Throughout the American occupation of Mexico City, attacks occurred on individual Americans and small groups of soldiers. Most commonly, these took place late at night when the US troops returned to their barracks from the red light district. Scott subsequently cautioned soldiers against leaving their quarters unless they were in small parties or were well armed.

47. George Gordon Meade, *Life and Letters of George Gordon Meade, Major General United States Army—Volume 1*, 109-110 cited in *Mexican War Diary of General George B. McClellan*, William Starr Myers, ed. (Princeton, NJ: Princeton University Press, 1917), 18-19. Meade argued that the regular troops of the US Army adhered to a much higher standard of conduct in civil-military relations than did the numerous self-trained and officered volunteer regiments of the Army. Numerous reports of other officers confirm that point.

48. *Pagina* 00641, *foja* 2868, *expediente* XI/481.3 and also *pagina* 00468, *foja* 2196, *expediente* XI/481.3; *pagina* 00015, *foja* 2229, *expediente* XI/481.3; *pagina* 00259, *foja* 2868, *expediente* XI/481.3; *pagina* 00301, *foja* 2868, *expediente* XI/481.3; *pagina* 00701, *foja* 2868, *expediente* XI/481.3; *pagina* 00526, *foja* 2868, *expediente* XI/481.3; *paginas* 00538-00539, *foja* 2868, *expediente* XI/481.3; *pagina* 00031, *foja* 2189, *expediente* XI/481.3; *foja* 2312, *expediente* XI/481.3; *pagina* 00004, *foja* 2349, *expediente* XI/481.3; *pagina* 00148, *foja* 2772, *expediente* XI/481.3, *pagina* 00154, *foja* 2772, *expediente* XI/481.3; *pagina* 00020, *foja* 2739, *expediente* XI/481.3; 00006, *pagina* 00023, *foja* 2773, *expediente* XI/481.3; *pagina* 00051, *foja* 2890, *expediente* XI/481.3 of the *Archivo de la Defensa Nacional*, Mexico City ,DF, Mexico City. Also see *foja* E3, *caja* 334, *Sin seccion* 1847; *foja* 3, *caja* 337, *Sin seccion* 1847; and *foja* E9, *caja* 326, *Sin Seccion* 1847 of the *Ramo de Gobernacion of the Archivo General de la Nacion*, Mexico City, DF.

Also see Jean Meyer, cited by Daniel Molina Alvarez, *La passion del padre Jarauta*, Mexico City, DF, *Gobierno de la Ciudad de Mexico*, 108-109; Leticia Reyna, *Las Rebeliones Campesinas en Mexico (1819-1906)*, (Mexico City, DF: Siglo Veintiuno, 1998), 363-65; Proclamation of 3 December 1847 From Governor Lorenzo Arellano of Guanajauto, *foja* E9, *caja* 326, *Sin seccion 1847, Ramo de Gobernacion, Archivo General de la Nacion*, Mexico City, DF; Veracruz State Document 67, Letter of 30 July 1848 from Governor Juan Soto, Box 347, *Sin seccion, Ramo de Gobernacion, Archivo General de la Nacion*, Mexico City, DF.

49. Letter of 9 May 1848 from Minister of the Interior and Exterior Luis de la Rosa to the Minister of War and Marine, folder 2772, section XI/481.3/2772, Archivo de la Defensa Nacional, Mexico City,DF, 00046-00048.

50. Ibid.

51. Jean Meyer, cited by Daniel Molino Alvarez, *La passion del padre Jarauta*, (Mexico City, DF: *Gobierno de la Ciudad de Mexico*), 108-109.

52. Letter of 14 June 1848 from Governor Barbachano to the Minister of War and Marine, folder 2820, section XI/481.3/2820, (Mexico City, DF: *Archivo de la Defensa Nacional*) 00004-00006.

53. Report dated 21 January 1848 from J. Naf. Guerra of the *Gobierno del Estado Libre y Soberano de Puebla* to the Minster of War and Marine 00006, folder 2773, section XI/481.3, (Mexico City, DF: *Archivo de la Defensa Nacional*) 00023.

54. *Memoria Del Secretario De Estado Y Del Despacho de Guerra y Marina Leide En La Camera de Diputados El Dia 9 Y En La De Senadores El 11 De Enero de 1849*, (Mexico, DF: *Imprenta de Vicente Garcia Torres en el Ex-Convento del Espiritu Santo*, 1849), 8-9, *Biblioteca Nacional, Archivo General de la Nacion*.

55. Justin H. Smith, *The War With Mexico, Volume II*, 142.

56. Sheet 3, folder 2, series *Milicia Nacional*, section *Guerra*, Group *Gobernacion*, *Archivo Historico de Estado de Mexico*, Toluca, Mexico.

57. James K. Polk, *Message From the President of the United States to the Two Houses of Congress at the Commencement of the Thirtieth Congress, December 7, 1847* (Washington, DC: Van Benthuysen, 1847), 16.

58. Winfield Scott, *Memoirs of Lieutenant General Scott, L.L.D., Volume II* (New York: Sheldon & Co. Publishers, 1864), 560.

59. From *The American Star,* 7 March 1848, *Hemeroteca Nacional de Mexico*, Mexico City, DF.

60. Letter of 8 April 1848 from Major Folliot T. Lally at Tampico to Major Lorenzo Thomas, *Letters Received From Officers A-K, Mexican War, Army of Occupation, Entry 133,* Entry Group 133, Records Group 94, Adjutant General's Office, National Archives and Records Administration, Washington, DC.

61. A receipt dated 7 June 1848 and signed by Juan Mugioa, *foja* 7, *caja* 349, *Sin seccion* 1848 (and filed in 1846), (Mexico City, DF: *Ramo de Gobernacion, Archivo General de la Nacion*).

62. *Pagina* 00003, *foja* 2582, *expediente* XI/481.3 (Mexico City, DF: *Archivo de la Defensa Nacional*).

63. *Special Order No. 39* of General Persifor F. Smith, found in *Orders, 1845-1848, Vera Cruz, May-August 1848, Volume 10 of 23,* found in *Mexican War, 1845-1850*, Records of the Adjutant General's Office, 1780-1917, Records Group 94 (Washington, DC: National Archives and Records Administration).

64. Richard Griswold del Castillo, *The Treaty of Guadalupe Hidalgo* (Norman, OK: The University of Oklahoma Press, 1990), 187.

65. Robert E. Lee to John Mackay in a letter dated 2 October 1847, *Robert E. Lee Papers* (Carlisle, PA: US Army Military Institute).

66. Major General John Ellis Wool in Order 94 dated 27 March 1848 and found in *General Wool's Orders and Special Orders, Mexican War, Army of Occupation,* Entry Group 44, Record Group 94, Office of the Adjutant General, National Archives and Records Administration, Washington, DC.

67. Letter From Cristobal Andrade to the Minister of Interior and Exterior Relations, *expediente* 1, *caja* 349, 1848, *sin seccion, Ramo de Gobernacion, Archivo General de la Nacion*, Mexico City, DF.

68. Secretary of State James Buchanan to Nathan Clifford, US Minister to Mexico in a dispatch of 7 August 1848, cited by William R. Manning in *Diplomatic Correspondence of the United States—Inter-American Affairs, 1831-1860, Volume IX—Mexico*, 4.

69. Census data is found in *foja* 1, *expediente* 3, *caja* 319, 1846, *Ramo de Gobernacion, Archivo General de la Nacion*.

70. The only exception to this occurred at Veracruz. There, the US Navy loaned Scott shipboard cannon firing 64-pound shot. As elsewhere, the artillery turned the tide of battle.

71. Lester R. Dillon, Jr., "American Artillery in the Mexican War, 1846-1847," Military History of Texas and the Southwest 11 (Austin, TX: Presidial Press, 1975), 59. "In the victory, artillery dominated the critical battles at Palo Alto, Buena Vista, and Vera Cruz. Coordinated infantry-artillery attacks vanquished the enemy at Cerro Gordo, Chapultepec, and the city of Mexico. The absence or improper use of artillery was disastrous at Monterey and Molina del Rey as unsuppressed Mexican fire inflicted excessive casualties on the attacking Americans."

72. Kenly, 264.

The Politics of War in the Department of the Missouri, 1861-1864

Donald B. Connelly

On the morning of 21 August 1863, the infamous William Quantrill and nearly 450 men attacked Lawrence, Kansas. Without suffering a single casualty, they killed more than 150 largely unarmed Kansas men and boys, looted the town, and burned 185 buildings. This raid was perhaps the worst atrocity in the Civil War. Four days later, Brigadier General (BG) Thomas Ewing, Union commander, District of the Border, issued an order that virtually depopulated four western Missouri counties. The notorious General Orders No. 11 required all loyal citizens in Jackson, Cass, Bates, and Vernon counties to move to a military post and all others to leave the region completely. While selective banishment or expulsion had long been practiced in the Civil War, depopulating entire counties was a radical step, perhaps the most severe step taken against the civilian population in the entire war.[1] Yet, Ewing and his superior, Major General (MG) John M. Schofield, defended the action as being necessary to preclude even greater violence and destruction as outraged Kansans cried out for an invasion of Missouri.[2]

The sacking of Lawrence and the Draconian response of General Orders No. 11 demonstrated just how violent warfare had become in the Department of the Missouri as atrocity and revenge threatened to overwhelm strategy and reasoned policy. The murderous politics of slavery in "Bleeding Kansas" and the Missouri border had produced an even more bloody-minded politics of guerrilla warfare. Kansas politicians competed with one another in calling for retaliation against Missouri, while radical Republicans in Missouri used the Lawrence raid to attack the conservative Unionist governor of Missouri as little better than a secessionist. If "war is the continuation of policy by other means," the Unionist politics in the Department of the Missouri was primarily about controlling the instruments of war.[3] Thus, department commanders in Missouri had to fight on four fronts: a war of Southern rebellion, a guerrilla war in Missouri, a war between the states of Kansas and Missouri, and a war among Unionist factions within Missouri. These four fronts were inextricably linked and inherently political. Military commanders were under unceasing and conflicting political pressure from local, state, and national political leaders and could not remain unaffected by politics.

The war of Southern rebellion in Missouri began when the Unionist Home Guard led by Congressman Frank Blair and Regular Army officer Nathaniel Lyon overthrew secessionist Missouri Governor Claiborne Jackson and the state militia commanded by Major General Sterling Price. By fall 1861, most of the secessionist state militias had been defeated and Price had withdrawn to southwestern Missouri. BG Samuel R. Curtis's victory at Pea Ridge, Arkansas, in March 1862 ended any real threat of a successful Confederate invasion of Missouri. Thereafter, the Confederate incursions were more often large-scale cavalry raids to hamper Union operations rather than genuine attempts to retake Missouri for the Confederacy. Price's great raid in fall 1864 was a last desperate attempt to "redeem" Missouri. Still, these Rebel incursions generated considerable tension between the state and federal governments. Missouri state officials were primarily interested in protecting the state, while the national government was more interested in defeating the Confederacy.

As the conventional military threat diminished, the guerrilla war expanded in Missouri. Again, the interests of state and federal officials diverged. State authorities sought to eradicate guerrilla activity, while the national government was content to contain it. In protecting Missouri from Confederate raids and guerrillas, most state officials and some military commanders were reluctant to transfer troops to other theaters to prosecute the war. The state and national officials disagreed over security forces' funding and control. Disputes over how to eradicate or how to contain guerrillas—a "hard" war versus a "soft" war—further splintered Union strategy.[4]

The divisions between a hard and soft war had their roots in initial attitudes about secession. Like the nation, Missouri in 1861 was badly divided. The state was primarily Democratic, while St. Louis, its largest city, was predominantly Republican. Although secessionists outnumbered Republicans, most Missourians were conservative Democrats who favored the status quo. Calling themselves "conditional Unionists," these conservatives hoped to avoid the impending conflict. They sought to stay in the Union, retain slavery, and remain neutral in "Lincoln's war" with the South. While a few conditional Unionists opted to join the secessionists, most remained loyal to the Union. In the early days of the war, they hoped, like most Democrats, that a moderate, conciliatory policy would end the war quickly with little bloodshed. The "unconditional Unionists" consisted largely of the Republicans and the large German community of Missouri who believed that stern, and even harsh, measures were required to suppress the rebellion. They often regarded the former conditional Unionists as little better than secessionists.

The question of loyalty permeated all antiguerrilla policies. When MG Henry Wager Halleck replaced John C. Fremont as commander in Missouri in November 1861, one of his first tasks was to come to grips with the legal implications of guerrilla warfare amid a civil war. Since various rebels' legal status and the military's legal authority to deal with them remained confused, Halleck the lawyer systematically revised military legal procedures. On 1 January 1863, Halleck issued General Orders No. 1, which delineated between using military courts-martial to try and punish military personnel and military commissions to try and punish civilians for military offenses. Both had similar rules and procedures.[5]

In the order, Halleck cautioned subordinates that civil offenses would remain the purview of civilian courts "whenever such loyal courts exist." While military personnel might be charged with the "Violation of the Rules and Articles of War," which were prescribed by statute, civilians would be charged with "violating the laws of war." Although admittedly general and not fully covered by statute, Halleck attempted to differentiate between the "duly authorized forces of the so-called Confederate States" and guerrillas. Duly enrolled soldiers, acting under proper authority, would be treated as prisoners of war, whereas "predatory partisans and guerrilla bands are not entitled to such exemptions." The distinctions between combatant and noncombatant and legal versus illegal combatant remained a vexed question throughout the war, but Halleck continued with his efforts to create a legal framework. While the partisans decried their treatment as outlaws, Halleck was threading a middle course to prevent all rebels or supposed rebels from being summarily punished. He hoped to suppress guerrillas without descending into atrocity and counteratrocity.[6]

Using military commissions was another novel and relatively successful innovation of the Civil War.[7] Historian Mark Neely has concluded that, although imperfect, "Trials by military commission restrained United States forces in the Civil War mainly by imposing systematic record-keeping and an atmosphere of legality on the army's dealings with a hostile populace." In addition to requirements for legal representation and record-keeping, department commanders had to review all sentences and the president reviewed all death penalties. These requirements were often not found in civilian courts. Neely estimated that nearly 5,000 different civilian prisoners passed through St. Louis' military prisons during the war and that the number held in other portions of the state would be a formidable figure. Yet, the thousands of men imprisoned in Missouri were generally not mere "political dissidents." The passions of civil war had erupted into murder well before 1861, and the proximity of Confederate support in Indian territory or Arkansas fanned the flames of further violence.[8]

In the Department of the Missouri records, very few men were charged with simply "uttering disloyal sentiments." Most were charged with "violating the oath of allegiance" or "violating the laws of war" for being Rebels or for aiding them. Punishments ranged from fines to banishment to prison. Despite the partisan accusations surrounding the tenures of Curtis and Schofield as department commanders, there was little difference in the number of charges or punishments their military commissions handed down. After 1862 military commissions in Missouri issued few death sentences.[9] President Abraham Lincoln's well-known reluctance to use capital punishment penetrated the adjudication process. Criticism of Lincoln's "kindheartedness" was sometimes bipartisan. Not only did radicals object to coddling treasonous murderers, Governor Hamilton Rowan Gamble complained to Attorney General Edward Bates that Lincoln's pardons deprived Missourians of justice. Bates was unable to change the President's mind and wrote Gamble that real consequences of Lincoln's policies would be to induce Union soldiers not to bother with military commissions. Too often, Bates' caustic assessment proved brutally accurate. The military commissions were only one tool of the war against the guerrillas, and many "bushwhackers" never made it to trial. Lincoln's disinclination to approve death sentences not only restrained their use by military commissions but also often resulted in a disinclination to take prisoners at all.[10]

Even the relatively moderate Schofield, whom radical Republicans called the "bushwhackers' best friend," occasionally lashed out, as in his general order of 29 May 1862.[11] While reiterating his policy to "be magnanimous in its treatment of those who are tired of the rebellion and desire to become loyal citizens," he declared that for those "caught in arms, engaged in their unlawful warfare, they will be shot down upon the spot." He required "All good citizens . . . to give their assistance to the military authorities in detecting and bringing to punishment the outlaws . . . and those who give them shelter and protection." Those who failed to do so would be "treated as abettors of the criminals." Finally, he reminded his command:

> All officers and men of this command are reminded that it is their duty, while punishing with unmeasured severity those who still persist in their mad efforts to destroy the peace of the State, not only to abstain from molestation, but to protect from injury all loyal and peaceable citizens.

> All will be held to a strict accountability for the just and proper execution of the important and responsible duties required of them by this order.[12]

Brandishing an olive branch and a sword while exhorting his men to destroy the guerrillas with both severity and restraint, Schofield, in his order, reflected the inherent contradictions and dilemmas of guerrilla warfare.

Another antiguerrilla policy was using assessments against disloyal persons. In December 1861, Halleck created a committee to collect $10,000 to take care of the refugees flooding into St. Louis. Residents or former residents of St. Louis who were "in arms with the enemy" or had "furnished pecuniary or other aid to the enemy" were assessed, and the excess monies were given to the state Sanitary Commission.[13] On 23 June 1862, MG Schofield, who commanded the District of Missouri and the Missouri State Militia, issued an even more drastic order. Schofield declared that "rebels and rebel sympathizers in Missouri will be held responsible . . . for the damages that may hereafter be committed by the lawless bands which they have brought into existence, subsisted, encouraged, and sustained." County boards, appointed by district commanders, would assess local rebel sympathizers $5,000 for each Union soldier killed, $1,000 to $5,000 for each wounded, and full value for stolen and destroyed property. The government would then distribute the sums collected to the persons so injured or their heirs. The boards were immediately to "enroll all the residents and property-holders of the county who have actively aided or encouraged the present rebellion." They could drop from the roll any person who took the oath of allegiance and satisfied the board of their loyalty. In making assessments, the boards would also take into account "the wealth of an individual and his known activity in aiding the rebellion."[14]

Although Halleck, Pope, and other commanders had previously assessed such fines, Schofield's order was a striking assertion of military authority.[15] Although Governor Gamble endorsed the plan, Schofield issued these orders as the federal commander of the District of Missouri and not as the Missouri militia commander. Schofield saw the use of local civilian/military boards to levy mass fines as an extension of martial law. Because he permitted persons to be dropped from the assessment rolls by demonstrations of loyalty suggests that his intent was to coerce good behavior as much as to punish bad behavior or fund the war.

The First Confiscation Act of 6 August 1861 that authorized property seizure, including slaves, used to aid the rebellion did not strictly apply but lent Halleck's and Schofield's actions a degree of legitimacy. The Second Confiscation Act of 17 July 1862 broadened military powers a bit by providing for confiscation and punishment related to six classes of rebels. What one historian has called a "confusing and poorly drawn" act was really a compromise between the radical Republicans in Congress who sought to punish rebels severely and use the act to emancipate African-Americans and President Lincoln who still favored a moderate policy and feared the effect that confiscation would have on the border states. After passage, Lincoln and his attorney general, Edward Bates, Missouri, made little effort to implement its provisions vigorously. Military commanders were given considerable leeway in its implementation. George B. McClellan ignored the law, while John Pope used it to justify his "hard war" policies.[16]

Implementing the confiscation acts in Missouri became politically contentious and was one more sore point between conservatives and radicals. Despite his earlier use of assessments, Schofield interpreted the confiscation law rather narrowly as requiring execution by normal judicial proceedings. His implementing order called for provost marshals to submit cases and supporting evidence to federal attorneys for prosecution, and condemnation and sale of property would take place after a court of competent jurisdiction established guilt. This suited one of his political allies, Attorney General Bates, as well as Bates' brother-in-law, Governor Gamble.[17]

Samuel Curtis interpreted the law far more expansively and gave his provost marshal, Franklin A. Dick, more latitude in employing it. Schofield later attributed Curtis' subsequent troubles in Missouri to his zealous implementation of the confiscation law. Curtis had to backtrack somewhat as abolitionist commanders used the acts to free slaves owned by men that no court had proven to be disloyal. Nevertheless, Curtis was more disposed to protect slaves fleeing to Army camps, and he believed the only objections came from "a few officers, a few slaveholders, and a few butternut politicians [who] are constantly trying to make a mountain out of a mole-hill." Curtis and Dick also made more liberal use of banishment. In one notorious case, Curtis ordered the banishment of a conservative Presbyterian minister, Samuel B. McPheeters, based on the allegations of a minority faction of his congregation. Lincoln was forced to intervene. While Lincoln suspected the reverend of Southern sympathies, there was no overt evidence of disloyalty. Although the president left the matter in Curtis' hands, he advised him "the churches, as such, take care of themselves."[18]

Curtis' fundamental trouble in implementing assessments was that Governor Gamble and the conservative Unionists did not trust him. They viewed Curtis, a former Republican congressman, as being in league with the radical Republicans and therefore distrusted his appointment of provost marshals and assessors who they viewed as their political enemies. Their suspicions were increased when radical Republican BG Benjamin Loan, who was also running for Congress, imposed $85,000 in fines on persons and towns in the Central District of Missouri shortly after Curtis assumed command of the department.[19]

Curtis was also caught in the backlash of implementing Schofield's $500,000 assessment on St. Louis to pay for the Enrolled Missouri Militia (EMM). Schofield had Gamble's approval for this initiative, but with the huge uproar the assessments created, even among Unionists, Gamble appealed to Lincoln to stop the program. Lincoln ordered the assessment on St. Louis suspended pending further examination. A few days later Halleck, while reserving the right to impose future assessments, permanently suspended the assessment on St. Louis. It was nearly a year before Lincoln repudiated the whole system. This was neither the first nor last time that the growing antagonism and distrust between the governor and the department commander would necessitate the president's intervention.[20]

Just as slavery was the fundamental reason for the war, it was also central to the war between Kansas and Missouri and the conflict among Missouri unionists. At the national level, abolitionist Republicans sought from the very beginning to use the war to destroy slavery. In August 1861, John C. Fremont, the 1856 Republican presidential candidate and new commander of the Department of the West declared martial law throughout Missouri and, more provocatively, announced that the property of those who took up arms would be confiscated and their slaves freed. President Lincoln learned of the proclamation from the newspapers and immediately dispatched his concerns to Fremont. Fearing the effect on other border states, he requested that Fremont modify his emancipation order to conform with the 6 August act of Congress.[21]

Fremont refused. By forcing Lincoln to countermand the policy publicly, Fremont was playing to the Abolitionist wing of the Republican Party. Lincoln recognized the politics behind the measure and the challenge, not only to his policies but also to his authority. This was but the first of many clashes with politically minded generals.[22] Although Fremont had created political problems for the administration, his lack of military success was the ultimate cause of his relief. Lincoln could have overlooked all the political problems if Fremont had produced some military successes to demonstrate his effectiveness. While ideology, partisanship, or friendship drove many politicians, Lincoln increasingly adopted the criterion of military effectiveness for appointing and retaining commanders.[23]

The hostilities that began over whether Kansas would be a slave or free state did not end with the outbreak of the Civil War and Kansas' admission to the Union. Kansas provided a safe haven for escaping slaves throughout the war. Kansans, such as Senator James Lane and Colonel Charles Jennison, revenged themselves on Missourians with little regard as to whether they were Unionists or not. To Lane and Jennison, all Missourians were bushwhackers. The two men staged punitive expeditions nominally to root out rebels, but they "liberated" African-Americans, horses, cattle, and even furniture. Some Kansans were motivated by more than political passion. As MG Schofield archly observed, a number were "not unwilling to steal themselves rich in the name of liberty." Even Jayhawkers used the verb "jayhawking" to mean stealing.[24]

The question of slavery and emancipation also splintered the Unionist cause in Missouri. Even more than the factional disputes over a hard versus soft war, the question of slavery and emancipation produced the greatest passion. By spring 1863 the number of proslavery "Snowflakes" had dwindled. The struggle was then between the Republican "Charcoals" who called for immediate emancipation and the conservative "Claybanks" who now advocated a gradual process. As the debate intensified, the radicals came to view anyone who did not favor immediate emancipation as "secesh," and conservatives regarded the radicals as "revolutionists."

For military officers, the struggle over guerrilla and emancipation policies entangled them willingly and unwillingly in the nastiest brand of politics.[25] Each faction attempted to enlist military authority to its position. Just as it was difficult for Missourians to remain neutral in the war, few officers could remain neutral in these debates. Lincoln's cautious approach to emancipation was often not matched in Congress, which in 1861 and 1862 passed laws forbidding the Army's use in apprehending runaway slaves. In Missouri, with most of the state militia federalized, this policy caused great concern among loyal slave owners. Military commanders were often caught between federal law, state law, their own political beliefs, white public opinion, and the initiative of daring runaway slaves.[26]

By summer 1863, recruiting for African-American regiments, Secretary of War Edwin M. Stanton's special project, became another point of contention between the state and federal governments. Recruiters often did not know or did not care about the status of

African-American recruits. Governor Gamble had granted permission for such recruitment as long as there was no "interference with the slaves of loyal owners" and no "violation of state laws." Schofield had to undertake yet another careful balancing act between Missouri conservatives' interests and the federal government's more radical policies. When Gamble subsequently complained of violations of state law, Schofield pledged to look into recruiting slaves of loyal men. However, the status of slaves, even of loyal men, was becoming increasingly uncertain as Kansans, radical Missourians, and now federal officials sought to evade Missouri laws and strike a blow against slavery.[27]

Caught in the middle, Schofield reminded the War Department of the sensitivity of the situation in Missouri and requested further guidance directly from Stanton. He even suggested the idea of compensated emancipation. Meanwhile, he temporarily suspended Negro recruitment to mollify the Missouri conservatives. The War Department, however, threw the problem back in his lap, and black recruitment continued. Neither Stanton nor Lincoln was disposed to instruct Schofield officially to disregard state laws in recruiting black troops. Nor was Congress disposed to underwrite compensated emancipation; Lincoln had already given up on the idea. By the end of the year, more than 2,400 African-Americans had been recruited in Missouri.[28]

Politics also pervaded the organization and structure of the military forces. The defense of Missouri was beyond state government resources, yet state officials were unwilling to turn the state's defense completely over to the federal government. To secure federal financial support, provisional Governor Hamilton R. Gamble agreed to appoint a federal officer to command the militia and subject it to Army regulations and the US Articles of War. The department commander, MG Halleck, became the ex officio major general of the state militia, and then BG John M. Schofield became his principal deputy in this area.[29] Schofield's job was to raise, organize, and train a force to defend the state. Although Schofield was officially a subordinate of the military department commander, he had to be responsive to the Governor, who believed he should have a say in the appointments and policy of the state militia. It was a delicate job, in which Schofield carefully had to balance local interests with the requirements of the national government.[30]

The MSM would eventually carry the primary burden of combating guerrillas, freeing up many US regiments for duty with the armies invading the South. By 15 April 1862, Schofield had raised a force of 13,800 men and organized them into 14 regiments and two battalions of cavalry, one regiment of infantry, and one battery of artillery. The preponderance of cavalry in the organized militia was an important part of the overall strategy. With infantry, Schofield wrote to BG Benjamin M. Prentiss, one "can do little more than hold a single point." With cavalry, "we can always strike the Rebels before they can collect in numbers sufficient to meet us" and frustrate their attempts to organize.[31]

In July 1862, beset by guerrillas and unable to get reinforcements from the Union armies moving south, Schofield persuaded Governor Gamble to call out the entire state militia. Using his authority as commander of the state militia, Schofield, in his General Orders No. 19 of 22 July, called up most of the free, white, adult males of the state for military service. Not since the American Revolution had there been such an extensive mobilization of the militia. To differentiate it from the full-time and federally funded MSM, this force was termed the Enrolled Missouri Militia (EMM). Schofield intended the EMM to supplement the MSM, not replace it. Rather than a full-time military force, the EMM was designed to provide local defense and to guard supply depots and bridges. But this mission was not easy. These relatively small, isolated units often became the targets of large guerrilla bands and Confederate raiders. By November 1862, 70 partial regiments had been formed; the number eventually totaled 89. Although this measure eased the manpower crisis, the EMM created problems of its own.[32]

Schofield acknowledged that the enrollment prompted many Rebel sympathizers either to join the local guerrilla band or to run "to the brush." While it increased guerrilla strength, it also unmasked many disloyal men. In heavily secessionist counties, enrollment likewise marked the loyal Unionists and left many of them at the mercy of the guerrillas, particularly while the companies were being armed and equipped. Unfortunately, enrollment also prompted many Unionists, especially in St. Louis, to flee the state to avoid militia service.

To avoid the problem of conscripting those who were unwilling to serve, Governor Gamble suggested that men might buy an exemption for $150 and thus help fund the force. Schofield proposed the far more modest amount of $10 and one-tenth of 1 percent on all taxable property as shown by the most recent assessment. He calculated that, in this way, more Southern sympathizers would not serve but would help pay for those who did. Unfortunately, Schofield misjudged the real effect of the policy. Radicals denounced his exemption because it permitted the rich—slave owners in the eyes of the radicals—to avoid service. Many moderates also viewed the $10 exemption as an unfair burden on poor citizens. Schofield hastily withdrew the order.[33]

If many complained about the call-up, still others detected a political opportunity. Although he initially opposed the enrollment, Congressman (and General) Frank Blair attributed the Republican success in the elections of 1862 to Schofield's General Orders No. 19. Writing to his brother, Montgomery, he acknowledged that "Schofield did not issue the order for that purpose and Gamble did not consent to it with any such idea but it did the work and no mistake." The order, according to Blair, forced the secesh to take to the bush while loyal men were drilled and organized. "Thus many thousands of secession votes were actually lost," he elaborated, "but the great point was that the armed organization was on our side giving protection to our voters."[34]

The EMM's most pressing problem was how to pay for it. Since the men were to remain state troops under state control, the federal government would not foot the bill. Halleck agreed to provide captured arms but recommended that the militia be "subsisted by requisitions on rebel sympathizers."[35] Schofield's bounty in place of service had been partially intended as a means to pay for the EMM. Initially, Schofield directed that the enrolled militia would subsist off Rebels and, if necessary, Union men, after giving a proper receipt. Schofield later had to amend the orders when the EMM began using any pretense to take provisions, further adding to the general fear and bitterness.[36] The $500,000 assessment on the Rebel sympathizers of St. Louis backfired badly on both Schofield and Curtis. Ultimately, the federal government agreed to fund the EMM while on active service.

The appointment of general and field grade officers was an important, politically charged subject. The ability of prominent men to attract recruits played an important role in the appointment to senior command, and thus senior officers were proportionally balanced between conservative Unionists and radical Republicans. Proslavery men generally commanded in proslavery sections of the state, while abolitionists tended to command in antislavery regions. The political and ideological fissures in the state were thus replicated in the militia. Schofield encouraged Governor Gamble and his subordinate commanders to postpone selecting field grade officers so that company grade officers could prove themselves. As the war progressed, Schofield even attempted to dissuade the state government from electing company officers.[37]

Mixing volunteer and militia units in Missouri occasionally created conflict and confusion. Those who possessed dual commissions could command both elements, but volunteer and militia officers squabbled over seniority and prerogatives. In 1862, when the state raised a new militia force called the EMM, the conflict over command authority further increased.[38] Furthermore, the militia was tied to the state unless sworn into federal service as state volunteers. On several occasions units mutinied when federal officers attempted to deploy them out of the state.[39] Conflicting authorities and interpretations meant that commanders on the ground could not automatically depend on command prerogatives, and they frequently had to rely on a spirit of cooperation.

The Germans were a particular problem. Since many were recent immigrants, they had little understanding of or sympathy for conservative Unionists and considered most of those who did not share their abolitionist views disloyal. Complaining to Lincoln, Gamble wanted them placed under state control or integrated into regular US regiments and consequently deployed out of the state. In January 1862, Schofield lamented that the only cavalry force at his disposal was "a battalion of Germans, utterly worthless for this kind of service. If I trust them out of my sight for a moment they will plunder and rob friends and foes alike." He had already arrested several officers and soldiers and asked Halleck to dismount and disarm the unit. The problem was not only with "foreign adventurers." As BG James Totten wrote to Schofield, "Private quarrels of long standing, originating out of matters connected with property, county politics, and neighborhood disagreement, are too often the cause of persecution of those in military power, and all is made to appear as connected with the rebellion." The war became an excuse for "personal revenge," and the desire for revenge increased as the war continued.[40]

The importance of politics can most readily be seen in creating and reorganizing the various military departments and the rise and fall of their commanders. Halleck once complained that it was hopeless "to separate military appointments and commands from politics."[41] In 1861 General William S. Harney, commander, Department of the West, was deposed in a conspiracy between Republican Congressman Blair, whose brother was Postmaster General in Lincoln's cabinet, and Abolitionist Regular Army Captain Nathaniel Lyon. They feared that Harney's impassivity in the face of secessionist Missouri Governor Claiborne Jackson's treasonous activity placed the St. Louis arsenal and all Missouri in jeopardy. Lyon briefly replaced Harney and drove Jackson from power but died in battle during a desperate effort to protect southwest Missouri from the combined forces of Missourian Sterling Price and Texan Ben McCulloch. The Blair family's choice as new commander in the Western Department was John C. Fremont. Fremont, however, lasted but a few months. The Blairs and Lincoln quickly became disillusioned with his radical political agenda and, more important, with his administrative and military incompetence.

In November 1861, Lincoln appointed Henry W. Halleck as commander of the new Department of the Missouri. To placate Republican Senator Jim Lane, Lincoln created the Department of Kansas, with Lane's political vassal, James G. Blunt, as the commander. Halleck's command was later expanded to become the Department of the Mississippi, with Missouri and Kansas becoming military districts under the command of John Schofield and James Blunt, respectively. When Halleck assumed command of the entire army, Schofield, as District of Missouri commander, stressed the importance of placing Missouri, Arkansas, and Kansas under one command. Halleck and Lincoln agreed, but to Schofield's chagrin, they appointed Samuel Curtis the commander. As the senior officer and the victor of Pea Ridge, Curtis was a logical choice. Yet, the conservatives in Missouri and Lincoln's cabinet distrusted him and sought his removal from the beginning.

By spring 1863, Halleck had also soured on Curtis because the Missouri commander first delayed launching an expedition to take Little Rock, via Helena, and later refused to provide reinforcements to Grant's Vicksburg campaign. In May 1863, Lincoln replaced Curtis with Schofield. In a letter to Schofield, Lincoln informed the new commander that he did not relieve Curtis because "he had done wrong by commission or omission." He did so because of the "pestilent factional quarrel" between Curtis and Governor Gamble, and "as I could not remove Governor Gamble, I had to remove General Curtis." The president went on to advise Schofield, "If both factions, or neither, shall abuse you, you will, probably, be about right. Beware of being assailed by one and praised by the other."[42]

Keeping above the political factions was easier said than done. If Curtis could not cooperate with Gamble, Schofield's cooperation with the governor outraged the radicals who became just as dedicated to toppling Schofield as the conservatives had been to replacing Curtis. Schofield replaced Provost Marshal Dick with James Broadhead and temporarily suspended African-American recruitment, pleasing the governor and conservatives; yet his efforts to broker a political compromise on emancipation irritated the conservatives without gaining any credit from the radicals.[43] As guerrilla activity increased in the summer, Schofield was under increasing pressure to take stern measures.

Upon assuming command, Schofield reorganized his command to provide for unity of command along the contentious Kansas-Missouri border. Just as he had recommended consolidating Kansas and Missouri into one department, he attempted to integrate command at the district level. He abolished Blunt's District of Kansas and created the District of the Frontier and the District of the Border. He gave Blunt command of the District of the Frontier, which included southern Kansas, Indian territory, western Arkansas, and nine counties in southwest Missouri.[44] The District of the Border comprised northern Kansas and eight counties around Kansas City and bordering Kansas.[45] Schofield appointed BG Thomas Ewing, Jr. to this sensitive command. Ewing was the brother-in-law and former law partner of William T. Sherman and a member of a politically powerful Ohio family. Although normally assumed to be aligned with the Jim Lane faction, Ewing attempted to keep his balance between the factions of Lane and Kansas Governor Thomas Carney. He was no friend of James Blunt and a declared enemy of Jayhawker Charles "Doc" Jennison. Schofield hoped that Ewing's moderate attitude and political skills would help defuse the simmering border war between Kansas and Missouri.[46]

Despite the continuing guerrilla threat, Schofield, by August 1863, had some reason for optimism with General Frederick Steele advancing on Little Rock and General Blunt about to capture Fort Smith. Then there was the Lawrence disaster. Quantrill's raid relied on boldness but also on a considerable amount of luck; he had been lucky to avoid Union patrols along the Arkansas, Missouri, Kansas border. Although his guerrilla force was the largest assembled since summer 1862, he had been fortunate to encounter accidentally 150 others along the way to Kansas.[47] Quantrill was further aided by an incompetent Union commander who spotted the guerrilla force the evening before but failed to notify the interior towns or to pursue closely.[48] Lawrence was the "citadel of Kansas abolitionism" and had been the target of three bushwhacker attacks in the 1850s. Still, the townspeople had grown overconfident, and the home guard and picket system had disintegrated. Schofield transferred units to support Grant, William S. Rosecrans, and Steele, thinning the troops stationed in the region. When the Union pursuit force of perhaps 200 did catch up with Quantrill's retreating band, their horses were near exhaustion, and the better-armed, better-mounted guerrillas easily fended them off.[49]

While General Thomas Ewing had issued General Orders No. 11 under pressure from Lane, Union policy had been drifting in that direction even before the massacre. On 18 August, Ewing issued two general orders designed to turn the screws on the Rebels and their sympathizers. General Orders No. 9 provided for confiscating slaves of those aiding the rebellion and for their safe escort to Kansas. General Orders No. 10 called for disloyal persons to be deported to the South. Former Rebels who had laid down their arms were required to leave the district. It prohibited unauthorized destruction of property, but it mandated the eradication of blacksmith facilities outside military stations.[50]

Ewing was not acting solely on his own authority. He had fully informed Schofield of his intentions two weeks earlier. Schofield, in turn, employed Frank Blair to approach Lincoln informally on these issues. At a 12 August meeting, Lincoln responded by telling Blair the story of the Irishman who asked for a glass of soda water, then adding that he would be glad to have a little brandy in it "unbeknownst to him." Blair inferred that Lincoln would be glad to have Schofield undertake these policies that could later be justified as military necessity. Lincoln's "hidden hand" approach to guerrilla policy enabled him to stay above the fray while his commanders took much of the political heat. This informal support gave Schofield confidence in pursuing more drastic policies.

On the same day Ewing issued General Orders No. 11 Schofield sent him a draft of his own proposal, which was remarkably similar to Ewing's order. Schofield's plan called for the expulsion of all disloyal persons and the destruction of houses and provisions that the guerrillas could use. To prevent retaliation against loyal persons, Schofield advised Ewing to remove them temporarily to places of safety. Schofield's willingness to resort to such harsh measures was in part due to the sting of radical condemnation. In an informal diary of the time, he lamented the unfairness of the criticism and recounted the stern measures he had decreed such as shooting guerrillas, banishment, and assessments.[51]

Halleck had warned Schofield that, at the first disaster, the politicians would attack "like a pack of hungry wolves."[52] Halleck proved prophetic. Missouri radicals began assembling a delegation to go to Washington to demand Schofield's relief. Radical Republican Senator James Lane, who barely escape death in the raid, declared war on

Missouri and called for Kansans to make "a large portion of western Missouri a desert waste."[53] MSM General Egbert B. Brown and Missouri Lieutenant Governor Willard P. Hall complained of Ewing's failure to control the Kansas border ruffians. Ten days after the raid and six days after Ewing issued his order, Schofield hurried to Leavenworth, Kansas, to forestall a full-fledged invasion. He met with Ewing, Kansas Governor Thomas Carney, and later with Senator Lane.[54]

Carney pledged to help Schofield defuse the situation and then reneged. Lane feigned a willingness to cooperate with Schofield while continuing to call for Ewing's relief and a punitive expedition. Schofield shrewdly recognized the partisan games these leaders played. He believed Lane's insinuations of making Ewing the scapegoat were for show and that as long as Schofield commanded the department, Ewing was the most pliant district commander Lane could expect. Schofield sensed that Lane's attacks on Ewing were really directed at him, and that Lane would renew his efforts to get rid of him. Carney, as Lane's rival for the Senate, saw the Senator's bloodthirsty calls for an invasion as a political opportunity for him. Since he knew Schofield would never permit such an action, he had no interest in helping Lane save face. Nor did he want to be seen as obstructing Kansas' righteous vengeance. Carney also criticized Ewing for supporting Lane's candidacy in the Senate.[55]

Despite the complaints of Lane, Carney, and the radical press about Ewing, Schofield seems to have never considered making Ewing the scapegoat. Ewing complained to him that "my political enemies are fanning the flames, and wish me for a burnt offering to satisfy the just and terrible passion of the people." Schofield attempted to reassure him and advised Ewing that a board of inquiry would exonerate him. Although Schofield might have preferred a less political commander, he believed Ewing was still the best man for the job. A new man would quickly fall prey to the snares and quicksand of border politics.[56] Since in Missouri Ewing was condemned by the radicals as a Schofield man and by the conservatives as a Kansas man, Schofield felt a degree of empathy for his embattled subordinate.[57] With both sides abusing him, Ewing conformed to Lincoln's model of proper command.[58]

During this trip, Schofield's anger had cooled, and he began to have second thoughts about some of the harsh measures in both his and Ewing's orders. Schofield still believed that given the passions aroused in Kansas General Orders No. 11 was necessary, but he ordered Ewing to modify it to exclude destroying property. He believed that destroying crops and buildings would do little to harm the guerrillas and would hamper loyal persons' return. While still severe, perhaps the greatest problem with the order was its implementation. Although Schofield had given him additional Missouri units, Ewing employed too many Kansas troops who had little interest in discriminating between loyal and disloyal Missourians. He even permitted the notorious "Doc" Jennison to participate in the operation. Schofield's amendment and cautions did not prevent much unnecessary property destruction and a few outright murders. Instead of unbridled devastation, Ewing conducted a kind of controlled mayhem, which only somewhat mitigated the destruction.

By November Ewing suspended the unpopular order, and by March 1864 many inhabitants began returning to their homes.[59] As extreme as the depopulation order was, it demonstrated the political contradictions and limits of radical antiguerrilla policies. While Missourians to this day denounce the order, Schofield and Ewing, both during and after the war, defended it as an act of military necessity to rid the area of guerrilla sympathizers and forestall Kansan retaliation.[60] Lincoln again gave his after-the-fact support: "I am not now interfering but am leaving [matters] to your own discretion."[61]

Assessments of the effects of General Orders No. 11 were equally mixed. Guerrilla activity certainly diminished, but some opponents and later historians have argued that the approaching winter diminished guerrilla activity and that the guerrillas simply moved to other areas, like central Missouri.[62] More supportive was the assessment of Confederate General Joseph O. Shelby who years later said that without General Orders No. 11 "the Confederates would shortly have found their way through the district into Kansas. . . . It not only cut off a large amount of supplies, but it removed a large number of our friends and sympathizers. . . . The order was fully justified and Ewing did a wise thing when he issued it."[63] Neither the Confederates nor guerrillas raided Kansas towns again, but 20,000 Missourians forced from their homes paid a high price for this "peace."

In September 1863, two delegations of Missouri and Kansas radicals met with Lincoln to demand Schofield's replacement with radical Republican General Ben Butler. In addition to Schofield's removal, they wanted the EMM disbanded and replaced with federal troops, and federal supervision of state elections. The radicals did not help their cause when, two weeks earlier, some had incited two St. Louis EMM regiments to mutiny rather than go to New Madrid to replace a volunteer unit marked to reinforce Steele in Arkansas. Radicals would get local judges to issue writs of habeas corpus to sabotage the EMM, as judges in other states sought to obstruct the draft. Lincoln backed up Schofield and Ewing and, far from condemning, he approved of the order to prevent a "remedial raid into Missouri." Lincoln told his trusted assistant John Hay that while he approved of their emancipation policies, he condemned the radicals' methods: "They are utterly lawless—the unhandiest devils in the world to deal with—but after all their faces are set Zionwards."[64]

Three months later the radicals used a more effective weapon to drive Schofield from his command. Just as they had done a year earlier, they obstructed Senate ratification of Schofield's nomination to Major General of Volunteers. Without confirmation, Schofield would again revert to the rank of brigadier general and would again be outranked by several other officers in the department. Just as Lincoln found it easier to replace Curtis than supplant a governor, it was easier to remove Schofield than depose the Senate. Lincoln had also concluded that the Department of the Missouri was just too fractious for a single command. With Steele's success in Arkansas and Blunt's gains in the Indian territory, the strategic rationale for the department had diminished. By giving Kansas to Samuel Curtis, Missouri to William Rosecrans, and Arkansas to Frederick Steele, Lincoln hoped to take care of these officers and to arrange a deal that would secure Schofield's promotion to major general. But Lane, Brown, and other senators who refused to support such a deal forced Lincoln's hand. Without obtaining Schofield's promotion, Lincoln reluctantly decided to divide the department into three separate departments. Even then, the factional infighting did not abate. When then radicals won control of the Missouri government, they forced out Rosecrans, who was replaced by General Grenville Dodge.[65]

In assessing the contributions of the various department commanders in Missouri, one should begin by emphasizing the continuity. They tried, often vainly, to discriminate between enemy soldiers and guerrillas, between organized guerrillas and "freebooters," between Confederate sympathizers and conditional Unionists, between bushwhackers and ordinary Missourians, and between lawful military action and partisan reprisal. More than Curtis, Schofield shared Halleck's view that Missouri was a supporting theater. Schofield readily responded to Halleck's troop levies for the fighting armies, even at the risk of weakening defenses in Missouri. Schofield's bold call-up of the EMM and his determined efforts to secure federal financial assistance greatly reduced the number of federal troops needed to safeguard Missouri. Curtis, Schofield, and Rosecrans did not end the guerrilla war. However, they did build up the defensive infrastructure of the state.[66] They raised, equipped, trained, and sustained thousands of Missourians to defend their state. In summer 1862, guerrilla bands in the thousands operated freely; in 1863 they were reduced to operating in the hundreds; by 1864 these bands generally consisted of several dozen men. Even though the hard-fighting, hard-riding district commanders and troops deserve most of the credit, the embattled department commanders had energetically directed and coordinated their efforts.

Quantrill's raid and General Orders No. 11 symbolize the brutality of war in the Department of the Missouri. Yet, their very rarity says something else about the war. Despite the murders, robberies, genuine atrocities, and bloodthirsty rhetoric many of the parties employed, the guerrilla war did not degenerate into ever-escalating atrocity. William Quantrill, "Bloody Bill" Anderson, and "Doc" Jennison remained exceptions. General Orders No. 11 was the result of exceptional circumstances and not the beginning of a new, more Draconian antiguerrilla policy. The American Civil War was neither a battle of chivalrous knights nor an explosion of homicidal frenzy. Appalling as many incidents were, Missouri and Kansas never reached the levels of violence seen in the Vendée during the French Revolution or in the guerrilla war in Spain, much less the staggering savagery of 20th-century civil wars. Despite the passions unleashed by the war, most Americans, especially the leaders, kept their heads.

For the modern military, it is easy to see the reflections of murderous divisions and sulfurous factionalism of the Department of the Missouri in Afghanistan, Iraq, Somalia, or Liberia. Rather than compare specific groups or policies, I think there are three broader lessons we can learn: the pervasiveness of politics, the need for flexibility, and the importance of fidelity. The Department of the Missouri was an inherently political command. Indeed, all military commands amid civil or guerrilla wars, or during occupation or "peacekeeping" missions, are inherently political. The organization and structure of the security forces are political. Commanders were and are required to make politically contentious decisions daily. Commanders at all levels will be buffeted by political factions from all levels. Commanders may strive to remain above politics but must accept the fact that such purity is often both impossible and undesirable. To be effective they must cooperate with those civil authorities in power, knowing full well that this cooperation will antagonize others. Sometimes, staking out a middle path merely means alienating all sides with no greater effectiveness.

Commanders in the Department of the Missouri proved remarkably flexible in responding to the myriad difficulties they encountered. They developed new and sometimes radical responses. Lincoln also showed tremendous flexibility in responding to various pressures without abandoning his overall objective. In the modern context, the importance of flexibility must begin with the measures of success. Imposing one's will on the enemy is satisfying to military men and ideologues but will generally not work in complex and contentious political environments. Success requires that commanders not only satisfy the president but also local political actors as well. However, bitter divisions can make harmony impossible. Commanders must accept the fact that many problems cannot be solved; they can only be handled, mitigated, fudged. Solutions bring their own problems and political reactions, and policies must be examined and readjusted continuously. Such flexibility requires great intellectual energy.

Flexibility sometimes required that Lincoln replace commanders who had become political liabilities. However, because men like Curtis or Schofield had faithfully tried to implement the commander in chief's policies, the president later rewarded them for their fidelity. Lincoln was not blindly loyal: Harney was retired and Fremont ended the war "awaiting orders." Department commanders also displayed great loyalty to subordinates as they grappled with difficult, often intractable, problems.[67] The need for fidelity goes up and down the chain of command. Subordinates, despite the complexities and uncertainties, need to be faithful to their duty, while superiors need to show loyalty, even when political expediency requires relief. Negotiating the treacherous crosscurrents of highly political military missions should not be the measure of all soldiers, and leaders must nurture and protect those who undertake such perilous tasks.

Notes

1. The "Great Hanging" of 40 to 50 Unionists at Gainesville, Texas, in October 1862 and the massacre of several hundred surrendering African-American soldiers at Fort Pillow, Tennessee, in April 1864 are also regarded among the great atrocities of the war. Many Southerners rank Sherman's expulsion of civilians from Atlanta, Georgia, and his ravaging of Georgia and South Carolina as equal or greater attacks on civilians.

2. For varying analyses of General Order 11 and the border war, see Donald L. Gilmore, "Total War on the Missouri Border," *Journal of the West* (July 1996), 70-80; Matt Matthews and Kip Lindberg, "'Better off in Hell': the Evolution of the Kansas Red Legs," *North & South*, 5/4 (2002), 20-31; Gunja SenGupta, "Bleeding Kansas," *Kansas History*, 24/4 (2001-02), 318-41; Barry A. Crouch, "'A Fiend in Human Shape?' William Clarke Quantrill and His Biographers," *Kansas History*, 22/2 (1999), 142-56; Lloyd Lewis, "Propaganda and the Kansas-Missouri War," *Missouri Historical Review*, 92/2 (1998), 135-48; James M. McPherson, "From Limited to Total War: Missouri and the Nation, 1861-1865," *Gateway Heritage*, 16/2 (1995), 4-17; Paul B. Hatley and Ampssler Noor, "Army General Orders Number 11: Final Valid Option or Wanton Act of Brutality? The Missouri Question in the American Civil War," *Journal of the West*, 33/3 (1994), 77-87; Gary L. Cheatham, "'Desperate Characters:' The Development and Impact of the Confederate Guerrillas in Kansas," *Kansas History* (Autumn 1991), 144-61; Ann Davis Niepman, "General Orders No. 11 and Border Warfare During the Civil War," *Missouri Historical Review* (January 1972), 185-210; Charles R. Mink, "General Orders, No. 11: The Forced Evacuation of Civilians During the Civil War," *Military Affairs* (December 1970), 132-37; Albert Castel, "Quantrill's Bushwhackers: A Case Study in Partisan Warfare," *Civil War History*, 13 (1967), 40-50. For an excellent survey of recent writings on Civil War guerrilla warfare see Daniel E. Sutherland, "Sideshow No Longer: A Historiographical Review of the Guerrilla War," *Civil War History*, 46/1 (2000), 5-23.

3. Carl von Clausewitz, *On War* (Princeton, NJ: Princeton University Press, 1976), 87-89.

4. The terms "hard" and "soft" war are useful expressions for understanding policy differences in dealing with rebellion and guerrilla war. They must, however, be employed cautiously. Different leaders advocated different policies about different issues during the war, most notably slavery. There was no bright line between hard and soft (conciliatory) war policies. Michael Fellman stressed the pragmatic nature and even desperate expediency of many policy decisions. See Michael Fellman, *Inside War: The Guerrilla Conflict in Missouri During the American Civil War* (New York: Oxford University Press, 1989), 81-97. Also see Mark Grimsley, *The Hard Hand of War: Union Policy Toward Southern Civilians, 1861-1865* (New York: Cambridge University Press, 1995), 1-22.

5. US War Department, *The War of the Rebellion: A Compilation of the Official Records of the Union and Confederate Armies* (hereafter cited as *OR*),128 vols. (Washington, DC: US Government Printing Office, 1880-1901), series I, vol. 8, 776-79.

6. Ibid., 476-79. Later, as Commanding General of the Army, Halleck issued War Department General Order No.100, 24 April 1863, which codified the laws of war. For a discussion of General Order No.100 and Halleck's guerrilla policy, see Fellman, 81-89. Also see Andrew J. Birtle, *U.S. Army Counterinsurgency and Contingency Operations Doctrine, 1860-1941* (Washington, DC: US Army Center of Military History, 1998), 32-36.

7. Military trials of civilians were not entirely unprecedented, but the scope of jurisdiction and scale of trials were unique. For a brief history of military commissions, see Mark E. Neely, Jr., *The Fate of Liberty: Abraham Lincoln and Civil Liberties* (New York: Oxford University Press, 1991), 167-68.

8. Neely, 32-50, 160-67.

9. General Court-martial Orders, Department of the Missouri, 1861-63, RG 153, National Archives and Research Administration (NARA).

10. "Our kind hearted president does not understand the problems created by indefinitely suspending these sentences." They encourage the offenders, and "promptitude in executing the sentences is absolutely necessary. . . . Can you help us change the rules to give approval authority to the CG, District of Missouri or Governor of Missouri?" H.R. Gamble, St Louis, to Edward Bates, 14 July 1862; Bates to Gamble, 24 July 1862, Bates Family Papers, Missouri Historical Society (MHS). Also see Fellman, 86-93.

11. *Daily Missouri Democrat*, 11 September 1863.

12. Missouri State Militia, General Order No. 18, 29 May 1862, *OR*, series I, vol. 13, 402-403.

13. Department of the Missouri, General Order No. 24, 12 December 1861, *OR*, series I, vol. 8, 431-32; series II, vol. 1, 170-71; William E. Parrish, *A History of Missouri, Volume III: 1860-1875* (Columbia, MO: University of Missouri Press, 1973), 68.

14. District of Missouri, General Order No. 3, 23 June 1862, *OR*, series I, vol. 13, 446-47; Special Orders No. 30, 29 June 1862, RG 393, Part III, E370, NARA.

15. For fines levied by Henry Halleck and John Pope also see *OR*, series I, vol. 3, 135, 422, 431.

16. James M. McPherson, *Battle Cry of Freedom: The Civil War Era* (New York: Ballantine Books, 1988), 500-501. Mark Grimsley recounted the political compromises that produced the "confusing" law. He also concluded that Pope's orders had little real impact. Grimsley, 68-71, 75, 78, 90. *Encyclopedia of the American Civil War: A Political, Social, and Military History* (New York: W.W. Norton & Co., 2000), 477-79.

17. Stanton to Schofield, 5 September 1862; District of Missouri, General Orders No. 19, 11 September 1862, Box 42, Schofield Papers, Library of Congress (LC); John M. Schofield, *Forty-Six Years in the Army* (New York: The Century Co., 1897), 56-58.

18. Schofield, *Forty-Six Years in the Army*, 56-58; Terry Lee Beckenbaugh, "The War of Politics: Samuel Ryan Curtis, Race and the Political/Military Establishment," Ph.D. dissertation, University of Arkansas, 2001, 83-85; *OR*, series I, vol. 22/1, 877-78; vol. 22/2, 6-7, 88-89; William E. Parrish, *Turbulent Partnership: Missouri and the Union, 1861-1865* (Columbia, MO: University of Missouri Press, 1963), 110-13.

19. *OR*, series I, vol. 13, 691, 693, 736, 800. For Loan's contested election see Bruce Tap, "'Union Men to the Polls, and Rebels to Their Holes': the Contested Election Between John P. Bruce and Benjamin F. Loan, 1862," *Civil War History* 46/1 (2000), 24-40.

20. *OR*, series I, vol. 13, 11-12; series I, vol. 22/1, 801-803, 805-806, 810-11, 826, 827, 832-33, 888; Schofield, *Forty-Six Years in the Army*, 57-58; Parrish, 113-16.

21. Even some Missourians who thought rebels "should be shot summarily by the thousands" recoiled at "Fremont's notion about the negroes." Barton Bates to his father, Edward Bates, 8 September 1861, Bates Family Papers, MHS.

22. Lincoln to Fremont, 11 September 1861, *OR*, series I, vol. 3, 485-85. William E. Parrish, *Frank Blair: Lincoln's Conservative* (Columbia, MO: University of Missouri Press, 1998), 121-22; Parrish, *Turbulent Partnership*, 60-63; David H. Donald, *Lincoln* (New York: Simon & Schuster, 1995), 314-17.

23. *OR*, series I, vol. 3, 477; Lincoln to Fremont, 11 September 1861, *OR*, series I, vol. 3, 485-85; Parrish, *Frank Blair*, 121-22; Parrish, *Turbulent Partnership*, 60-63. In defending his position, Lincoln wrote to his friend Orville Browning that Fremont's proclamation was "purely political" and "not within the range of military law or necessity." Further, "the general may not do anything he pleases." See Donald, 314-17.

24. John M. Schofield, "The Border War Between Missouri and Kansas," handwritten manuscript, Box 91, Schofield Papers, LC; "'This Regiment Will Make a Mark': Letters From a Member of Jennison's Jayhawkers, 1861-1862," *Kansas History*, 20/1 (1997), 50-58.

25. Parrish, *Turbulent Partnership*, 126; *OR*, series 1, vol. 22/2, 301. In June 1863 Schofield inserted himself into the debate that divided the Unionist cause. He began by having the *New York Tribune* publish a letter on his support for "the speedy emancipation of slaves." Schofield next attempted to influence the state convention's deliberations by enlisting Lincoln's support. Lincoln responded cautiously by saying he could accept gradual emancipation if the transition period were "comparatively short" and if the act included protection against selling slaves "into a most lasting slavery." Schofield then visited the meeting hall and personally urged a "speedy" gradual emancipation. Schofield's hope that he could engineer a compromise on emancipation that would heal the factional divisions was a forlorn one. In the end, no compromise was acceptable. The conservatives adopted neither of Lincoln's provisions and approved a plan that would end slavery in 1870. The "Charcoals" continued to press the cause of immediate emancipation and in 1864 won the state election. On 11 January 1865 a new state convention declared the immediate and unconditional emancipation of all slaves. See Schofield, *Forty-Six Years in the Army*, 74-75; *Tri-Weekly Missouri Democrat*, 12 June 1863; Lincoln to Schofield, 22 June 1863, *The Collected Works of Abraham Lincoln*, Roy P. Basler, ed., vol. VI, 291; Parrish, *Turbulent Partnership*, 123-48, 200-201.

26. The court-martial of Colonel W.P. Robinson, commander, 23d Missouri Infantry, for disobedience of orders is a good example of this problem. On 11 July 1863 Constable John McBride came to arrest an enslaved woman named Lethe at Camp Edwards. McBride had a lawful warrant and letters from Generals Curtis and Schofield. Colonel Robinson refused McBride entry, stating that doing so would be a violation of congressional law in assisting with apprehending runaway slaves. The court-martial found Robinson guilty. In reviewing the case, Schofield confirmed the finding and sentence saying, "Officers are prohibited from employing their forces for the purpose of returning fugitives from service or labor, but they are not required to employ their forces to prevent such return." Schofield, in a typical act of political juggling, then remitted Robinson's sentence and restored him to duty. See the *Daily Missouri Democrat*, 2 September 1863; General Order 87, 26 August 1863, RG 153, Records of the Office of the Judge Advocate General, NARA.

27. Schofield to Gamble, 3 July 1863, RG 393, E2579, NARA. Schofield to L. Thomas, 10 June 1863, RG 393, Part 1, E2571, NARA; "Enlistment of Colored Troops," *Missouri Democrat*, 10 June 1863.

28. Schofield to Stanton, 17 July 1863, RG 393, Part 1, E2571, NARA; Schofield to BG Thomas, 26 September 1863, RG 393, Part 1, E2571, NARA; Schofield to Townsend, 29 September 1863, RG 393, Part 1, E2571, NARA; Schofield to BG L Thomas, 10 June 1863, RG 393, Part 1, E2571; "Enlistment of Colored Troops," *Missouri Democrat*, 10 June 1863; Schofield to Gamble, 3 July 1863, RG 393, E2579; Schofield to Townsend, 29 September 1863, RG 393, Part 1, E2571; *Annual Report of the Adjutant General of the State of Missouri*, 31 December 1863 (Jefferson City, MO: W.A. Curry, 1864), 531.

29. In the American system, Schofield, at this point, possessed three commissions: captain in the Regular Army, Brigadier General of US Volunteers, and Brigadier General of the Missouri State Militia.

30. *OR*, series I, vol. 8, 354-56, 389; Schofield, *Forty-Six Years in the Army*, 54-56; James L. McDonough, *Schofield: Union General in the Civil War and Reconstruction* (Tallahassee: Florida State University Press, 1972), 29-41.

31. *OR*, series I, vol. 8, 493-94.

32. Missouri State Militia, General Order No.19, 22 July 1862, *OR*, series I, vol. 13, 10, 506-508. Schofield's report of 7 December 1862 explains and justifies his actions. *OR*, series I, vol. 13, 7-22, 513-15; Schofield, *Forty-Six Years in the Army*, 56; Parrish, *Turbulent Partnership*, 92; Mark Lause, "A Brief History of the Enrolled Missouri Militia: Forgotten Citizen-Soldiers of the Civil War," at <http://www.geocities.com/College Park/Quad/6460/CW/s/emmhist html>.

33. Stanton to Schofield, 26 July 1862, Box 42, Schofield Papers, LC; *OR*, series III, vol. 2, 294; *OR*, series I, vol. 13, 518-19; Colonel J.M. Glover to Scho-field, 30 July 1862, RG 393, Part III, E367, NARA; Gamble to Schofield, 24 July 1862, RG 393, Part III, E367, NARA; Missouri State Militia, General Order No. 23, 28 July 1962, *OR*, series I, vol. 13, 518-19.

34. William E. Smith, *The Francis Preston Blair Family in Politics*, vol. II (NY: MacMillan Co., 1933), 219.

35. Halleck to Schofield, 30 July 1862, Box 40, Schofield Papers, LC.

36. Schofield endorsement to BG J. Totten to Lieutenant Colonel C.W. Marsh, 3 August 1862, RG 393, Part III, E367, NARA; General Order 23, 22 September 1862, RG393, Part III, E369, NARA.

37. Schofield to Lieutenant Governor Willard P. Hall, 21 November 1863, RG393, E2579, NARA.

38. See Schofield to COL John Gray, Adjutant General of Missouri, 28 July 1863, E2571, RG393, Part I, NARA. Since EMM officers could not command US troops and juniors should not command seniors, Schofield directed Gray to ensure that the US officer is senior where there are combined US and EMM troops.

39. *OR*, series I, vol. 8, 422-23; *OR*, series I, vol. 13, 7-9, 436, 439; Schofield, *Forty-Six Years in the Army*, 54-56. For Governor Gamble's complaints about US Volunteer officers assuming command of state troops and Halleck's hair-splitting response, see *OR*, series III, vol. 2, 579, 591. Also Halleck to Gamble, 27 September 1862, Gamble Papers, MHS.

40. Parrish, *Turbulent Partnership*, 55; *OR*, series I, vol. 8, 478, 482, 502; *OR*, series I, vol. 8, 663, 607.

41. *OR*, series I, vol. 13, 654.

42. *OR*, series I, vol. 22/2, 293; *The Collected Works of Abraham Lincoln*, vol. VI, 234. Lincoln replaced Curtis with General Edwin Sumner on 10 March 1863, but Sumner died on his way to Missouri, so Curtis got a temporary reprieve.

43. Ironically, Dick had been a longtime ally of Frank Blair before the war, but he was now identified as a Curtis man. See Parrish, *Turbulent Partnership*, 27, 110, 155.

44. "The Indian Territory, the State of Kansas south of the 38th parallel, the western tier of counties of Missouri south of the same parallel, and the western tier of counties of Arkansas will constitute the District of the Frontier, and will be commanded by Maj. Gen. James G. Blunt; headquarters at Fort Scott, or in the field. The State of Kansas north of the 38th parallel, and the two western tiers of counties of Missouri north of the same parallel and south of the Missouri River will constitute the District of the Border, and will be commanded by Brig. Gen. Thomas Ewing, Jr.; headquarters at Kansas City." Later in July Schofield reconsidered this action and returned

these Missouri counties to the District of Southwestern Missouri. See General Orders No. 48, 9 June 1863, *OR*, series 1, vol. 22/2, 315.

45. These counties were Jackson, Cass, Bates, Lafayette, Johnson, Henry, Saint Clair, and the northern part of Vernon. On 23 September 1863, after the Quantrill raid and General Order No. 11, Schofield transferred Lafayette, Johnson, and Henry to the District of Central Missouri.

46. Charles Blair to Ewing, 18 November 1863; Ewing to Jennison, 25 November 1863; Thomas Ewing, Jr. to Thomas Ewing, Sr., 22 September 1863; H.G. Fant to Ewing, 18 and 20 July 1863; Ewing to Schofield, 24 July 1863, Thomas Ewing Papers, LC. After Schofield's removal from command of the Department of the Missouri and Curtis' appointment as commander of the Department of Kansas in January 1864, Ewing was transferred to St. Louis and fought Sterling Price at Pilot Knob on 27 September 1864. Ewing returned to Ohio after the war and served two terms in Congress (1877-1881) as a Democrat. He later practiced law in New York City and died in 1896.

47. Fifty bushwhackers from the Osage River region and 100 Confederate recruits under COL John Holt who refused to participate in the massacre and looting. See Albert Castel, *A Frontier State at War: Kansas 1861-1865* (Lawrence: Kansas Heritage Press, 1958), 126.

48. In his report, Thomas Ewing faulted Captain J.A. Pike's "error in judgement" for not following Quantrill "promptly and closely." Had Pike done so, he believed that "Quantrill would never have gone as far as Lawrence, or attacked it, with 100 men close to his rear." See *OR*, series I, vol. 22/1, 580. While Pike's reluctance to pursue a superior force in the dark is somewhat understandable, his failure to raise the alarm in the area, especially at the two prime targets of Lawrence and Olathe, is less so.

49. Once into Missouri, Quantrill's men dispersed into small groups and hid. Over the next week, Union commanders claimed to have tracked down and killed 100 of them. See Castel, *A Frontier State at War*, 124-41; Richard S. Brownlee, *Gray Ghosts of the Confederacy: Guerrilla Warfare in the West, 1861-1865* (Baton Rouge: Louisiana State University Press, 1958) 121-25; *OR*, series I, vol. 22/1, 578-90.

50. *OR*, series I, vol. 22/2, 460-62.

51. Mark E. Neely, Jr., "'Unbeknownst' to Lincoln: A Note on Radical Pacification in Missouri During the Civil War," *Civil War History*, vol. XLIV/3, 212-16; *OR*, series I, vol. 22/2, 471-72; "Diary of Events in Department of the Missouri," Schofield Papers, Box 1, LC; Schofield, *Forty-Six Years in the Army*, 80-84. According to William Wherry's 1884 note this diary was dictated by Schofield to his brother and aide George W. Schofield. The Schofield Papers contain several such "diaries" for relatively narrow time periods. Rather than a regular chronicling of events, Schofield seems to have felt the need to put his side of controversial events down on paper for future reference.

52. Halleck to Schofield, 7 July 1863, Schofield Papers, Box 40, LC.

53. *OR*, series I, vol. 22/1, 573.

54. "Diary of Events in Department of the Missouri," Schofield Papers, Box 1, LC.

55. Ibid.

56. Schofield's continued support probably also contained a political dimension. Although Ewing's relationship with Lane was deteriorating, he was a member of a powerful political family and remained well connected enough to aid in Schofield's promotion to major general. Ewing also had powerful military connections such as brother-in-law William T. Sherman. Schofield's

staunch support of Ewing undoubtedly contributed to Sherman's good opinion of his future subordinate.

57. T. Ewing to Schofield, 25 August 1863, Thomas Ewing Papers, LC; T. Ewing to (Secretary of the Interior) J.R. Usher, 28 August 1863, Thomas Ewing Papers, LC; Schofield to Ewing, 28 August 1863, Thomas Ewing Papers, LC; "Diary of Events in Department of the Missouri," Schofield Papers, Box 1, LC.

58. While at Leavenworth, Kansas, Schofield also attempted to conciliate yet another delicate problem of civil-military relations by making peace between Ewing and the town mayor. Leavenworth had become the center of a vast "fencing" operation for Redleg looters. One of Ewing's detectives, ironically named Jennison, had confiscated horses stolen by runaway Missouri slaves. Mayor Daniel R. Anthony ordered his arrest for disturbing the peace. The local court fined Jennison $50 and costs. Ewing objected to Anthony's attempt to use the local courts to obstruct his officers and declared martial law. The mayor challenged Ewing's authority to impose martial law, responding, "Our people prefer to have all violations of city and state laws settled by the civil authorities." Yet few Kansas courts were disposed to punish those who committed crimes against Missourians. Schofield was able to negotiate a truce, if not a peace, in which Mayor Anthony pledged not to obstruct federal authorities, and Ewing agreed to lift martial law. "Diary of Events in Department of the Missouri," Schofield Papers, Box 1, LC; D.R. Anthony to T. Ewing, 17 July 1863; A.H. Jennison to Ewing, 19 July 1863, Schofield Papers, Box 1, LC; Anthony to Ewing, 8 September 1863, Thomas Ewing Papers, LC.

59. Schofield told Ewing that "the test of loyalty should be rather liberal than severe, the object being to permit those, and only those, to return who will hereafter be faithful to the Government. Under the reign of terror which has so long existed on the border, active loyalty could not be expected. All who return should be enrolled, and their names registered at the nearest military post." See *OR*, series I, vol. 22/2, 693-94.

60. Parrish, Turbulent Partnership, 158. "Diary of Events in Department of the Missouri," Schofield Papers, Box 1, LC; Schofield, Forty-Six Years, 80-84. Draft review by Thomas Ewing of book on Order No. 11, Thomas Ewing Papers, LC.

61. *The Collected Works of Abraham Lincoln*, vol. VI, 492.

62. See Gilmore, 70-80; Cheatham, 144-61; Niepman, 185-210; Mink, 132-37.

63. LTC R.H. Hunt, "General Orders No. 11," 15th Kansas Cavalry, Kansas Commandery, Military Order of the Loyal Legion of the United States, February 1908, 6. Shelby supposedly made the statement in 1897.

64. Halleck to Schofield, 7 July 1863, Schofield Papers, Box 40, LC. *Daily Missouri Democrat*, 11 September 1863; *Columbia Missouri Statesman*, 18 September 1863; Schofield, *Forty-Six Years in the Army*, 84-87; Neely, *The Fate of Liberty*, 68-74; *OR*, series 1, vol. 22/2, 558, 563; "Enrolled Militia" *Daily Missouri Democrat*, 9 September 1863; Lincoln to Schofield, 1 October 1863; Lincoln to Charles D. Drake and others, 5 October 1863; *The Collected Works of Abraham Lincoln*, vol. VI, 492-93, 499-504; Parrish, *Turbulent Partnership*, 166.

65. Lincoln to Stanton, 18 and 21 December 1863; *The Collected Works of Abraham Lincoln*, vol. VII, 61, 62, 78-79, 84-85; *Lincoln and the Civil War in the Diaries and Letters of John Hay*, Tyler Dennett, ed. (New York: Dodd, Mead, 1939), 139-40; Schofield, *Forty-Six Years in the Army*, 107-112. Senator B. Gratz Brown's 20 January 1864 opposition speech to Schofield's promotion to major general included a petition that 64 members of the Missouri legislature signed. "'Confirmation of General Schofield' Speech of Hon. B. Gratz Brown of Missouri," 20 January 1864, Sampson Family Papers, Western Historical Manuscript Collection, Columbia, MO. Lincoln

appointed Schofield to command another department—the Department of the Ohio. Schofield's enemies did not relent even after his departure from Missouri, and Schofield and his friends had to continue lobbying for his promotion. On 12 May 1864 the Senate finally approved Schofield's promotion to Major General of Volunteers with a date of rank of 29 November 1862. Schofield got his promotion and just as important, a field command—the Army of the Ohio.

66. As of 31 December 1863 Missouri had contributed 104, 927 troops (nearly 10 percent of the state's population) to the Union cause. Missouri Volunteers: 35, 355; Missouri State Militia: 16, 918; Enrolled Missouri Militia: 46,893; Sundries: 5,761 (including 2,409 colored troops). See *Annual Report of the Adjutant General of the State of Missouri*, 31 December 1863 (Jefferson City, MO: W.A. Curry, 1864), 531.

67. For example, Schofield returned COL W.P. Robinson to duty after his court-martial for disobeying orders (see endnote 25) He also stood by Ewing, and even after Schofield's fall, Rosecrans gave Ewing a new command in eastern Missouri.

The US Army in the South: Reconstruction as Nation Building

Joseph G. Dawson III

Reconstruction and military government in the South during the Civil War era helped complete the foundation for American military government and "nation building" in other eras. The US Army's soldiers and officers were directly involved in physically rebuilding the infrastructure of the South. They also fulfilled a peacekeeping role as a constabulary. Based on extraordinary laws the US Congress passed in 1867, Army officers supervised local and state governments; they instituted various changes designed to bring about significant social and political reforms. Motivated by ideological goals, Republican leaders in Congress sought these changes, including defining citizenship and political and civil rights for African-Americans. Thus, an important ethnic and racial element entered into the Army's assignment, with implications not only for the former Confederate states but, eventually, for the rest of the United States.

The Army's assignment in the South merits evaluation, both short term and long term. In two short blocks of time the Army had more success than not. It was successful in assisting physical rebuilding and partially successful in peacekeeping from May 1865 to March 1867. From March 1867 to summer 1870 soldiers successfully implemented the provisions of the congressional Military Reconstruction Acts, limited violence, and restrained major civil disorders in the South. For the long term in the years after 1870, violence continued to be a factor, and the Army was unable to transform Southern society in the ways specified or implied in the Reconstruction acts. Moreover, the federal government stationed too few soldiers in the South to protect those put at risk by former Confederates and their supporters or to implement all of the changes implied by Reconstruction. Nevertheless, looking at the century after 1870, it can be argued that the Army achieved partial success. It contributed to important first steps in reshaping (or rebuilding) both Southern and American society. The Army helped initiate significant political and social changes in Southern society, even if some of those changes were qualified, undercut, or put aside from the 1870s to the 1960s.

Every army likes to rely on its strengths, but as the American Civil War concluded, few veterans in the Union Army and few civilians, North or South, would have placed military occupation or military government on a list of the US Army's accomplishments. Most Americans, including Army officers, paid little attention to the Army's experience in such matters. Within only a few weeks, from Robert E. Lee's surrender at Appomattox, Virginia, in April 1865 to the capitulation of the Confederacy's Trans-Mississippi forces at Galveston, Texas, in June, the Confederate States of America and its military forces had ceased to exist. How the Union Army's wartime experiences with occupying and governing hostile territory would apply to the postwar remained to be seen. Since 1861 members of Congress had debated the ways to reunite the nation, variously called "Restoration" or "Reconstruction." In December 1863, President Abraham Lincoln had recognized a pro-Union government for Virginia and created three pro-Union state governments in Tennessee, Arkansas, and Louisiana where "military governors" (civilians holding commissions as Union Army generals) took charge.[1] But no detailed federal plans—either congressional or executive—existed for postwar Reconstruction.[2]

When the Army administered military government in the former Confederacy in 1865, it was not the first time its officers had been given such duties. During the US-Mexican War of 1846-48, Regular and volunteer units had captured and occupied several towns and cities and patrolled the countryside near them.[3] The most prominent occupation took place in Mexico City from September 1847 to June 1848. Major General (MG) Winfield Scott commanded about 10,000 American soldiers to police a city containing 200,000 Mexicans.[4] Scott issued a series of orders establishing his temporary authority. Soldiers cleaned streets and acted as police. American Army officers supervised courts, officiated at elections, collected taxes, and regulated businesses, including issuing liquor licenses. In contrast to the South in 1865, a state of declared international war still existed in Mexico and diplomats negotiated a treaty that formally ended hostilities. At stake were lands that President James K. Polk and a majority in Congress agreed would come under US control, later ratified in the Treaty of Guadalupe Hidalgo in March 1848.[5]

Longer occupations took place elsewhere in former Mexican provinces, lasting more than three years. In 1846 American soldiers occupied New Mexico, and volunteer officers wrote laws and a constitution for the territory. In January 1847 Mexicans at Taos, New Mexico, attempted to regain control of the province, killing the acting civil governor. Some Mexicans signaled their support for the resistance, but US volunteer soldiers suppressed the rebellion in three weeks.[6] The American military government lasted in New Mexico until 1850. During most of that period, from 1846 to 1849, the Army also conducted a loose occupation of California. Combat there concluded in January 1847, and the Californians offered no conventional or guerrilla resistance thereafter. Meanwhile, two US Army officers helped draft a constitution for the new state. Thus, the American Army had a record of military government before 1861.[7]

From 1861 to 1865, Union Army officers gained experience that would prove valuable during Reconstruction. As the Civil War unfolded, Southern towns and cities fell to Federal forces, including Nashville, Tennessee (February 1862); New Orleans, Louisiana (April 1862); Norfolk, Virginia (May 1862); Memphis, Tennessee (June 1862); and Little Rock, Arkansas, and Chattanooga, Tennessee (September 1863). Union troops established garrisons and patrolled the countryside. Army officers supervised many aspects of daily life in the occupied places. These included approving newspapers and their editors, permitting churches to remain open and authorizing ministers to preach, reopening or establishing schools, and improving public health. Officers also operated major businesses, especially railroads and banks, where new legal currency had to be put into circulation. They carried out all of these actions as combat continued elsewhere in the South.[8]

Meanwhile, agents of the US Treasury Department conducted punitive actions in the occupied areas. Cooperating with the Union Army and Navy, and operating under the congressional Confiscation Acts, treasury agents confiscated huge quantities of cotton and sent it to northern mills.[9]

While treasury agents confiscated cotton, the War Department established a legal framework for the Army's operations pertaining to Reconstruction, issuing General Orders No. 100 on 24 April 1863. Drafted by Francis Lieber, a noted legal scholar, at the request of the War Department, these "Instructions for the Government of the Armies of the United States in the Field" became one of the principal foundations for the modern law of land warfare in Europe as well as America. Amended and approved by MG Henry

W. Halleck, the Union Army's chief of staff, General Orders No. 100 drew upon the American experience in Mexico. Lieber's Code, as the orders were also called, observed; "war has come to be acknowledged not to be its own end, but the means to obtain great ends of the state."[10] Lieber intended that, as much as possible, civilians should be protected and property rights should be respected, especially such culturally valuable institutions as libraries, museums, and colleges. However, enemy buildings could be used as barracks or depots, for instance. Enemy soldiers in uniform were to be fairly treated as prisoners of war and the wounded given medical care, but combatants fighting in civilian clothes were liable to be summarily executed. Key features of the code spelled out how Federal commanders could work with or replace local southern civil officials. Civil laws could function or be overridden by military governors, but charges against US soldiers would be tried in military courts. Although Confederate leaders condemned General Orders No. 100, Union commanders understood that Lieber's Code set significant operational standards for military government.[11]

General Orders No. 100 laid a foundation for the Army's authority, but as was the case throughout the 19th century, the Army still had no official doctrine or institutional procedure for its roles as an occupying force. During the war the methods of occupation varied from place to place, depending in part on the officers in charge. In 1865 there were no detailed plans for postwar Reconstruction, and no one knew how long the Army would be administering military government, which was operating in a rebellious region of the United States rather than in a foreign nation. Likewise, no one knew how soon most white southerners would renew their loyalty to the Union. Unlike the continuing existence of the Republic of Mexico in 1847-48, the death of the Confederacy in 1865 removed the contentious element of Confederate nationalism from the South's postwar years, although ex-Confederates displayed a long-lasting residual affection for the "lost cause." By occupying numerous southern towns, garrisoning forts, and patrolling roads—simply by being in the South—officers and soldiers, especially African-American soldiers, became objects of scorn, hatred, and anger. Seeing Federal soldiers wearing blue uniforms in the states of the former Confederacy caused most white southerners frustration, bitterness, and anxiety.[12] When the war ended, ex-Confederates wished the Union soldiers to be gone, and many Federals wished to go home.

Many northern veterans returned home soon enough, and a parsimonious Congress reduced the Army's budget to a modest level, typical of the small US peacetime military establishment. The Union Army dropped from about 1 million soldiers in May 1865 to around 220,000 in October.[13] Mustering out continued. By 1867 about 60,000 officers and men remained in the entire Federal Army, and about one-third of them were in the former Confederate states. By 1870 the total had declined to only 37,000 and dropped lower in years to come.[14] Having only part of such a modest military force to garrison and patrol 13 states containing some 10 million civilians (including thousands of Confederate veterans) presented serious challenges for the postwar Army that faced a potentially more hostile population in the South than in Mexico in the 1840s.

Using the Army as an occupation force seemed to be one of the last things on Andrew Johnson's mind, the succeeding president who took office upon Lincoln's death. Seizing the advantage while Congress was not in session, Johnson inaugurated his own plan of Restoration. As they had during the war, treasury agents continued to confiscate cotton.[15] Only a handful of federal marshals or deputy marshals in each state were available to make arrests or guard prisoners.[16] It became clear to everyone that only the Army was present in such numbers across the former Confederacy that it could patrol the South and police its cities. In places untouched by Union forces before the war ended some public officials abandoned their offices when the Army arrived. Army officers reopened courts or became judges and either asked mayors to return or took their places.[17] In much of the former Confederacy, damage to infrastructure was widespread. Soldiers began a process of physical reconstruction, repairing or rebuilding roads, bridges, and public buildings. Many railroads had broken down or been ripped up. Several railroad companies were bankrupt, and some owners had fled, leaving locomotives and railcars dilapidated.[18] Having operated the US Military Railroads during the war, Army officers directed soldiers to lay track, refurbish or replace railcars, and set timetables.[19] Parts of the military railroad were sold to civilian investors. Under the Army's direction, southern trains began to roll again.[20]

Hoping for a social transformation, the freedmen were uncertain about their status, socially and politically. The Army continued its wartime labor rules for nearly 4 million former slaves while members of Congress puzzled over social policy.[21] The Army also began to cooperate with a new federal agency established in March 1865 by an act of Congress, the Bureau of Refugees, Freedmen, and Abandoned Lands. Known to everyone as the Freedmen's Bureau, it was administered from the War Department and designed to provide federal assistance to former slaves. Its commissioner was MG Oliver O. Howard, a US Military Academy (USMA), West Point, New York, graduate and an Army officer on active duty. Moreover, many bureau agents were Army officers or former Army officers.[22]

For months after Confederate armies surrendered, Congress and President Johnson disputed about Reconstruction. Johnson implemented his own moderate plan, levying few requirements for the former Confederate states. The president called for them to nullify secession, cancel wartime debts, and ratify new state constitutions that abolished slavery. However, Johnson outlined no plans for the freedmen but issued hundreds of pardons to ex-Confederates or wealthy Southern civilians who had supported the Confederate cause. Thus, Johnson's plan was a speedy way for white southerners to resume governing themselves at the local and state levels as well as returning their representatives to Congress.[23]

Like a shadow, the Army stood behind the Johnson government. Soldiers acted as a constabulary in the South while white southerners proceeded to implement Johnson's plan. In many cases, pardoned ex-Confederates led the restoration efforts. Some Confederate veterans, most southern Unionists, and many former slaves recognized that the Army's hand rested lightly on the South. Obviously, slavery ended with the ratification of the 13th Amendment to the US Constitution in December 1865. In response, each southern state legislature passed "Black Codes." These laws regulated former slaves' lives in many ways such as their types of jobs, employment contracts, testimony in court, vagrancy, and property rental. Furthermore, the freedmen were not enfranchised. If the Black Codes were allowed to stand, many ex-Rebels mistakenly concluded, that Southern states would be restored with few penalties. Some former Confederates realized, however, that "self-reconstruction" would end if President Johnson and most Republicans in Congress had a serious falling out.[24]

In spring and summer 1866 significant events transformed northern attitudes on Reconstruction. Riots racked two major southern cities—Memphis in April and New Orleans in July. Although there had been troops in both cities at the time of the riots, their commanding officers—George Stoneman in Memphis and Absalom Baird in New Orleans—had not taken effective measures to prevent bloodshed, misunderstood local circumstances, and harbored unfounded hopes that violence would be avoided.[25] Dozens of freedmen were killed or injured in the two riots, and the civil authorities, some of them ex-Rebels, were clearly implicated. Elected or appointed officials in the two cities had failed to stop the unrest, and some, including policemen, had participated in the mayhem. A few months earlier President Johnson had decided to veto a civil rights bill, and in the meantime, numerous former Confederates had been elected to office, including seats in Congress. These events pushed moderate and radical Republicans together to oppose Johnson's restoration plan. Many northerners now pictured the South, led by former Rebels, as unwilling to abide by the changes the war brought. The Republican majority in Congress refused to seat the ex-Confederates elected to the House and Senate and had earlier passed a bill to recharter the Freedmen's Bureau. In the meantime, continuing its extraordinary role as constable and its influence in southern economic and social life, the Army assumed an unusual position in American civil-military relations.[26]

Introducing a measure that might have concluded Reconstruction, in June 1866 the congressional Republicans proposed the 14th Amendment to the US Constitution. Almost all ex-Confederates, most northern Democrats, and President Johnson immediately opposed the proposed amendment. It contained several provisions. It defined as citizens all persons naturalized or born within the US borders ("citizens" had not been defined before), including African-Americans. Republicans wanted all male citizens to be eligible to vote (although the amendment did not include such a provision), and all citizens, black and white, would be counted to determine the number of members for each state in the US House of Representatives rather than three-fifths of blacks counted in antebellum times.

A state temporarily could deny the right to vote to citizens who had engaged in rebellion, but if a state denied other citizens (such as African-Americans) the right to vote, the state's representation in the House of Representatives could be reduced accordingly. Most ex-Confederates objected to the fact that antebellum southern officials who supported or assisted the rebellion were temporarily denied the chance to hold either state or federal offices until Congress removed such disability. Asserting long-held views on states' rights and his interpretation of the Constitution, President Johnson had already vetoed the recharter of the Freedmen's Bureau, contending that the agency was unconstitutional and unnecessary.[27] Johnson now urged all states to reject the 14th Amendment as treading on states' rights. Ironically, the legislature of Tennessee, Johnson's home state, was the only former Confederate state to ratify the 14th Amendment at its first opportunity. To show how its plan was supposed to work, Congress seated Tennessee's US senators and congressmen.[28]

A solid Republican majority in Congress confronted President Johnson by passing a series of measures, all vetoed by the executive, then passed over his veto. The Freedmen's Bureau was rechartered. In March 1867 Congress passed the first of four congressional Military Reconstruction Acts to "Provide for the More Efficient Government of the

Rebel States." Thus, nearly two years after Lee had surrendered and six months after Johnson officially had declared the Civil War ended in August 1866, the word "Rebel" formed part of the title of major national legislation. Northern and southern Democrats termed the laws "Radical" Reconstruction Acts, and they were indeed radical to many 19th-century Americans. Congress could not rely on a few treasury agents, US marshals, or federal prosecutors to implement its ambitious and complicated plan. The Reconstruction Acts' far-reaching provisions required several actions of the former Confederate states but radically departed from all previous American experience by officially placing Army generals in charge of most of the former Confederacy.[29]

The laws divided 10 of the former Rebel states into five military districts, and state governments elected or operating under Johnson's plan ceased to have legal standing. Coming out of the shadow of previous months, Army generals were granted sweeping authority to keep or cancel all state laws and to maintain or replace all state and local officeholders in the military districts. Moreover, the generals were to implement the requirements of the Reconstruction Acts, including registering voters, conducting elections for constitutional conventions, certifying election results, supervising the operation of constitutional conventions, and conducting more elections to ratify the constitutions and elect officeholders. Meanwhile, in accordance with civil rights laws Congress passed, the Army would protect the rights of all citizens, including African-Americans and southern Unionists. The Reconstruction Acts authorized the generals to determine the eligibility of voters, indicating that anyone who had sworn to uphold the US Constitution before 1861 but then supported the Confederacy could be blocked from registering. Furthermore, these acts not only required the new southern state constitutions to make blacks eligible to vote but also the new southern state legislatures were informed in advance that they must ratify a proposed amendment to the US Constitution (the 14th) before Congress would seat their states' US senators and congressmen. Seating of senators and congressmen would symbolize the end of Reconstruction in each state.[30] After March 1867 Reconstruction meant that 10 former Confederate states would complete these steps under Army supervision.

Assigning the Army to carry out exceptional political procedures certainly was radical. The civil rights laws and Reconstruction Acts changed freedmen's lives in numerous ways. In contrast to the years of slavery, the freedmen could legally marry, legally possess firearms, choose to change jobs, decide to move from one place to another, routinely testify in courts of law, attend schools, own real estate and other property, serve on juries, pay taxes, enroll in the state militia, and enlist in the peacetime US Army. Many Americans concluded that black men having the right to vote was radical; it would begin to transform the South and, eventually, politically and socially rebuild the entire nation.[31]

These were remarkably ambitious plans, and no one could predict how long the political rebuilding and social transformation through military government would last: only several months or as long as a few years. As usual, Americans were impatient. Reconstruction's supporters and detractors wanted the steps completed as soon as possible.

Congressional leaders based the Reconstruction process on several actions and assumptions. First, they levied temporary political penalties on the ex-Rebels to allow citizens loyal to the Union to run the southern governments. Second, the Reconstruction Acts called for political procedures familiar to Americans—procedures that had been *state* responsibilities, including registering voters, conducting elections, certifying ballots, drafting and amending state constitutions, and having state legislatures consider and either reject or ratify amendments to the US Constitution. In 1867, therefore, the Reconstruction Acts temporarily replaced state rights with federal directives. Third, if ex-Confederates used force to oppose the process of Reconstruction, the process could fail or last indefinitely. Confederate soldiers in 1865, however, had not resorted to guerrilla warfare, so it seemed unlikely that southerners would become guerrillas in 1867. Still, for Reconstruction to be completed with any success, it was necessary for civil order to prevail. Army troops in state capitals and a few other towns formed the thin blue line between law and disorder. Furthermore, success would be contingent upon expecting minimum levels of acquiescence, compliance, or even cooperation from ex-Confederates. Some former Confederates, smarting under temporary political penalties, realized that by acting individually or in groups they might forestall the changes, especially black participation in politics, that Republicans sought.[32]

All of these steps and concepts generated controversy within the constitutional framework, federal-state relations, system of courts, and two-party politics understood by Americans.[33] Some opponents in the North, such as President Johnson, as well as the South doubted the constitutionality of all the Republicans' measures, including civil rights laws, the Freedmen's Bureau, the 14th Amendment, and the Military Reconstruction Acts. Furthermore, opponents questioned the efficacy of using the Army to bring about these social and political changes. Others, especially ex-Rebels, simply opposed all political and social changes taking place as a result of the Civil War.

It appeared that Congress had cut President Johnson out of Reconstruction, but he maintained authority as commander in chief of the armed forces, although he was at odds with Secretary of War Edwin Stanton. In 1867 the Army had primary missions of defending national borders, including the coasts of southern seaboard states facing the Atlantic and the Gulf of Mexico; protecting settlers and campaigning against Indian tribes in the trans-Mississippi region; and carrying out Reconstruction. Obviously, Republicans in Congress were concerned that the president might interfere with Reconstruction.[34] Officially, Johnson picked the generals for the Southern military districts, but General in Chief Ulysses S. Grant exercised influence on the choices. The initial group of commanders included Brevet MG John M. Schofield who graduated from the USMA in 1853 for the First Military District (Virginia). The Second District (North Carolina and South Carolina) commander, Brevet MG Daniel E. Sickles, was a volunteer officer and, like Johnson, a prewar Democrat. The Third District (Alabama, Georgia, and Florida) commander, Brevet MG John Pope, was a USMA graduate in 1842, and the Fourth District (Mississippi and Arkansas) commander, Brevet MG Edward O.C. Ord, was an 1839 West Pointer and a veteran of California occupation duty. The Fifth District (Texas and Louisiana) commander, MG Philip H. Sheridan, graduated from the USMA in 1853.[35] At first glance, Sheridan, Pope, and Sickles could be classified as "radical"—they appeared to favor civil and political rights for the freedmen—but the other district commanders were moderate or conservative, giving no outward support for the Republicans' agenda.

Implementing that agenda displayed some contrasts with military government in New Mexico and California after the US-Mexican War. A notable feature of Reconstruction was that Army officers did not draft the new southern constitutions, and the Army did not face residents of another nation or another culture.[36] In six of the 10 southern states, the Army's direct control lasted only a few months, running from spring 1867 to summer 1868. The remaining states were reconstructed by 1870. While the Army exercised influence in the South into the 1870s, some historians left an influential, though exaggerated, description of "bayonet rule," writing as if military despots dominated for several years.[37] In addition, southern resistance to Reconstruction, beginning slowly and becoming occasionally intense in some states, grew more widespread than in Mexico's former provinces of California and New Mexico.

Receiving copies of the Reconstruction Acts, the generals in charge of the military districts went right to work, and each had their own ideas about how to implement them. Each district commander sought to carry out the Reconstruction process expeditiously, which would allow the Army to return to its traditional missions on the seacoasts and the frontier. Except for Sickles, a former Democrat, none of the five district commanders had held political office or been aligned with a political party. Indeed, most Regular Army officers were politically conservative, standing a considerable distance from most of the Republicans in Congress. In 1867 only about 21,000 soldiers were stationed in the former Confederate states, and the generals logically had concerns about keeping the peace, given such modest numbers of soldiers in their commands.[38] It was obvious the Army could not be everywhere. Acts of violence against black and white southern Republicans occurred sporadically, but for several months, there was no concerted or widespread violence across the South. In the military districts, some former Confederates decided to show their displeasure with Reconstruction by not registering or not participating in politics.[39] Otherwise, voter registrars, many of them Army officers or former Army officers, blocked numbers of ex-Rebels from registering who had sworn to uphold the US Constitution before 1861 and then supported the Confederacy.

In each military district, the process of Reconstruction proceeded along similar lines but with idiosyncrasies. Rather than seeking strength in unity, southern Republicans often split into political factions.[40] Democrats struggled to find an effective political strategy and achieved notable early electoral successes in two southern states, putting Louisiana and Georgia in the column for the Democratic presidential candidate in 1868. Violence occurred against individual Republicans, such as schoolteachers and officeholders of both races, and occasional riots flared up, events that can be likened to a low level of guerrilla war. However, no matter the ex-Confederates' electoral ploys or violent tactics, they avoided direct confrontations with the Army. In other words, opponents of Reconstruction declined to engage in more intense levels of guerrilla war.[41] In the meantime, the district commanders and their subordinate officers, most of whom were conservative men who were uncomfortable with their assignments, proceeded to implement the terms of the congressional laws.

MG Schofield, commander, First Military District opposed the 14th Amendment and was skeptical about political rights for African-Americans. He got along well with many white southerners and found ways to express his sympathy or respect for them. In unpublished essays, Schofield spelled out his conservative views on Reconstruction. He was uncertain about the powers the Military Reconstruction Acts gave him. Still, while some white Virginia officeholders rejected Reconstruction or tried to impede its progress, Schofield decided that national laws must be enforced. Thus, the Army helped to initiate the Republicans' social and political agenda. Schofield carefully divided his district into subdistricts; thoroughly supervised voter registration, including thousands of blacks; and guaranteed the drafting of a new state constitution. Furthermore, for a conservative, Schofield seemed to take a more radical path in some ex-Confederates' eyes. For example, the general announced that there could be no discrimination against blacks on trains and trolley cars in Virginia. Virginia's governor turned out to be uncooperative, prompting Schofield to remove the governor in April 1868 and appoint a former Union officer from Michigan to take his place. Schofield also removed some officials and appointed hundreds of other officeholders to vacant offices. Obviously, when an Army officer removed elected or appointed civilians, many Americans considered such actions to be radical. A velvet glove covered Schofield's iron hand. Appearing reluctant and deferential made him more palatable to former Confederates than other military district commanders. In public he declined to use caustic rhetoric. His private writings revealed more radical tones: "If we can not trust them [ex-Confederates] there is nothing left but to hold the Southern States under military government until a new generation can be educated."[42]

In June 1868 Schofield accepted President Johnson's offer to become secretary of war, and the president replaced him in the South with Brevet MG George Stoneman, USMA 1846 and a Democrat.[43] Stoneman also enforced the Reconstruction Acts, appointing triple the number of men to office as Schofield. Nevertheless, the Army began to learn how opponents' clever ploys, political obstruction, intimidation, and violence could delay Reconstruction goals. Completing the process more slowly than some states, Virginia was not readmitted to the Union until January 1870.[44]

Second District Commander Daniel Sickles had been a flamboyant, even notorious, Democratic congressman before the war, but by 1867 he had become a Republican. In contrast to Schofield, Sickles was tactless, self-important, and impatient. He immediately interpreted the First Reconstruction Act to give him full authority over state officials (such authority was confirmed by the subsequent acts), announcing that he could remove officeholders at any time. He also decreed that all adult black men who had paid taxes would be eligible to serve on juries. Like Schofield, in June 1867 Sickles banned discrimination against African-Americans on all public conveyances in the Carolinas. To determine if judges' verdicts in major criminal convictions had been fair, Sickles reviewed state court decisions. When Sickles determined that a judge had been unfair, the general established a military court to take his place. Making further use of his extraordinary powers, the general removed civil officials from office and put in his appointees. In June North Carolina Governor Jonathan Worth complained to President Johnson about Sickles' actions, which obviously advanced the Republican agenda. Exercising his authority as commander in chief, in August 1867 Johnson removed Sickles from command, replacing him with Brevet MG Edward R.S. Canby.[45]

Belonging to no party and considered by some to be fair-minded, General Canby took up his post in Charleston, South Carolina, in September.[46] Worth regretted Canby's posting and accused the general of instituting a "military despotism." Naturally, the governor complained to President Johnson.[47] As voter registration and preparations for elections progressed, supervised by the Army's Bureau of Civil Affairs, Canby transferred some criminal cases to military judges. He reiterated that blacks would serve on juries and assumed duties in the Carolinas as assistant commissioner of the Freedmen's Bureau.

On his order, food was distributed to hundreds of destitute freedmen. Canby began removing civil officials, including city council members and the mayors of Charleston and Columbia, South Carolina, branding them "impediments to Reconstruction." Canby replaced seven of the Charleston city councilmen with African-Americans. Meanwhile, Reconstruction proceeded apace: voters cast ballots, conventions assembled, and delegates drafted constitutions. Voters, blacks among them, went to the polls to approve the constitutions and elect state officials, including legislators. They also ratified the 14th Amendment. In June 1868 the Carolinas were readmitted, and the Second Military District ceased to exist.[48]

In the Third Military District, with headquarters at Atlanta, Georgia, Brevet MG John Pope claimed to behave with restraint and even reluctance, but to most white southerners, Pope seemed radical. In Alabama, Georgia, and Florida, Pope faithfully executed federal laws and therefore advanced the Republican social and political agenda. Naturally, he fell afoul of President Johnson. Georgia Governor Charles Jenkins unsuccessfully brought suit in federal court to block action under the Reconstruction Acts, and ex-Confederates denounced Pope as a despot. Following street violence in Mobile, Alabama, Pope decided that numerous civil officials were impeding Reconstruction, and he began removing 100 judges, city councilmen, and mayors in all three states of his district. Acting under the authority of congressional laws, he appointed men to fill vacant offices and voided an election in Tuscumbia, Alabama. He also handed out specific guidelines on publishing newspapers. Like Schofield, Sickles, and Canby, Pope ordered that all jurors must be registered voters. Not only did this step mean that black men would take on a civil right with political implications, it also meant that, for an indefinite time, some former Confederates would not serve on juries if they could not register to vote. In December, a few weeks after voters in the Third District approved calling for constitutional conventions, President Johnson removed Pope, sending him to the Great Lakes and replacing him with Brevet MG George G. Meade.[49]

A USMA graduate of 1835 and a Union hero at Gettysburg, Pennsylvania, Meade wanted Reconstruction to be short and as painless as possible for the South and the nation. Even knowing Meade's conservative views, some white southerners in the Third Military District refused to cooperate. Meade acted with restraint, usually favoring conservative or moderate politicians opposed to radicals but found himself, like Pope, removing officials who were, in his estimation, "impediments to reconstruction." In Georgia, Meade's removals included Governor Jenkins and the state treasurer. Unlike Pope, Meade replaced these civilians with active duty Army officers, Colonel Thomas Ruger and Captain (CPT) Charles Rockwell. Likewise, when he decided to remove the mayor of Columbus, Georgia, Meade replaced him with an Army captain. After disputes arose in Florida's constitutional convention, Meade sent an Army colonel to chair the meeting, and that officer seemed to favor the moderates. Furthermore, Meade curried favor with ex-Confederates. Meade authorized that a pardoned ex-Confederate general, John B. Gordon, could be a Georgia gubernatorial candidate and failed to look closely at the background of more than 20 conservatives elected to the Georgia legislature who could not qualify to hold office under the 14th Amendment. Nevertheless, by June 1868 Congress deemed that all three states in the Third Military District had carried out the Reconstruction laws and readmitted their senators and representatives.[50]

Showing that the process of Reconstruction was far from foolproof, in September 1868 Meade failed to head off a riot in Camilla, Georgia, that killed nine blacks and wounded 30 others. Reports reached Congress of numerous acts of violence by the Ku Klux Klan against Georgia Republicans. When the Georgia legislature abruptly voted to eject its 28 black members, Congress placed Georgia back under military government in December 1869. President Grant assigned Brevet MG Alfred H. Terry, an antebellum attorney and wartime volunteer Union officer, to supervise the district of Georgia. Terry was unsure of his authority under these odd circumstances, but eventually he appointed a military review board to evaluate legislators' credentials. The officers ruled that three legislators were ineligible and 19 others could not take the prescribed federal oath, thereby losing their positions. The expelled black representatives returned to the legislature, and new elections were held to fill the empty seats. Even with those changes, Republicans held only a narrow majority in both houses. Congress exacted an additional penalty, calling for Georgia to ratify the proposed 15th Amendment to the Constitution. The legislature completed that requirement in February 1870, and Congress approved the state's readmission again in July.[51]

Mississippi and Arkansas formed the Fourth Military District commanded by Brevet MG Edward Ord. A conservative officer who approached his assignment with an attitude similar to Schofield's, Ord was opposed to black suffrage and skeptical of the powers allotted to district commanders. Like Schofield, Canby, and Meade, Ord did not intend to rearrange the state governments in his district or carry out many removals. He displaced only one state official, the treasurer of Arkansas, and closely supervised that state's finances. Removals at the county and local levels were another matter. Ord pulled out more than 50 white officeholders, replacing some of them with qualified blacks, appointments that stunned ex-Confederates who thought that the general was their friend. Doubtful that state courts were competent, Ord moved some cases to military commissions. William McCardle, a newspaper editor in Vicksburg, Mississippi, was so harsh in his editorial criticism of Ord that the general ordered his arrest on charges of impeding Reconstruction, sparking a case that went to the US Supreme Court.[52] Meanwhile, Ord, who also had served as assistant commissioner of the Freedmen's Bureau for Arkansas, worked closely with Brevet MG Alvan C. Gillem, an active duty officer who was assistant commissioner of the Freedman's Bureau for Mississippi. Like President Johnson, Gillem was a Tennesseean who graduated from West Point in 1851. Pending the arrival of MG Irvin McDowell, USMA 1838, Gillem became district commander in January 1868 when Ord gained approval from President Johnson and General Grant to transfer to California.[53]

Ex-Confederates in Mississippi and Arkansas watched with concern as Reconstruction pressed ahead. Although some observers considered Gillem President Johnson's friend, the general spurred on voter registration and continued Ord's pattern of using Army officers as voter registrars in both states in the Fourth Military District. Attending to levee repairs along the Mississippi River and filling vacant political offices occupied much of Gillem's time. An unusual example was his appointment of two Army majors in succession to be mayor of Jackson, the state capital of Mississippi.[54]

In June 1868 Arkansas met the requirements for readmission, but numerous problems delayed Mississippi, prompting MG McDowell to appoint one of his subordinates, Brevet MG Adelbert Ames, USMA 1861, as acting governor. Ames set himself apart as one of two generals (the other was Joseph J. Reynolds in Texas) who took the strongest public stand favoring Reconstruction. Ames swept out hundreds of state officials, some of them Republicans, thus adding to party factionalism. Numerous black Mississippians gained town and county offices under Ames' regime. Careful voter registration drives finally prepared the state to hold state elections, although ex-Confederates did all they could to impede the Reconstruction process. In February 1870 Mississippi was readmitted. In a bold act of partisanship, Ames called on the state legislature to elect him to the US Senate. Following his election, he resigned from the Army.[55]

In the Fifth Military District, MG Sheridan carried burdens other generals did not. Based on his controversial Shenandoah Valley campaign in 1864, critics characterized Sheridan as a ruthless soldier who took the war to Confederate civilians and caused widespread damage to civilian property. Thus, many white southerners hated Sheridan, who did nothing to allay their hatred. At the outset of Military Reconstruction, and perhaps more than any other general, Sheridan may have represented exactly the kind of district commander Johnson despised.[56] Interpreting the Reconstruction Acts to his satisfaction and after carefully weighing his options, Sheridan removed dozens of former Confederates or their sympathizers from office or authorized his subordinates to do so. Removals included the governors of Texas and Louisiana, the Louisiana state attorney general, and the mayor of New Orleans and most of the city council. Sheridan appointed a former Union Army officer to be the police chief in New Orleans. Registering voters became a top priority, with the idea that many ex-Confederates would be excluded. Causing distress to many white southerners, in May 1867 Sheridan also integrated New Orleans' streetcars. Sheridan's actions became too much for the president.[57] In August 1867 Johnson removed Sheridan and announced that he would be replaced by MG Winfield S. Hancock, USMA 1844, an avowed Democrat who wanted his party's presidential nomination.[58]

In fact, several generals followed Sheridan in the Fifth Military District. Serving as interim commander for three months until Hancock arrived, Joseph A. Mower perpetuated Sheridan's close enforcement of the Reconstruction Acts. Then Hancock, one of the Union's heroes at the Battle of Gettysburg, made every effort to reverse or cancel Sheridan's approach. Hancock manipulated the Reconstruction Acts to the Democrats' favor, removing some of Sheridan's and Mower's appointees from office and replacing them with conservative civilians who were more accommodating to former Confederates' views. Hancock permitted men to register to vote who Sheridan or Mower had blocked from registering. Many white southerners cheered Hancock, overlooking the fact that he was an Army general removing civilians from office. Hancock may have been the conservatives' and ex-Confederates' favorite district commander; even more so when Grant required him to reinstate some of Sheridan's appointees.[59] This dispute led Hancock to request a reassignment to the east, and he left the Fifth Military District in March 1868.[60] An interim replacement, Brevet MG Robert C. Buchanan, was remarkably even-handed. He gained no support from ex-Rebels; most of them believed Buchanan's even-handedness seemed too helpful to southern Republicans. Overcoming numerous difficulties, Louisiana was readmitted by Congress in July 1868.[61]

Hancock, a Democrat, was a sharp contrast to Brevet MG Joseph J. Reynolds, USMA 1843. Someone who may be ranked among the most radical of all the generals, Reynolds not only insisted that ex-Rebels in Texas comply strictly with the Reconstruction laws but he also exercised his discretionary powers, removing Democrats and ex-Confederates and putting more than 800 Republicans and Unionists in office. Of course, Reynolds saw to the necessary steps of holding elections and having a convention draft a new state constitution. Considerable violence between whites and blacks in East Texas challenged the Army's ability to keep the peace, and Reynolds also had to devote attention to Indian raids. President Johnson removed Reynolds in November 1868, replacing him with Brevet MG Edward R.S. Canby.[62]

Democrats and ex-Confederates were disappointed in March 1869 to see President Grant reassign Reynolds as provisional governor of Texas. Using removals and appointments, Reynolds played politics by first taking one Republican faction's side and then moving to aid another one. Voter registration drives continued, with Army officers serving on registration boards. A convention finally drafted a new state constitution, and a civil government was installed. While still an officer on active duty, Reynolds sought to have the Texas legislature elect him to the US Senate. Unlike Ames in Mississippi, Reynolds failed in his ploy, and he withdrew as a candidate. Overcoming many problems, Texas was readmitted in March 1870.[63]

General William T. Sherman, USMA 1840, provided a sharp contrast to Reynolds' evident support for Reconstruction. Among the Army's most prominent conservatives, Sherman replaced Grant in 1869 as commanding general, an honorary office with little authority. Thus, Sherman found it difficult to influence the Reconstruction process for the states still under military government in 1869 and 1870. He became frustrated with political machinations in the capital, although he was the brother of one of the leading Republican senators, John Sherman, Ohio. Consequently, he relocated his headquarters to St. Louis, Missouri.[64]

Even before Congress readmitted all of the former Confederate states, the House of Representatives impeached President Andrew Johnson in February 1868, followed by a bitter trial in the Senate from late March through May. Johnson had vetoed civil rights bills and the Reconstruction Acts and had opposed the 14th Amendment. He also had exercised his authority as commander in chief to remove or reassign all five of the original military district commanders. Johnson had removed Sickles, Pope, and Sheridan and replaced them with officers, such as Canby, Meade, and Hancock, who either favored the Democrats or opposed the radical agenda. Most Republicans concluded that Johnson's reassigning generals worked against Republican reforms by undermining Reconstruction's continuity. In addition, Johnson had tried to circumvent Grant's influence, even after Congress passed the controversial "Command of the Army Act" in March 1867. Although it was his removing Secretary of War Stanton that brought on his impeachment, Johnson removing military districts commanders generated resentment among Republicans and contributed to their willingness to support his impeachment.[65]

Before winning the presidential election in November 1868, General Grant watched all Reconstruction developments closely. In early 1866 he handed out General Orders No. 3, "To Protect Loyal Persons Against Improper Civil Suits and Penalties in [the] Late Rebellious States." Designed to discourage frivolous lawsuits that ex-Confederates brought against soldiers and Freedmen's Bureau agents, Grant's orders also specified that the Army would protect "colored persons from prosecutions in any of said States charged with offenses for which white persons are not prosecuted or punished in the same manner and degree." Grant followed up with General Orders No. 44 in July, authorizing the Army to arrest those accused of committing crimes against soldiers, bureau agents, and other persons if local or state law officers failed to act. Grant committed the Army to enforce civil rights.[66]

After Congress passed the Reconstruction Acts, Grant stated his support for the basic goals of Reconstruction, sometimes directing district commanders to observe specific paragraphs of these laws.[67] Sometimes Grant prescribed caution to the district commanders.[68] He urged no hasty removals and did not want any elected officials removed unless "absolutely necessary."[69] He worried that many months of military government in the South would cause "a reaction against the army." Grant wrote to Edward Ord, "I am exceedingly anxious to see reconstruction effected and Military rule put an end to. . . . The best way, I think, to secure a speedy termination of Military rule is to execute all the laws of Congress in the spirit in which they were conceived firmly but without passion."[70]

No matter the district commanders' personal politics, from 1867 to 1870 most of them exercised their authority under the Military Reconstruction Acts to produce radical results. Adding to the complications in carrying out these federal laws, the generals not only acted contrary to antebellum American traditions but also infuriated most ex-Confederates and many northern Democrats. Generals who appeared to most southern whites to be either vindictive or radical, such as Sheridan in the Fifth Military District and Pope in the Third, carried out the congressional Reconstruction laws forcefully. Even the "moderate" or "conservative" generals, such as Schofield, Meade, Ord, and Canby, clearly accepted one of the basic but also radical concepts of Military Reconstruction: the Army was in charge of southern governments and responsible for implementing the political steps returning 10 former Confederate states to the status of loyalty. In other words, the ex-Confederates had to fulfill what the Republican majority in Congress wanted, and the Army would see to it that they did. Schofield and Meade were personally more palatable than Sheridan and Pope, but during the years the Army administered military government, all four generals' results turned out to be much the same.

In the late 1860s and early 1870s, southern Democrats combined two approaches in their efforts to regain political power. They effectively employed threats, intimidation, and selective violence against vulnerable, unprotected, or isolated black and white Republicans, and they exploited Republican factionalism to regain their prewar status and power. Violent acts of terrorism by ex-Confederates, such as murdering Republican officeholders and burning down their homes, churches, and schools, highlighted the fact that, in most cases, those opposing the results of Reconstruction continued to avoid confrontations with the Army, which could not protect everyone. As support for enforcing federal laws waned in the North, by overt or covert means southern opponents of Reconstruction significantly reduced the impact of Reconstruction laws and amendments by 1876.[71]

After the Southern states were readmitted, the Army's role changed. Military units served across the South, often in the same forts, barracks, and arsenals where they had been stationed in the antebellum years. It was natural for Republican politicians to look to the Army to help maintain order, but the small numbers of soldiers in the South made peacekeeping difficult and hindered them in enforcing federal laws. Although the appearance of soldiers in blue uniforms could still defuse a crisis or discourage violent acts, politically motivated civilian depredations and murders mounted, and several major disturbances occurred. In September 1868 President Johnson's friend, Brigadier General Lovell H. Rousseau, failed to prevent a riot and murders of Republicans in St. Landry Parish, Louisiana. At Eufaula, white attackers killed seven and wounded 70 blacks. In summer 1873 a riot at Colfax, Louisiana, resulted in the deaths of dozens of African-Americans. During 1874, in Arkansas, factional rivalry produced the so-called "Brooks-Baxter War." In the same year Louisiana hit a new low when conservatives murdered several blacks at Coushatta, and Democrats took to New Orleans streets to overthrow the elected Republican governor, William Kellogg. Charleston, South Carolina, was the scene of violence during the November 1876 elections. In each case, Army units restored order or arrived after the violence subsided, but these and other violent outbreaks after 1870 indicated that the Army could not be counted on to maintain complete social stability among a white populace largely opposed to Reconstruction and willing to perpetrate violence, especially at selected times and places where there were no soldiers.[72]

Actions by ex-Confederates and their sympathizers also took other forms, with the Ku Klux Klan, the Knights of the White Camellia, and the "White Leagues" making threats and inflicting violence against southern Republicans. The Klan and similar organizations perpetrated violent acts across the South, prompting Congress in 1870 to pass the Ku Klux Acts, also known as the Enforcement Acts. President Grant demonstrated his willingness to use federal forces to uphold those congressional laws and cracked down in South Carolina. Soldiers assisted US marshals in arresting klansmen and guarded courthouses while federal prosecutors tried their cases. Federal authorities arrested hundreds of klan members and put dozens on trial. Other klansmen absconded to avoid confronting the Army or prosecution. Thus, the Army played a major role in suppressing the Ku Klux Klan.[73]

Contributing to maintaining law and order in the reconstructed states, it became routine during elections for Army squads or companies to guard ballot boxes, patrol county roads, and march through city streets. Moreover, Army officers and a few soldiers sometimes became a posse comitatus, accompanying state law officers carrying warrants to arrest men charged with crimes. All of these martial displays were controversial and out of the ordinary in American political life, especially when the Army assisted in serving arrest warrants.[74] In the 1870s Democrats raised numerous criticisms and called for an end to using the Army as a posse comitatus. By 1876 fewer congressional Republicans supported the Army's continued influence, even if many southern Republicans wanted the Army's presence to serve as a reminder of federal authority.[75] In June 1878 the Democrats were able to have Congress pass the Posse Comitatus Act prohibiting the Army's direct involvement in "executing the laws" without the express authorization of Congress.[76] When President Rutherford B. Hayes made it clear that troops would no longer directly support the last remaining southern Republican governors in 1877, hundreds of soldiers continued to be stationed in the former Confederate states.[77]

During Reconstruction, the US Army carried out its responsibilities of military government as mandated by Congress. These postwar responsibilities related to the numerous and various administrative and constabulary duties in the South from 1861 to 1865 and were associated with peacekeeping and posse comitatus during the 1870s. Combined with its occupying New Mexico, California, and Mexico and drafting laws and constitutions in the annexed lands following the US-Mexican War, Reconstruction gave the Army a considerable, if unappreciated, record in military government by 1870. Most officers disliked their duties in the South and, conservative by the standards of the day, were uncomfortable enforcing the social and political changes indicated by the Reconstruction Acts.

The Army learned firsthand that the prospects for success in postwar occupation duties relied in part on a population that was ready to comply or cooperate with the occupying forces. Social stability was needed for the Army to implement reforms. Based on the Army's experiences during the U.S.-Mexican War and Reconstruction, CPT William Birkhimer wrote a book to provide a guide to military government for officers at the Army's Leavenworth, Kansas, schools. Revised for a third edition in 1914, Birkhimer's treatise indicated that the Army had gained additional experience as an occupation force during and after the Spanish-American War.[78] Still, in the 1870s and even after the turn of the century, it was difficult for the Army to acknowledge that postwar military government and occupation had become a part of its professional duties. The next step would be for the Army to incorporate these experiences into some sort of official doctrine.[79]

Reconstruction in the South was not the Army's first experience with postwar "nation building." Reconstruction had much in common with occupation and nation-building duties after other wars. It lasted longer than expected, was sometimes dangerous, became more controversial the longer it lasted, and indicated how opponents' selective use of violence could undermine the social and political changes the Army was trying to implement. Reconstruction helped to lay the foundation for the future of postwar military governments, and in the 1940s and after training and field manuals began to prepare the Army better for military government. Nation building during Reconstruction was among the most difficult noncombat duties the Army performed during the 19th century.[80]

Notes

1. Richard Lowe, *Republicans and Reconstruction in Virginia, 1856-70* (Charlottesville: University Press of Virginia, 1991), 12-13, 18-24. Lincoln's original military governors were Andrew Johnson in Tennessee, John Phelps in Arkansas, and George Shepley in Louisiana. As a resident of Tennessee, Johnson had held several offices, including governor, member of Congress, and US senator. Phelps had been a congressman from Missouri and a Union volunteer army officer. Shepley had been a federal district attorney in Maine and a Union volunteer army officer. All three were prewar Democrats. See William C. Harris, *With Charity for All: Lincoln and the Restoration of the Union* (Lexington: University Press of Kentucky, 1997), 40-57, 72-86, 105-12, 116-18, 126-28, 171-85, 190-228; *The Louisiana Governors*, Joseph G. Dawson III, ed. (Baton Rouge: Louisiana State University Press, 1990), 145-48.

2. Herman Belz, *Reconstructing the Union: Theory and Policy during the Civil War* (Ithaca, NY: Cornell University Press, 1969); Harris.

3. An army captain of volunteers, Samuel Curtis, left a significant description of occupation duty in *Mexico Under Fire: Being the Diary of Samuel Ryan Curtis*, Joseph E. Chance, ed. (Fort Worth: Texas Christian University Press, 1994).

4. Laura H. Serna, "Mexico City," *The United States and Mexico at War*, Donald S. Frazier, ed. (New York: Macmillan, 1998), 252.

5. In his significant study, *Military Government and Martial Law* (Washington, DC: Chapman Co., 1892; 2d ed., Kansas City, MO: Franklin Hudson Co., 1892; 3d ed., Kansas City, MO: Franklin Hudson Co., 1914), Major William E. Birkhimer took note of Scott's actions in Mexico City (pages 138-39, 141, 351, 355) and provided a verbatim appendix with one of Scott's general orders (pages 581-83). H.A. Smith, *Military Government* (Fort Leavenworth, KS: General Service Schools Press, 1920), 12-13, 21-22, 59-64, 105-111 indicates that Army officers in the early 20th century had access to examples of Scott's orders. See also Edward S. Wallace, "The U.S. Army in Mexico City," *Military Affairs* (Fall 1949), 158-66; Henry O. Whiteside, "Winfield Scott and the Mexican Occupation: Policy and Practice," *Mid-America*, 52 (1970), 102-18; George T. Baker, "Mexico City and the War With the United States: A Study in the Politics of Military Occupation," Ph.D. dissertation, Duke University, 1969, especially iii-v, 44-79, 91-115, 339-60.

6. Robert E. Shalhope, *Sterling Price, Portrait of a Southerner* (Columbia, MO: University of Missouri Press, 1971), 63-66.

7. In regard to drafting laws and constitutions in New Mexico and California and administering states in ways that apply to post-Civil War Reconstruction, see Joseph G. Dawson III, *Doniphan's Epic March* (Lawrence, KS: University Press of Kansas, 1999), 80-102; Joseph Ellison, "The Struggle for Civil Government in California, 1846-1850," *California Historical Quarterly* (March 1931), 96-115; Theodore Grivas, *Military Governments in California, 1846-1850* (Glendale: Arthur H. Clark Co., 1963), 79-220; Neal Harlow, *California Conquered: The Annexation of a Mexican Province, 1846-1850* (Berkeley: University of California Press, 1982; revised ed., 1989). Regular Army officers prominent in California were Brigadier General Stephen Kearny, Colonel (COL) Persifor Smith, COL Richard Mason, and COL Bennet Riley. None were available to apply their experience during the Civil War; all four had died by 1858. Two lieutenants serving in California, Henry W. Halleck and Cave Couts, were members of the constitutional convention. Couts left the Army in 1851, but Halleck was prominent in the Civil War and Reconstruction. Other lieutenants serving in California during military government who became notable later included William T. Sherman, E.O.C. Ord, and E.R.S. Canby. See also Birkhimer's references to New Mexico and California in *Military Government and Martial Law*, 55-56, 63, 80, 81, 94, 137, 364.

8. General overviews include A.H. Carpenter, "Military Government of Southern Territory, 1861-1865," *American Historical Association Annual Report for 1900*, 2 vols. (Washington, DC: American Historical Association, 1901), vol. 1, 465-98 and Robert F. Futrell, "Federal Military Government in the South, 1861-1865," *Military Affairs* (Winter 1951), 181-91. For the gulf and Louisiana see Frank L. Byrne, "A Terrible Machine: General Neal Dow's Military Government on the Gulf Coast," *Civil War History* (March 1966), 5-22; Gerald M. Capers, *Occupied City: New OrleansUunder the Federals* (Lexington: University of Kentucky Press, 1965); Jo Ann Carrigan, "Yankees versus Yellow Jack in New Orleans, 1862-1866," *Civil War History* (September 1963), 248-60; Joseph G. Dawson III, *Army Generals and Reconstruction: Louisiana, 1862-1877* (Baton Rouge: Louisiana State University Press, 1982), 5-23. For Tennessee, see Gilbert E. Govan and James W. Livingood, "Chattanooga under Military Occupation," *Journal of Southern History* (February 1951), 23-47; Joseph H. Parks, "A Confederate Trade Center Under Federal Occupation: Memphis, 1862-1865," *Journal of Southern History* (August 1941), 289-314; Peter Maslowski, *"Treason Must Be Made Odious": Military Occupation and Reconstruction in Nashville, Tennessee, 1862-65* (Millwood, NY: KTO Press, 1978). See also Robert C. Morris, *Reading, 'Riting, and Reconstruction: The Education of the Freedmen in the South, 1861-1870* (Chicago: University of Chicago Press, 1981), 12-32; Stephen V. Ash, *When the Yankees Came: Conflict and Chaos in the Occupied South, 1861-1865* (Chapel Hill: University of North Carolina Press, 1995), 44, 45, 57, 88-90, 98, 104, 114, 173, 175; Jerrell H. Shofner, *Nor Is It Over Yet: Florida in the Era of Reconstruction, 1863-1877* (Gainesville: University Presses of Florida, 1974), 27, 55, 83-85, 95.

9. Ludwell H. Johnson, *The Red River Campaign: Politics and Cotton in the Civil War* (Baltimore, MD: Johns Hopkins University Press, 1958; reprint, Kent, OH: Kent State University Press, 1993); Ludwell H. Johnson, "Northern Profit and Profiteers: The Cotton Rings of 1864-1865," *Civil War History* (June 1966), 101-115; A.S. Roberts, "The Federal Government and Confederate Cotton," *American Historical Review* (January 1927), 262-75.

10. In other words, Lieber's Code described something close to Carl von Clausewitz's postulation in *On War* that war is "politics by other means."

11. Francis Lieber, "Instructions for the Government of the Armies of the United States in the Field," *War of the Rebellion: A Compilation of the Official Records of the Union and Confederate Armies* (Washington, DC: US Government Printing Office), series III, vol. 3, 148-64. Richard S. Hartigan, *Lieber's Code and the Law of War* (Chicago: Precedent Publishing Co., 1983) also contains the code in full on pages 45-71, with a quoted passage on pages 50-51. In *Military Government and Martial Law*, Birkhimer also provided the text of the code on pages 633-53 and discussed some of its points on pages 26-31, 584-614. Context is provided in Frank Freidel, "General Orders 100 and Military Government," *Mississippi Valley Historical Review* (March 1946), 541-56; Frank Freidel, *Francis Lieber, Nineteenth Century Liberal* (Baton Rouge: Louisiana State University Press, 1947), 317-41; Phillip S. Paludan, *A Covenant With Death: The Constitution, Law, and Equality in the Civil War Era* (Urbana, IL: University of Illinois Press, 1975), 95-108; Mark Grimsley, *The Hard Hand of War: Union Military Policy Toward Southern Civilians, 1861-1865* (Cambridge: Cambridge University Press, 1995), 149-51, 178-79.

12. For the memoir of a conservative junior officer, see James Chester, "Recollections of Reconstruction," *United Service* (August 1895), 122. See generally Ash and Grimsley. See also Harry W. Pfanz, "Soldiering in the South During the Reconstruction Period, 1865-1877," Ph.D. dissertation, Ohio State University, 1958, 21-82, 100-26, 160-213, focusing on 1865-1866.

13. Ulysses S. Grant to Edwin M. Stanton, 20 October 1865, *Papers of Ulysses S. Grant*, 25 vols., John Y. Simon, ed. (Carbondale: Southern Illinois University Press, 1967-2000), vol. 15, 358, hereafter cited as *Grant Papers*.

14. Russell F. Weigley, *History of the United States Army* (enlarged ed., Bloomington, IN: University Press, 1984), 598; James E. Sefton, *The United States Army and Reconstruction, 1865-1877* (Baton Rouge: Louisiana State University Press, 1967), 261.

15. Grant to Stanton, 30 October 1865, *Grant Papers*, vol. 15, 374; William C. Harris, *Presidential Reconstruction in Mississippi* (Baton Rouge: Louisiana State University Press, 1967), 66-68; Sefton, 38.

16. Frederick S. Calhoun, *The Lawmen: United States Marshals and Their Deputies, 1789-1989* (Washington, DC: Smithsonian Institution Press, 1989), 7, 107-109.

17. Grant to Kentucky Governor T.E. Bramlette, 18 October 1865, *Grant Papers*, vol. 15, 353-54; Kenneth E. St. Clair, "Military Justice in North Carolina, 1865: A Microcosm of Reconstruction," *Civil War History* (December 1965), 341-50; Elizabeth J. Doyle, "New Orleans Courts Under Military Occupation, 1861-1865," *Mid-America* 42 (1960), 185-92.

18. Robert C. Black III, *Railroads of the Confederacy* (Chapel Hill: University of North Carolina Press, 1952), 290-91 and passim; Grimsley, 105, 111, 142-43, 154-57, 159-64, 166, 169-70, 190, 197-98, 200, 203.

19. David S. Heidler and Jeanne T. Heidler, *Encyclopedia of the American Civil War* (New York: W.W. Norton, 2000), 1595-98.

20. Sefton, 10, 90; Ash, 87, 88; Elizabeth J. Doyle, "Greenbacks, Car Tickets, and the Pot of Gold: The Effects of Wartime Occupation on the Business Life of New Orleans," *Civil War History* (December 1959), 347-62; Harris, *Presidential Reconstruction in Mississippi*, 197-98, 208; Edward G. Campbell, "Indebted Railroads: A Problem of Reconstruction," *Journal of Southern History* (May 1940), 167-88. The Army's interest in railroads lasted for years. See, for example, Grant to E.R.S. Canby, 5 June 1868, *Grant Papers*, vol. 18, 278 and *Report of the Secretary of War, 1870-71*, House Executive Document No. 1, 41st Congress, 3d Session, Serial 1446, 149-51.

21. Fred H. Harrington, *Fighting Politician: Major General N.P. Banks* (Philadelphia: University of Pennsylvania Press, 1948); James G. Hollandsworth, *Pretense of Glory: The Life of General Nathaniel P. Banks* (Baton Rouge: Louisiana State University Press, 1998). Banks' labor plan for former slaves, managed by Army inspectors, set the example in the Mississippi Valley during the war. See Louis Gerteis, *From Contraband to Freedman: Federal Policy toward Southern Blacks, 1861-1865* (Westport: Greenwood Press, 1973); Ronald Davis, "The U.S. Army and the Origins of Sharecropping in the Natchez District: A Case Study," *Journal of Negro History* (January 1977), 60-80; J. Thomas May, "Continuity and Change in the Labor Program of the Union Army and the Freedmen's Bureau," *Civil War History* (September 1971), 245-54.

22. For broad coverage, see George R. Bentley, *A History of the Freedmen's Bureau* (Philadelphia: University of Pennsylvania Press, 1955); William S. McFeely, *Yankee Stepfather: General O.O. Howard and the Freedmen* (New Haven, CT: Yale University Press, 1968); *The Freedmen's Bureau and Reconstruction*, Paul A. Cimbala and Randall M. Miller, eds. (New York: Fordham University Press, 1999). An important account by a former officer as bureau agent is in John W. DeForest, *A Union Officer in the Reconstruction* (New Haven, CT: Yale University Press, 1948). See also J. Thomas May, "The Freedmen's Bureau at the Local Level: A Study of a Louisiana Agent," *Louisiana History* (Winter 1968), 5-19.

23. Eric McKitrick, *Andrew Johnson and Reconstruction* (Chicago: University of Chicago Press, 1960), 158-213; Eric Foner, *Reconstruction: America's Unfinished Revolution, 1863-1877* (New York: Harper & Row, 1988), 176-84.

24. Dan T. Carter, *When the War Was Over: The Failure of Self-Reconstruction in the South, 1865-1867* (Baton Rouge: Louisiana State University Press, 1985).

25. After the riots, Stoneman later served during Reconstruction in Virginia. Baird was ordered to Washington, DC and served for the rest of his long career in the Inspector General's Office where he had been posted before 1861. In 1885 he rose to become the Inspector General of the Army, holding the rank of brigadier general. See Ezra J. Warner, *Generals in Blue: Lives of the Union Commanders* (Baton Rouge: Louisiana State University Press, 1964), 15-16.

26. George C. Rable, *But There Was No Peace: The Role of Violence in the Politics of Reconstruction* (Athens: University of Georgia Press, 1984), 33-58; Bobby L. Lovett, "Memphis Riots: White Reactions to Blacks in Memphis, May 1865-July 1866," *Tennessee Historical Quarterly* (Spring 1979), 9-33; James G. Ryan, "The Memphis Riots of 1866: Terror in a Black Community During Reconstruction," *Journal of Negro History* (July 1977), 243-58; James G. Hollandsworth, *An Absolute Massacre: The New Orleans Race Riot of July 30, 1866* (Baton Rouge: Louisiana State University Press, 2001); Dawson, *Army Generals and Reconstruction*, 36-43.

27. Johnson's veto came on 19 February 1866.

28. James E. Sefton, *Andrew Johnson and the Uses of Constitutional Power* (Boston: Little, Brown, 1980), 133-36. See also Foner, 247-61. Foner observes that in defining national citizenship, "Republicans carried forward the state-building process born of the Civil War" (emphasis added), Ibid., 258.

29. Congress excluded three ex-Confederate states from its plan: Tennessee, readmitted as a reward for ratifying the 14th Amendment, and Missouri and Kentucky, which had not taken formal steps to secede in 1861. The Army had established its presence in those three states, mostly at posts that had existed in the antebellum years. See Dawson, *Army Generals and Reconstruction*, 46-51; Sefton, *The US Army and Reconstruction*, 109-13, 116 note, 135-36, 142-43, 185; Foner, 273-91.

30. Sefton, *The US Army and Reconstruction*, 109-13, 135-36, 142-43, 185; Birkhimer, 481-82, 485. The text of the Military Reconstruction Acts are in *Documentary History of Reconstruction*, Walter L. Fleming, ed., two vols. (Cleveland, OH: Arthur H. Clark Co., 1906-1097; reprint, Gloucester, MA: Peter Smith Co., 1960), vol. 1, 401-419.

31. Foner, 278, states clearly, "Black suffrage, of course, was the most radical element of Congressional Reconstruction," without also emphasizing the radical nature of Congress using the Army to implement the steps to bring about black suffrage and other social changes.

32. See the discussion in Michael Perman, *Reunion Without Compromise: The South and Reconstruction, 1865-1868* (Cambridge: Cambridge University Press, 1973), 137, 277-78; Harold M. Hyman and William M. Wiecek, *Equal Justice Under Law: Constitutional Development, 1835-1875* (New York: Harper & Row, 1982), 443; Brooks D. Simpson, *The Reconstruction Presidents* (Lawrence: University Press of Kansas, 1998), 115.

33. Opposed to the Reconstruction acts and the Army's roles in the South, ex-Confederates took several cases to federal courts, including the Supreme Court. See Hyman and Wiecek, 381-85, 453-55, 460-63; Stanley Kutler, *Judicial Power and Reconstruction Politics* (Chicago: University of Chicago Press, 1968), 37-40, 65-75, 78-99, 100-111, 163-64.

34. Harold M. Hyman, "Johnson, Stanton, and Grant: A Reconsideration of the Army's Role in the Events Leading to Impeachment," *American Historical Review* (October 1960), 85-100.

35. Grant to Ord, 1 March 1867, and Grant's General Orders No. 10, 11 March 1867, *Grant Papers*, vol. 17, 66, 80-81. For short essays on Pope, Schofield, and Sheridan, see *Dictionary of American Military Biography*, Roger J. Spiller, ed. and Joseph G. Dawson III, associate ed., three vols. (Westport, CT: Greenwood Press, 1988), vol. 2, 872-75; vol. 3, 956-60, 989-93. For essays

on Ord and Sickles, see *Biographical Dictionary of the Union*, John T. Hubbell, ed. (Westport, CT: Greenwood Press, 1995), 383-84, 478-79.

36. Although some Southerners spoke in dialects and some of the evangelical religious expressions of both black and white Southerners differed from those of Northerners, residents of the military districts spoke versions of the English language, and most professed to be Protestant Christians. Thus, the Army needed no translators or advisers about religion.

37. William A. Dunning, *Reconstruction, Political and Economic* (New York: Harper, 1907), esp 109; Claude Bowers, *The Tragic Era* (Boston: Houghton Mifflin, 1929); E. Merton Coulter, *The South During Reconstruction* (Baton Rouge: Louisiana State University Press, 1947), esp 119-38. See also William A. Dunning, *Essays on the Civil War and Reconstruction* (New York: Macmillan, 1897), chapter on "Military Government During Reconstruction," 136-75.

38. Sefton, *The US Army and Reconstruction*, 261.

39. Dubbed "masterly inactivity," such a tactic posed a problem in Reconstruction's early months. The original Reconstruction act called for most of those registered to vote in elections. Subsequent laws stipulated that the steps of Reconstruction could be approved by a majority of those voting rather than by a majority of those who were registered. See Perman, 229-47.

40. Michael Perman, *The Road to Redemption: Southern Politics, 1869-1879* (Chapel Hill: University of North Carolina Press, 1984), 22-56.

41. Ex-Confederates and their sympathizers did not employ such tactics as randomly shooting into Army camps or barracks, sniping at soldiers, or assassinating Army officers in town or in the countryside; shooting at moving trains; setting fire to Army barracks; ambushing small Army patrols; attacking squads guarding ballot boxes; blowing up railroad bridges; dynamiting rail lines; or assaulting Army outposts. Guns and ammunition appear to have been so widely available that those opposing Reconstruction did not have to get them by attacking Army camps or taking them from dead soldiers.

42. "Aristotle in Blue and Braid: General John M. Schofield's Essays on Reconstruction," Civil War History, (March 1971), 45-57, quotation on 49; John M. Schofield, *Forty-Six Years in the Army* (New York: Century Co., 1897), 394-405. Samples of Schofield's orders and correspondence are in House Executive Document No. 342, 40th Congress, 2d Session, Serial 1,346, 7-35, and *Report of the Secretary of War, 1867-68*, House Executive Document No. 1, 40th Congress, 2d Session, Serial 1,324, 240-99, 381-414. James L. McDonough, *Schofield: Union General in the Civil War and Reconstruction* (Tallahassee: Florida State University Press, 1972), 170-88; Sefton, *The US Army and Reconstruction*, 15, 18, 102-103, 115, 121, 129-30, 132, 138, 145, 167-68, 182.

43. After serving as Secretary of War, Schofield was promoted to major general in the Regular Army and held numerous senior posts, eventually rising to be Commanding General of the Army in 1888 before retiring in 1895. See Warner, 426.

44. Samples of documents related to Stoneman's tenure are in *Report of the Secretary of War, 1868-69*, House Executive Document No. 1, 40th Congress, 3d Session, Serial 1,367, 320-27. Lowe, 157-59, 161, 166, 169, 228, note28. Stoneman retired from the Army in 1871, settled in California, and in 1882 was elected governor of the state as a Democrat. See Heidler and Heidler, 1,875.

45. Johnson's Order, 26 August 1867, *The Papers of Andrew Johnson*, LeRoy P. Graf and Paul H. Bergeron, et al., eds., 16 vols. (Knoxville: University of Tennessee Press, 1967-2000), vol. 12, 514 hereafter cited as *Johnson Papers*. Samples of documents related to Sickles' tenure are in House Executive Doctrine No. 342, Serial 1,346, 35-60, 85-93. James R. Morrill III, "North Carolina and the Administration of Brevet Major General Sickles," *North Carolina Historical Review*

(Summer 1965), 291-305. In 1869 Sickles left the Army and returned to politics in various capacities, including being appointed by President Grant as US Ambassador to Spain and being elected to Congress. See *Biographical Dictionary of the Union*, 479.

46. Canby gained wide experience as a senior Reconstruction commander, eventually serving in Louisiana (1865-66), the Carolinas (1867-68), Texas (1868-69), and Virginia (1869-70). As the government reduced the Army after the war, in 1866, Canby became one of only eight Regular Army brigadier generals assigned to the field (not on the General Staff in Washington), serving in that rank until his death in 1873. See Max L. Heyman, Jr., *Prudent Soldier: A Biography of Major General E. R. S. Canby* (Glendale: Arthur H. Clarke Co., 1959), passim.

47. Jonathan Worth to Johnson, 31 December 1867, *Johnson Papers*, vol. 12, 402-23. The use of "military despotism" is on 402, 423.

48. Samples of Canby's orders are in House Executive Document No. 342, Serial 1,346, 60-85, 93-99, and *Report of the Secretary of War, 1867-68*, Serial 1,324, 299-320. Heyman, 305-32, and Sefton, *The US Army and Reconstruction*, 20, 159, 161-62, 186, 190-93, 197.

49. Samples of Pope's orders and correspondence are in House Executive Document No. 342, Serial 1,346, 99-126; *Report of the Secretary of War, 1867-68*, Serial 1,324, 320-74. See Peter Cozzens, *General John Pope: A Life for the Nation* (Urbana: University of Illinois Press, 2000), 279-94; Shofner, 103, 105, 161-64, 176; Merlin G. Cox, "Military Reconstruction in Florida," *Florida Historical Quarterly* (January 1968), 219-28; Sefton, *The US Army and Reconstruction*, 114, 122-26, 130-32, 137-39, 144-50, 165-69. Pope continued his military career, holding several department commands in the north and west until retiring in 1886.

50. George Meade, *The Life and Letters of George Gordon Meade*, two volumes (New York: Scribner's, 1913), vol. 2, 290-94; House Executive Document No. 342, Serial 1,346, 126-31; *Report of the Secretary of War, 1868-69*, Serial 1,367, 74-129; Alan Conway, *The Reconstruction of Georgia* (Minneapolis: University of Minnesota Press, 1966), 156-59, 162, 169, 171, 221; Shofner, 177, 181, 184, 191, 193; Cox, 230-33; Sefton, *The US Army and Reconstruction*, 11, 17, 116, 169-73, 186. In 1872 Meade died while on active duty, commanding the Division of the Atlantic. See Warner, 317.

51. *Report of the Secretary of War, 1869-70*, House Executive Document No. 1, 41st Congress, 2d Session, Serial 1,412, 83-95; Lee W. Formwalt, "The Camilla Massacre of 1868," *Georgia Historical Quarterly* (Fall 1987), 399-426; Sefton, *The US Army and Reconstruction*, 198-207. Terry remained in the Army until he retired in 1888 with the rank of major general. See Warner, 498.

52. *Ex parte McCardle*, 6 Wallace 320 (1867). McCardle asserted that he should not be arrested by the Army or threatened with a trial before a military commission when civilian courts were operating and sought a writ of habeas corpus. Congress acted to limit the Supreme Court's jurisdiction, and the case was dropped. See also note 35.

53. House Executive Document No. 342, Serial 1,346, 141-59; *Report of the Secretary of War, 1867-68*, Serial 1,324, 375-78; William C. Harris, *Day of the Carpetbagger: Republican Reconstruction in Mississippi* (Baton Rouge: Louisiana State University Press, 1979), 1-2, 6-7, 11-12, 15-20, 31, 43, 62, 67-70, 74, 76; Sefton, *The US Army and Reconstruction*, 114, 118-19, 130, 139-40, 151-52, 173-74; Bernarr Cresap, *Appomattox Commander: The Story of General E.O.C. Ord* (San Diego: A. S. Barnes & Co., 1981), 239, 242-43, 247-77, 290-91; General Orders 104, 28 December 1867, *Grant Papers*, vol. 18, 87-88. Ord served in the west until his retirement in 1880.

54. *Report of the Secretary of War, 1868-69*, Serial 1,367, 531-704; Cresap, 273; Harris, 18, 31, 35, 40, 50-56, 134-38, 181, 190-91; Sefton, *The US Army and Reconstruction*, 174, 185-86, 190, 195. Gillem served on frontier assignments until his death in 1875. See Warner, 176.

55. *Report of the Secretary of War, 1869-70*, Serial 1,412, 99-101. In 1874, Ames was elected governor of Mississippi. See Harris, 50-58, 62-63, 180, 191-96, 253-56, 264-70; Sefton, *The US Army and Reconstruction*, 190, 195-97.

56. Johnson to Grant, 19 August 1867, *Johnson Papers*, vol. 12, 494.

57. House Executive Document No. 20, 40th Congress, 1st Session, Serial 1,311, 7, 16, 62-66, 75, 79, 83, 92-94; House Executive Document No. 342, Serial 1,346, 159-73; *Report of the Secretary of War, 1867-68*, Serial 1,324, 378-80; Philip H. Sheridan, *Personal Memoirs of P.H. Sheridan*, two volumes (New York: Charles Webster Co., 1891), vol. 2, 233-34, 251, 253, 262, 264, 272-74, 277; Dawson, 46-62; William L. Richter, *The Army in Texas During Reconstruction, 1865-1870* (College Station: Texas A&M University Press, 1987), 109-13.

58. Johnson to Grant, 26 August 1867, *Johnson Papers*, vol. 12, 511. A friend of Grant's with a substantial combat record, Sheridan was promoted to the rank of lieutenant general in 1869 and supervised Army campaigns in the Trans-Mississippi. He was Commanding General of the Army from 1884 until his death in 1888. See *Biographical Dictionary of the Union*, 472. See also Roy Morris, Jr., *Sheridan: The Life and Wars of General Phil Sheridan* (New York: Crown, 1992), 260-96. Although willing to be nominated earlier, Hancock accepted the Democratic nomination in 1880, losing a close election to James A. Garfield. See David M. Jordan, *Winfield Scott Hancock: A Soldier's Life* (Bloomington: Indiana University Press, 1988), 213-26, 274-82.

59. In a letter to President Johnson, Governor Jonathan Worth of North Carolina complimented Hancock on his policies of "sensible statesmanship," much in contrast to Worth's opinions of other district commanders. See Worth to Johnson, 31 December 1867, *Johnson Papers*, vol. 12, 423. Johnson praised Hancock, likening him to George Washington. See Johnson to Senate and House, 18 December 1867, *Johnson Papers*, vol. 12, 350. See views of other Southern conservatives favoring Hancock, Ibid., 39, 573.

60. House Executive Document No. 342, Serial 1,346, 179-188; Jordan, 200-12. After 1868, Hancock held important assignments on the frontier and in the Department of the East until his death on active duty in 1886. Ibid., passim.

61. *Report of the Secretary of War, 1868-69*, Serial 1,367, 202-208; Dawson, *Army Generals and Reconstruction*, 63-79; Richter, 114-39; Sefton, *The US Army and Reconstruction*, 175-78.

62. House Executive Document No. 342, Serial 1,346, 206-208; *Report of the Secretary of War, 1868-69*, Serial 1,367, 704-716; Richter, 119-56.

63. *Report of the Secretary of War, 1869-70*, Serial 1,412, 143-45; Richter, 166-86; Dale Baum, *The Shattering of Texas Unionism: Politics in the Lone Star State During the Civil War Era* (Baton Rouge: Louisiana State University Press, 1998), 183-84, 204-205, 219-20. Reynolds was posted to the frontier, but his controversial decisions during the 1876 campaign against the Sioux led to a court martial. He left the Army in 1877. See *Biographical Dictionary of the Union*, 434.

64. George C. Rable, "William T. Sherman and the Conservative Critique of Radical Reconstruction," *Ohio History* (Summer-Autumn 1984), 147-63; John F. Marszalek, *Sherman: A Soldier's Passion for Order* (New York: Free Press, 1993), 364-76, 390-91, 429.

65. Hyman, "Johnson, Stanton, and Grant"; Simpson, 120; Sefton, *Johnson and the Uses of Constitutional Power*, 145, 150-51, 174-84; Michael L. Benedict, *Impeachment and Trial of An-*

drew Johnson (New York: W.W. Norton, 1973), 57-60; Hans L. Trefousse, *Impeachment of a President* (Knoxville: University of Tennessee Press, 1975), 80, 82-83, 100-105, 111, 116-17, 120, 142.

66. General Orders No. 3, 12 January 1866 and General Orders No. 44, 6 July 1866, *Grant Papers*, vol. 16, 7-8, 228. See the discussion by Brooks Simpson, *Let Us Have Peace: Ulysses S. Grant and the Politics of War and Reconstruction, 1861-1868* (Chapel Hill: University of North Carolina Press, 1991), 128-29, 138-39, 146, 161, 166-67, 180.

67. See, for instance, Grant to President Johnson, 17 August 1867, *Johnson Papers*, vol. 12, 489, 491. Demonstrating how closely Grant supervised enforcing the Reconstruction acts are many communications in *Grant Papers*, 18. Pertaining to the Second District, see Grant to Canby, 18 December 1867 and 13 May 1868, Ibid., 60, 253. For the Third District, see Grant to Pope, 30 October 1867 and 2 November 1876, Ibid., 22, 30 and Grant to Meade, 6 January 1868, 12 February 1868, 29 April 1868, 29 June 1868, Ibid., 91-92, 152, 236-37, 303. For the Fourth District, see Grant to Ord, 1 October 1867, Ibid., 4 and Grant to McDowell, 5 June 1868, Ibid., 279. For the Fifth District, see Grant to Mower, 2 November 1867, Ibid., 28; Grant to Hancock, 29 November 1867, 7 February 1868, 29 February 1868, Ibid., 39, 132, 175-76; Grant to Buchanan, 8 May 1868, Ibid., 247-48.

68. See, for example, Grant to Ord, 23 June 1867, *Grant Papers*, 17:192. See also McDonough, 185-86; Sefton, *The US Army and Reconstruction*, 140; Cozzens, 282-83.

69. Grant to Sheridan, 5 April 1867 and Grant to Pope, 21 April 1867, *Grant Papers*, vol. 17, 95-96, quote on 96, 117-18. See also Grant to Schofield, 3 April 1868 and Grant to Meade, 7 April 1868, Ibid., vol 18, 217-18, 227-28.

70. Grant to Ord, 22 September 1867, Ibid., vol. 17, 354.

71. Rable, 73, 101-21, and passim.

72. Simpson, *The Reconstruction Presidents*, 133-73; Foner, 342, 528-30, 550-52; Rable, 101-62; Melinda M. Hennessey, "Reconstruction Politics and the Military: The Eufaula Riot of 1874," *Alabama Historical Quarterly* (Summer 1976), 112-25; William Gillette, *Retreat From Reconstruction, 1869-1879* (Baton Rouge: Louisiana State University Press, 1879), 110-33; Dawson, *Army Generals and Reconstruction*, 86-87, 144-47, 162-82; Melinda M. Hennessey, "Racial Violence During Reconstruction: The 1876 Riots in Charleston and Cainhoy," *South Carolina Historical Magazine* (April 1985), 100-12; Sefton, *The US Army and Reconstruction*, 236-50.

73. Simpson, *The Reconstruction Presidents*, 150, 155, 173-96; Everette Swinney, "Enforcing the Fifteenth Amendment, 1870-1877," *Journal of Southern History* (May 1962), 202-18; Lou F. Williams, *The Great South Carolina Ku Klux Klan Trials, 1871-1872* (Athens: University of Georgia Press, 1996); Alan W. Trelease, *White Terror: The Ku Klux Klan Conspiracy and Southern Reconstruction* (New York: Harper & Row, 1971), 189-418; Gillette, 133-85, 230-99; Sefton, *The US Army and Reconstruction*, 191-92, 220-26. For a contrasting interpretation see Richard Zuczek, *State of Rebellion: Reconstruction in South Carolina* (Columbia: University of South Carolina Press, 1996), 88-153.

74. Calhoun, 14, 87-88, 119.

75. Simpson, *Reconstruction Presidents*, 153, 158.

76. Cassius M. Dowell, *Military Aid to the Civil Power* (Fort Leavenworth, KS: General Service Schools Press, 1925), 203.

77. Clarence C. Clendenen, "President Hayes' 'Withdrawal' of the Troops—An Enduring Myth," *South Carolina Historical Magazine* (October 1969), 240-50; Vincent P. DeSantis, "Ruth-

erford B. Hayes and the Removal of the Troops and the End of Reconstruction," *Region, Race, and Reconstruction: Essays in Honor of C. Vann Woodward* (New York: Oxford University Press, 1982), 417-50; Simpson, *Reconstruction Presidents*, 209-12.

78. William E. Birkhimer, *Military Government and Martial Law* (Washington, DC: Chapman Co., 1892; 2d ed., Kansas City, MO: Franklin Hudson Co., 1892; 3d ed., Kansas City, MO: Franklin Hudson Co., 1914).

79. See for example, Smith; Dowell.

80. See Ralph H. Gabriel, "The American Experience With Military Government," *American Historical Review* (July 1944), 632-37; William E. Daugherty and Marshall Andrews, *A Review of U.S. Historical Experience With Civil Affairs, 1776-1954* (Bethesda, MD: Operations and Research Office of Johns Hopkins University, 1961). See also Morris Greenspan, *The Modern Law of Land Warfare* (Berkeley: University of California Press, 1959), 210-77.

The Frontier Army and the Occupation of the West, 1865-1900

Robert Wooster

The US Army's association with the American West vividly demonstrates its historic involvement in nation building and counterinsurgency. As Francis Paul Prucha has explained, the American Army was a "child of the frontier," acquainted since its very inception with wars against indigenous peoples as well as the political, economic, social, and cultural development of frontier regions. In essence, the 19th-century Army usually performed two roles: frontier security and national development.[1]

No military organization operates in a vacuum, and the Army's mixed relations with the more general American society certainly influenced its frontier operations. Most of the officers who dominated the post-bellum Army understood that volunteers had numerically dominated both Union and Confederate forces but believed that they, the professionals, deserved credit for transforming those masses of humanity into functioning armies. Having undergone four years of dreadful trial by fire, many emerged from the war confident that society as a whole could benefit from their experience and leadership. As Major General (MG) William Sherman confided to a subordinate tasked with overseeing Reconstruction in North Carolina, "If left alone, I know you could guide the state of North Carolina into a path of peace, loyalty and security in three months . . . but I doubt whether those who were so slow to come to the fight will permit you to act." Or as MG (and soon to be Secretary of War) John Schofield told Ulysses S. Grant on the occasion of the latter's Republican Party nomination for president in 1868, "I have always believed that the Union could be fully restored only by the men who put down the rebellion."[2]

Civilians typically held a different opinion. In their eyes, volunteers, not professionals, had defeated the Confederacy. Traditional fears that a large Regular Army threatened liberties and overburdened taxpayers remained popular political fodder. Sherman's petulant 1874 decision to transfer his offices from Washington to St. Louis—in the process leaving the regulars without their commanding general to defend their political interests—hardly enhanced the Army's reputation. Representative Fernando Wood (Democrat, New York) dismissed officers as "idle vagabonds who are so well paid and do nothing." To these concerns now loomed the additional specter of Reconstruction, and fears of the Army's involvement in politics were hardly limited to unreconstructed former Confederates. As Representative Milton I. Southard (Democrat, Ohio) later complained, "During the last ten years not one-half of our Army has been employed for legitimate purposes. Its use has consisted mainly of running elections and keeping the dominant party in power." Congress vividly demonstrated its disdain for the regulars in 1877 when its delay in passing an Army appropriations bill left soldiers without pay for five months.[3]

These political realities ensured reductions in the size of the Regular Army. In 1866, Congress had set the Army's maximum strength at 54,000. "The legislative temper of Congress at this time does not indicate a very flattering prospect," acknowledged Secretary of War Schofield in early 1869. Indeed, budget cuts that year reduced the Army to 37,313, and renewed attacks the following year sliced off another 4,000. In 1874, Congress limited its funding to support only about 27,000. Although friends of the Army fought off any further reductions, the Army had been reduced by fully one-half in eight years.[4]

From these attacks, one might conclude that Americans were consistent in their desire to restrict the Army's role in the life of the nation. Such, however, was hardly the case. Although wary of a standing army, Americans of the late 19th century were pragmatists. In addition to limiting the size of the Regular Army, they wanted to keep the federal government small, but they also expected the very same government to provide them with services, assistance, and protection. Specialized federal or state bureaucracies were rare. Thus, despite their distrust of military professionals, Americans happily relied on the Regular Army for a diverse array of public functions.

Although the average soldier probably never saw any American Indians in anger, he almost undoubtedly engaged in some form of nation building. Establishing national sovereignty, maintaining order, and keeping the Army's peace were the most basic responsibilities. Reconstruction remained a huge obligation, consuming about 40 percent of the Army in 1867. As late as 1876 15 percent of the entire Army was still billeted in the South. On average about 12 percent guarded federal arsenals and coastal defenses. Although there was no repetition of the armed occupation of Utah in 1857, the government also kept a wary eye on Deseret, the provisional state organized in 1849 by a convention of Mormons. Voicing the fears of many, one officer complained that "the Mormons alone could now gather more men capable of bearing arms than you could muster in your whole army, and that in the Switzerland of America." As such the government maintained strong garrisons in Utah and in 1886 provided a federal marshal who had arrested a leading Mormon official with a strong escort.[5]

The federal government also used the Army to reestablish domestic order. During the fugitive slave controversies of the early 1850s, President Franklin Pierce's attorney general, Caleb Cushing, had given federal marshals broad authority to employ "any and all armed forces" as a posse comitatus when threatened "by unlawful combinations." Thus, when massive railroad worker strikes in 1877 sparked ugly rioting, the federal government deployed more than 3,500 Regulars (about 15 percent of the entire Army) to restore order. Violent clashes between regulars and strikers were rare; under strict instructions from President Rutherford B. Hayes to avoid becoming involved in actual strikebreaking, the troops confined their activities to guarding federal property, escorting trains, and protecting railroad company property.[6]

Concerned that summoning the troops was too easy, Congress responded in 1878 by including the so-called Posse Comitatus Act as part of that year's Army appropriations. Written by Representative James Proctor Knott (Democrat, Kentucky), the new measure effectively repealed the old Cushing doctrine by limiting the authority to deploy Regulars to the president, who could do so only after first issuing a "cease and desist" order. Even under the more restrictive law, soldiers continued to be used in civil disturbances west of the Mississippi River. Detachments of bluecoats, for example, were deployed in New Mexico's Lincoln County War (1878-79); on several occasions in Cochise County, Arizona Territory (1881-82); and in Wyoming's Johnson County range war (1892). They occupied Omaha, Nebraska; Seattle, Washington; and Rock Springs, Wyoming in response to riots against immigrant Chinese workers during the 1880s. And under the pretext of protecting the mail, fully two-thirds of the entire Regular force was involved in the widespread labor unrest of 1894. The greatest tensions came in Chicago where the strikes had originated. Openly aligning himself with corporate interests, MG Nelson A. Miles, commander, Department of the Missouri, nearly transformed a dangerous situation into a full-fledged massacre. "Rioters or anarchists have 6000 Winchester rifles and bushels of dynamite bombs," went one of Miles' breathless missives to superiors in Washington. "Shall I give the order for troops to fire on mobs obstructing trains?" went another. Fortunately, cooler heads in Washington prevailed, and a bloody slaughter was avoided.[7]

In the absence of other federal bureaucracies, the Regular Army also continued to engage in numerous scientific ventures across the frontier. Post surgeons had been keeping regular weather records since 1814; following the Civil War, the Signal Corps took up meteorological studies with a vengeance. Under the able leadership of Colonel (COL) Albert J. Myer, himself a former surgeon in antebellum Texas, Signal Corps personnel supplied farmers, shippers, and various business trade associations throughout the country with weather predictions and information. In 1871, the Signal Corps budget had been $15,000; by 1880, it had risen to $375,000. Internal accounting scandals and continuing budget pressures took away some of the luster and led Congress to transfer all meteorological activities to the Department of Agriculture in 1890, but the Army had provided the United States with what amounted to its first national weather service.[8]

Individual soldiers contributed mightily to frontier science. William H. Corbusier—a surgeon whose remarkable military service included three years of the Civil War, postings at 17 posts in the continental United States, two tours in the Philippines, and an inspection of Alaska—became a prominent linguist who specialized in Yavapai dialects and the use of sign languages among Plains Indian tribes. Similarly, Major (MAJ) Washington Matthews helped to pioneer ethnological studies of the Navajos, Arikaras, and Hidatsas. Equally prominent was Captain (CPT) John Gregory Bourke, who wrote several important memoirs and ethnological studies based upon his frontier experiences. As noted anthropologist Adolph Francis Alphonse Bandelier once admitted, "much of the work now attributed to civilians is in fact due to Army officers who have disinterestedly loaned it away."[9]

Similarly, the Army had long been a major player in the great scientific surveys of the West. Before the Civil War, officers from the Corps of Topographical Engineers had helped to blaze numerous trails west in a spectacular combination of scientific investigation and public showmanship. Although the topographical engineers were dissolved as an independent entity in 1863, the Army continued to help map the terrain and geology of the American West. Regulars in blue almost inevitably provided the escorts for the great scientific studies of the age. Lieutenant George M. Wheeler was among the most impressive of the soldier-surveyors. Overseeing teams of soldiers, civilian scientists, and adventurers, Wheeler's explorations, officially known as the US geographical surveys west of the 100th meridian, methodically mapped and categorized more than 175,000 square miles of the American West between 1872 and 1879. This was in addition to his earlier reconnaissance surveys of 1869 and 1871, from which he produced maps depicting nearly 100,000 square miles.[10]

And the Army played other roles. Scores of military posts served as the genesis for non-Indian settlement. Post libraries and schools helped to educate not only soldiers but also many in the surrounding civilian communities. Regulars often distributed emergency supplies to destitute settlers, and when fire ravaged much of Chicago in 1871, four companies of the 8th Infantry Regiment were dispatched to help restore order. Similarly, Congress's elimination of special funding for Yellowstone National Park employees in 1886 led military officials to send in the cavalry. Military management was later extended to Yosemite, General Grant, and Sequoia National Parks. Until the creation of the National Park Service in 1916, Regulars extinguished forest fires, conducted scientific observations, provided rudimentary interpretative programs, and shielded many of the nation's most spectacular natural areas from the transgressions of ignorant tourists. "Blessings on Uncle Sam's soldiers," proclaimed naturalist John Muir. "They have done the job well, and every pine tree is waving its arms for joy."[11]

The Army also fostered better western communications. The Corps of Engineers improved rivers and Pacific coast harbors. Army escorts, especially in western Texas, Kansas, Colorado, and Wyoming, ensured that mail service was reasonably safe and reliable. Thanks to a $100,000 congressional grant, soldiers built more than 1,200 miles of military telegraphs in western Texas during the mid-1870s. Relations between Army officers and railroad companies were famously (or infamously, depending on one's view) close. The top Army brass knew that railroads would cut supply costs and make it possible to deploy troops quickly on a previously unimaginable scale; railroad officials understood that they needed the soldiers to protect exposed construction parties and to convince wary Easterners that a move west would be reasonably safe. Though somewhat less prevalent than had been the case before 1865, the Army continued to build frontier roads. In 1881, for example, COL Benjamin Grierson bragged that troops under his command had, in addition to collectively marching more than 135,000 miles chasing Indians, established more than 1,000 miles of wagon roads in the past three years alone. "A rapid and permanent increase of the population and wealth" was sure to follow, Grierson predicted.[12]

With the Army came money. As a practical farmer just outside Fort Riley, Kansas, put it, "Uncle Sam . . . will soon make money more plenty here." Indeed, an army presence meant an influx of federal dollars—jobs, construction projects, building and land leases, horse and mule purchases, transportation contracts, contracts for animal forage, and soldiers who provided a captive market for all ilk of frontier entrepreneurs. An instructive example of the Army's economic impact may be seen in a typical year—1876—at a typical post—Fort Davis, Texas. The civilian community there numbered about 400; the garrison included 298 officers and men. Military salaries exceeded $100,000, and contracts for forage and heating fuel for the post totaled another $44,463. Assuming that most of the money went directly into the Fort Davis economy, the Army brought about $360 per resident. In 2002 dollars, this meant $5,800 for every man, woman, and child in this remote frontier settlement.[13]

Regional examinations of the frontier army's economic impact further illustrate its importance to Western nation building. Historian Darlis Miller has estimated that the Army injected between $1.25 and $2 million per year into the New Mexico (population 153,593 in 1880) and Arizona (population 59,620) economies during the late 1860s and early 1870s. Lieutenant Colonel (LTC) Thomas ("Ty") T. Smith, whose groundbreaking work, *The U.S. Army & the Texas Frontier Economy*, provides the most systematic effort to calculate the financial effects of the Army's presence, concludes that it disbursed about $70 million into the Lone Star state between 1849-1900. The Army, suggests Smith, was responsible for roughly 8 per cent of the increased valuation of the state's real and personal property over that half-century.[14]

What did frontier Army personnel think of their roles as nation builders? Most took pride in their accomplishments but were frustrated that such duties consumed so much of their time and energy. As Sergeant Henry McConnell (1866-1871) put it, "frontier troops in our army were simply 'armed laborers,' nothing less, nothing more." Enlisted men resented the labor details that could dominate their lives on the frontier. "Us sent to Fort Stockton to guard de line of Texas," explained one ex-soldier, "but all us do am build adobe houses." Officers understood that the constant fatigue duty contributed to alarmingly high desertion rates, which could be as high as 25 percent annually. As the officer investigating one such case explained, the deserter insisted "he had enlisted to be a soldier and not a slave." Most soldiers would have agreed with the complaints of Brevet MG Christopher C. Augur on his efforts to police the new hamlets springing up along the Union Pacific Railroad in his Department of the Platte: "It is a very delicate and unpleasant duty, and one from which we would gladly be relieved."[15]

Involvement in these noncombat activities certainly had a negative impact on the Army's efforts to pursue its primary task in the West: destroying all American Indian military resistance. Even in the best circumstances the thin lines of underfunded bluecoats could hardly be everywhere. The government's inconsistent and paternalistic Indian policies lent further confusion. In 1867, for example, planned offensives along the Bozeman Trail were shelved to allow a special peace commission to complete its task. In Arizona, similar peace initiatives in 1871 and 1872 also delayed major Army campaigns. In 1877, LTC William R. Shafter was warned to "act cautiously" against Indian raiders along the Rio Grande until the troops engaged in that year's railroad strikes could be transferred to Texas. In other cases, eccentricities of government policy and organization thrust the Army into conflict situations it had sought to avoid.

Since most tribes dismissed international boundaries as simply more evidence of the white man's inability to grasp the realities of western geography, their migrations into Canada and Mexico frequently brought the State Department into the messy stew of Indian policy. Further, the Bureau of Indian Affairs, which administered the reservations, was housed in the Department of the Interior. Theoretically, Interior Department officials dealt with the tribes with the Army held in abeyance until someone (sometimes the president, sometimes an Indian agent, sometimes a soldier) judged the use of force to be necessary. Several wars, most notably those against the Modocs (1872-73) and the Nez Percés (1877), resulted from Indian Bureau insistence that tribes be moved from one reservation to another. Army officers bitterly complained that civilian agents were dishonest, inexperienced, or impractical.[16]

The brutal complexities of the wars against the Indians rivaled the intricacies of Indian policy. Separating Indians labeled "friendly" from those dubbed "hostile" was difficult and often dangerous. Attempts to disarm the tribes were especially perilous. Ousting the Modocs from the rugged lava beds of southern Oregon and northern California represented challenges completely different from those encountered when tracking down the mounted Comanches of the southern plains. Some campaigns occurred in the winter; some in the spring, summer, or fall. Some campaigns included cavalry; some included infantry; some included artillery.

Mindful of the hazards of oversimplifying 1,000 combat actions (during which about 2,000 soldiers and 6,000 Indians were killed or wounded) over 25 years, a few generalizations can nonetheless be made.[17] At the operational level, successful large-scale campaigns against Indians after the Civil War included a team of Indian auxiliaries to provide information, a series of loosely coordinated columns designed to move into a particular region from several different points and extraordinarily stubborn leadership by the strong-willed colonel or lieutenant colonel who led one of the columns. The most effective such operations culminated in a sudden attack on an Indian encampment, which almost invariably devolved into a confusing melee of bullets, arrows, men, women, and children.

At the tactical level, scholars are now on a little surer ground thanks to the orderly research of the indefatigable Smith. Smith has assessed and categorized the 81 Army-led Indian fights in Texas from 1866-1881 for which sufficient information can be gathered. Forty-three percent of these encounters resulted from routine patrols or scouts, typically including a detachment of 50 or fewer men. Large-scale operations (including several companies engaged in field operations over several weeks or months) comprised 32 percent of the post-Civil War Indian fights in Texas. Pursuits (in which a detachment was sent out in response to specific information about an Indian raid) made up 15 percent of these actions, with combat involving military escorts for mail stages, supply trains, paymasters, etc., comprising the remaining 10 percent. Officers were present 88 percent of the time.[18]

To look at the wars against the Indians from still another perspective, the example of Fort Davis, Texas, is again instructive. Davis-based troops were involved in 12 combat actions against the Indians after 1865, more than those from any other post in the Lone Star state. Seven of these engagements were the result of Indian attacks against Regulars holding defensive positions or on mail escort duty. Typically, these long-ranged skirmishes produced few casualties. The other five combat actions resulted from the 33 scouts and expeditions organized from Fort Davis during that period. Four other columns that did not actually engage the enemy either recovered some stolen property or destroyed Indian livestock, meaning that troops engaged in some sort of aggressive move stood about a 27-percent chance of inflicting tangible punishment upon their foes.[19]

Little evidence suggests that the Army attempted to disseminate the lessons learned from these experiences in any systematic fashion. The experiences of Lieutenant Alonzo Gray offer a simple illustration of this neglect. Born in Wisconsin, Gray graduated from West Point in 1887, an unremarkable 40th in his class. The freshly minted lieutenant found himself thrust into service at Fort Bayard, New Mexico. "I was ordered out on an Indian scout with ten men for ten days," wrote Gray. "At this time, field service was not taught at West Point and, being decidedly green, I went out very poorly equipped."[20]

Such an admission, while seemingly innocuous, seems at closer scrutiny a damning indictment of the old Army. What about Gray's assessment of his alma mater? The US Military Academy, which supplied about three-fourths of the vacancies in the officer corps after 1867, taught young officers a good deal of science and engineering; a smattering of liberal arts; and the basics of riding, shooting, and linear small-unit tactics but almost nothing about fighting Indians or frontier conditions. For a brief period before the Civil War, Professor Dennis Hart Mahan had added a lesson in his "Engineering and the

Science of War" capstone course (the engineering section of the course took 112 lessons; "The Science of War" segment numbered only six) titled "Indian Warfare." Apparently, Mahan based the lesson on the near-annihilation of an unfortunate column commanded by MAJ Francis L. Dade as the Second Seminole War (1835) opened. However, even this temporary foray seems to have been the only formal lesson ever included in the official curriculum.[21]

What about other influences that might have assisted the bewildered Gray? Surely veteran frontier Regulars shared their experiences with their junior colleagues in informal settings. At tradition-bound West Point, the rotating roster of instructors included notable frontier personalities like William J. Hardee, William B. Hazen, John Gibbon, Richard Dodge, Charles King, and Edward S. Godfrey. At social events, eager audiences often sought out Godfrey, a dashing 7th Cavalryman who had been with MAJ Marcus Reno at the Little Bighorn and would later earn a Medal of Honor for heroism against the Nez Percé for his tales of the West. "He saw everything in the cosmos," wrote one starstruck cadet. "Godfrey's black eyes flashed as he was telling us of this. We all sat close about him." The old Army's officers were extraordinarily chatty letter writers, leaving voluminous descriptions, not necessarily analyses, of their frontier combat experiences.[22]

And what about the burgeoning Army reform movement of the late 19th century? The reformers always remained a distinct minority among the officer corps and devoted more of their energies to things more useful for fighting the Prussians or the French than the Lakotas or the Apaches. Ironically, some of the "lessons" learned fighting Indians were belatedly integrated into new regulation manuals in 1891, soon enough to be of use to an officer destined to serve in the Philippines but 100 years later than the situation on the American frontiers actually demanded.[23]

Had Gray been extraordinarily conscientious and known exactly where to look he might have found some guidance. In 1871, for example, the headquarters of the Department of Texas issued a lengthy commentary on Indian fighting in its General Orders No. 77. The *Army and Navy Journal* later reprinted these orders under the heading, "Hints for Frontier Service." And in a brilliantly researched revisionist work, historian Andrew J. Birtle has demonstrated that the diligent historian can find traces of the development of what might loosely be called counterinsurgency doctrine during the second half of the 19th century. A few typical titles and publication dates are instructive of this theme: COL John Gibbon, "Arms to Fight Indians," *United Service* (1879); CPT Arthur L. Wagner's chapter, "Indian Scouting," in his *The Service of Security and Information* (1893); and CPT Edward S. Godfrey, "Cavalry Fire Discipline," *Journal of the Military Service Institution of the United States* (September 1896). The most detailed effort was a book written by Lieutenant Edward S. Farrow, who had fought against the Nez Percé in 1877, the Bannocks in 1878, and the Sheepeater Paiutes in 1879-80. After leaving the West for a tour of teaching duty at West Point, Farrow published his *Mountain Scouting: A Handbook for Officers and Soldiers on the Frontiers*, in 1881. Among the 16 chapters of Farrow's work were essays on "Indian Character"; "The Trail, Signs, and Signals"; and "Skirmishing."[24]

But these infrequent public discussions—most of which occurred after the largest wars against the Indians had been concluded—seem to have had little practical effect among contemporaries. Nelson Miles, arguably the most effective of the old Army's post-bellum campaigners, had done well in the Red River War, ground down the Northern Cheyennes, chased Sitting Bull into Canada, caught Chief Joseph, and helped to wear down Geronimo. As notable for his lack of interest in meaningful Army reform as for his incredible ego, Miles published two autobiographies and a memoir of his experiences during a tour of European armies. Miles also critiqued the government's Indian policy in essays for the *Journal of the Military Service Institution of the United States* and the *North American Review*. But Miles failed to leave behind much record of the reasons for his battlefield successes other than the occasional cryptic comment heralding the value of his "perfect spy system," his "properly organized command," or, more frequently, his own personal genius. Nor did Miles appear to have modeled his actions on Army guidelines or practice.[25]

Miles' most prominent rivals were Ranald Mackenzie and George Crook. The enigmatic Mackenzie seems to have owed his success to instinct, force of personality, and a stubborn desire to succeed and never shared the methods he had used in his successful campaigns with a general audience. Wracked by the physical and emotional pain stemming from seven wounds, nearly two full decades of combat, and possibly syphilis, Mackenzie was committed to a mental asylum at the age of 43 before he could do any publishing. More than either Mackenzie or Miles, Crook made serious efforts to understand his enemies' ways and habits and, in 1885, began writing an autobiography (still unfinished when he died five years later) that has greater depth than any of Miles' multiple efforts. But Crook's growing dependence on Indian auxiliaries hardly won the acceptance of his peers and was a key factor in Commanding General Philip Sheridan's decision to accept his request for a transfer in the midst of a campaign against Geronimo.[26]

As Robert Utley, dean of frontier military historians, has noted, the Army generally saw the wars against the Indians as a "fleeting bother," unworthy of serious scrutiny. In part, the Army was too busy doing other things, including nation building, to devote much attention to fighting Indians. Racism also helps to explain the Army's negligence. The Regulars viewed American Indians as many things—noble savages, primitive wanderers, despicable murderers, and thieves. Some even went to great lengths to assist their defeated foes, but almost none viewed Indians as equals. MG John Schofield put it bluntly in 1875: "There is no glory to be won in savage warfare."[27]

There was virtually no correlation between successful leadership in the Indian wars and promotion, which occurred according to seniority within one's regiment (through captain) or branch (through colonel). Exceptions to the rule of seniority were rare, making President Grant's appointment of LTC George Crook as brigadier general in recognition of his successful Tonto Basin Campaign of 1873 all the more divisive among the latter's jealous rivals. "If Indian warfare was only regarded as legitimate warfare there would be encouragement for hard work and successful campaigning such as you have done," rued the long-suffering wife of CPT Frank Baldwin who would eventually be honored with two Medals of Honor. LTC Emory Upton, recognized as the post-bellum Army's premier theoretician, sniped that "the proposition that 'bushwacking' and Indian fighting with one or two companies do not qualify an officer for the position as General." Or as MG Winfield Hancock told Congress in 1876—the same year as LTC George A. Custer's defeat along the banks of the Little Bighorn—Indian service should be "entitled to no weight" in assessing the proper organization of the Army.[28]

Training programs were practically nonexistent. With line units chronically understrength, recruits received almost no military instruction before being rushed to their regiments. There the demands of fatigue detail continually interrupted training exercises. Often citing its inability to afford ammunition, the Army rarely encouraged marksmanship practice until after the Little Bighorn defeat. Most of the branch schools for instruction and application were not established until the 1880s, and even those would devote much of their time to remedial activities for another decade. As one officer remembered, conversations among his peers were "apt to run rather among the marches and battles of the Civil War . . . than upon the details of garrison life."[29]

What may we learn from the frontier Army's experiences? One must be extremely careful about drawing simplistic or fallacious parallels between the present and the past. Further, 21st-century concepts of doctrine would have seemed alien to the US Army officer of the 19th century.[30] After all, the Army "won": organized Indian resistance was obliterated, the West was occupied, and national expansion continued.

Mindful of these caveats, several conclusions nonetheless seem apparent. As an institution, the late 19th-century Army encouraged its officers to be adaptive and experimental, valuable traits for the underdeveloped areas in which they so often served. The Army also excelled in helping its soldiers to become engineers and scientists. Further, its garrisons fueled Western economic growth and offered security to the civilian communities they often fostered. In so doing, the Army materially eased the non-Indian occupation of the American West. Except for the Corps of Engineers, the Army did little to prepare its enlisted men or officers for the realities of their frontier service, whether keeping the peace, assisting civilians, or fighting Indians. As Jerry Cooper, author of a pioneering work on the Army's role in domestic disorders, noted, "The Army was totally unprepared for strike duty. It had no mobilization plan . . . nor did it have a well-conceived policy to guide officers in the field conducting strike duty." Adds the historian who examined the Army's role in saving the national parks, "No well-defined policy of protection had been promulgated; no judicial machinery had been provided. The average cavalryman had no previous training in protecting nature from man."[31]

The Army's wars against the Indians and its nation-building activities along the frontiers were neither new nor exceptional. After all, the Regular Army, which had cut its teeth at Fallen Timbers in 1793, would soon be called upon to perform such services on a much larger scale in the Philippines. But, more often than not, the Army was either unwilling or unable to respond to the realities of its frontier service in a timely manner. The Army's refusal to acknowledge its history hurt its Western operations after the Civil War, and its failure to integrate frontier conditions into preparing and training its soldiers had costs. Most of its field campaigns did not do what they were designed to do—either "overawe" or "seek and destroy" the enemy. For every expedition or operation that actually came to grips with tribes deemed hostile, there were countless others that found nothing. The lack of systematic attention accorded to the realities of the Army's twin roles as agent of nation building and guardian of frontier security made the implementation of these tasks more difficult, more lengthy, and more dangerous.

Notes

1. Francis Paul Prucha, *The Sword of the Republic: The United States Army on the Frontier, 1783-1846* (Bloomington: Indiana University Press, 1969), 394; Prucha, *Broadax and Bayonet: The Role of the United States Army in the Development of the Northwest, 1815-1860* (1953; reprint, Lincoln: University of Nebraska Press, 1967); Durwood Ball, *Army Regulars on the Western Frontier, 1848-1861* (Norman: University of Oklahoma Press, 2001); Michael L. Tate, "The Multi-Purpose Army on the Frontier: A Call for Further Research," *The American West: Essays in Honor of W. Eugene Hollon*, Ronald Lora, ed. (Toledo: University of Toledo Press, 1980); Tate, *The Frontier Army in the Settlement of the West* (Norman: University of Oklahoma Press, 1999).

2. Sherman to Schofield, 6 May 1865, Box 28, Hiram Barney Collection, Huntington Library, San Marino, CA; Schofield to Grant, 25 May 1868, Box 53, Eldridge Collection, Huntington Library.

3. *Congressional Globe*, 40th Congress, 3d Session, 1 March 1869, Part 2, 925-27; *Congressional Record*, 45th Congress, 2d Session, 1878, Part 4, 3677.

4. Schofield to Lowe, 11 February 1869, Box 49, John M. Schofield Papers, Library of Congress, Washington, DC.

5. Robert Wooster, *The Military and United States Indian Policy, 1865-1903* (New Haven: Yale University Press, 1988), 14-15; Miles to Sherman, 12 December 1881, Roll 30, William T. Sherman Papers, Library of Congress; McCook to Adjutant General, 3 December 1885, Box 17, Schofield Papers; Clayton D. Laurie and Ronald H. Cole, *The Role of Federal Military Forces in Domestic Disorders, 1877-1945* (Washington, DC: Center of Military History [CMH], 1997), 77.

6. Robert W. Coakley, *The Role of Federal Military Forces, 1789-1878* (Washington, DC: CMH, 1989), 132; Jerry M. Cooper, *The Army and Civil Disorder: Federal Military Intervention in Labor Disputes, 1877-1900* (Westport, CT: Greenwood Press, 1980), 59-61; Ari Hoogenboom, *Rutherford B. Hayes: Warrior and President* (Lawrence: University Press of Kansas, 1995), 326-35.

7. Coakley, 344; Cooper, 100; Laurie and Cole, 20, 57-109; Miles to Lamont, 10 July 1894, Box 72, Schofield Papers; Miles to Adjutant General, 5 July 1894, Box 72, Schofield Papers; Robert Wooster, *Nelson A. Miles and the Twilight of the Frontier Army* (Lincoln: University of Nebraska Press, 1993), 198-200.

8. Tate, *The Frontier Army in the Settlement of the West*, 169-73.

9. William Henry Corbusier, *Soldier, Surgeon, Scholar: The Memoirs of William Henry Corbusier, 1844-1930*, Robert Wooster, ed. (Lincoln: University of Nebraska Press, 2003); Joseph C. Porter, *Paper Medicine Man: John Gregory Bourke and His American West* (Norman: University of Oklahoma Press, 1986); Tate, *The Frontier Army in the Settlement of the West*, 14-17.

10. William H. Goetzmann, *Army Exploration in the American West, 1803-1863* (New Haven, CT: Yale University Press, 1959); Richard A. Bartlett, *Great Surveys of the American West* (Norman: University of Oklahoma Press, 1962), 333-72.

11. Gilbert Fite, "The United States Army and Relief to Pioneer Settlers, 1874-1875," *Journal of the West* (January 1967), 99-107; H. Duane Hampton, *How the U.S. Cavalry Saved Our National Parks* (Bloomington: Indiana University Press, 1971), 190.

12. "Lt. A. W. Greely's Report on the Installation of Military Telegraph Lines in Texas, 1875-1876," *Southwestern Historical Quarterly*, L. Tuffly Ellis, ed. (July 1965), 69, 85-86; General Orders No. 1, District of the Pecos, 7 February 1881, Roll 1, Grierson Papers, Newberry Li-

brary, Chicago, Illinois. For examples of the cozy army-railroad relationship, see Schofield to Drake, July 4, 1868, box 39, Schofield Papers; Dodge to Schofield, Dec. 19, 1868, ibid.

13. William A. Dobak, *Fort Riley and its Neighbors: Military Money and Economic Growth, 1853-1895* (Norman: University of Oklahoma Press, 1998), 69; Manuscript Returns, U.S. Census, 1870, 1880, Presidio County, Texas; Registers of Contracts, Entry 1242, Fort Davis, TX, 1876, 232, 253, 262; Record Group 92, National Archives; Edward M. Coffman, *The Old Army: A Portrait of the American Army in Peacetime, 1784-1898* (New York: Oxford University Press, 1986), 346-47; Jerome A. Greene, *Historic Resource Study: Fort National Historic Site* (Denver: National Park Service, 1986), 39. Enlisted men received a base pay of $13 per month, with additional bonuses for longevity and extra-duty work. Noncommissioned personnel made between 25-50 percent more. Officers' pay ranged from $125 per month for a second lieutenant of infantry to $291 for a colonel. For rough calculations, I used averages of $15 per month per enlisted man and $190 per month for officers.

14. Darlis A. Miller, *Soldiers and Settlers: Military Supply in the Southwest, 1861-1885* (Albuquerque: University of New Mexico Press, 1989), 354; Thomas T. Smith, *The U. S. Army and the Texas Frontier Economy, 1845-1900* (College Station: Texas A&M University Press, 1999), 11-13, 176.

15. H.H. McConnell, *Five Years a Cavalryman; or, Sketches of Regular Army Life on the Texas Frontier, Twenty Odd Years Ago* (Jacksboro, TX: J.N. Rogers, 1889), 104; William A. Dobak and Thomas D. Phillips, *The Black Regulars, 1866-1898* (Norman: University of Oklahoma Press, 2001), 105; Report on John Smith, 14 September 1883, Separate Special Reports (Reports of Individual Deserters) 1883-1890, Box 15, Fort Davis Records, RG 393, NA; Report of Augur, 30 September 1867, Annual Report of the Secretary of War, 1867, 60.

16. Ord to Shafter, 25 August 1877, Roll 1, William Shafter Papers; Wooster, *The Military & United States Indian Policy, 1865-1903*.

17. Robert M. Utley, *Frontier Regulars: The United States Army and the Indian, 1866-1891* (1973; reprint, Lincoln: University of Nebraska Press, 1984), 410.

18. Thomas T. Smith, *The Old Army in Texas: A Research Guide to the U. S. Army in Nineteenth-Century Texas* (Austin: Texas State Historical Association, 2000), 12-45; Smith, "Fort Inge and Texas Frontier Military Operations, 1849-1869," *Southwestern Historical Quarterly* (July 1992), 1-25.

19. Smith, *Old Army in Texas*, 17-38; Fort Davis, TX, July 1867-January 1871, Roll 297, M 617, Returns From US Military Posts, National Archives; "Tabular Statement of Expeditions and Scouts," Fort Davis, TX, Box 14, Part V, Entry 16, RG 393.

20. "Service on the Vanishing Frontier, 1887-1898," *Military History of Texas and the Southwest*, Maclyn P. Burg, ed. (Number 3, 1976), 8.

21. Thomas T. Smith, "West Point and the Indian Wars, 1802-1891," *Military History of the West* (Spring 1994), 31, 40, 41, 48, 51.

22. Ibid., 43-47.

23. Perry D. Jamieson, *Crossing the Deadly Ground: United States Army Tactics, 1865-1899* (Tuscaloosa: University of Alabama Press, 1994), 53; Mark R. Grandstaff, "Preserving the 'Habits and Usages of War': William Tecumseh Sherman, Professional Reform, and the U.S. Army Officer Corps, 1865-1881, Revisited," *The Journal of Military History* (July 1998), 530-31. For reforms and reformers, see also Timothy K. Nenninger, *The Leavenworth Schools and the Old Army: Education, Professionalism, and the Officer Corps of the United States Army, 1881-1918*

(Westport, CT: Greenwood Press, 1978); Carol Reardon, *Soldiers and Scholars: The U.S. Army and the Uses of Military History, 1865-1920* (Lawrence: University Press of Kansas, 1990); and T.R. Brereton, *Educating the U. S. Army: Arthur L. Wagner and Reform, 1875-1905* (Lincoln: University of Nebraska Press, 2000).

24. Jerome A. Greene, foreword to Edward S. Farrow, *Mountain Scouting: A Handbook for Officers and Soldiers on the Frontiers* (1881; reprint, Lincoln: University of Nebraska Press, 2000), 7 n. 2; Andrew J. Birtle, *U.S. Army Counterinsurgency and Contingency Operation Doctrine, 1860-1941* (Washington, DC: CMH, 1998); Brereton, 40-44. Perhaps Greene, who wrote the introduction for a reprint of Farrow's intriguing volume, put it best: "The book is something of a phenomenon, for treatises dealing with the formal methodology of Indian warfare are virtually nonexistent." "Nonetheless," he adds, "elements of Indian fighting methodology crept tangentially into the broader military curriculum, albeit late."

25. Wooster, *Nelson A. Miles and the Twilight of the Frontier Army*; Miles to Sherman, 5 February 1877, Roll 23, Sherman Papers. Miles once promised Sherman, "Some time when I get time, I will write you my plan of Indian campaigning for it may interest you, and as it enables me to know the strength and design of my enemy, to always find, defeat and follow him." Miles to Sherman, 1 February 1877, Roll 23, Sherman Papers. No record of such a detailed follow-up has been found. For a more favorable portrayal of Miles, see Peter R. DeMontravel, *A Hero to His Fighting Men: Nelson A. Miles, 1839-1925* (Kent, OH: Kent State University Press, 1998).

26. For Sheridan's disapproval of Crook's methods, see Paul Andrew Hutton, *Phil Sheridan and His Army* (Lincoln: University of Nebraska Press, 1985), 364-66. On Crook, see *George Crook: His Autobiography*, Martin F. Schmitt, ed. (revised edition, Norman: University of Oklahoma Press, 1986); Charles M. Robinson III, *George Crook and the Western Frontier* (Norman: University of Oklahoma Press, 2001). Recent biographies of Mackenzie include Michael D. Pierce, *The Most Promising Young Officer: A Life of Ranald Slidell Mackenzie* (Norman: University of Oklahoma Press, 1993 and Charles M. Robinson III, *Bad Hand: A Biography of General Ranald S. Mackenzie* (Austin, TX: State House Press, 1993).

27. Robert M. Utley, "The Frontier and the American Military Tradition," *The American Military on the Frontier: The Proceedings of the 7th Military History Symposium*, James P. Tate, ed. (Washington, DC: Office of Air Force History, 1978), 9; Report of Schofield, 20 September, SW, AR, 1875, 122.

28. Utley, *Frontier Regulars: The United States Army and the Indian, 1866-1891*, 19-20, 45, 198; Alice to Baldwin, 31 March 1877, Box 9, Frank D. Baldwin Papers, Huntington Library; Upton to Greene, 3 October 1879, Box 2, F.V. Greene Papers, New York Public Library.

29. Coffman, 279-80, 336-37; Jamieson, 119; Grandstaff, 530-31. See also John M. Gates, "Indians and Insurrectos: The U.S. Army's Experience With Insurgency," *Parameters* (March 1983), 59-86.

30. Jamieson, 37.

31. Cooper, 47; Hampton, 81.

The US Army and Nation Building and Pacification in the Philippines

Brian McAllister Linn

In a recent *Atlantic Monthly* article on "Ten Rules for Managing the World," Robert Kaplan lists as rule number 7, "Remembering the Philippines." Among the lessons of the United States' first successful encounter with overseas guerrilla warfare, Kaplan draws special attention to the importance of soldiers destroying military resistance. Civic action and nation building are important, even vital, elements of occupation and a long peace, but the military defeat of the enemy must come first. He also stresses the vital role military officers played, particularly junior and field grade, who, lacking both the means and inclination to follow a centrally directed, one-size-fits-all counterinsurgency strategy, structured their own local pacification campaigns. By adjusting to the nature of the enemy resistance and the geographic and socioeconomic conditions in their areas of operations, officers were able to develop effective local counterinsurgency policies for what was, essentially, a localized resistance. He concludes, "given the challenges ahead, our experience a century ago in the anarchic Philippines may be more relevant than our recent experience in Iraq."[1]

This paper addresses two areas of the American military experience in the Philippines that may be relevant to today's officers. The first is perhaps better described as a "nonlesson," in that it discusses some of the dangers of interpreting past lessons in the context of today's terminology. Specifically, it addresses whether the US military mission in the Philippines can be characterized as nation building. The second topic is a short summary of the nature of pacification in the Philippines, with special attention to the methods, techniques, and approaches that the Americans used.

Nation Building or Benevolent Assimilation

In assessing the lessons of the Philippines for today's peacemakers, historians, if not journalists, must first deal with the issue of terminology. Today's audiences are familiar with terms such as "peace enforcement" and "nation building" that officers a century ago did not use and, in some cases, did not conceive of as missions. The question of whether historians should continue to use archaic, but historically correct, terminology or adapt to current usage is not just academic hairsplitting; it has important ramifications when assessing historical lessons and, indeed, with the entire question of the utility of history. I should say at the beginning that I am not enamored with the terms "nation building," "military operations other than war" (MOOTW), or "peace enforcement," which I think have been adopted because they are politically correct, bureaucratically directed, and so vague that they are more often sources of confusion than clarity. In most cases the terms the imperial forces used—savage warfare, pacification, punitive expeditions, chastisement, imperial policing—are far more accurate.

Only by the most convoluted reasoning can the US military mission in the Philippines be termed nation building. President William McKinley had no intention of either preserving or creating a separate Philippine nation. His position, which he maintained in the face of much evidence to the contrary, was that George Dewey's victory at Manila Bay had effectively shattered Spanish government in the Philippines and "rendered it necessary . . . to send an army of occupation to the Philippines for the twofold purpose of completing the reduction of Spanish power . . . and of giving order and security to the islands while in the possession of the United States."[2] McKinley was emphatic that the United States held the Philippines, not for its own benefit but for the good of the Filipinos. American rule would provide the inhabitants with as much individual freedom, government, education, internal development, and legal protection as they could safely absorb.

This policy was perhaps best summed up in December 1898 as "benevolent assimilation, substituting the mild sway of justice and right for arbitrary rule." Within this context, the Army's mission was to occupy the rest of the archipelago and "to protect the natives in their homes, in their employments, and in their personal and religious rights."[3] It might be argued, and some did, that implicit in McKinley's rhetoric was the promise that if the Filipinos had demonstrated their fitness for self-government they would have been freed of American tutelage. But this was a long way off. From the beginning the administration denied the archipelago the territorial status it accorded Hawaii and Puerto Rico (ultimately the Philippines were governed as an "insular possession") and made it clear that "between the people of the ceded islands and the United States the former are subject to the complete sovereignty of the latter."[4] To McKinley, the Philippines was essentially a colony, not a nation in the making.

For the most part, the US Army's officer corps' views reflected that of the political leadership. Most officers, including the minority who opposed annexation, held paternalistic and racist attitudes that were inimical to nation building.[5] Indeed, to these officers, the numerous civic projects—constructing schools, roads, and markets and suppressing banditry, slavery, and violence—were justified, both officially and personally, because the "natives" were unfit to rule themselves and would continue to be so for the foreseeable future.[6] The numerous parallels Army officers drew between their service against Native Americans and the inhabitants of the Philippines, particularly the Moros, are further evidence of the Army's view of its mission. Officers like Hugh Lenox Scott, who had extensive civil and military duties with both Indians and Moros, argued that both were "children of the world," requiring "paternal forbearance." His task was not to create a nation but to serve as "preceptor to those whom, from the point of view of civilized mankind, our government regarded as less advanced than we."[7] Scott served with great distinction for three years as governor in the Sulu archipelago and worked, at considerable cost to his health, to bring social, political, and economic benefits to the Moros. But when a new professional opportunity arose, Scott had no qualms in leaving colonial service, for as he said, "I was not a missionary but a soldier."[8]

Although nation building is inadequate to describe US military policy in the Philippines, the contemporary term "benevolent assimilation" must also be used with some caution. Certainly it was one of the pillars of American military policy in the Philippines, and in some regions, it was perhaps the most important single aspect of US occupation. For example, in Manila the US Army rapidly turned one of the pestholes of Asia into a model city. Millions of dollars and man-hours were expended dredging Manila's harbor, hiring crews to clean the streets, flushing out the sewers and canals, building roads, and instituting a host of other civic reforms. Between July 1899 and June 1900 the Board of Health vaccinated 114,000 Filipinos for small pox, contained an outbreak of bubonic plague, and cut the death rate by disease from 1,090 in November 1899 to 599 in June

1900.⁹ This emphasis on civic action continued as the Army expanded into Luzon's countryside and into the other islands. Wherever military garrisons were stationed, they built schools, roads, health clinics, police, and other tangible signs of American progressivism.

A related aspect of benevolent assimilation was manifested in the perception and treatment of Filipino civilians. According to McKinley, the Americans should act in such a manner "that our flag may be no less beloved in the mountains of Luzon and the fertile zones of Mindanao and Negros than it is at home, that there as here it shall be the revered symbol of liberty, enlightenment, and progress in every avenue of development."¹⁰ After fighting broke out on 4 February 1899, he insisted that armed resistance was due to a combination of ignorance and the "sinister ambition of a few leaders of the Filipinos." As he told Congress:

> We are not waging war against the inhabitants of the Philippine Islands. A portion of them are making war against the United States. By far the greater part of the inhabitants recognize American sovereignty and welcome it as a guarantee of order and of security for life, property, freedom of conscience, and the pursuit of happiness. To them full protection will be given. They shall not be abandoned. We will not leave the destiny of the loyal millions in the islands to the disloyal thousands who are in rebellion against the United States.¹¹

In this and other declarations, McKinley made it clear that both uplifting and protecting the civilian population were central to the Army's mission in the Philippines. He was equally clear that the United States had an absolute right to direct the future of the inhabitants of the Philippines; there would be no compromise with those who opposed American authority.

The remaining aspect of the Army's mission in the 28 December 1898 benevolent assimilation policy often superseded establishing a colonial government or social reform—and that was McKinley's order that military government "be extended with all possible dispatch to the whole of the ceded territory."¹² This directive imposed a timetable on the US forces and worked in contradiction to McKinley's own belief that armed resistance to American authority would collapse as a result of internal contradictions. The orders to extend military control, together with McKinley's refusal to recognize the legitimacy of Emilio Aguinaldo's government, contributed to the outbreak of fighting on 4 February 1899. Moreover, it greatly influenced military strategy.

For example, in early 1899, the commanding general in the Philippines, Major General (MG) Elwell S. Otis, despite his wish to concentrate on military objectives in central Luzon (i.e., Aguinaldo's army), had to dispatch precious troops to a number of subsidiary theaters: Negros, Mindanao, Panay, the Sulu archipelago. His rationale was not military—correct or not Otis remained convinced that Aguinaldo's army was the center of gravity—but rather to fulfill McKinley's orders to provide government, stability, and protection to the inhabitants. With the destruction of Aguinaldo's army in December 1899, the need to extend military government became more paramount, and the number of American garrisons increased from 53 in November 1899 to more than 400 a year later. Despite Otis's successor, Arthur MacArthur, accusing Otis of squandering his manpower and failing to concentrate sufficient forces to secure decisive results, he increased the number of garrisons by almost 100.

In summation, the Army's mission can only with great difficulty be defined as nation building. This is not to say that some aspects of the Army's mission did not involve tasks very similar to those performed by today's nation builders. One prominent example was restoring law and order. This was done on a variety of levels, from MG Otis drawing up a new legal code for the archipelago to the individual garrison commander establishing police forces; providing security for merchants and public officials; and suppressing bandits, religious sects, and guerrillas. Army officers were also deeply involved in restoring the Philippine economy and worked hard to establish markets, encourage investment, remove oppressive tariffs, and open up trade—in the process often running into strong opposition from colleagues who sought to use economic warfare as a tool to crush resistance. Moreover, many of these efforts in the field of education, in government, in diminishing the influence of the Church, in establishing a functioning bureaucracy and an independent judiciary can all be seen as essential steps in creating a Philippine state. Thus, the Philippine experience provides important practical lessons about nation building that today's officers should study. At a fundamental level, the US military was not engaged in nation building because that was not what it was ordered to do. Neither President McKinley, nor his subordinate senior commanders in the Philippines, nor the officers charged with enforcing government policy in the archipelago envisioned an independent Philippine nation emerging from their efforts.

The Nature of the War

For American officers to follow Kaplan's stricture to "remember the Philippines," they must first understand the nature of the war. This is a considerable challenge. The current American academic orthodoxy, promulgated in textbooks, journals, and television documentaries, is that the war was little more than an early exercise in racism, cruelty, and perhaps even genocide.[13] Philippine nationalist scholars present an equally distorted view of a revolutionary people in arms rising up against both imperial rule and the plutocrats who collaborated. To appreciate the war and to draw lessons from it effectively, one must understand the nature of both the insurgent challenge and American pacification.

The Insurgent Challenge

Sanctions against collaborators. Because benevolent assimilation placed such a premium on willing Filipino cooperation, it was incumbent on the insurgents to prevent collaboration and impose their own control on the population. In many respects, this was but an extension to the entire archipelago of policies and methods that had already been practiced in the small area of American control in 1899. As the Americans moved into the provinces, the local guerrilla commanders issued proclamations that emphasized the duty of all Filipinos to resist the invaders and declared that any who assisted the enemy were traitors and would be subject to the most severe sanctions. The insurgents had learned that terror was a potent counterargument to what they termed the Americans' "policy of attraction." Indeed, within four days of the outbreak of the war, they had executed the mayor of a Manila suburb who attempted to surrender to the United States.[14] Collaborators' property was singled out for destruction, although often devastation was indiscriminate and intended as much to intimidate entire communities as to punish individuals. As the Americans occupied more towns, attacks on collaborators became more common and public, and the reported burnings, kidnappings, tortures, and killings eventually numbered in the hundreds, with thousands of incidents unreported.[15]

Shadow governments. From the beginning, the revolutionaries/insurgents sought to deny the Americans the means to implement local government. In some areas they were able to create a "shadow government" that paralleled the American colonial government. These shadow governments collected taxes, enforced the law, and provided social services to supporters. In other areas the same individuals served on both the American and insurgent governments, cooperating wholeheartedly with the occupiers in social reforms such as sanitation, schools, and roads while punishing collaborators and raising taxes to support local guerrilla forces.[16]

Although some Americans were convinced that virtually every Filipino office holder was playing a double game, there were a number of factors that inhibited the establishment of shadow governments. The first, and perhaps greatest, factor was the lack of central direction—or in all too often any direction—over the resistance. From December 1899 on, Aguinaldo remained a fugitive who had little control over, or even communication with, his subordinates on the island of Luzon, much less with the even more decentralized resistance movements in the rest of the archipelago. As a result, there was no concerted effort to establish the requisite organization to oversee and coordinate the actions of the local revolutionary governments.

Second, Aguinaldo and his supporters were slow to recognize their potential and pursued instead a policy of strict noncompliance with the occupiers. All civic officials were expected to refuse to serve in American-controlled governments; indeed, all contact between the Filipino population and the Americans was discouraged. Many insurgent commanders issued proclamations declaring that all towns that accepted US rule would be destroyed and their populations killed. In some areas, this even took the form of depopulating towns and removing their inhabitants to "safe" districts. Although these measures achieved some temporary success, in the long run, they greatly helped the Americans. Unable to survive in the countryside, refugees drifted back to their ancestral homes and fell under US authority. In part due to insurgent attacks, they soon found their lives depended on cooperating with the military. So, too, the rural and civic elites who provided the core of insurgent leadership soon found that life in the boondocks was not only physically debilitating but it also separated them from their businesses and families. As the Americans increased pressure on the elites through confiscation, fines, and arrests, the policy of noncompliance proved harder and harder to sustain.

Third, the fractious, even fratricidal, nature of local resistance movements meant that local government officials were often caught between rival guerrilla chiefs. In one province, for example, a local commander protested that his rivals were undercutting his efforts to establish shadow governments by murdering anyone who took civic office.[17]

Finally, shadow governments were extremely vulnerable: one informant, one captured document, one botched entry in the civic accounts, one suspicious incident—any of these could alert the military garrison. This vulnerability greatly increased over time, especially after it became clear the Americans were winning and the number of Filipinos with a vested interest in the new colonial government increased.

American Pacification

Like Filipino resistance, American pacification or counterinsurgency was essentially regional. But unlike Filipino resistance, it always had an element of centralized control and direction exercised by Army and Navy headquarters in Manila. The basic outlines of American military strategy were twofold. The first, which occurred in 1899, was to eliminate the Filipino conventional forces. The second, which began even as the Americans were defeating those forces, was to establish military government, pacify—that is, impose control, law, and order—the population, and suppress armed resistance. This required US forces to do more than occupy the major cities; it required them to take the war into the boondocks.

Importance of local commanders. The Philippine war overwhelmingly confirms the absolute necessity of having officers of character, initiative, and humanity in guerrilla conflicts. From Manila, the American high command promulgated policies, but the key to their implementation was the company officers who dealt with the population daily. Indeed, Henry T. Allen concluded, "It is a fact that the disposition of nearly every town in the archipelago depends upon the officer or officers who have been commanding in that town."[18] Scattered into hundreds of small garrisons, isolated and surrounded by a hostile or apathetic populace, garrison commanders had to establish order in their immediate neighborhoods. They were the men who led the patrols in the mountains and jungles, fought the guerrillas, and rooted out the shadow governments in their towns. On their own initiative, they raised and armed irregulars; established working relations with local political figures, negotiated surrenders with guerrilla chiefs; built intelligence networks; and constructed roads, schools, and dispensaries. To both villagers and guerrillas they came to represent the United States and its promise of honest, effective, and progressive government. In a war that was fought essentially by local forces for local control, the garrison commander's role was crucial to securing American victory.

Garrisoning. US pacification in the 1900s was based as much on the occupation of hostile territory as upon active field operations. Ultimately, American troops would occupy more than 600 towns, in the process imbedding themselves deeply into Philippine society. With few exceptions, companies were stationed in one or two posts their entire 12- to 16-month tour of duty, regiments were stationed in the same one or two provinces, and brigadier generals commanded the same military districts. This continuity had a number of very important results. One result was that it made soldiers familiar with the terrain; they learned to move efficiently through such natural obstacles as hemp, jungle, swamp, mountains, and rivers. They learned where the guerrilla hideouts were, where the best sites for ambushes or observation stations were, and how the seasons affected the roads. Over time, soldiers learned the best methods of patrolling in their areas; they learned the best formations for preventing ambushes, surrounding a village, or sweeping through sugar cane. Finally, the long service in one garrison area provided soldiers with extensive local contacts with the population to learn enough of the language to communicate; to develop a network of spies and guides; and to augment their meager manpower with Filipino paramilitaries such as police, armed guards, and local militia. Local officers could develop and implement reforms that would appeal to the people in their areas. In some places, it might be a road network that allowed farmers to bring their produce to markets; in others, it might be suppressing bandits and sects or removing corrupt and oppressive officials.

Integrating civil and military duties. In contrast to today's Army, which makes clear distinctions between "warfighting" and every other mission, the Army of 1900 had extensive duties in civil administration. Until July 1901, the Army's commanding general was also the governor of the Philippines. This dual command extended downward to colonels, who served both as regimental commanders and provincial governors, and to lieutenants and captains, who both led their troops in the field and at the same time served as town mayors, customs officials, police chiefs, tax collectors, civil judges, chief engineers, and sanitation inspectors and performed other such duties. The Army in the Philippines was able to make such transitions smoothly and quickly, and without a lot of complaining that it was not their real mission or that constabulary duty was destroying their combat effectiveness. At the same time they hunted guerrillas, soldiers continued to teach school, build roads, provide medicine and treatment, ensure religious toleration, and in other ways demonstrate the benefits of colonial rule. As part of its efforts to minimize opposition, the Army sought to avoid actions that would alienate either Americans or Filipinos.

Most Army officers proved to be highly effective civil administrators—they were honest, they could handle paperwork and detail, and they were not afraid to make immediate decisions. Many also showed a surprising grasp of people skills—there is no reason to doubt the sincerity of the popular testimonials that many officers garnered from the local population. They might not like the Filipinos, and they might view them as racial inferiors, but that did not prevent them from doing a great deal of good. Many soldiers saw no contradiction between detesting the Filipinos as a people and liking individuals or between advocating strong measures against guerrillas and protesting any imposition on "their" townspeople. Indeed, the American victory in the Philippines depended a great deal on the willingness of a sufficient number of officers to accept that civil responsibilities were an essential part of pacification.

Coercion. However great their emotional satisfaction with building schools and eliminating sickness, American officers recognized that "the military objective, the defeat of the guerillas, was the most essential of their tasks."[19]

Destruction. Since the guerrillas used the population as a source of logistics, information, manpower, and shelter, the Americans were soon driven to punish individuals and communities. US soldiers destroyed crops, farms, boats, and livestock in areas suspected of aiding guerrillas and exacted what one officer termed "most just retribution and retaliation" for attacks on American troops. Such destruction grew in frequency and scope.[20] While these sanctions were justified under military law, they also reflected the conviction among many officers that "the judicious application of the torch is the most humane way of waging such a war."[21] However, it is important to note that the level of retaliation reflected officers' perceptions of both the strength of the guerrilla forces and their popular support.

One officer, in a province widely, if mistakenly, believed to be pacified, wrote to his wife, "I have never burnt a house yet or cut a tree, or whipped a native or hung one, and I don't intend to. If we can't conquer these savages without resorting to Spanish methods, my notion is that we had much better quit these islands, and let them have them."[22] On

Panay for much of 1900, there appears to have been an effort to restrict punishment only to the guilty.[23] In southeastern Luzon, an area where the level of resistance was perhaps the greatest in the archipelago, there was far more support for retaliation. As early as February 1900 the district commander ordered that "communities that harbor criminals and permit them to operate against the United States will have to suffer in some way for the acts of the criminals themselves."[24]

Despite some protest, most officers in the area appear to have accepted this principle of collective responsibility. One officer commented of an especially recalcitrant area that "it will be extremely difficult to control that section of the district except by burning all the towns where Insurgents are harbored thereby compelling people to come into the towns during the wet season."[25] Similarly, another officer directing a sweep through the countryside commented, "My suggestion is to burn freely and kill every man who runs."[26] By 1901 the amount of American destruction had grown considerably; one patrol burned 180,000 pounds of rice and 60,000 pounds of corn in slightly more than a week.[27] Such measures imposed great hardships on both the guerrillas and noncombatants, but they proved essential in shattering guerrilla resistance and winning popular acceptance, however grudgingly, of American rule.

Joint operations. The nature of the Philippine archipelago forced the Army and Navy to collaborate on amphibious operations. After a rocky start that was largely caused by the respective senior commanders' egos, the US Navy and Army cooperated very well. The most important Navy contribution was its blockade of all nonoccupied ports and its amphibious capacity. The Navy's blockade effectively ended interisland trade; moreover, the rebels could not communicate with each other or receive outside support. The Navy thus was a key factor in making the Philippine war a series of regional struggles and not a national revolution. The Navy also gave the Americans the ability to land and strike all along the coast. One such operation captured Aguinaldo.

Innovation and adaptation. The Army went to war with tactics that had been designed for European battlefields but proved well suited for fighting in the jungles, mountains, and rice paddies. Moreover, officers and men were able to adapt these tactics to local conditions. In one province, the threat might be small groups of snipers who kept up a constant harassing fire on the occupied towns; in another province it might be primitive headhunters; in a third it could be hordes of machete-wielding religious fanatics; in a fourth province it might be Muslim tribesmen who fought behind stone fortresses and practiced ritual suicide. With few exceptions, the Americans' flexibility, small-unit cohesion, and from-the-front leadership by officers and noncommissioned officers proved sufficient to overcome these many and varied challenges.

Intelligence. It is commonplace to say that in low-intensity wars intelligence is the most important asset, but the Army's effort in the Philippines was very uneven. From the beginning, the intelligence services were small—usually one or two officers and a few translators—and their duties were unclear. The high command, especially MG Otis, was slow to establish a more efficient or accurate system. Otis relied for most of his information on upper-class Filipino collaborators who tended to tell him what he wanted to hear —that the Filipino people desired US rule and that only a small group of warlords, brigands, and terrorists were opposed—misinformation he passed on to McKinley. Arthur MacArthur, who took over in May 1900, had a far better grasp of the need for intelligence; nevertheless, it was not until 13 December 1900 that intelligence was reorganized under the Division of Military Information, which was charged not only with translating documents but also with relaying vital information promptly to field units. The most productive Army intelligence came from the local town and provincial officers. Because the benevolent assimilation policy placed so much insistence on civil affairs, post commanders were required to collect an impressive amount of data on local conditions that often had great military value. Thus, in creating civil governments or police forces; in auditing town finances; or in making alliances with town counselors or clergy, officers often were able to destroy shadow governments, arrest guerrillas posing as "amigos," and secure hidden weapons.[28]

Logistics. One of the great strengths of the US Army in the Philippine war was that it could put most of its forces into combat infantry units, not into logistics and other support. Logistics was primitive by our standards; indeed, it was often appallingly bad. Thousands of troops were sent home as invalids, many of whom subsequently died because of the Army's inability, and outright incompetence, to provide decent food, shelter, and medicine to American soldiers. Yet, having said that, the Americans could do what their opponents were not doing: sustaining troops in the field. Indeed, Filipino guerrillas who had managed to avoid military defeat often surrendered because of starvation and disease. Moreover, the very primitiveness of American logistics enabled it to put roughly 60 to 70 percent of its manpower into its combat formations, whereas in Vietnam, it required nine service troops to support one combat infantryman.

Filipino auxiliaries. Throughout the Philippine war the US military forces were terribly undermanned. At their peak the American forces numbered 70,000, and usually they totaled no more than 45,000. Moreover, because of Army accounting practices, transfers, detached duty, and sickness, the average rifle strength of Army forces was about 26,000—and this to occupy, pacify, and administer nearly 8,000,000 Filipinos. From the beginning the Americans relied on Filipino help, first with logistics (which employed more than 100,000 Filipinos in 1899 alone), then as scouts and police, and finally as armed units. The American military was able to enlist Filipino auxiliaries through a number of ways. Many Filipinos opposed the Republic of the Philippines and the nationalist/regional revolutionary leadership for tribal, religious, or personal reasons.

The Philippine Scouts owed their origin to the irregular warriors raised from the Macabebes for service against guerrillas in the swamps of central Luzon. Having served the Spanish for decades, the Macabebes were brutally persecuted by Aguinaldo's predominantly Tagalog supporters when the latter took over Pampanga province. On Samar, the Americans raised a scout unit from among the hemp merchant families who were losing both economic and political power as a result of insurgent exactions. By the end of the war, there were more than 15,000 Filipinos serving in officially recognized scout or constabulary units. These Filipino soldiers did very well under American officers. By 1905, except for the Moro provinces, locally raised forces carried out most military operations in the archipelago.

Local officers also raised a number of paramilitary units whose existence was often kept secret from their superiors and who were occasionally in direct violation of orders from Manila. A combination of revenge, religious zeal, and self-preservation prompted the sectarians of the *Guardia de Honor* to join the Americans against the anticlerical revolutionaries in La Union province. In western Mindanao, local Muslim chiefs viewed the Catholics in the revolutionary forces with hatred born of centuries of warfare and did such a good job of suppressing them that the Americans faced very little armed resistance. In many towns officers could solicit help from landowners, businessmen, or political figures who had been abused by the local guerrillas. These elites raised militias that freed American forces from town security duties and joined with the garrisons to hunt guerrillas in the boondocks. The town police forces, much maligned in some areas, proved efficient counterinsurgency forces in others. As in so much of successful American counterinsurgency, it was the ability of local officers to adapt, adjust, and innovate that often determined whether local forces would play a significant role in pacification.

Conclusion

Robert Kaplan is correct in his assertion that today's military officers should "remember the Philippines." The US military's pacification of the archipelago offers both a treasure trove of lessons on counterinsurgency procedures and an unsurpassed case study of the dynamics of non-Marxist agrarian regional insurgency. Thus, at all levels, from the creation and implementation of broad civil-military policies, to the vital role played by civil-military projects, to the utilitarian techniques of bush warfare, the Philippines can teach a great deal. But there is a reason that virtually all American officers have ignored the Philippine experience for more than a century. The war was a complex and confusing conflict that defies conventional military analysis. To learn the lessons, officers must truly think outside the box, to be willing to engage in intensive study and self-reflection. The Philippine experience does not fit easily into conventional frameworks of MOOTW or nation building, and efforts to do so will probably lead to conclusions that will be so simplified as to be either useless or dangerous.

These disclaimers aside, there are five essential lessons that a study of the Philippine war can teach today's officers. First, there is the absolutely vital lesson that guerrillas are not invulnerable, that they are often disunited and divided, that they have a great deal of difficulty sustaining continued popular support, that their leadership is often militarily and politically inept, and that time is often on the side of the occupying forces. A second lesson holds that in a war that is essentially a struggle over local control, the role of the local commander—both insurgent and American—is crucial. In addition to the importance of the early and constant integration of civil and military duties, it is crucial to recognize the importance of local issues. Central government gets all the attention—everyone knows who Paul Bremer is. But I would hazard a guess that, in the long run, Paul Bremer may be far less important than the dozens of officers who are helping to build local governments and trying to put Iraq together.

A third lesson concerns the unavoidable necessity of controlling punitive or retaliatory policies. Quite frankly, it is either naive or dishonest to pretend that soldiers will continue to take casualties without responding, and that in some (probably in many) cases, this retaliation will either accidentally or deliberately lead to physical abuse, property destruction, and even death. Moreover, the likelihood is that such punitive measures will increase over time. Punitive measures have always been part of American counterinsurgency, and they have often been cited, by both American commanders and their opponents, as highly effective. I am not advocating mindless destruction, but I am warning against unrealistic rules of engagement that essentially prohibit troops from performing their most important missions. If soldiers cannot strike back, they will simply avoid combat, resulting in US troops hunkering down behind wire and waiting for the gymnasiums and fast-food courts to arrive while the guerrillas control the countryside. A fourth lesson stresses the need for local auxiliaries, even if it means embracing rather unsavory allies. We need more Macabebes, and we have to be willing to accept the fact that their behavior will sometimes be motivated by revenge, tribal vendettas, or just bad character.

Finally, there must be a serious effort by the US Army as an institution to study guerrilla/revolutionary/insurgent/unconventional warfare. To an outsider, the Army's distaste for professional education in anything other than large-scale conventional conflicts approaches the pathological. The Chief of Staff, US Army's reading list includes virtually nothing on unconventional warfare nor do the curriculums at West Point, the US Army Command and General Staff College, and the US Army War College. Indeed, US Marine students at the School of Advanced Warfighting spend far more time studying the Army's greatest counterinsurgency campaign than do the Army students at the School of Advanced Military Studies, Fort Leavenworth, Kansas. It is no contradiction to praise the initiative, common sense, and practicality that American soldiers have demonstrated in recent nation-building and pacification operations and, at the same time, maintain that with a stronger institutional commitment and more professional education they might have done even better. If and when the Army does decide to focus on the "small war" duties it is actually performing rather than the hypothetical "big war" it spends so much time preparing for, then it could do far worse than begin with Robert Kaplan's advice: "Remember the Philippines."

Notes

1. Robert Kaplan, "Supremacy by Stealth: Ten Rules for Managing the World," *Atlantic Monthly* (July-August 2003), 80.

2. William McKinley to Wesley Merritt, 19 May 1898, US Army Adjutant General's Office, *Correspondence Relating to the War With Spain . . . April 15, 1898 to July 30, 1902*, (1902: reprint, Washington, DC: Center of Military History: 1993) vol. 2, 676, hereafter cited as *CWS*.

3. William McKinley to Secretary of War, 21 December 1898, in Henry C. Corbin to Elwell S. Otis, 21 December 1898, *CWS*, vol. 2. 858-59.

4. US War Department, *Annual Reports of the War Department* (Washington, DC: US Government Printing Office, 1899) vol. 1, 24, hereafter cited as *RWD*.

5. For a sample of the diverse opinions among soldiers who opposed US annexation of the Philippines, see Joseph I. Markey, *From Iowa to the Philippines: A History of Company M, Fifty-First Iowa Volunteers* (Red Oak, IA: Thos. D. Murphy Co., 1900), 184; James Parker, "The Philippine Campaign," n.d., Box 28, Clarence Edwards Papers, Massachusetts Historical Society, Boston, MA; "Memoir," John Henry Parker Papers, Archives, U.S. Military Academy Library, West Point, NY; H. Roger Grant, "Letters From the Philippines: The 51st Iowa Volunteers at War, 1898-1899," *Palimpsest* (November-December 1974), 174-75. In contrast, one author argues there were "numerous oblique references" against expansionism in military writings. See James L. Abrahamson, *America Arms for a New Century: The Making of a Great Military Power* (New York: Free Press, 1981), 76.

6. For a sample of Army views on the unfitness of Filipinos for self-government, see J. Franklin Bell to Henry C. Corbin, 17 May 1902, Box 1, Henry C. Corbin Papers, Manuscripts Division, Library of Congress (hereafter MDLC); P.S. McGovern, "The Philippines: Let us Take Them Out of the Political Football Arena," Command and General Staff School Individual Research Paper, 1930, Combined Arms Research Library, Fort Leavenworth, KS; "Notes on the Philippines," Box 20, Matthew F. Steele Papers, Military History Institute, Carlisle, PA (hereafter MHI); Leonard Wood to Theodore Roosevelt, 18 November 1906, Box 37, Leonard Wood Papers, MDLC; Raymond E. Lee, "The Philippine Defense Problem," 1 March 1927, Study for US Army War College (AWC) Course, AWC 1926-27, File 235-82, MHI.

7. Hugh Lenox Scott, *Some Memories of a Soldier* (New York: Century Co., 1928), 461. On parallels between the Philippines and the Western frontier, see Brian McAllister Linn, "The Long Twilight of the Frontier Army," *Western Historical Quarterly* (Summer 1996), 141-67.

8. Scott, 400.

9. Guy L. Edie to Assistant Adjutant General (AAG), Provost Marshal General, 31 July 1900, *RWD*, 1900, vol. 1, 283-88. John M. Gates, *Schoolbooks and Krags: The United States Army in the Philippines, 1899-1902* (Westport, CT: Greenwood Press, 1975), 57-63.

10. William McKinley, "To the Senate and House of Representatives," 3 December 1900, *Compilation of the Messages and Papers of the Presidents*, James L. Richardson, ed., 19 vols. (New York: Bureau of National Literature, 1897-1922), volume 10, 222.

11. William McKinley, "Second Inaugural Address," 4 March 1901, *Compilation of the Messages and Papers of the Presidents*, vol. 10, 244.

12. William McKinley to Secretary of War.

13. For a critique of current interpretations of the war, see Brian McAllister Linn, "Taking Up the White Man's Burden," *1898: Enfoques y Perspectivas*, Luis E. Gonzales-Vales, ed. (San Juan: *Academia Puertorriqueña de la Historia*, 1997), 111-42.

14. John M. Stotsenburg to AG, 2d Brigade, 8 February 1899, Box 2, Entry 764, Record Group (RG) 395, National Archives, Washington, D.C. Hereafter, all RG citations refer to National Archives collections.

15. For a summation of some of the worst atrocities, see US Senate, *Affairs in the Philippine Islands: Hearings Before the Committee on the Philippines of the United States Senate*, 57th Congress, 1st Session, Document No. 331, April 1902, 993-1376.

16. For examples of such a "shadow government," see William Tutherly to AG, 21 February 1901, Letter Sent 201, Co's. A-F Letter Sent Book, 26th Infantry, Entry 117, RG 94; Edgar Z. Steever to Commanding Officer Vigan, 20 July 1900, Letter Received 1286, Entry 5583, RG 395; J.M. Thompson to AG, Department of Northern Luzon, 4 January 1901, Letter Sent 62, Entry 2312, RG 395.

17. *Buenaventura Dimaguila* to Mariano Trias, 30 November 1900, Exhibit 1125, John R.M. Taylor, *The Philippine Insurrection Against the United States, 1898-1903: A Compilation of Documents and Introduction*, 5 vols. (1906: reprint, Pasay City, PI: The Eugenio Lopez Foundation, 1971), vol. 5, 281-88.

18. Henry T. Allen to [John A. Johnston?], 21 January 1902, Box 7, Henry T. Allen Papers, MDLC. For similar sentiments, see Dean C. Worcester to Mrs. Henry W. Lawton, 5 May 1901, Box 2, Henry W. Lawton Papers, MDLC.

19. Brian McAllister Linn, *The U.S. Army and Counterinsurgency in the Philippine War, 1899-1902* (Chapel Hill: University of North Carolina Press, 1989), 170.

20. Charles J. Crane, *The Experiences of a Colonel of Infantry* (New York: Knickerbocker Press, 1923), 340.

21. Samuel B.M. Young, "Our Soldiers in the Philippines," 13 November 1902, Box B, Samuel B.M. Young Papers, MHI.

22. Matthew F. Steele to Stella, 15 August 1900, Box 7, Matthew Steele Papers, Institute for Regional Studies, North Dakota State University, Fargo, ND.

23. A.A. Barker to AAG, Department of Visayas, 16 September 1900 and Edward D. Anderson to AG, Department of Visayas, 7 June 1900, both in 26th Infantry Regimental Letters Sent Book, Entry 117, RG 94; Walter H. Gordon to AG, 15 May 1900, in Walter Henry Gordon, 3927 ACP 1886, RG 94.

24. AAG to Commanding General, 2d Brigade, 2d Division, 5 February 1900, Entry 4330, RG 395.

25. Benjamin F. Cheatham to AG, 2d District, Department of Southern Luzon, 29 May 1900, Letter Sent 192, 37th Infantry Letters Sent Book, Entry 117, RG 94.

26. 2 June 1900, Diary, William Carey Brown Papers, MHI.

27. On the campaign in this area, see Linn, *The U.S. Army and Counterinsurgency in the Philippine War, 1899-1902*, 119-61.

28. Brian McAllister Linn, "Intelligence and Low-Intensity Conflict in the Philippine War, 1899-1902," *Intelligence and National Security* (January 1991), 90-114.

Lost in the Snow: The US Intervention in Siberia During the Russian Civil War

Major Jeff Stamp, US Air Force

Part I: Overview

Part I: Overview and Thesis

Part II: Summary of Events

Part III: Ill-informed—US intelligence failures before intervention

Part IV: Ill-conceived—Idealism vs realpolitik

Part V: Ill-advised—Intervene without interfering?

Part VI: Conclusions

> # Part I: Thesis
>
> The US military intervention in Siberia was ill-informed about the situation, ill-conceived by an administration that refused to admit that national security demands and the doctrine of self-determination clashed, and ill-advised by deliberately vague orders that turned out to be impossible. The interplay of these factors resulted in an exceedingly complex operation that was doomed to fail from the start.

If one was to summarize this page in one sentence, it would probably be, "How **not** to conduct a foreign intervention."

Part II: Summary of Events

March 1917	Czar ousted
November 1917	Kerensky government ousted at beginning of Russian Civil War
1917-1922	Russian Civil War
August 1918	United States agrees to intervene
December 1919	United States withdraws

This is a brief timeline of major international events affecting the US intervention in Siberia. A key point to remember is what is not listed: the Allies' continuing efforts in World War I will affect their decision-making process toward intervention in the Russian Civil War in ways they might not otherwise have contemplated. In particular, the British and French were particularly keen to try to reestablish some kind of Eastern Front against Germany. The United States agreed to intervene almost exclusively because of Allied pressure resulting from various "side effect" concerns of the Great War; for example, to "protect war materials sold to the czar's government."

US Area of Responsibility on the Trans-Siberian Railway, 1918

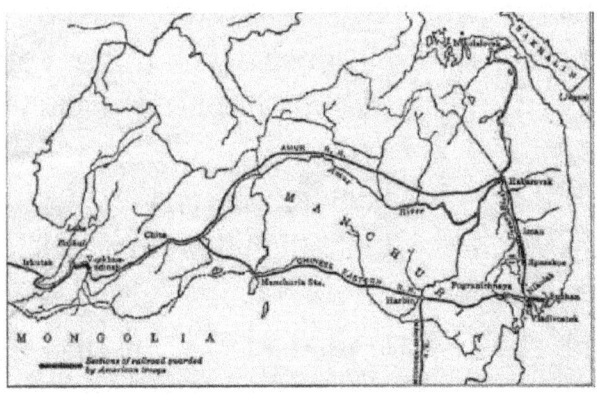

ttp://hsecretwar.hhsweb.com/

This map helps give some idea of not just where the intervention's theater of operations was but the sheer, staggering **size** of the area in question.

Part III: Ill-Informed

- **Lack of formal intelligence collection**
  - Resulted in incomplete information
  - *Cheka* defeated informal organization
  - Informal reporting biased, incomplete
- **Wilsonian ideal of open diplomacy runs into real-world problems**
  - Democracies may not like secret services, but tyrannical opponents make them necessary.

One of the key difficulties the United States, and more specifically the Wilson administration, encountered in contemplating intervention in Russia was the near-total intelligence vacuum it faced. At the time the United States had no formal foreign intelligence-collection mechanism, either civilian or military, other than reporting by the Ambassador or attaches, upon which to base decisions. Ambassador David Francis' (at the time) reporting, naturally, did not take into account other opinions of what was happening in Russia; was easily frustrated by the nascent *Cheka* (Soviet secret police) in the capital; and resulted in a biased, incomplete picture of what was going on in the areas the Soviets controlled.

Of note, President Woodrow Wilson's own idealism—as manifested by his preference for "open" diplomacy—ran counter to trying to establish some sort of functioning intelligence-collection and analysis system.

> # Part III: Ill-Informed
>
> Lack of alternate sources of information
> - Allies' intelligence skewed to affect US decision making
> - No SIGINT or IMINT capabilities
> - Odd combination of near anarchy and budding Bolshevik police state prevented reliable open-source collection
>
> Conclusion: Incomplete data on which to base decisions

The Allies—the French, British, and Japanese—were usually willing to provide intelligence from their own sources, but naturally, that intelligence was slanted to attempt to persuade the United States; that is, Wilson, to accede to the Allies' wishes in Russia. (General William S. Graves, the US commander in Siberia, was particularly plaintive about the reporting of his British counterpart, General Alfred W.F. Knox.)

The United States had no signals intelligence (SIGINT) or imagery intelligence (IMINT) capabilities in Russia at all, and the odd combination of budding police state (in areas the Bolsheviks controlled) and near-anarchy (almost everywhere else in Russia) made "open source" collection—from newspapers, for instance—either extremely suspect or flat-out impossible. The conclusion is that Wilson and his Cabinet had incomplete information on which to base decisions, and information—at a premium in any type of war—is the basis of any successful intervention.

> # Part IV: Ill-Conceived
>
> Dilemma: Wilsonian self-determination versus Bolshevik menace
> - Fundamental question: What **is** self-determination? Do Reds count in this case?
> - Wilsonian answers conflicted with US interests
>   —Bolsheviks aided Germany, if only indirectly
>   —Bolsheviks threatened Europe, eventually the world
> - Dilemma compounded by Allies' imperial ambitions in the Far East
>   —Heavy pressure on United States to intervene anyway

The question at the heart of the U.S. Siberian intervention is, "What is self-determination?" What, exactly, constitutes the will of any given people? This principle, proclaimed near and dear by Wilson, actually begged several questions arising from the unique nature of the Russian Civil War: Is a revolution led by would-be tyrants (the Bolsheviks) really an expression of the Russian people's will, even if it replaces an older tyranny? Even if this is the case, and Wilson admitted that was not certain, that still leaves another question: By taking Russia out of the war, the Reds indirectly assisted America's enemies, and all this still leaves aside the problem of the Bolsheviks' self-proclaimed goals of world domination. The height of America's first "Red scare" was not far off when the Wilson administration was considering the issue.

Add to this the question of America's Allies' imperial ambitions in the Far East. The Japanese, in particular, were more than ready to intervene, apparently in the hopes of taking over resource-rich Siberia for themselves. The French and British were also very much in favor of intervention for a number of reasons—to prevent the collapse of the Eastern Front against Germany, to keep Japan from gobbling up Siberia by giving any intervention there an Allied flavor, and, last but not least, to stem the perceived Bolshevik menace (although there was internal dissent of how severe that menace was in Paris and London).

> # Part IV: Ill-Conceived
>
> "Solution"—a series of compromises to assuage Wilson's conscience but were not necessarily practical
> - Self-delusion—not intervention, just protecting stockpiles, helping Czech legion
> - Complex reasoning lost on US, Russian publics
> - Results: No one really satisfied, but doing nothing seemed worse
> - Wilson's moral morass results in unworkable orders to US commanders

This is reminiscent of a classic debate in American politics between liberal idealism and "realpolitik." After months of agonizing, Wilson, aided by Allied prodding, finally acquiesced and agreed to send US troops to Russia as part of an Allied intervention. Wilson justified the move by what, in hindsight, can only be called self-delusion rooted in idealism almost totally detached from military realities.

In July 1918, Wilson wrote an *aide-mémoire* that wound up becoming the only orders, guidance, or instructions General Graves ever received. The *aide-mémoire* laid forth the reasons the United States was sending troops to Russia (although it deliberately avoided the word, "intervention"). It would protect the Czech legion (former prisoners of war who had agreed to fight with the Allies against Germany, then found themselves awash in a sea of near-anarchy in western Siberia); protect stockpiles of military supplies shipped to the czar's government and sitting on the docks in Vladivostok, Murmansk, and other ports; keep open the Trans-Siberian Railway to this end; and assist the Russians in establishing such self-government as they chose. US forces were supposed to do all of this, however, without interfering with Russian self-determination and do so in the middle of a multiple-sided civil war.

Wilson's complex reasoning was lost on both the US and Russian publics. Whatever the *aide-mémoire* said, the indisputable fact was that US soldiers were in Russia without being invited by a de facto Russian government. That could not be construed as anything other than intervention by anyone other than a reality-challenged idealist. The real problem, though, lay in General Graves' attempt to implement essentially unworkable orders. In sum, he interpreted them as "go to Siberia and be neutral."

> # Part IV: Ill-Conceived
>
> Were other solutions available?
> Two possibilities for certain:
> - Declare war against Bolsheviks
> - Simply do nothing at all
>
> Wilson rejected both.
> Both were politically impossible, given US public sentiment, and morally difficult, given Wilson's personal beliefs.

Of course, a reasonable question, given the circumstances, is, "Did Wilson have any other realistic options?" Yes, there were two. The first would have been to, along with the rest of the Allies, declare war against the Bolshevik government because the separate peace negotiated by the Reds in the Treaty of Brest-Litovsk would certainly constitute a sufficient *casus belli*. This might have made it possible to reinstate the short-lived Kerensky government that the Bolsheviks ousted, given the latter's relative insecurity in 1918. The other option would have been to simply do nothing at all because, from a purely accounting perspective, given the titanic scale of combat on the Western Front, the loss of the Czech legion and the military stockpiles in Russia's ports represented a minor problem and could be argued was only distracting from the real issue at hand. The Department of War made this argument vociferously before Wilson's agreement with the Allies to intervene.

In the end, however, Wilson rejected both arguments. The first solution would be difficult, however firm the legal and diplomatic ground, to justify to the American people, given that imperial Germany was still very much in the war. Moreover, Wilson could not convince himself that the Bolsheviks—despite his personal loathing of them—did not represent the will of the Russian people. Likewise, American popular sympathy for the Czechs at the time and Wilson's fear of unchecked Japanese imperial ambitions made the second option nonviable as well. So Wilson opted for a morally convoluted, militarily impossible mission.

> # Part V: Ill-Advised
>
> Graves' determination: "noninterference" to avoid "mission creep."
> - Worried about getting dragged into anti-Bolshevik war by Allies
> - Concerned that Whites just as bad as Reds
>
> Concerns well-grounded but how to do?
> - Kolchak regime unpopular, brutal
> - Trying to "protect" something in the middle of a civil war means combat, period
> - More difficult than modern peacekeeping missions, as no "peace" in place between Whites and Reds

General Graves had two apparently outstanding characteristics: a strong sense of integrity and a complete lack of imagination, which made him about as good a choice for the Siberian mission as Wilson could have hoped for. Graves, seeing himself as a good soldier, never questioned the suppositions of his orders (such as the *aide-mémoire* was), only how to implement them, which was enough of a problem.

Graves' chief concern was to avoid what nowadays is called "mission creep." He had no intention of exceeding his orders and getting dragged into an anti-Bolshevik war by the Allies. In particular, his concern that the Whites were just as brutal as the Reds led him to attempt to interpret the *aide-mémoire* scrupulously. As it happened, his concerns were well founded. British General Knox on the scene was rabidly anti-Red, and the regime of White Russian Admiral Aleksandr V. Kolchak, who controlled most of Siberia during the US presence there, was at least as corrupt and brutal as the communists. The reality of **how** to accomplish the *aide-mémoire's* instructions proved elusive.

The particularly thorny part of the problem lay in the inescapable fact that attempting to protect something—be it Czechs, military supplies, the railway, or anything else—in the middle of a shooting war means combat will be involved. Combat, in turn, means two other problems: casualties (the reasons for which may not be apparent to the home public) and whichever side one is shooting at will claim a violation of neutrality, even if those doing the complaining started the shooting. In short, Graves' situation was actually more difficult than modern peacekeeping operations because there was certainly no peace between the Whites, Reds, and various Cossack bands roaming Siberia at the time.

> # Part V: Ill-Advised
>
> ## Limited Intervention Serves Red Purposes
> - Makes propaganda easier; demonstrates that the United States lacks resolve; makes unconventional tactics easier to implement
> - US troop morale suffers; public pressure to return troops
> - Graves must then contend with little home support, an increasingly difficult situation, and little help from the State Department
> - Withdrawal and mission "failure"

Another angle to the US intervention in Siberia—and many other interventions besides—is the question of, scruples aside, whether intervening will further your purposes or your (potential) opponents'. This point, probably more than any other, is where Wilson's decision would return to haunt the United States.

Landing comparatively small contingents in Siberia and northern European Russia was, in many ways, the worst of all possible decisions. Far from being large enough to defeat Bolshevik (or White) armies and constrained by Wilson's *aide-mémoire* from doing so, all US forces could do in Siberia was to help keep the Trans-Siberian Railway operating in the middle of a civil war. While the Allies did keep the railway operating, naturally, this meant the United States would take casualties for no easily discernible reason to the American taxpayer—or the soldiers themselves, for that matter.

Moreover, the real tragedy was how all this played into the Bolsheviks' hands. After discerning that the US presence did not constitute a credible threat, the Reds easily made propaganda use of the intervention, claiming it was counterrevolutionary, and gained recruits and public support in the process.

Meanwhile, naturally US troop morale suffered, and public pressure mounted at home to end the mission, particularly after the Armistice ending World War I. This made Graves' situation increasingly untenable because he had to contend with all of the above, on top of receiving little to no help from the State Department (Ambassador Francis was at odds with Wilson's Russian policy). When the United States finally withdrew from Siberia in 1920, even General Graves would term the entire mission a "debacle."

Part VI: Conclusions

Three Primary Contributors to Failure

- Bad intelligence combines with...
- Wilson's idealism and leads to dilemma; "solution" to dilemma orders...
- Essentially impossible mission: How does the US military intervene without interfering?
    —Anyone reminded of Heisenberg's Uncertainty Principle?

The U.S. mission in Siberia was about as "doomed from the start" as it is possible to be. A series of cascading effects, produced initially by a lack of intelligence, compounded by Wilsonian idealism in an extremely complex sociopolitical situation, resulted in an unworkable mission. An unworkable mission, by definition, is going to fail. The fundamental questions at stake in the situation—how to intervene without interfering and how to help a people without taking away their right to self-determination—was never fully answered by Wilson's policy and, in many ways, reflects some of the fundamental questions surrounding any foreign intervention. However, while most foreign interventions involve enough force and definitive purpose to succeed (at least in the planning stage), in the hope that "the end would justify the means," Wilson's uncompromising idealism prevented even that.

Every time a major power, even for the noblest of reasons, considers intervention, that power must confront the politico-military equivalent of Werner K. Heisenberg's uncertainty principle: to inject yourself into the situation is to change the situation and, at least temporarily, will probably mean some liberal idealistic principles taking the proverbial back seat to realpolitik. Wilson's Siberian misadventure demonstrates that attempting to avoid that unpleasant reality, particularly when one is ill- or misinformed about the situation at hand, is to invite mission failure.

Bibliography

Printed Publications

Foglesong, David S. *America's Secret War Against Bolshevism: U.S. Intervention in the Russian Civil War, 1917-1920*. Chapel Hill, NC: University of North Carolina Press, 1995.

Goldhurst, Richard. *The Midnight War*. New York: McGraw-Hill Book Co., 1978.

Graves, William S. *America's Siberian Adventure*. New York: Peter Smith, 1941.

Melton, Carol Wilcox. *Between War and Peace*. Macon, GA: Mercer University Press, 2001.

Somin, Illya. *Stillborn Crusade: The Tragic Failure of Western Intervention in the Russian Civil War 1918-1920*. New Brunswick, NJ: Transaction Publishers, 1996.

Internet Sources

Leifheit, Daniel A. *America's Secret War*. 5 March 2004. http://secretwar.hhsweb.com/

State Department Soldiers:
Warlords, Nationalists, and Intervention

Katherine K. Reist

The era in China from the first Opium War (1839) to the end of the civil war (1949) was one of revolts, revolutions, foreign interventions, and civil wars. China faced the need for modernization of its philosophical systems, government, industry and military. Lacking an effective government for most of this period, many Chinese became increasingly vocal in their demands for order and stability, the hallmarks of a good Chinese government, and sought to support those who claimed to have the key to its establishment. In this period also the many foreigners who had established businesses, schools, hospitals, and churches in China wished to be protected from the violence that was endemic to the political instability. Their positions were protected by the series of treaties between China and various Western nations, Russia, and Japan that followed from the first Opium War and subsequent military and diplomatic confrontations: the unequal treaties. By and large the foreigners sought to maintain the treaty system. The Chinese viewed it as a symbol of China's humiliation and determined to end it. The American position was that the treaties should remain in effect until the Chinese government demonstrated its ability to protect American lives and interests.

The State Department's concept of China mixed together in almost equal parts myth, morality, and model—the myth of the enormous market in China open to opportunity and the morality of encouraging and supporting the emergence of a Christian, republican nation with the United States as the obvious model. American interests were commercial, educational, moral, and paternalistic. In the view of policy makers, The United States was not like other nations with interests in China; it would help China help itself. The result would be a country sufficiently strong that it could enforce treaties and protect foreign nationals and their commercial interests. When these goals were accomplished, the United States would end China's treaty privileges. Moreover, American actions—or more accurately, its lack of action—would maintain a balance of power in Asia that would discourage other powers from aggressive actions, particularly those that would close American opportunities for commerce.

None of these perceptions was accurate. The market in China was restricted for various reasons, among them the lack of interest in most of the goods offered for sale. Trade with China was minimal—1 to 3 percent of exports in this period. The most successful companies were British-American Tobacco and Standard Oil, both of which ignored general "wisdom" on doing business in China. The missionaries in China were a fairly large group, but they were scattered throughout the country, representing a variety of mission organizations and denominations. While their influence was significant in education, health care, and publications, they were not successful in Christianizing China. China's political goal was to achieve stability, modernization, and, sporadically, a republican form of government. While foreign assistance would be appreciated, the Chinese had not adopted any one model. Insistence on treaty privileges weakened China, both economically and politically; waiting until China was strong enough to negotiate perpetuated the system. American interests in China were not of sufficient importance to defend them militarily. There was neither popular support, unless lives were directly threatened, nor that of Congress, or of many in the State Department for actions that could be regarded as actions of imperialism.

The problems sparked by the Boxer Uprising enhanced the American minister's authority in Beijing. As the Boxers had made all foreigners enemies, the foreigners, in turn, acted as allies. Therefore the minister, in his view, needed to have the same status and recognition as those representing the other powers, specifically the United Kingdom, France, Russia, Japan, Germany, Austria-Hungary, and Italy. In 1900, American Minister Edwin M. Conger had been reluctant to inflame anti-foreign sentiment by requesting additional troops. When he did make that request, the admiral commanding the Asiatic Fleet had had no instructions regarding his role in such an instance.[1] The State Department had insisted that the repetition of such a misunderstanding would not occur. As a result, in subsequent crises, neither the War nor Navy Departments could reinforce, move, withdraw, or alter the mission of forces in China without the consent of the Secretary of State.[2] Military forces in China were "State Department forces."

In the turmoil following the Chinese revolution of 1911, which overthrew the Qing dynasty and established the Republic of China, many foreigners feared that the new Chinese nationalism would make itself popular by advocating anti-foreignism. Fearing another Boxer-type uprising, American Minister to China W.J. Calhoun requested that an army unit be sent to Tianjin to control the rail link to the capital to evacuate the legation personnel should another attack be launched on the Legation Quarter. Under the Boxer Protocols (1901), the eight nations that had taken part in suppressing this movement received the right to increase the number of their legation guards and to establish a force in Tianjin to protect the railroad, the most effective means of evacuation, from "the capital to the sea." The Americans, while reinforcing the legation guard, had not established a military presence at Tianjin. The United States did not have a concession area there. The State Department, while protecting all the rights of the treaty system, tried to disassociate itself from the formal trappings of an imperial presence and identification with the other treaty powers, not always an effective endeavor.

The State Department, having replaced the 9th Infantry with Marine Corps legation guards, did not request marine reinforcements but requested those of an army regiment. The minister believed the troops would enhance his position among his peers, allow him to play the War Department against the Navy, and allow a more visible deterrent to any attacks on foreigners. Some viewed the deployment of an army unit as a more permanent commitment than that of the marines. Perhaps the minister was reflecting on recent instances when he had requested marine reinforcements and when the admiral commanding the Asiatic Fleet decided that the crisis was past, he was able to reembark the marines over the minister's objections. Perhaps an army unit would be less independent. Of course, to be effective, the army commander would have to maintain good relations with the other powers and the Navy, yet maintain an element of noninvolvement so that the American presence differed, at least in degree, from the other powers.

The 1st Battalion, plus machine gun platoon, of the 15th US Infantry Regiment was sent from Manila to Tianjin in January 1912. The 3d Battalion and the headquarters arrived in March. The 2d Battalion was held in reserve in Manila. For the first decade of its presence in China, the 15th Infantry Regiment experienced few problems with the Chinese. Its existence fell into the pattern of colonial forces everywhere—parades, reviews, dining-ins, formal calls, and much entertaining. There were classes until noon and sports activities in the afternoons. Then the problems were, in (then) Lieutenant Colonel George C. Marshall's words, "cheap booze and cheaper women."[3] When the bars closed, free rickshaws were provided to lessen the attractions of the latter. This effort met with varying success.

The real problem was the lack of training, although over time various commanders dealt with the problem with some ingenuity. Marching was possible, although the city was not conducive to supporting much of this activity, and the land surrounding the city was planted. Marches across country could only be held between harvest and planting. Therefore, the usual line of march was along the railroad right of way. One commanding officer was so focused on forced marches to prepare the troops for a possible rescue mission in Beijing that there was a movement to have him relieved for mental incompetence.[4] Annual weapon requalification was finally solved by purchasing land near Qinhuangdao. Each battalion spent part of the summer in camp there.

Because the Americans did not hold a concession in Tianjin, housing the regiment posed something of a problem. At first the officers and men were scattered among the facilities available in the French and British concessions. When, in World War I, China declared war on Germany, the German (and Austro-Hungarian) concession became available to the Americans. Although ownership reverted to the Chinese, the Americans were able to rent the former German barracks area and additional warehouses and stables as needed. The Army, then, had a fairly close working relationship with several Chinese entrepreneurs as well as with those the regiment hired as servants. were handled by who Each squad, noncommissioned officer (NCO), or officer hired the Chinese to handle many fatigue details—to prepare meals, keep quarters clean, and perform laundry and maintenance duties. The servants were not supposed to clean individual weapons, but this prohibition was more honored in the breach than not. In addition to casual labor for unloading supplies, the quartermaster hired skilled workers such as carpenters, masons, and drivers. Each employee received an identity card and a "uniform"; many remained with their units for 15 to 20 years. In recognition of the immediate lack of a threat, the 2d Battalion, which had been sent to China in 1914, was returned to Manila in 1921 with the Department of State's approval.

These interactions, as well as the threat of future anti-foreign actions, made several commanders aware of the need for language skills for at least some of their unit members. Some commanding officers encouraged the interested officers, NCOs, or enlisted men to learn the colloquial language. Marshall required officers and members of the mounted patrol to learn Chinese.[5] The patrol, mounted on Mongol ponies, warned those Americans living outside of the concession boundaries of impending danger. The patrol consisted of one officer, 27 enlisted men, and 52 ponies. Competency was encouraged for all others. Language lessons were sometimes published in *The Sentinel*, the paper of the 15th. Those who were proficient were granted a special device to wear on their sleeves—the Chinese character "zhong," the first syllable of the Chinese term for China. There had developed along the coast a business *lingua franca* called "pidgin," a mixture of Malay, Portuguese, Chinese, and English. Although the regiment's motto, "Can Do," was pidgin, it was not a medium for serious discussion or negotiation. Therefore, the language training was in *bai hua*, or colloquial Chinese.

Some problems were apparent with the mission as originally stated—protecting the railroad from Beijing to the sea. Railroad security was necessary because the roads were poor to nonexistent any distance from the cities, and the climate produced either thick dust or thicker mud. Protection meant guarding the more important rail stations and bridges and frequently inspecting the track. Because the foreign garrisons were established in Tianjin, inspecting the line from there to Beijing, approximately 80 miles, was not overly difficult at first. But this stretch of the line did not actually accomplish the Protocol goals. Tianjin was not on the sea. Thus, another part of the rail line to Tanggu also needed to be guarded.

Debarking at Tanggu, 113 miles from Beijing, was difficult because a bar across the river mouth prevented all but the smaller ships from crossing it. Oceangoing ships had to anchor several miles offshore and send people and supplies in by lighter. Obviously this situation would be dangerous should it become necessary to evacuate the legation personnel from Beijing. Therefore, the phrase "from the capital to the sea" was interpreted to mean from Beijing to Qinhuangdao—more than 260 miles from Beijing—to take advantage of a long pier in deep water developed by the Kailan British-Chinese Mining Administration.[6] (The port remained ice free year-round.) Yet to protect access to the pier, the foreign forces would need to control the railroad to Shanhaiguan, approximately 25 miles farther. The solution the foreign forces in Tianjin agreed on was to divide responsibility for sections of the rail line among the troops of the various powers. The Americans would be responsible for a 55-mile section from Lutai to Lanzhou.

An officer and 40 men were stationed at various outposts between these two stations, with a company in Tangshan, a fairly large town with a major rail yard. The British, French, Japanese, and Italian garrisons made similar arrangements to protect the line. At first these arrangements sufficed. However, as the instability in China accelerated and various warlord factions began to compete for power, the situation for the foreign troops in China changed. The richer provinces were the obvious targets for warlord acquisition, but the key was Beijing.

The foreign governments tended to recognize the holder of power in the capital, whether represented by a parliament, or simply his own staff, as the government of China. This recognition allowed the resident power holder to negotiate loans and other assistance. Although a weapons embargo was proclaimed for weapons shipments to China, such shipments arrived with some regularity. Thus, some of the warlords obtained the latest in weaponry such as Renault tanks, Krupp artillery, Western aircraft, and personal weapons. Others joined the fortunate in ever-shifting coalitions. The Chinese had also developed 20 large arsenals and several smaller ones; obtaining weapons for most of the contenders for power in China was not a major concern. The foreign forces, in general, and the Americans, in particular, did not have tanks, aircraft, or heavy artillery. They were equipped with pre-World War I and war surplus arms and supplies. Their mission was based more on their ability to "show the flag" and bluff.

By the early 1920s, warlord conflicts had begun to pose a threat to the mission of the troops in Tianjin, the second most important commercial center in China. Control of the Beijing-Tianjin area meant control of a major transportation hub. Rail lines stretched west and south from Beijing, and south and northeast from Tianjin. Control of the railroads meant control of North China. The sine qua non of a warlord was an armored train, on which he could travel in some comfort and safety. Other trains were loaded with men, weapons, and supplies. Obviously, then, a successful warlord needed to control access to the trains in his area, and deny their use to rivals.

The problem for the foreign troops was to keep the rail line free and unencumbered by parked warlord trains. At first "International Trains" flying the flags of the various powers, and with detachments of one officer and a dozen men from each garrison representing them, were run up and down the line as a show of treaty rights and the powers' intention to enforce them.[7] There were some challenges. Some shots were fired at the trains and some track displaced, but most incidents were minor. For most warlords, fighting each other for control of China took precedence. They could not also handle a war with one or more foreign forces, and indeed, such a war would severely limit their ability to succeed in controlling China. For the first few Chinese military confrontations, the foreign forces were spared any serious threat.

A threat always simmered under the surface, however. The threat of anti-foreignism was one element upon which any warlord could call to appeal to the people in his area of actual or potential control. All of them did so but always with a concern for the need to keep the foreigners neutral. Some foreign governments tried to limit the force of this appeal by helping one or more likely contenders for power with advice, financial aid, or military advisers. The most obvious beneficiary of such foreign aid was Zhang Zuolin, the "old Marshal" of Manchuria, who received money and military advice from Japan. The peak of these warlord coalition conflicts occurred in 1924-25, when victory seemed possible for either side. Not only did the various northern warlords competing for control of the capital area engage huge armies (from 125,000 to 250,000 men) equipped with modern (and heavy) weapons, but also much of the fighting centered around the Beijing-Tianjin area, requiring control of the railroad by one or another of the factions. Foreign attaches described the military encounters as resembling those of World War I.

Tianjin was particularly difficult to defend because it was situated in flat terrain and (post-Boxer) lacked walls. Access from the city to rail and water transportation meant that no faction could bypass it. The International Trains were no longer effective in the face of Chinese military necessity. As the Americans refused to participate in further attempts to keep the lines free in this way, the International Trains were discontinued. At times, as many as 80 trains belonging to a single warlord clogged the rail lines and sidings in and around Tianjin.[8] Telegraph lines were cut, and communication was interrupted temporarily. The real danger for the concession areas was posed by retreating troops who were unorganized, dispirited, and armed. Many tried to enter the foreign area to find shelter or for the purpose of looting.

In response, the foreign military commanders worked on a mutual defense plan for the foreign areas of the city; the goal of the plans was to protect the foreigners until reinforcements arrived. Each garrison, depending on size, was given a section of a defined perimeter to protect. It was to deny Chinese troops admittance to this area, persuading them to go around, not through the foreign area. The 15th tried several approaches to guarding its section. It set up small outposts on the road leading to the concessions. These small detachments had weapons but lacked ammunition to prevent any "incidents." The outposts, instead, offered a free meal of rice, cabbage, tea, and bread to any soldier who would turn in his weapon and who, unarmed, was then free to traverse the city.[9] Those who refused to turn in their arms were denied access to the urban area. This ploy worked fairly well for a time. The Americans' mounted patrol was sent to warn nationals living outside the concession area of danger and to escort them into the shelter of the foreign lines. The 15th maintained a census of Americans in the area.

Additional challenges arose. Occasionally large units of Chinese troops tried to come through the American lines because the American area had officially reverted to Chinese control.[10] Then the language training that several of the commanding officers had encouraged paid off in the encounters. Single officers, with a few enlisted men, met the first of the Chinese soldiers and demanded, in authoritative Chinese, that an officer be produced. After arguing with the Chinese officer, the Chinese forces sought another way around the American area. The foreign forces became aware that these encounters, based on bluff and the Chinese commanders' desire not to complicate their already hazardous situation, would not be similarly successful for long. The 15th began to request transfer from China following these encounters. The State Department, admitting that the unit's mission was "in abeyance," nonetheless denied permission for withdrawal.

Meanwhile in south China, the *Guomindang* (*GMD*), or Nationalist Party, in alliance, initially, with the Communist Party, began a military drive to unify the country and to eliminate the warlords and the unequal treaties. Due to a number of factors, the rise of anti-foreign feelings led to their expression in protests, demonstrations, boycotts, riots, kidnapping, and violent acts. For most of the foreign community, these tensions peaked when the *GMD* began to approach the larger cities of the lower Yangzi River. The Nationalist forces' assault on Nanjing necessitated that British and American gunboats protect and evacuate the nationals. This act included landing naval and marine personnel and firing naval guns.

The *GMD's* next target was Shanghai where there was a large international settlement. Again, the Americans did not hold a concession area there. But many Americans lived in the area, and many businesses had headquarters in the city. In response to the perceived danger, American Minister J.V.A. MacMurray and other diplomats requested additional forces (to double the number already available) to protect the lives and interests of their nationals.[11] The 3d Marine Brigade, with aircraft, light tanks, and artillery, was sent to Shanghai to assist in defending American interests but not to defend, per se, the settlement area. Although the settlement area was threatened more than once, the Chinese, whether victor or vanquished, did not attempt to openly attack the area.

The presence of reinforcements from the various nations, at least doubling the available forces, obviously played a role in deterring further directed *GMD* attacks on foreigners in the Shanghai area. At the height of the crisis, 171 warships of the various nations, with eight flag officers aboard, were anchored off Shanghai. The senior officer was Admiral C.S. Williams, even though the British had the largest naval force, including a carrier, present. The American naval presence included four cruisers, four destroyers, an oiler, a transport, and a minesweeper.[12]

With the *GMD's* success in displacing the local warlords who had opposed their forces, the Northern Expedition continued toward Beijing. The necessity of holding the capital for any group that labeled itself as nationalist was apparent. However, the danger to the foreign nationals and diplomatic representatives, after the problems at Nanjing and elsewhere, was also apparent. Minister MacMurray consulted the State Department regarding the implementation of Special Plan YELLOW. YELLOW was not a plan for war against China, although the War Plans Department developed it within the color-coded war planning efforts. Rather, it was an evacuation plan to follow should anti-foreign hostility actively threaten American lives in China. The plan called for evacuating Americans from the interior of the country, by gunboat where possible, to one of the larger coastal cities, either Shanghai or Tianjin. *Guangzhou* (Canton) was mentioned in one iteration of the plan, but most Americans lived in central and northern China, and available forces might not stretch to include those in the south. While marine and naval personnel would be landed to assist in the evacuation, most of the protection and fighting, if necessary, would be handled by Army forces from the Philippine Department, reinforced from Hawaii, and ultimately from the mainland. (Later versions of this plan were less practical.) A force of three to five divisions was detailed in the plan to adequately protect the specified cities and the rail line from Beijing.[13]

Anticipating that this or other plans might need to be implemented, the Army had attempted to establish a general headquarters and staff for the "American Forces in China" (AFIC) in 1922 in conjunction with, but separate from, the command of the 15th Infantry. The 15th now would be part of the AFIC and no longer would be under the Philippine Department (over much protest from its commanding general).[14] However, the headquarters was established as the US Army Forces in China (HQUSAFIC), thereby denying the Army control of joint forces. In case of a joint operation, the Army already would have a general officer and staff who were familiar with the local conditions on the ground and operating.

It was hoped, but not established as part of the special plan, that the HQUSAFIC would control all ground forces. The established headquarters would give the Army at least equal status with the admiral commanding the Asiatic Fleet in the estimation of the minister and perhaps more influence regarding its mission. It would also enhance the American forces' status in combined consultations among the military establishments in Tianjin, although the ranking foreign officer was Japanese. The Department of State did not authorize the special plan. The US Marine 3d Brigade remained a separate entity, not directly tied to the legation's protection nor required to cooperate with other nations' forces. In addition, the brigade commander, General Smedley D. Butler, was senior to Army General Joseph C. Castner, which might have complicated the Army's claim to joint force command.

The *GMD* campaign for the north did not meet with the anticipated heavy fighting; the city, although on alert, did not experience the expected violence. The marine brigade was recalled, minus the 4th Marine Regiment that remained in Shanghai. The 31st Infantry, which had replaced some of the marines in Shanghai, returned to Manila. The HQUSAFIC was disestablished; the 15th remained in Tianjin, although it had once again requested reassignment.

Although China regained a measure of relative stability, the *GMD* began a series of campaigns against the Chinese Communist Party that, along with the Nationalist capital moving to Nanjing, focused attention on the central and southern parts of China. This shift of focus from the north had unintended results. Most of the foreign diplomats maintained their legations in Beijing, waiting to analyze the degree of control the new government exercised and its success against the communists. Chiang K'ai-shek (Jiang Jieshi), however, wished to enhance his government's prestige by having the foreign diplomatic missions upgraded to embassies and established in Nanking. Movement in this direction was slow but steady.[15] But the legality of the foreign troops in Tianjin rested on the phrase "between the capital and the sea." This provision obviously did not apply to Nanjing as it is on the Yangzi, accessible from the sea. The 15th requested to return from China because its mission was no longer necessary. The ambassador refused, arguing that embassy staff remained in Beijing and might require evacuation. In addition, the diplomats argued that the regiment's modified mission was to protect the lives and property of nationals. This statement was later amended to protecting American lives. As manpower levels eroded throughout the 1920s and the depression had not improved the military budgets or the supply situation, the success of such a mission was arguable.

The other continuing problem was the actions of the Japanese. In September 1931, the Kwantung army, stationed along the railroad right of way in southern Manchuria, had declared that the Chinese had blown a railroad bridge on the Japanese-controlled Southern Manchurian Railroad. They therefore moved to take control of all of Manchuria, subsequently declaring it to be an independent country, "Manchukuo." Although the Chinese protested through the League of Nations and to the signatories to the Nine-Power Treaty and Kellogg-Briand Pact, little action was taken. (The Japanese withdrew from the league when their actions were labeled as being aggressive.) To protect their investment in Manchuria, the Japanese began to extend their control into Inner Mongolia and north China. They also began to reinforce, beyond treaty limits, their forces in the north in response to claims of anti-Japanese incidents. Their diplomats were less responsive to the protests of those of other nations.

During this period, the War Department became increasingly concerned regarding its force in China. The costs of maintaining this force were not worth the interests being protected. Public opinion was against a "colonial force" overseas. The Philippine Department commander wished the troops to be available there until the independence of the islands occurred. The efficacy of stationing a small force in an area of conflict, where its numbers were sufficient to annoy but not to achieve anything of use, was argued. The State Department replied that although the force was small, the mission for which it had been employed had ceased to exist, and the Japanese did not seem to moderate their demands on China due to its presence, the time was psychologically inappropriate for withdrawal because negotiations were ongoing with the Chinese government. Even if such negotiations regarding the treaty privileges were successful, the State Department wished to observe the Chinese government's actions for a while before withdrawal was warranted.

As Japanese control of the five northern provinces of China was extended, the commanding general of the Philippine Department wrote to the War Department that if ever there existed a reason for stationing troops in China, it had passed. He further likened the situation there to having a powder magazine near a fire. He recommended, if necessary, to reinforce the marine guard and to withdraw the infantry from Tianjin.[16] Secretary of State Cordell Hull replied that the troops' presence was psychologically stabilizing and that because their mission was neither combat nor coercion withdrawal might be misunderstood. Minister Nelson T. Johnson stated that he had no reason to be concerned about a possible outbreak of conflict between the Japanese and the Americans.

The tenor of communications between the War and State Departments increased in intensity as well as number through the mid-1930s. Even when war broke out between China and Japan in 1937, the State Department remained somewhat sanguine. Reports that the American troops were guarding their barracks and adjacent American homes only as other forces were guarding their concessions and that hope of international cooperation was unrealistic failed to change Ambassador N.T. Johnson's mind. When the Navy Department began to issue orders removing dependents from China, the State Department followed suit and permitted Army dependents to be sent home as well. The actions of the Japanese finally brought to a head the issue of control of the 15th Infantry. Assistant Secretary of War Louis Johnson wrote to President Franklin D. Roosevelt of the danger in which the State Department's actions had placed these troops.[17] In February 1938, the War Department issued orders for the 15th to return Fort Lewis, Washington. The regiment sailed on 4 March 1938.

How effective was the State Department soldiers' military mission in an era of revolution, warlords, nationalists, and intervention? The troops were in China as a symbol of a desire for order, the intent to protect the nationals, and a deterrent to foreign nationals becoming involved in China's internal disorders. They also served as a visible demonstration of American interests in Asia. There was no repetition of the siege of the legation quarters (or the Embassy), although anti-foreign sentiment used by both the militarists and nationalists was more widespread. Beijing was not isolated for more than a day or so before communications were restored. The presence of troops enhanced, in the minister's assessment, his ability to conduct diplomacy on equal terms with the Europeans and the Japanese. The Tianjin garrison protected foreign nationals, and not just a few Chinese, from the chaos of civil war. The garrison commanders worked with their opposite numbers in the city, the ministers in the capital, and the admirals and marine commanders as the situation required. In their 25 years in China, they did not fire a shot in anger.

However, this entire set of relationships developed through a series of ad hoc measures. The joint and combined plans were a reaction to a series of events. The major problems occurred in the State Department's control of the mission and the troops with very little consultation with the War or Navy Departments. Without consultation, it was difficult for the military to plan, train, or even understand its responsibilities. Since the foreign troops were not the target of attack from Chinese forces and only rarely did anti-foreign incidents threaten the area under the regiment's direct control, there was a certain leeway that allowed these informal arrangements to function with some effectiveness.

The major problems were in the discrepancy between show of force and commitment. The United States was not committed to a military defense of its policies or position in East Asia. It was hoped that a show of force would be sufficient to allow for both. By 1937, the stated goals had failed. The State Department soldiers were placed in a frustrating situation with little control over mission, staffing, safety, or planning. The situation was resolved by the actions of another power that resulted in war, not by consultation, negotiation, or mutual interest.

Notes

1. Captain Jesse D. Cope, "American Troops in China—Their Mission," *Infantry Journal* (March-April 1931), 174-78.

2. Louis Morton, "Army and Marines on the China Station: A Study in Military and Political Rivalry," *Pacific Historical Review* (February 1960), 51-73.

3. Forrest C. Pogue, *George C. Marshall: Education of a General*, vol. 1. (New York: Viking Press, 1963), 240.

4. Barbara W. Tuchman, *Stilwell and the American Experience in China, 1911-1945* (New York: Bantam Books, 1983), 148.

5. Dennis L. Noble, *The Eagle and the Dragon—The United States Military in China, 1901-1937* (New York: Greenwood Press, 1990), 53; *Report on Chinese Language Course*, 1 May 1927, File 350, Box 294, World War I Organization Records, National Archives and Records Administration (NARA), Washington, DC.

6. *Goodbye to Old Peking: The Wartime Letters of U.S. Marine Captain John Seymour Letcher, 1937-1939*, Roger B. Jeans and Katie Letcher Lyle, ed. (Athens, OH: Ohio University Press, 1998), 201, n 20. Kailan was Herbert Hoover's old company.

7. Charles W. Thomas III, *The United States Army Troops in China, 1912-1927*, monograph, US Army Military History Institute, Carlisle Barracks, PA.

8. George C. Marshall to Lt. Col. Hjalmer Erickson, 29 January 1925, *The Papers of George Catlett Marshall*, vol. 1, The Soldierly Spirit, December 1880-June 1939, Larry I. Bland, ed. (Baltimore, MD: The Johns Hopkins University Press, 1981), 272.

9. The American defense line consisted of 7 miles of canals, dikes, railroad branches, bridges, and roads. See Noble, 194, and Tuchman, 127.

10. Captain William B. Tuttle, with nine enlisted men, met the lead elements of 5,000 Chinese troops who had fixed bayonets as they moved forward. See Pogue, 229-30.

11. As of 1 April 1927, military forces available were 14,000 British, 2,400 Americans, 1,900 Japanese, 1,200 Italians, and 500 French. See Brigadier General J.C. Castner, USAFC, to the AG, 10 April 1927, AG 370.5, Box 483, RG 407, NARA, Washington, DC.

12. Rear Admiral Kemp Tolley, US Navy, Retired, *Yangtze Patrol—The U.S. Navy in China* (Annapolis, MD: Naval Institute Press, 1984), 165.

13. Military attaches filed Situation YELLOW reports regularly. The number of Americans in China for planning purposes were north China, 2,743; central China, 6,510; and south China, 1,596. Situation Monograph YELLOW, 1 March 1926. 242-55 1-60, Box 299, RG 165, NARA, Washington, DC; *American War Plans, 1919-1941*, vol. 1, Stephen T. Ross, ed. (New York: Garland Press, 1992), xii.

14. The Secretary of War to the Secretary of State, 21 October 1922, *Foreign Relations of the United States, 1922* (Washington, DC: US Government Printing Office); Morton.

15. Nelson T. Johnson presented his credentials as the first American Ambassador to China in September 1936. See Tuchman, 184; Jeans, 201, n 20.

16. Major General E.E. Booth, Commanding, Philippine Department to the Adjutant General, 2 October 1931, 093.5, Box 44, RG 407, NARA, Washington, DC.

17. Morton. The China station was considered to be a career enhancer for diplomatic and military personnel. Of those officers serving in China in this era, 25 were promoted to general officer in the Army. Six became commandants of the US Marines. See Noble, 53.

There and Back Again: Constabulary Training and Organization, 1946-1950

Robert Cameron
Armor Historian

This presentation addresses the training, organization, and operation of the US zone constabulary in occupied Germany immediately following World War II. The constabulary itself illustrates how a mid-20th-century modern professional army sought to address an operation most definitely "other than war." Providing security in war-torn Germany with its civilian infrastructure and economy in ruins was not a familiar mission for an American Army that had just fought its way across Europe. The US Army opted to create a specially trained and organized force to conduct what was, in modern parlance, a stability operation. The resultant success of the constabulary stemmed from its orientation upon a unique operational environment, the attention given to soldier training, the emphasis on accountability throughout the chain of command, and overall adaptability. The constabulary experience also embodied a transition from combat to peace operations and back again to combat—precisely the type of transition today's Army regularly makes.

(Reference to US Commission on National Security in 21st Century consideration of "constabulary" units to handle peace operations without impacting the conventional force's readiness.)

Agenda

Need
Creation
Operations
Issues and challenges
Reorientation

Key areas addressed are depicted here.

Germany 1945: US Zone of Occupation

Problem
- 40,000 square miles
- 1,400 border miles
- 16,000,000 Germans
- 500,000 displaced persons
- No civil infrastructure
- Shortages of food, fuel, shelter
- Demobilization ongoing

Nazi support
Resistance potential
Force level versus disturbances
Underground activity

??? Unknowns

Large-scale static deployment
versus
Small, mobile detachments

Following the end of the war in Europe, the United States military found itself responsible for occupying and policing a large segment of wartime Germany. Large numbers of refugees and displaced persons, coupled with a civil infrastructure in ruins, complicated the task facing the US military, itself in the midst of demobilizing. Discussions regarding the best method to provide security in the occupied zone varied from a large-scale static occupation to creating a special police force that would rely on mobility rather than mass to conduct security operations throughout the American zone. The extent of Nazi support, likelihood of resistance to occupying forces, underground activities—especially those dedicated to helping Nazi and SS personnel—were all unknown factors. Civilian uprisings triggered by food scarcity and the general chaos of postwar Germany also seemed likely. No clear idea existed on what force level would be required for occupation duties.

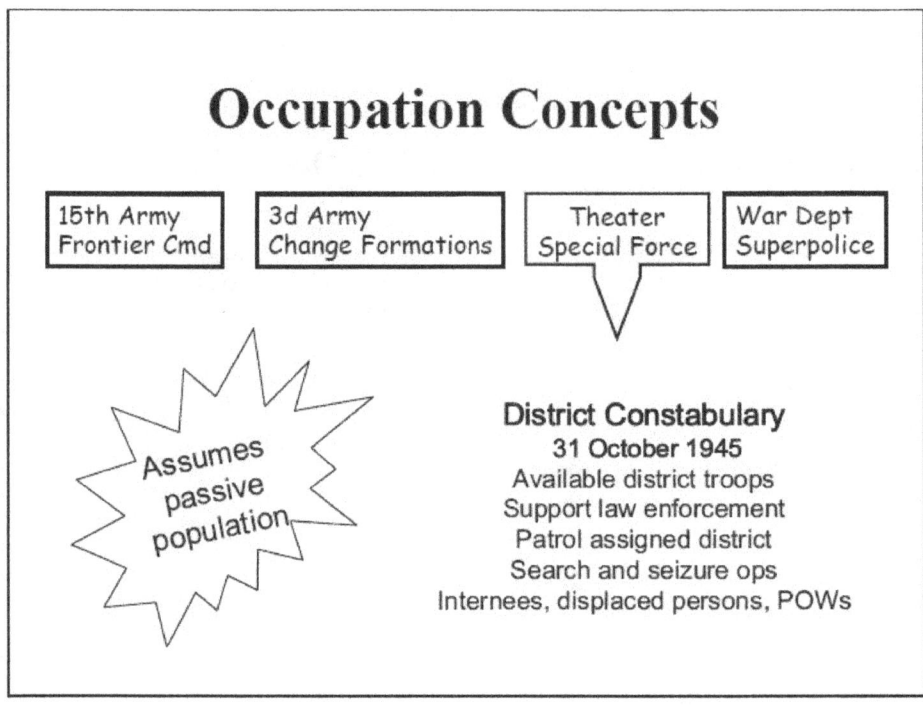

The idea for a constabulary evolved from the separate efforts of several commands. In 1944 the Fifteenth Army began preparing plans for occupying the Rhineland. It envisioned an ad hoc police force divided into a city and frontier command. The latter was actually implemented to control movement across the Franco-German border. The Third Army recommended that units on hand be modified for police duties. The War Department, drawing on the parallel efforts in the Pacific Theater, advocated relying on local police agencies supported by a super police force. The European Theater command, however, recommended a specially organized and trained police force. The District Constabulary represented a trial run of this concept, using available units with minimal preparation. Lessons learned from its operations were applied to the subsequent US zone constabulary. Inherent to all occupation plans, however, was the assumption that the German population would prove largely passive.

> # Theater Command Guidance, November 1945
>
> Trained constabulary commences operations, July 1946
> Absorb district constabulary
> Cavalry reconnaissance squadrons basis
> Occupation infantry divisions form tactical reserve
> Mobile operations with fixed patrol areas
>
> **Assumptions**
> - German government stabilizing
> - Relief from temporary postwar duties
> - No major security problem
> - *No need for operations outside US zone*

In November 1945 the theater command issued detailed guidance on creating a special police force. It would rely on mobility and fixed patrol areas to provide a US presence throughout the American zone. The emphasis on mobile, dispersed operations made the cavalry reconnaissance squadrons natural models for the new constabulary units. In actual operations, they would be supported as necessary by the three infantry divisions under theater command. In opting for a special, mobile police force, the theater command chose mobility over mass. While early occupation plans had called for a large, static occupation force, the public pressure to demobilize and downsize the Army encouraged economies in personnel. Planners estimated that relying on a constabulary force would allow an additional 100,000 soldiers to be removed from occupation duties. However, creating the constabulary assumed that US forces would not be called on to meet contingencies outside the American zone and that the German population would stage no major uprisings or outbreaks of violence. These assumptions were calculated risks taken on the basis of developments in Germany to date, especially the gradual rebuilding of German police organizations.

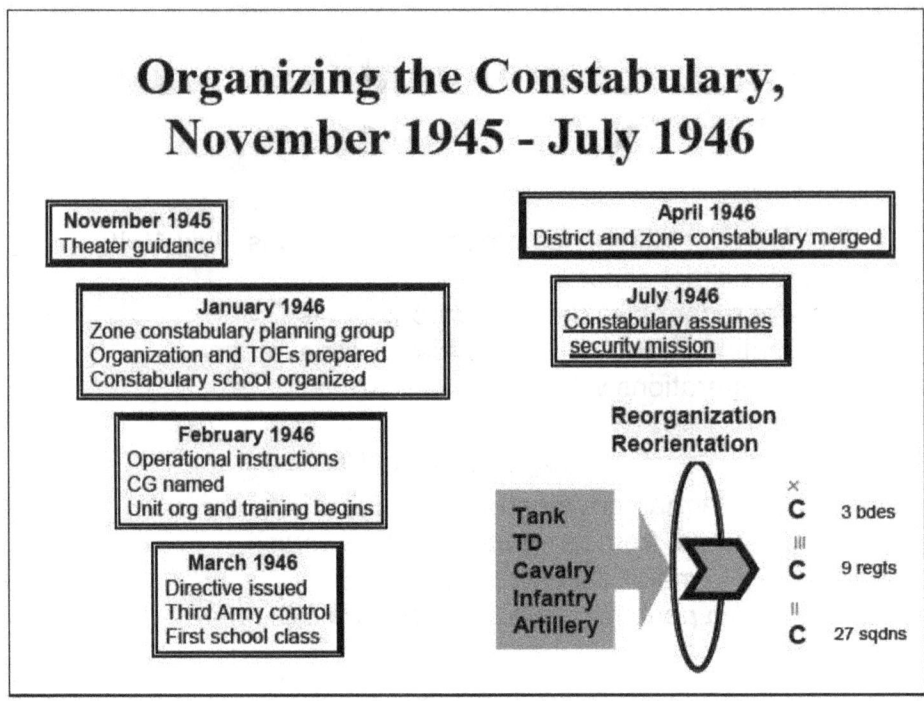

Following theater guidance, preparation of the Constabulary occurred at a frenzied pace between November and the implementation date in July. In this period, unit tables of organization and equipment (TOEs) had to be created; personnel and materiel had to be found to fill the units; commanders had to be selected; a disposition scheme had to be determined; and a training program complete with school, instructors, and a program of instruction (POI) had to be established. Moreover, constabulary operations also had to be integrated into the overall occupation policy. The Third Army headquarters bore primary responsibility for these measures, partially due to the anticipated early inactivation of the Seventh and Fifteenth Army headquarters. Consequently, a Zone Constabulary Planning Group was established under the direction of MG Ernest N. Harmon to address the detailed planning for the new force. In February Harmon became the commander of the zone constabulary, and the VI Corps Headquarters and Headquarters Company became the Headquarters, US Constabulary on 15 February 1946, marking the new force's formal birth date. A March directive authorizing the constabulary's creation and outlining its scope of activities largely formalized already ongoing actions. On 1 July 1946 the constabulary formally assumed its security mission. On paper the constabulary comprised 38,000 soldiers organized into brigades, regiments, and squadrons. Most soldiers and equipment came from armored or cavalry reconnaissance units due to their familiarity with mobile, dispersed operations.

- The constabulary's end strength was 38,000 based on separate estimates of the military government and the theater command. Simple estimates used military government: 1 constable : 450 Germans; theater command: 140-man unit : 225 square miles—delta included administrative, signal, and supply elements.

- Throughout the planning process, the issue of using foreign nationals in American units was urged to offset personnel shortfalls and economize on the number of US soldiers required. The theater command considered the idea but ultimately rejected it: "It was felt, however, that while this sort of organization might be efficient, the building up of German military force and thinking would likely result in serious criticism of our objectives and ethics both in Europe and the United States." [theater view]

Constabulary Mission

- Maintain general security
- Assist accomplishment of military government objectives
- Proactive measures against riots, rebellions, and acts prejudicial to US forces' security
- Cooperate with MPs, Intelligence Corps, and military government
- Support German police without supplanting

The constabulary existed to provide security in the American occupied zone. It supported the military government and coordinated its actions with other intelligence, military, and law enforcement agencies within the zone, including the German police. The constabulary assisted the German police but did not replace them. Indeed, the Germans' ability to take over their own law enforcement would prove to be a key determinant in the constabulary's longevity. The latter's responsibility was limited to the occupied zone in Germany. Separate efforts were implemented to deal with security issues in Austria, the Bremen enclave, and Berlin.

Constabulary Training

MG Ernest N. Harmon

Phased Training Feb-Jul
Phase I   Individual
Phase II Unit
Phase III Operational

Trooper's Manual

**Operation
GRAB BAG**
- 21 May 1946
- Debut
- Danube River Activities

As the first commander of the constabulary, MG Harmon exerted a major influence over its creation and initial operations through May 1947. Harmon was an armor officer during World War II who had risen to command the 1st and 2d Armored Divisions and later the XXII Corps. As constabulary commander, his ability to make rapid decisions and cope with unpleasant developments and his emphasis on discipline helped ensure the constabulary's effectiveness. During the trainup phase, Harmon sought out capable personnel both as commanders and instructors. A three-phased training program was implemented: initial organization and individual training, organizational and unit training, and operational training and assumption of responsibilities. During the final phase, all constabulary units participated in at least one operation and conducted command post exercises. The *Trooper's Manual* proved invaluable in acquainting constabulary personnel with their mission, jurisdiction, and the fundamentals of police procedures. Its prinicipal author was Colonel (COL) J.H. Harwood, a former state police commissioner for Rhode Island, and it was written specifically for soldiers. The manual's content found application during Operation GRAB BAG, the constabulary's debut. In this operation, 4,000 constabulary solders worked with intelligence and Criminal Investigation Division personnel in a large-scale search and seizure of some 400 vessels on the Danube River. Black market activities and shutting down a reputed SS lifeline were the operation's principal objectives.

Constabulary School

Sonthofen, GE, Jan 46
COL Henry C. Newton
Introduced police activities

Initial "train the trainer" role
POIs adjust to field needs
5,700 students, Mar-Dec 46

Critical to establishing a viable constabulary was organizing a special school at Sonthofen, Germany, site of a former Hitler youth school, in January 1946. The school suffered from shortfalls in supplies and experienced personnel yet nevertheless began its first class in March 1946. It, too, bore the influence of MG Harmon, who played a guiding role in the school's early organization and early operation. Instructors were drawn from those officers who had experience in the Army's existing school system and could provide expertise. Among the most important of these officers was COL Henry C. Newton, who became the assistant commandant and was largely responsible for the school's curriculum and daily operations. Newton had been influential in the armored force's school system and the Armored Force Replacement Training Center. He also commanded the 12th Armored Division and saw combat in the M theater of operations and European theater of operations. In shaping the Constabulary School, Newton used the Armored Force School as a model. In its early weeks of operation, the Constabulary School focused on training a nucleus of personnel who would return to their units and impart their knowledge there. The first POIs represented little more than educated guesses as to what soldiers would require. The basic courses for officers and enlisted men offered training in German history and culture, police procedures, tactics, maintenance, and soldierly conduct. As the constabulary gained field experience, changes occured to align training curricula to meet demonstrated needs. The most significant change was expanding instruction in police procedures and activities.

Startup Challenges

Short startup time (6 months)
Unfamiliar mission
Unit availability
Quarters
Personnel

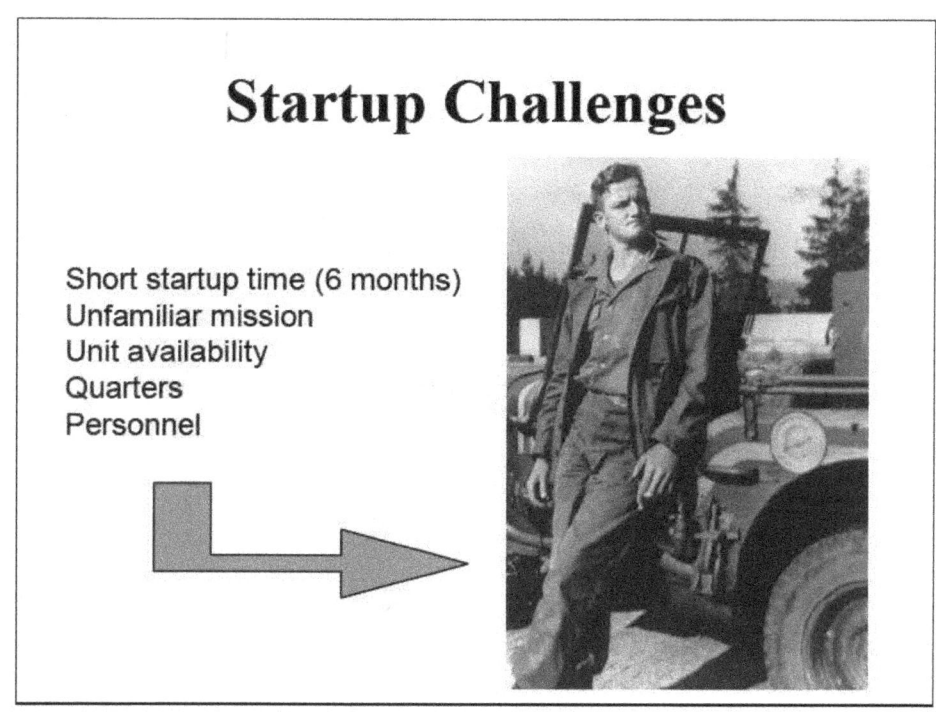

The constabulary faced considerable difficulties in its first months of existence. With barely six months available, it had not only to be created but also to assume responsibility for transforming units and soldiers into new organizations with an unfamiliar mission. It had to do so amid public clamoring to rapidly return overseas forces back home; calls for demobilization; and a host of immediate postwar problems in Germany, including dispositioning POWs, refugees, displaced persons, etc. Although units were earmarked for incorporation into the constabulary early, often their reorganization lagged behind schedule and was hampered by other responsibilities. Although constabulary units were intended to be deployed in their patrol areas, often units could not find sufficient quarters. While awaiting availability, they often shifted from one set of temporary lodgings to another. The most pressing problem, however, lay in securing sufficient numbers of desired personnel. Too often the best soldiers were those who were about to depart the Army and return home. Personnel turbulence stemming from redeployments and winnowing undesirable elements disrupted training and the creation of effective cadres for constabulary units. Worse, significant numbers of replacements proved illiterate, of low intelligence, and lacked the rigid discipline born of war. Many new soldiers possessed minimal military experience and were subject to the popular trend toward relaxed discipline. Many such soldiers came to Germany on their first overseas tour and were about to be deployed in remote locations with considerable authority. Discipline posed a critical threat to the constabulary's effectiveness from day one of its operations.

Molding an Elite Force

Need discipline and esprit de corps

⬇

- High-profile armor divisions basis
- Higher ratings
- Strict discipline
- Regular rotations
- Training

Mobility, Vigilance, Justice

To ensure that the constabulary did not become a rabble, or worse, armed thugs, special efforts were made to make the force an elite one and to instill pride in its members. Constabulary units were formed from the 1st and 4th Armored Divisions, high-profile mobile divisions with distinguished combat records. Soldiers were offered higher ratings than if serving in regular line units. A special patch was issued to distinguish the constabulary, drawing on its armor lineage and a motto determined, emphasizing key aspects of constabulary duty. Similarly, a distinctive uniform was designed, and considerable personal training was given in soldierly bearing. Regular rotations and training became a routine feature of the constabulary experience to avoid trooper burnout and complacency. MG Harmon sponsored and supported these efforts and applied his own rigid discipline standards to both officers and enlisted personnel.

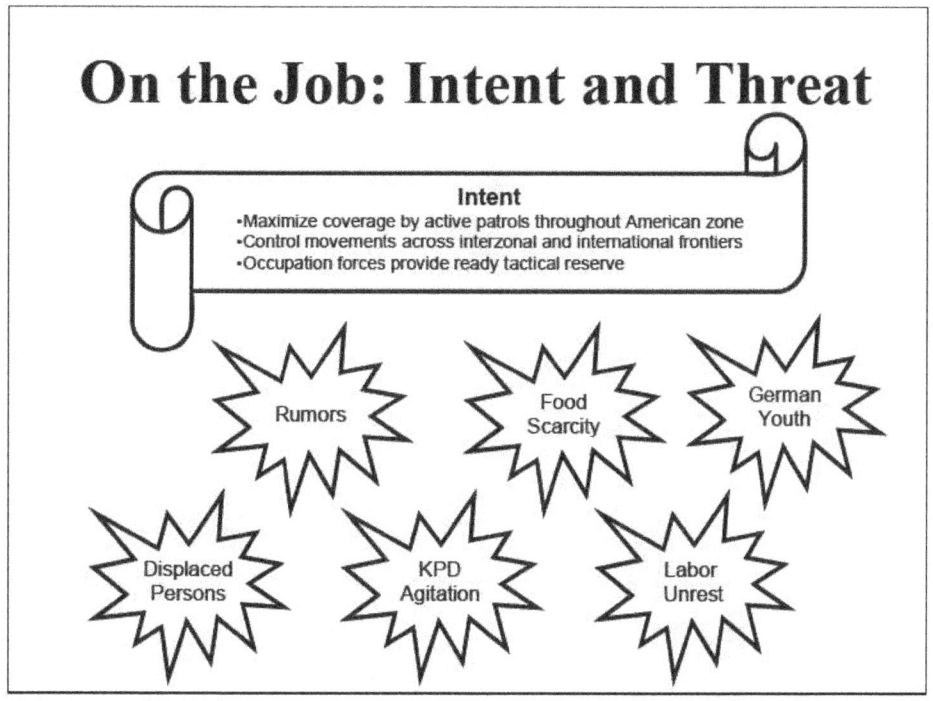

Once organized, the constabulary sought to maximize its presence through vehicle, foot, horse, and aerial patrols. Initially, these patrols covered major urban areas, roadways, and border areas. Special effort was made to access more remote areas to ensure the entire zone was covered. Behind the constabulary stood the occupational forces, serving as a tactical reserve in the event of a major disturbance. In conducting its daily operations, the constabulary faced multiple real or potential dangers. Rumors counteracted efforts toward stability and normalization. The rumors also depicted the constabulary as an American SS, their shows of force as really preparing for a coming war, and in 1947 they prophesied the constabulary's departure. Food scarcity, or more accurately the lack of an effective distribution system, resulted in urban areas suffering shortages while rural areas had ample food. Sometimes city crowds went to the country to take what they needed directly from the farmers. Youth suffered from unemployment and an upbringing in a Nazi culture, making it a potentially destabilizing influence. Displaced persons posed another source of discontent and trouble, with large numbers of people confined to camps while awaiting the determination of their future status. The German Communist Party, having been marginalized under Nazi rule, now made a comeback, organizing workers and seeking to make a united front spanning all occupied zones. Food strikes and work stoppages were also common in the early postwar era, and noticeable by its prevalence lay the black market and related theft.

Operations

Activities
Patrols
Border Control
(Operation SCOTCH, Nov 46)
Black Market
(Search and seizure)
Show of Force
("Everyone loves a parade.")
Displaced Person Camps
(Operation CAMEL, Nov 46)
US Military Personnel
(Operation TRAVELER, Mar 47)
Civilian Disturbances
Traffic Control
("Slow down!")

Deployment parallels civil government org
Close linkage with mil and civ police/intel

Constabulary deployment paralleled the geographic organization of the civil government. The constabulary maintained close ties with American intelligence agencies and the German police, with stops at the local offices incorporated into patrol routes. Threat management entailed a variety of activities of which patrols represented the most common. They ensured a presence in potential trouble spots. Periodically, large groups of constabulary were brought together in a show of force to deter violence and criminal action. These events also served as a unit formation, or parade, otherwise impossible given the dispersal of the constabulary. Border control was primarily accomplished through establishing checkpoints; vehicular patrols; and periodic mass checks of personnel, papers, and potential contraband. Based on intelligence reports, search-and-seizure operations targeted black market operations. The latter, however, proved almost impossible to eliminate due to the general dearth of goods available in the German economy. The constabulary was also responsible for security in the displaced persons camps where riots sometimes occurred and black market activity thrived.

Periodic raids such as the dawn strike of Operation CAMEL kept camp residents off balance, but the constabulary preferred the more subtle method of establishing a low-profile cordon around a camp and checking all movement into and out. As the traffic level in Germany began to rise, constabulary speed traps became more common. Civilian and military personnel became frequent targets. In the case of the latter, revoking driving privileges sometimes followed. Ensuring the proper conduct of American soldiers also fell to the constabulary. Drunken and disorderly conduct, harassing Germans or displaced persons, randomly firing weapons, and harassing women proved the most common disturbances. Constabulary indiscipline rates tended to be higher than line units, partially due to the better system of documenting each such infraction. One of the more bizarre incidents follows:

29 April 1947. Frankfurt. A US soldier started a fight with a zoo keeper who tried to prevent the soldier from handing a broken bottle to an ape and attempting to climb into the ape's cage. The soldier was arrested and turned over to military police in Frankfurt.

Items

- Reconnaissance, surveillance, and target acquisition squadron operations emphasize human intelligence (HUMINT) and multidimensional reconnaissance, including infrastructure and society.
- Mission, enemy, terrain and weather, troops, and time available (METT-T) to current mission, enemy, terrain and weather, time, troops available, and civilians (METT-TC).
    —HUMINT—information gleaned from local law enforcement, civil authorities, and intelligence elements were key in planning and conducting operations.
    —Patrols and actions oriented on society and infrastructure.
    —Constabulary guiding force in developing German police.
- Operation SCOTCH, November 1946
    —US-French operation versus illegal commerce on US-French border.
    —Cordon and confiscate black market activities and goods.
- Operation CAMEL, November 1946
    —Target black market activities in displaced persons camp.
    —676 soldiers involved.
    —Unannounced dawn raid on entire complex.
    —114 arrests—army clothes; ammunition; knives; and a suitcase full of morphine, codeine, and penicillin seized.
- Operation TRAVELER, March 1947
    —Roundup of AWOL military and unauthorized civilians in zone.
    —Start at reveille with checkpoints and spot-checks of messes, clubs, theaters, PXs, railroad stations, border.
    —27 AWOLs, including one murderer.
    —Success led to repetition—periodically cleaning up and rounding up unauthorized personnel and escaped POWs.

Trends and Issues

- Intensified vehicle patrols within 10 miles of border
- Regular rotations—avoid burnout and provide training
- Regular inspections of all constabulary—the Harmon train
- Jul 46 agreement with Soviets about mutual zonal boundary
- Oct 46 squadron reduction aligns paper and real strength

- Overstretched command and control span
- Continuous personnel shortfalls
- Voluntary reduction of squadron size
- Consolidation around cities and trouble spots
- Pressure to economize fuel consumption
- Poor combat readiness

Constabulary effectiveness benefited from lessons learned through experience and the attentiveness of the command chain to the trooper's responsibility. MG Harmon established a mutual working relationship with the Soviets to control border traffic between the US and Soviet zones. He also pointedly visited constabulary units throughout the zone, using a train once belonging to Hermann Göring. Appearing with little warning, Harmon would conduct spot-checks of troopers and their units. Officers considered incapable were relieved of command. Units were routinely rotated back into training to preserve their edge. Early efforts to control unauthorized personnel traffic across zone boundaries discovered that fixed checkpoints were routinely bypassed. Consequently, increased vehicle patrols in a 10-mile swath behind the borders were implemented with considerable effect. To offset shortfalls in men and materiel, the constabulary, on its own authority, reduced squadron size from five to four, consolidated headquarters and service elements at regiment to reduce overhead, and streamlined its organizations. Such actions actually allowed troop strength to increase and realized a better tooth-to-tail ratio. However, no amount of command improvisation could eliminate the personnel shortages within the constabulary. The dispersion of troopers into so many small section and squad elements taxed the officers' ability to supervise and command their men. By early 1947 the constabulary was under orders to conserve fuel. It also suffered further cutbacks in its end strength. To compensate, patrol activities became more focused around urban areas and known trouble spots. Intelligence gleaned to date on criminal activity trends enabled the constabulary to better use its diminishing assets.

Reorientation, 1947-48

Theater Concerns
Occupational troop basis cuts
Building a tactical reserve
Improving combat readiness
External aggression > internal security

The Threat

- HQ, US Army, Europe established
- Army training center at Grafenwoehr
- Constabulary part of theater reserves

Warsaw Pact
Berlin Airlift

1947 Cuts
1/3 brigades
4/9 regiments
11/27 squadrons
Light tank units

1947 Training
2d Constab Regiment
Individual to platoon
School theater asset

1948 Reorganization
Armored division equivalent
2d, 6th, 14th ACRs formed
School closed
Tank training center opened
Troop-level training and FTXs

In 1947 the absence of a major disturbance, coupled with the resurgence of German police and civil infrastructure, encouraged that the constabulary be reduced by nearly one-third. Simultaneously, theater concerns began to influence the constabulary's development. Tension with the Soviet Union, coupled with the absence of significant security problems within the American zone, underscored the importance of some tactical force capable of military operations. In 1947 combat forces fell from one infantry division to one regimental combat team plus the constabulary. Readiness for combat was rated at 20 percent for the former and 65 percent for the latter. With insufficient forces even to conduct a zone evacuation, the theater command sought to reestablish a tactical reserve and stiffen combat training efforts. In March, Headquarters, US Army, Europe (USAREUR) activated, and work began on a training center at Grafenwoehr. The constabulary became part of the theater reserve. Although constabulary units lost their light tanks in early year reductions, the 2d Constabulary Regiment was concentrated at Augsburg, reinforced with light tank and recoilless rifle troops, and began training as a combat reserve. Constabulary training began to shift away from the individual and toward the platoon. Administratively, the constabulary assumed greater roles within the American zone, and its training facilities began to serve as theater assets.

1948, however, marked a watershed in the constabulary's evolution. That year the need for a specialized school ended, and the Constabulary School closed. Within theater command, a consensus existed for the need to build an armored division equivalent from constabulary units, to include three armored cavalry regiments (ACRs), two field artillery battalions, one maintenance battalion, and one engineer battalion. Its headquarters would be structured as an ad hoc corps headquarters in the event of an emergency. Related actions included creating a tank training center (later redesignated the USAREUR Tank Training Center to reflect its theaterwide use) at Vilseck, Germany. The center was modeled after the US Army Armor School, Fort Knox, Kentucky, emphasizing gunnery, tactics, and maintenance; involving constabulary units in troop-level exercises; participating in field training exercises (FTXs); and the organization of the ACRs. Constabulary units' increased involvement in combat training, however, resulted in a decrease in patrols and general presence. While German civil authorities bemoaned the gradual disappearance of the constabulary, German police had assumed many of the roles formerly assigned to them without mishap. Indeed, the same police had benefited from constabulary guidance and support in their own operations.

Constabulary Transformed
1949-1950

Korean War

November 1950
Constabulary inactivated
Seventh Army HQ activated

1949 Training
New equipment
22-week training program
African-American unit training
NCOA established
FTXs and maneuvers

1950 Training
Annual proficiency tests
Career field training
FTXs and maneuvers

The period 1949-50 witnessed the constabulary's continued transformation into a combat organization. New equipment deliveries begun the previous year continued (jeep photo to tank photo), providing visible proof of the constabulary's new orientation. To prepare soldiers and units for combat missions, a 22-week training program was designed and implemented, receiving high praise from Chief of Staff, US Army General Omar N. Bradley. Increased participation in FTXs and maneuvers, including operations with allied troops and regular training at Grafenwoehr, highlighted the constabulary's change in mission. German organizations assumed constabulary functions. Consolidation reduced the number of different constabulary stations from 200 in 1946 to 20 by late 1949. Intelligence gathering and special operations remained the principal police functions still being performed. Training responsibilities, however, increased. In 1949 the constabulary assumed responsibility for training three African-American infantry battalions, marking their transformation from post security elements into combat-ready organizations.

In September 1949 the constabulary established the Noncommissioned Officer Academy (NCOA). Its original mission included teaching NCOs in constabulary techniques, but this focus quickly expanded to general instruction for NCOs to improve their capabilities and leadership skills. This academy soon became a model for subsequent NCOAs in the Army and Air Force. In 1950 implementation of proficiency tests assessed the combat capability of armor, engineer, artillery, and infantry units. Its capstone event included a three-day training exercise at Vilseck. A career field training program also placed soldiers in the military occupational specialty best suited to their individual talents. Reclassification and/or specialized training ensued. By November 1950 the constabulary was a police force in name only. Only two squadrons remained in the original constabulary configuration. The remaining units had all converted into tactical units with police functions very much a secondary mission.

With the outbreak of the Korean war and the related danger of a global conflict, USAREUR needed combat elements rather than policemen. Moreover, the German government and civil infrastructure had revived and could assume the responsibilities once entrusted to the constabulary. Consequently, on 24 November 1950 the constabulary inactivated. Its headquarters and staff became part of the newly activated Seventh Army headquarters whose deputy commanding general was MG I.D. White, the last constabulary commander. The two remaining constabulary squadrons continued to function under Seventh Army control until they were inactivated in 1952. Training assets and installations the constabulary had established transferred to USAREUR control. During this period of final reorganization, the constabulary had no difficulty securing recruits or retaining them. Moreover, the command considered its efforts on behalf of the soldiers a success: most had opened creditable life insurance accounts, special savings accounts increased from 1 percent to 54 percent, and the venereal disease rate plummeted.

Conclusions

Constabulary Successful

- Finite mission parameters
- Clear jurisdictional guidance
- Focused training
- Discipline emphasized in all operations
- Deliberate creation of esprit de corps
- Import of experienced officer nucleus
- Constabulary purpose built for stability operation
- Organizational and command flexibility

The constabulary successfully completed its mission of providing security in the American zone of occupation until the appropriate German authorities were able to assume this task. Despite numerous unknowns and challenges facing the organization, the specially trained and organized constabulary maintained an American presence and guided the rebirth of the German police. As its internal security mission came to a conclusion, the constabulary successfully transformed itself back into a combat force. It is this process of changing from a tactical force into a police force and back again that deserves some attention in view of the Army's current deployment trends. Moreover, the US Commission on National Security for the 21st Century has also considered using some form of constabulary force to cope with the broad range of peace operations likely to remain a principal Army function into the foreseeable future.

- The constabulary mission is not open-ended; there is no intent to remain indefinitely.

- Careful limitation of mission—police with precise geographic limitations; no theater commitment.

- Rely on allied nations to ensure security in their respective zones.

- Not a multipurpose organization, although a flexible one.

- Great care in training, discipline, and ensuring that soldiers properly conduct themselves when executing their duty; build respect.

Reconstructing the Civil Administration of Bremen, US Enclave

Bianka J. Adams

"Bremens Selbständigkeit ist die Voraussetzung dafür, damit es überhaupt in der Lage ist, die ihm gestellten Aufgaben als Seehandelsstadt zu erfüllen." ("Bremen's independence is the prerequisite for its ability to fulfill its responsibilities as a seaport city.")

—Wilhelm Kaisen, campaign speech,
12 October 1946, Bremen

Introduction

Reconstructing a civil administration within a conquered nation is not an easy mission for the victors under the best of circumstances. This complicated task was exacerbated in Bremen by the changing administrative control between the United States and Great Britain. Located entirely within the British occupation zone, the Americans and the British attempted to pass off responsibility for Bremen to each other during the first two years of military government.

This paper examines how reconstructing a civil administration in Bremen proved to be a challenge to both the American and the British military governments. Since neither territorial boundaries nor administrative powers had been clearly defined in the Yalta Agreement, the two had to invest time and energy to decide these issues while simultaneously trying to establish an efficient military government.

The administration of the US enclave in Bremen was an afterthought for military government planners in the United States and the United Kingdom. Required as a port for the US Zone of Occupation in southern Germany, the Bremen enclave had to contend with the fact that it owed its existence to necessity but was otherwise unwanted. Although British forces initially occupied the city, the American Army was the first to establish a military government for it in April 1945. After this opening phase in which the military government operated mainly according to American directives and instructions, the second phase—December 1945throughout 1946—placed Bremen under British control. A third phase began on 1 January 1947, when the enclave became the fourth state within the US Zone of Occupation. Under the circumstances, Bremen thus became a field for experimentation by the United Kingdom and the United States, with each using different approaches in re-creating the civil administration. Although ultimately successful, the differing policies retarded the development of democratic institutions within the enclave.

The first historical report of the US military government described Bremen as a "miniature republic within the Reich."[1] Indeed, the city had a long history of struggling for independence within the larger political community stretching back to the time of Charlemagne in the eighth century. First established as a bishopric, it grew steadily as a trading center in large part due to its harbor at the mouth of the Weser River. In 1358, it joined the Hanseatic League, a powerful free trade federation of northern European cities, and soon its merchants became wealthy enough to challenge the bishop for control of the city. The merchants' efforts to gain independence from the church and the right to govern themselves would continue for another three centuries. By the end of the Thirty Years' War in 1648, Bremen had gained the status of a free city that answered only to the emperor of the Holy Roman Empire.[2]

Bremen retained its independence until 1871 when it became a free Hanseatic city with a standing equivalent to that of a federal state within the newly founded German Reich. Twenty years earlier, in the wake of the revolution of 1848, Bremen gave property owning male citizens the right to vote for the city council, called *Bürgerschaft*, which in turn elected a government, or *Senat*, with a mayor, or *Bügermeister*, as its president.[3]

Bremen was the last state or *land* with a democratically elected government in Adolf Hitler's Germany. It only ceded its independence to the Nazi government in March 1933. Although it remained nominally independent, from then on, a Nazi-appointed governor ruled over the city.[4]

Bremen was one of the centers of the German armaments industry during the Third Reich. Its shipyards and factories supplied the regime with warships, submarines, airplanes, and motor vehicles. As a result, the city of 280,000 suffered close to utter destruction in Allied bombing raids. About 60 percent of its residential dwellings and up to 90 percent of its harbor infrastructure were destroyed. Among Bremen's war dead were 4,000 residents who perished in Allied bombing raids.[5]

The Bremen Enclave

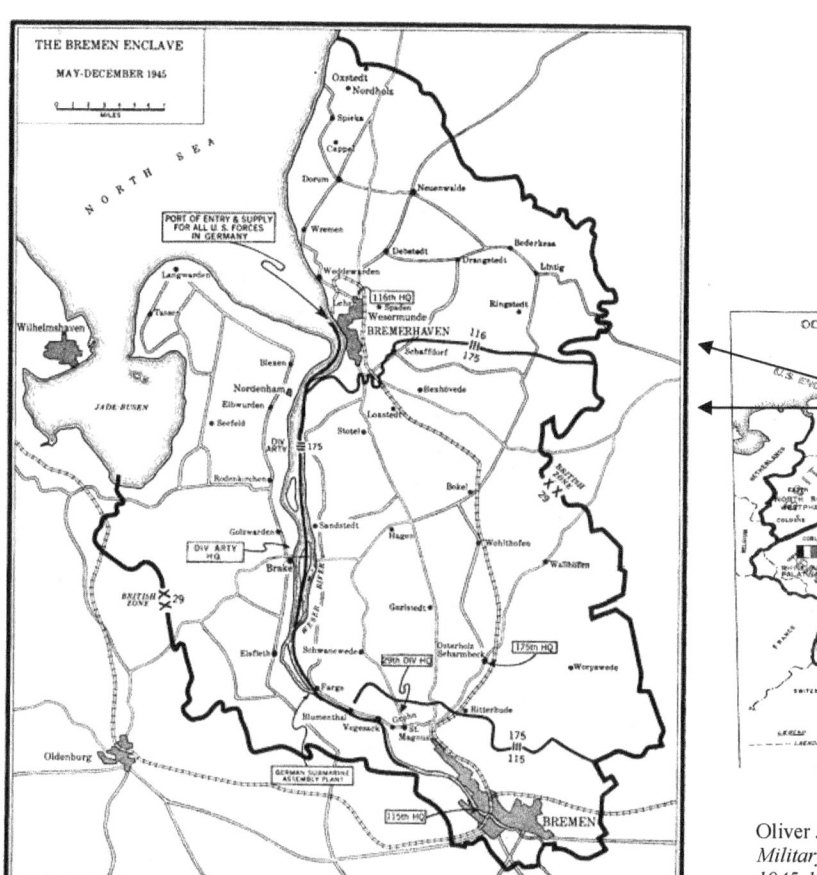

Source: Joseph H. Ewing, *29 Let's Go: A History of the 29th Infantry Division in World War II* (Washington, DC: Infantry Journal Press, 1948), 260.

Oliver J. Frederiksen, *The American Military Occupation of Germany, 1945-1953* (Heidelberg, GE: Historical Division, Headquarters, US Army, Europe, 1953), 15.

Surrender and First Steps

Bremen surrendered on 26 April 1945 to British forces from the 21st Army Group under Field Marshal Sir Bernard I. Montgomery. Accompanying the Army Group, Lieutenant Colonel (LTC) Bion C. Welker's US military government detachment E 2 C 2 entered the city. Welker's group was the first of six established in the area, including the counties of Osterholz, Wesermünde, and Wesermarsch.[6]

By the end of June all detachments were in place. The 29th Infantry Division under Major General (MG) Charles H. Gerhardt had assumed responsibility for Bremen's security. At that time, Bremen Port Command, under American MG Harry B. Vaughan, took charge of rebuilding and operating the city's port and its facilities.[7]

After administering critical services in heavily damaged urban areas of Bremen and Wesermünde, Welker's detachment had to turn its attention toward recreating a functioning civil administration. The British forces entering Bremen had already undertaken first steps toward this end. They removed the Nazi-appointed governor and replaced him with the "conspicuously cooperative" police president, Johannes Schroers, who became mayor.[8] Only four days later, on 30 April 1945, Welker ordered Schroers' removal and internment because he had been a leading member of the elite Nazi *Schutzstaffel* (*SS*).

Erich Vagts became Schroers' successor because he impressed Welker with his "senatorial stature" and seeming administrative experience. Vagts assembled a cabinet of key officials, or *Senatoren*. In an interview with Counterintelligence Corps (CIC) officers charged with investigating appointments to the government of Land Bremen, he explained the principles he followed in selecting personnel: "Insofar as positions are vacant and the dismissed people are to be replaced, my first consideration will always be their technical and administrative qualifications. As far as their political qualifications are concerned, my first concern will be that they have not had any connections with the Nazis."[9]

At the beginning of May 1945, Dr. Walter Dorn of Columbia University, who was Deputy Military Governor Lieutenant General Lucius D. Clay's adviser on the denazification program, arrived in Bremen to assist Welker with establishing a city government. He objected to Welker's choice of Vagts because of Vagts' close ties to the Nazis during the war.[10] Thus, as soon as he was settled, Dorn used a list the Office of Strategic Services compiled and began contacting politicians who had served in the Bremen legislature before the Nazis took control of the city. The two most important men were Social Democrat Wilhelm Kaisen and Conservative Theodor Spitta, both of whom had participated in underground, anti-Nazi political activities during the Hitler years.[11]

Dorn "invited and urged" both Kaisen and Spitta to assume responsibility in the new city government. He also convinced two independent candidates, three liberals, three social democrats, and two communists, who were the leaders of the antifascist movement in Bremen, to join the newly appointed Senate on 6 June 1945.[12] In the process, Dorn replaced five of Vagts' appointees with his own choices because CIC background investigations proved those individuals had Nazi Party affiliations.[13]

Bremen's Postwar Leadership

Erich Vagts, 1933

Source: Herbert Schwarzwälder, *Das große Bemen-Lexikon*, (Bremen: Edition Temmen, 2002), 749.

Wilhelm Kaisen, 1951

Source: Herbert Schwarzwälder, *Bremer Geschichte*, (Bremen: Johann Heinrich Döll. 1993). 261.

Source: Herbert Schwarzwälder, *Das große Bemen-Lexikon*, (Bremen: Edition Temmen, 2002). 677.

Theodor Spitta, 1945

Despite Dorn's objections, when CIC investigators concluded that Vagts was honest and reliable, Welker continued to support him and endowed him with even more extensive powers than his position as mayor would normally have entailed.[14] At the end of July 1945, however, the CIC began investigating Vagts for allegedly shielding Nazis. At this point Vagts became a liability to Welker, who finally agreed to replace him with Wilhelm Kaisen as the new mayor and president of the senate on 1 August 1945. Spitta became Kaisen's deputy. Kaisen would govern Bremen in this capacity for the next 20 years.[15]

Several days after establishing Bremen Detachment, an advanced team under Major Raymond M. Davis' command formed Detachment G 1 C 2 Wesermünde.[16] The unit found the Wesermünde city administration functioning under the leadership of Dr. Walter Delius, who the CIC arrested and interned. After initially replacing Delius with an unsuitable candidate, Davis appointed Dr. Helmuth Koch as mayor. His deputy became Gerhard Van Heukelum, leader of the *SPD* (German Social Democratic Party) before 1933 and editor of the Social-Democratic newspaper. Both received orders to establish a new city administration and begin denazification of all governmental agencies.[17]

Even though the new administration delivered community services satisfactorily, the Wesermünde Detachment had to struggle with organizational obstacles that were symptomatic of problems the enclave faced. Originally consisting of three separate administrative entities, Wesermünde was a postwar artificial construct of the Allies with unclear administrative channels and venues. The functional history Detachment G 1 C 2 submitted in October 1945 describes the confusion that resulted:

> Stadtkreis [city] Wesermünde includes the borough of Bremerhaven (not to be confused with the port of Bremerhaven). The borough of Bremerhaven formerly belonged to the Land [state] Bremen, but was incorporated into the community of Wesermünde under the Nazi government; it is now being called Wesermünde-Mitte. The other boroughs constituting the community of Wesermünde are Geestemünde and Lehe, the latter previously belonging to Hannover.[18]

The boroughs formerly belonging to Hanover were cut off from their traditional administrative channels and lacked new ones to replace them. This led to substantial confusion among German administrators about who was in charge of vital areas such as rationing, payment of labor, and economic control.[19]

To complicate the situation further, the Acting Superior President of the Province of Hanover, who operated under British supervision, maintained that all communities outside the port area remained "Hanover communal unions" in the Province of Hanover. He interpreted this to mean that only his office could issue orders to agencies located in Wesermünde. He refused to acknowledge the Americans' right to govern Bremen as an enclave in the British Zone. In his opinion, American interests in Bremen should be confined to using the port, which did not necessitate control over administrative issues.[20] These circumstances rendered city agencies in Wesermünde virtually without any higher echelons.[21]

After the first few months of occupation, the need to reorganize the administrative control in the enclave became apparent. In addition, the CIC's investigation of Vagts also brought to light serious deficiencies in the enclave's administration. On 30 July 1945, a combined US-UK committee was established and charged with determining and recommending the proper structure for the administrative control of the Bremen enclave.[22] During the negotiations, the committee discovered that, strictly speaking, Bremerhaven was just a small uninhabited dock area and that the city of Wesermünde was only as a staging area for the port. With the approval of the Allied Control Council in Berlin, the committee decided to "include Stadt Wesermünde as part of the territory remaining under U.S. control."[23]

On 10 December 1945, Clay and British Deputy Military Governor Sir Brian Robertson signed an "Agreement of Military Government Responsibility in the Bremen Enclave" to take effect at the beginning of 1946.[24] The pact redrew the borders of the enclave and placed it under British administration:

> (a) The administration of military government in the Enclave less Bremen and Bremerhaven will be turned over to the British Zone Commander.
> (b) The United States Military Government teams at Bremen and Bremerhaven, as well as British military government teams to be stationed in the Enclave, will follow the policy instructions issued by the British military government authorities, subject to the condition that if the team receives instructions from the British which interfere with the carrying out of the effective operation of the Bremen Port, or interfere with area security, all military government teams may, and upon the request of the U.S. Sub-District Commander, will suspend action on such instructions. . . .[25]

Within the enclave, the agreement assigned responsibility for security and military government to the commanding general, Bremen Port Command. Since the Port Command had not thus far dealt with civil affairs, it had to establish a G5 section. This process was finished in early January 1946 when a newly created G5 section assumed control over the Bremen and Wesermünde Detachments.[26] This situation lasted until 15 April 1946 when the Bremen Port Command was dissolved. Colonel Welker assumed command of the newly created Office of Military Government for Bremen Enclave (US).[27]

Initially, the Bremen Detachment looked forward to a "new era" that promised changes in the enclave's administrative setup. A historical report covering from 10 December 1945 to the end of January 1946 dealt exclusively with problems that original boundaries and distribution of responsibility in the enclave created. According to this history, Bremen's dilemma was due to three circumstances: lack of unified command for the enclave, some higher echelons' lack of awareness that the enclave existed, and the necessity of constant coordination with British forces and German civilian agencies.[28]

The first of these points, in particular, led to many interrelated problems for military government in the enclave. Because major generals commanded both the Port Command and the 29th Infantry Division, military government was already at a disadvantage because it was commanded by a lieutenant colonel.[29] More important, the Bremen Port Command had priority on practically everything, including material, labor, and housing, because it was the reason why the enclave existed. Next in line for distribution of resources was the 29th Division, which had to assure the "comfort and welfare" of its 15,000 officers and men. Military government received the goods and services it needed from what remained after the other commands had taken their share. This circumstance complicated implementing military government's mission significantly. Housing shortages and the lack of materials slowed down rebuilding industry for civilian production.[30] In Bremen, military government detachments and tactical units remained under the same command. By contrast, in the US Zone, Deputy Military Governor Clay insisted on separating military government from tactical commands to ensure military government's control over resources.

Yet other difficulties arose because of the distance of several hundred miles between the enclave and the American Zone in south Germany. Directives from the control council or the deputy military governor frequently lacked provisions for the special situation in Bremen. An example of this was Clay's order to increase food rations for Germans in December 1945. The historical report for this period expressed the sheer exasperation officers of Detachment E 2 C 2 felt in contemplating the time and energy they would have to expend in negotiations with the British military government and German civilian authorities when they received the order:

> The Enclave was not independent. Food, labor, power, fuel—practically everything must come from without the Enclave and there was very little to be sent out in exchange. The Enclave was a beggar with nothing to give in return. The Enclave was not included in deals made for the entire US Zone. Problems had to be worked out on the ground by just going across the boundary into the British Zone and discussing the matters which had to be coordinated with the British at Oldenburg, Stade, Hamburg or Hannover.[31]

Military government's task of providing higher food rations was even more difficult because Bremen's population grew steadily due to an influx of refugees and returning soldiers. A British census dated 29 October 1946, which included the US Enclave Bremen, showed Bremen's population at 753,518 residents.[32]

The "New Era"

The citizens of Bremen characterized the last two months before the change from American to British military government as a "period of pressures." Rumors about American plans to surrender the enclave entirely to British control persisted throughout the city.[33]

On 2 January 1946, the enclave experienced the full impact of its new circumstances. A conference between American and British military government representatives scheduled for that day was canceled. The British merely informed the Americans that decisions affecting the reorganization of the former Reich administrations in Bremen had "already been arrived at" and that the conference would not serve a useful purpose. The British decisions altered the old system of controls for the State Economics Office (*Landeswirtschaftsamt* now renamed *Wirtschaftsamt*), the Finance Office (*Oberfinanzpräsidium* now *Finanzamt*), and the State Labor Office (*Landesarbeitsamt* now *Hauptarbeitsamt*).[34]

In effect, the changes the British imposed restricted the venue of these offices and in many cases placed them under control of the Hanover Province government. This led to considerable confusion not only among German administrators but also among American military government personnel. An example of this was an order to transfer all revenues the Bremen Finance Office collected to Hanover Finance Office, which then would allocate funds for occupation costs back to Bremen. The commentary of an American finance officer on this new procedure expressed strong skepticism:

> If the British are willing to agree that they will pay all expenses of the port operation, meeting promptly without question all demands for funds from Bremen Port Command, then they are more than welcome to the funds collected here. Otherwise it is obvious that to conduct an efficient port operation adequate funds must be available, without the necessity of persuading someone in Hannover or any other place that money should be provided for that expense.[35]

Despite directives from Berlin ordering compliance, the Bremen Enclave Finance Section still had not transferred revenues by September 1946.[36]

While in other parts of the American Zone communities and cities elected their municipal governments between January and May 1946, the Bremen military government had to establish a Nominated Representative Council for the city of Wesermünde because the British preferred appointed administrations. By April 1946, a nominated city council consisting of 40 members had been appointed. All political parties, as well as spokespersons for labor, professions, trade, and industry, were represented. The council held its first session on 16 April. The council appointed two commissions—one to prepare a new city constitution and one to appoint city officials. On 6 June, when the city council met again, these tasks were completed.[37] The military government approved the new city constitution on 1 July 1946. The inauguration of City Council and Management was scheduled for the following day.[38]

On 13 October, the citizens of Bremen elected members of the city council in the city's first free elections since 1933. The elections were carried out according to the British modified individual candidate system. Candidates for the council competed for three-fourths of the seats directly in 16 electoral districts. The remaining seats were distributed according to the proportional share of electoral votes each of the participating political parties received. The parties chose their candidates from a reserve list that the party leaders had assembled earlier. The result was a landslide victory for the *SPD*, which won 51 of 80 seats in the council.

On 14 November the council decided on the distribution of functional committees or departments. Ten would be permanent and three others, among them a Committee on Denazification, were designated as special. At the end of the month, the council formally elected members of the senate to head the various committees. Kaisen remained head of the administration as president of the senate and became Senator for Police and Interior Administration.[39]

In his acceptance speech, Kaisen elaborated on the program for his administration. His foremost concern was the recovery of the economy that, according to him, depended on massive infusions of materiel and investments from foreign countries. He also pointed out that Bremen had delivered more than its share of reparations and urged the Allies to stop dismantling factories "if every hope of finding a way out of our misery is not to be killed."[40] As an essential part of rebuilding Bremen into a democratic society, Kaisen mentioned denazification. Commenting on the noticeable difference in interest in the program between the victors and the vanquished, he quipped that according to the military government denazification could be finished in Bremen inside of six months while "German branches speak of six years."[41]

From the beginning of the new era there was evidence that the American military government acted according to American as well as British directives, depending on the situation.[42] This somewhat confusing state, with the fact that Bremen's status compared to that of the newly created states in the US Zone was as yet unclear, triggered high-level discussions of the city's future. They began in June 1946 when the British military government made no secret of its desire to make Bremen part of a soon-to-be created state of Lower Saxony.[43]

Opinions about British intentions differed widely within the Bremen Detachment. The director of the Civil Government Division, Harold H. Crabill, argued that the United States had an obligation to defend Bremen's right to self-determination because of the American belief in freedom.[44] Major John W. Boyd, Internal Affairs and Communications Division, pointed out that safety in the enclave would be better served if Bremen were to return to American control entirely.[45] Chief Legal Officer Robert W. Johnson, on the other hand, argued that creating a state in the enclave would be inconsistent with agreements reached with the French and the Soviet Union. In his opinion, Bremen had never ceased to be part of the Northwestern or British Zone:

> 28. An incorporation of the Enclave into the American Zone as an integral part thereof would require not only UK and US consent, but French and USSR as well. And since it is geographically, administratively, sociologically and economically a part of the Northwestern Zone, its severance therefrom might well cause difficulties far greater than those already caused to Germany by the four present Zonal divisions.[46]

After his return from an inspection trip to Bremen in early June 1946, Deputy Military Governor Clay charged Henry Parkman, Director, Civil Administration Division, Office of Military Government, United States (OMGUS), with preparing a study of Bremen's future status. Parkman went to Bremen, where he interviewed Welker and Kaisen.[47] In their answers, both agreed that Bremen had to remain under American control as a free city state with direct representation on the Council of States of the US Zone and on soon-to-be-established Bizonal Agencies. According to Parkman, Welker "was emphatically of the opinion" that Bremen should not be turned over to the British because he believed the British would build up Hamburg to the detriment of Bremen.[48] Kaisen shared Welker's assessment of British intentions and added that "living under split dual military government" had proved to be impossible. Kaisen continued that Bremen should be fully under the US military government and should return to its status as an independent city-state with a direct relationship to the central government.[49]

Parkman summarized his findings in a memorandum that argued for continued US control of Bremen because of the economic importance of the Bremen port for American interests in central Europe:

> The outlines of British policy in the Bremen area are not clear, but from the evidence, it is apparent that the present intention is to deflate the significance of Bremen both economically as a port and politically as a Land.
>
> Looking at German economy solely from the German point of view it may be noted that Bremen provides the only competition to the port Hamburg for overseas traffic.
>
> British control of the port of Hamburg, and British pressure to obtain the control of Bremen, give evidence that this control is being and will be used to serve primarily British interests. It cannot be doubted that under British control American interests for the long future would be definitely subordinated.[50]

In reaching his conclusion that Bremen should come exclusively under American control, Parkman acknowledged considerable reluctance because the "natural solution would seem to be a withdrawal of U.S. Military Government." He decided, however, that neither Bremen's nor US interests would be served by such a step.[51] On 18 September 1946, Parkman submitted his final report to Clay: "I reached the conclusion that the proper solution is for the U.S. to resume full Military Government responsibility in the Enclave, with the eventual prospect of creating a new Land government for the area with certain additions and modifications."[52]

Under the circumstances, Deputy Military Governors Robertson and Clay had to reach a satisfactory arrangement concerning Bremen. They decided that Parkman, who was already familiar with the situation in Bremen, should work with his British colleague, Austin Albu, Deputy President, Governmental Sub-Commission of the Control Council for Germany (British Element), to recommend solutions.

After a fact-finding mission in Bremen, Parkman and Albu submitted a report to the deputy military governors. They agreed that because of "the progressive development of German governmental controls at higher levels and the crystallization of units of government of Land status in the British Zone," Bremen's status had to be clarified. They recommended new territorial boundaries, help with economic problems, a clear legal status for the enclave as a state, and continued U.S. military government:

- Territorial Boundaries. Land Bremen should consist of *Stadt* [city] Bremen, Land *Gebiet* [state area] Bremen, and *Stadtkreis* [city] Wesermünde.
- Economic Problem. Land Bremen should be represented on the bizonal committees equally with Hamburg.
- Political Problems.

—Bremen should provisionally have the full powers of a Land government.

—Bremen should be directly represented at the Zonal Advisory Council, but informal representation should be continued at the *Laenderrat* [Council of States].

- Military Government Problems.

    —An integrated staff is not desirable.

    —The 10 December agreement should be reviewed.

    —The US military government should operate under US military government rules.

    —It is not desirable to extend the US military government's area of jurisdiction to include the intermediary ports on the Weser because of German civil administration problems.[53]

Clay and Robertson approved the recommendations and instructed Parkman and Albu to work out an agreement for the military governors. Not everyone at Clay's headquarters agreed with the recommendations. Secretary General Colonel William Whipple, for one, was concerned that the United States would have to assume full responsibility for the state of Bremen's economic supply in case "anything should happen" and the bizonal economic agencies should not materialize. He also feared that Bremen would naturally vote with the other North German states and that this would "overbalance the Executive Committees in a manner detrimental to our interests." He was referring to the political influence of the Council of States in the US Zone and the compliant spirit the US military government had built up in its state governments.[54] Replying, Parkman agreed with some of Whipple's concerns but argued that if the economic and political unification of all Germany were accomplished, it would be inconceivable that anyone would be satisfied with a system in which the identity of the four zones was preserved. The principle, he said, would be to let Germany act as Germany with elections reflecting the constituent units' interests.[55]

As those discussions continued, the military government in Bremen also underwent organizational changes. On 20 September 1946, LTC Gordon Browning succeeded Welker, who had stayed on in a civilian capacity after he retired from active service. When Browning, a former Congressman from Tennessee, was elected governor in his home state, Thomas F. Dunn became his successor. Dunn transferred from the War Shipping Administration on 11 December 1946 to assume his position as Director of Military Government in Bremen. In January 1947, Capt Charles R. Jeffs, US Navy, became deputy director, a position that had been vacant until that date.[56]

Land Bremen

Thus, by the end of 1946, Bremen was governed by democratically elected administrative agencies and faced the prospect of becoming a state within the US Zone very shortly. The city's senate had received notice of the agreement between Clay and Robertson on 5 November 1946, but when the Allies had taken no steps in that direction by the end of the month, Kaisen reminded Dunn of the urgency of this matter, especially regarding bizonal agencies. He pointed out that the town was denied access to preparatory meetings on the subject because of its still undecided status.[57] It would be another two months before Military Governor General Joseph T. McNarney issued Proclamation No. 3 formally announcing Bremen's statehood as part of the American Zone of Occupation.

From then on, the state of Bremen would encompass the city of Bremen, the area surrounding it, and the city of Wesermünde, including Bremerhaven. The city's democratically elected administration continued as a state government until a new constitution could be ratified.[58]

The final version of the Anglo-American agreement established Bremen as a provisional state and part of the US Zone while the enclave remained in place. The United States reserved control of the harbor and all facets of the shipping industry for itself. As a state within the U.S. Zone, the city attained direct representation in the Council of States while at the same time becoming informally affiliated with the Zonal Advisory Council for the states within the British Zone. It also became a member with full rights in all bizonal agencies.[59]

After a prolonged period of legal and administrative uncertainty, Bremen entered the end phase of military government with stabilized borders, democratically elected government agencies, and a clear relationship with the occupying powers. Also effective 1 January 1947, the town area of Wesermünde, which had been part of the state of Prussia, became permanently attached to it. On 7 February, the city council of Wesermünde decided to rename the town "Bremerhaven" after the adjacent harbor.[60]

With Land Bremen formally part of the US Zone, the new state needed a constitution. To speed up the process, Dunn requested that OMGUS waive the requirement for an election of a constitutional assembly and instead accept Bremen's city council as a constitutional assembly.[61] When OMGUS did not object, the council drafted a new constitution that passed into law on 21 October 1947.

Bremen's new status brought changes for the military government. In April 1947, the Office of Military Government for Bremen Enclave was renamed the Office of Military Government for Bremen (OMG Bremen).[62] At the same time, because control over the harbor at Bremerhaven poised to go to OMG Bremen, the Bremerhaven Detachment became simply a Liaison and Security Detachment.[63]

By 1948, OMG Bremen's role had changed once again, this time from governing an occupied territory to advising the German government. In May, eight of 11 military government divisions had assisted the city's senate in establishing German agencies. A Committee on the Interior took charge of the police and fulfilled the tasks of the Civil Administration and Public Safety Divisions. A Committee on Economics, Ports, and Transportation assumed the role of the Economics, Waterfront, Manpower, and Transport Divisions. Committees on Public Health and Public Welfare took over from the Public Health and Welfare Division. A Committee on Finance replaced the Finance Division and Committees on Public Schools, Vocational Schools, Physical Training, and Youth Welfare assumed responsibility from the Education Division. A Committee on the Constitution with charge of constitutional and legal affairs, as well as ecclesiastical affairs, also came into being, but the Legal Division supervised it. A Committee on Denazification continued the work of the Denazification Division. Land Bremen was also solely responsible for housing construction, food procurement, and agriculture.[64]

With the OMG's mission nearing completion, the organization's personnel fell from 104 in January 1948 to 61 in July. By 30 November, the number of US personnel had been cut to 57 for OMG Bremen.[65] Similarly, the Bremerhaven Liaison and Security

Detachment had eight US soldiers at the end of December 1947. A year later, after transitioning from a military to a civilian operation, only one civilian remained.[66]

Between September and November 1948, OMG Bremen underwent several reorganizations that consolidated divisions' functions. On 15 September, it consisted of six divisions: the Information Service Division, Education and Cultural Relations Division, Legal Division, Governmental Affairs Division, Waterfront Division, and Bipartite Division. The next organizational change took place on 30 November when the military government established a new advisory agency, the Public Affairs and Legal Division, with six civilian advisers for legal affairs, civil administration, public health, public welfare, public safety, and denazification matters. By this time, US military personnel in Bremen consisted of just one officer.[67] OMG Bremen ceased to exist in fall 1949 and was replaced by the Office of the State Commissioner.[68]

Conclusion

American and British attempts to rid themselves of responsibility for Bremen, in effect, slowed the development of the area's political institutions and deprived it of representation in the Council of States for a year. The military government in the Bremen Enclave had to deal with difficulties arising from its insular existence within the British Zone while facing the same challenges civil affairs detachments encountered in other urban centers in Germany. The confusion over legal and territorial boundaries often prevented the flexible and efficient operation of military government divisions because time-consuming negotiations with German agencies operating under practices that were well established in the British Zone preceded any decision or action of significance.

Notes

1. Functional History of Military Government in the Bremen Enclave (FHMG), 26 April 1945-30 September 1945, 1; Records of the Public Information Office, Functional Histories of Military Government in Bremen, April 1945-March 1948, Box 68, Record Group (RG) 260, National Archives and Records Administration (NARA), College Park, Maryland.

2. Michael Scherer, "*Freie Hansestadt Bremen,*" *Der Bürger im Staat*, 1/2, 1999, (*Landeszentrale für politische Bildung Baden-Württemberg*) at <http://www.lpb.bwue.de/aktuell/bis/1_2_99/laender7 htm>, 2-4.

3. Herbert Schwarzwälder, *Das große Bemen-Lexikon* (Bremen: Edition Temmen, 2002), 128.

4. Scherer, 5; Herbert Schwarzwälder, *Die Machtergreifung der NSDAP in Bremen 1933* (Bremen: Carl Schünemann Verlag, 1966), 24-29 and 35. Schwarzwälder points out that the NSDAP in Bremen had gained 32 seats in the 120-seat *Bürgerschaft* in the election in November 1930. In the next two years it tried to overthrow the *Senat* in three unsuccessful votes of no confidence. According to Schwarzwälder, Bremen's Nazis finally had to enlist Berlin's help because they knew their chances to take the *Senat* by democratic means were as slight as winning an election in Bremen. Ibid.

5. Herbert Schwarzwälder, *Bremer Geschichte* (Bremen: Johann Heinrich Döll, 1993), 251.

6. Andreas Röpcke, "*Entstehung, Status und Verwaltung der amerikanischen Enklave Bremen,*" *Bremisches Jahrbuch*, Band 66, 1988, 432-33.

7. Ibid., 437; FHMG, 10 December 1945-31 January 1946, Records of the Public Information Office, Functional Histories of Military Government in Bremen, April 1945-March 1948, Box 69, RG 260, NARA, 1 and 3-4.

8. Almuth Meyer-Zollitsch, *Nationalsozialismus und Evangelische Kirche in Bremen, Veröffentlichungen aus dem Staatsarchiv der Freien Hansestadt Bremen*, Band 51, 1985, 314.

9. Secret Report No. L-360 from OSS Concerning Erich Vagts, Lord Mayor of Bremen, Luther Stevens Smith, Director, Civil Administration Division for Deputy Military Governor, US Group, Control Council/Germany (USGCC/G), 9 August 1945 in Office of Military Government, United States (OMGUS), Adjutant General (AG), 1945-1946, Box 57, RG 260, NARA. Vagts succeeded in convincing interviewers from the Counterintelligence Corps of not only his own reliability and honesty but also his appointees' reliability and honesty.

10. As chair of the ultraconservative German National People's Party (*DNVP*), Vagts became a member of Bremen's *Bürgerschaft* in 1928. In March 1933, he became Senator for Health until he left the *Senat* in September. Two years later, the Nazis appointed him Bremen's representative with the Reich government, a post he held until 1945. Even though Vagts had close ties to the Nazis, they distrusted him enough to turn down his application for membership in the National Socialist German Workers Party (*NSDAP*) because they deemed him politically unreliable. Schwarzwälder, *Das große Bemen-Lexikon*, 749.

11. In the 1920s, Kaisen was the leader of the Social Democratic Party (*SPD*) in Bremen's *Bürgerschaft* (state parliament), an editor of the party's newspaper, and the Senator for Welfare from 1928 until 1933. When the Nazis came to power, he had to resign his office and withdraw from public life. He survived the Nazi dictatorship unmolested as a subsistence farmer in Borgfeld, a suburb of Bremen. Karl-Ludwig Sommer, *Wilhelm Kaisen. Eine politische Biographie* (Bonn: Dietz, 2000), 122. Spitta, a lawyer who specialized in constitutional law, was in 1920 one of the authors of a new constitution for Bremen. He was first elected a member of Bremen's

Bürgerschaft in 1905 and served on several law and order committees. As a member of the moderately conservative *Deutsche Demokratische Partei* (German Democratic Party), he became a state senator in 1919 and a year later the deputy mayor of Bremen. Forced into retirement by the Nazi regime, he survived the Third Reich on his state pension. Schwarzwälder, *Das große Bemen-Lexikon*, 678. Meyer-Zollitsch, 315; *Walter L. Dorn. Inspektionsreisen durch die U.S.-Zone. Notizen, Denkschriften und Erinnerungen*, Lutz Niethammer, ed. (Stuttgart, Deutsche Verlags-Anstalt, 1973), 41.

12. Ibid., 40 and Meyer-Zollitsch,.314.

13. Secret Report No. L-360.

14. Röpcke, 439.

15. Ibid., 440. In a Senate session on 3 August 1945, Kaisen explained the circumstances leading to Vagts' dismissal and announced that the title of Reigning Lord Mayor, a creation of the National Socialists, had been abolished in favor of the traditional title, President of the Senate. *Aussage aus der Senats-Sitzung vom 3*, August 1945, Seite 267ff, Verhandlungen über den Erlaß eines bremischen Gesetzes wegen ihrer Zugehörigkeit zur NSDAP und über Neueinstellung 1945, Mai 8-, Entnazifizierung 3-B.10.b.29, 2, hereafter cited as *Entnazifizierung* 3-B.10.b.29,2, *Staatsarchiv der Freien Hansestadt Bremen* (StAB), 2-4.

16. Historical Report, undated, Records of the Bremerhaven Liaison and Security Detachment, Central Office, Subject File, Box 546, RG 260, NARA, 1-3. Davis stayed in command of this detachment until LTC Luther S. Diggs arrived on 7 August 1945.

17. Ibid., 8-9.

18. Functional History, October 1945, Headquarters, Military Government Detachment G1C2 Wesermünde, Records of the Public Information Office, Functional Histories of Military Government in Bremen, April 1945-March 1948, Box 68, RG 260, NARA, 2. The uninhabited dock area, during the early period of the occupation called Bremerhaven, always belonged to Bremen.

19. Major Raymond M. Davis, Inf, Commanding, to LTC B.C. Welker, Commanding Officer, Military Government Detachment E2C2, Bremen, 20 July 1945, Records of the Bremerhaven Liaison and Security Detachment, Central Office, Subject File, Box 541, RG 260, NARA.

20. *Der Oberpräsident der Provinz Hannover to the Oberbürgermeister, Wesermünde, the Landrat Dr. Arps, Lokstedt, Wesermünde-Land, the Regierungsvizepräsident Dr. Benken, Stade*, 6 September 1945, Records of the Bremerhaven Liaison and Security Detachment, Central Office, Subject File, Box 541, RG 260, NARA.

21. Historical Report, undated, Records of the Bremerhaven Liaison and Security Detachment, Central Office, Subject File, Box 546, RG 260, NARA, 7.

22. Röpcke, 437; Brigadier General Bryan L. Milburn, GSC, Chief of Staff to Secretary General, USGrCC, 30 July 1946, OMGUS, AG, 1945-1946, Box 54, RG 260, NARA.

23. FHMG, October-November 1945, 1-10. Dezember, Records of the Public Information Office, Functional Histories of Military Government in Bremen, April 1945-March 1948, Box 68, RG 260, NARA, 1-2. According to the report, Berlin had been under the impression that *Stadt* Wesermünde was a part of Bremerhaven. Ibid.

24. Agreement of Military Government Responsibility in the Bremen Enclave, OMGUS, AG, 1945-1946, Box 54, RG 260, NARA.

25. Agreement of Military Government Responsibility in the Bremen Enclave, OMGUS, AG, 1945-1946, Box 54, RG 260, NARA, 1.

26. FHMG, October-November 1945, 1-10. Dezember, Records of the Public Information Office, Functional Histories of Military Government in Bremen, April 1945-March 1948, Box 68, RG 260, NARA, 2.

27. Röpcke, 443.

28. FHMG, 10 December 1945-31 January 1946, Records of the Public Information Office, Functional Histories of Military Government in Bremen, April 1945-March 1948, Box 69, RG 260, NARA, 3.

29. Ibid., 4.

30. Ibid.

31. Ibid., 8-9.

32. German Census, 29 October 1946, British Zone, Records of the Bremerhaven Liaison and Security Detachment, Records of the Central Office, Subject Files 1945-1949, Box 558, RG 260, NARA.

33. FHMG 10 December 1945-31 January 1946, 16.

34. Ibid., 17.

35. As quoted in Röpcke, 445.

36. Ibid.

37. Historical Report, undated, Records of the Bremerhaven Liaison and Security Detachment, Central Office, Subject File, Box 546, RG 260, NARA, 9-11. Captain Kenneth R. Moul, Adm. O. for the Oberbürgermeister Gerhard van Heukelum, 1 July 1946, Records of the Bremerhaven Liaison and Security Detachment, Central Office, Subject File, Box 541, RG 260, NARA.

38. Ibid.

39. Memo, Waterman and Fletcher for Director, Information Control Division, 5-7.

40. "Bremen Today and Tomorrow," Speech by Bürgermeister Kaisen after the election of the new Senate, translated from "*Weser-Kurier*," 30 November 1946, Records of the Bremerhaven Liaison and Security Detachment, Records of the Central Office, Subject Files 1945-1949, Box 532, RG 260, NARA, 4-5.

41. Ibid., 5.

42. Röpcke, 448. Röpcke draws this conclusion from a remark Kaisen made in an opening address before the Bremen *Bürgerschaft* (City Administration). Kaisen eluded to Bremen's "very peculiar" position and the fact that rules and regulations for both the American and British Zones were applied in Bremen. Ibid.

43. Ibid., 447.

44. Ibid.

45. Major John W. Boyd, CMP, Communications Officer, to Director, Office of Military Government for Bremen Enclave (US), 15 July 1946, Records of the Public Safety Division, General Correspondence and Other Records. 1945-1949, Box 234, RG 260, NARA.

46. Robert W. Johnson, Chief Legal Officer, to COL Welker, Director of OMG for Bremen Enclave (US), Records of the Denazification Division, Box 168, RG 260, NARA, 8.

47. Memorandum, Henry Parkman, Director, Civil Administration Division, for the Secretary General, 27 November 1946, OMGUS, AG, 1945-1946, Box 54, RG 260, NARA, hereafter cited as Parkman Memorandum for the Secretary General.

48. Memorandum, Views of Colonel Welker in Respect to Bremen, Henry Parkman, Director, Civil Administration Division, 16 September 1946, OMGUS, AG, 1945-1946, Box 88, RG 260, NARA.

49. Memorandum, Views of Bürgermeister Kaisen on the Status of the Free City of Bremen, Henry Parkman, Director, Civil Administration Division, 18 September 1946, OMGUS, AG, 1945-1946, Box 88, RG 260, NARA.

50. Major Erwin W. Bard, AUS, to Director, Civil Administration Division, OMGUS, 19 August 1946, OMGUS, AG, 1945-1946, Box 88, RG 260, NARA, 3 and 5.

51. Henry Parkman for Deputy Military Governor (DMG), 18 September 1946, OMGUS, AG, 1945-1946, Box 88, RG 260, NARA.

52. Ibid.

53. Memorandum, Austin Albu and Henry Parkman for General Robertson and General Clay, Military Government Administration in the Bremen Enclave, 29 October 1946, OMGUS, AG, 1945-1946, Box 109, RG 260, NARA.

54. Memorandum, COL William Whipple, GSC, Secretary General, for Chief of Staff, Administration of Bremen, 25 November 1946, OMGUS, AG, 1945-1946, Box 54, RG 260, NARA.

55. Parkman Memorandum for the Secretary General.

56. FHMG, 1 September-1 December 1946, Records of the Public Information Office, Functional Histories of Military Government in Bremen, April 1945-March 1948, Box 71, RG 260, NARA, 1; FHMG in Land Bremen, 1 July 1946-30 June 1947, Records of the Public Information Office, Functional Histories of Military Government in Bremen, April 1945-March 1948, Box 74, RG 260, NARA, 1-2. Captain Jeffs succeeded Dunn as Director of the Office of Military Government for Bremen on 30 November 1948.

57. Kaisen, Bürgermeister, for Director, OMGUS Bremen Enclave, Bremen Participation in Bizonal Administrative Committees [sic], 23 November 1946, Records of the Bremerhaven Liaison and Security Detachment, Records of the Special Branch, Denazification Records, 1945-1949, Box 601, RG 260, NARA.

58. *Weser Kurier*, Donnerstag, 23 Januar 1947, Records of the Bremerhaven Liaison and Security Detachment, Records of the Central Office, Subject Files 1945-49, Box 546, RG 260, NARA. The proclamation went into effect retroactively on 1 January 1947.

59. Ibid.

60. G. v. Heukelum for American Military Government Wesermünde, Alteration of the Name of the City of Wesermünde, 10 February 1947, Records of the Bremerhaven Liaison and Security Detachment, Records of the Central Office, Subject Files 1945-1949, Box 532, RG 260, NARA.

61. Thomas F. Dunn, Director, Office of Military Government for Bremen Enclave (US), for the Deputy Military Governor, Office of Military Government for Germany (US), Constitutional

Assembly of Land Bremen, 10 March 1947, OMGUS, AG, 1947, Box 173, Memorandum, Henry RG 260, NARA.

62. Brigadier General C.K. Gailey, GSC, Chief of Staff, Office of Military Government for Germany (US), General Orders, 14 April 1947, OMGUS, AG, 1947, Box 173, RG 260, NARA.

63. Röpcke, 452.

64. Organizational Chart, Office of Military Government Bremen, 1 May 1948, Records of the Denazification Division, Box 177, RG 260, NARA; FHMG, 1 July 1946-30 June 1947, Appendix 3, Civil Administration Land Bremen as of 1 April 1947, Records of the Public Information Office, Functional Histories of Military Government in Bremen, April 1945-March 1948, Box 74, RG 260, NARA. The exceptions were the Information Control Division, which monitored everything from radio broadcasts to newspaper publication to theater and film productions, the Liaison and Security Bremerhaven Division, and the Transport Division.

65. Annual Functional History of Military Government in Land Bremen, January-December 1948, 7.

66. Ibid., 8.

67. Ibid., 9. The practical implication of the creation of bizonal agencies and the Joint Export-Import Agency was that the military government relinquished control over traffic, economic issues, finance, and export-related matters. Annual Functional History of Military Government in Land Bremen, January-December 1948, 5; Records of the Public Information Office, Functional Histories of Military Government in Bremen, April 1945-March 1948, Box 75, RG 260, NARA.

68. Röpcke, 452. The State Commissioner represented the Office of the High Commissioner for Germany that had been created by the Occupation Statute signed by the United States, Great Britain, and France in April 1949. US Department of State, *Documents on Germany 1944-1985*, 212.

Victors and Vanquished: Americans as Occupiers in Berlin, 1945-1949

William Stivers

From July 1945 until September 1949, the American sector of Berlin was under military government rule. These years saw profound developments in the city's internal affairs as well as its emergence as the "front city" of the Cold War. One such development was a fundamental shift in the US relationship with the leaders and people of West Berlin. What began as an encounter between victors and vanquished ended as an association of friends and allies. The punitive features of the occupation had first receded and finally disappeared. Distance and distrust had yielded to partnership and respect.

There was little in the initial circumstances of the occupation that would have predicted that shift. In the first years of the US presence in Berlin, relations between Americans and Berliners were fraught with difficulties. US forces entered Berlin in July 1945 to occupy the capital city of a defeated state. The occupation's aim was neither liberation nor reconstruction but control of that enemy to prevent Germany's resurgence as a threat to world peace.[1] US officials experienced the local population as resentful, manipulative, and anti-Democratic. Its people were wallowing in self-pity, denying guilt, and bent on restoring Germany's status by seeking to embroil the United States in conflict with the Soviet Union. Yet, if Berliners were resentful, they had good cause. For residents of the US sector, American occupation did not stop with its one clearly positive side—protection from the Soviets—but signified arbitrary confiscation of property, eviction from dwelling space, physical and verbal abuse by US troops, and moral degradation. Leaders of pro-Western parties in Berlin were kept at arm's length through a policy of "aloofness" that depreciated their credentials as democrats and held them indirectly responsible for Germany's guilt.

After four years of the occupation, the situation had changed beyond recognition. Events had bridged the chasm separating victors from vanquished. Repressing memories of the occupation's punitive phase, West Berliners saw Americans as benefactors. In their eyes, the US military government had promoted democracy and ensured civil rights. The Berlin blockade had confirmed the worst fears of Soviet intentions, and the legendary airlift had established the United States as West Berlin's indispensable protector. For Americans, Berlin was no longer the capital city of Adolf Hitler's Germany but was now Europe's outpost of freedom. The common people of Berlin, asserted *Time* magazine, had won the battle of the blockade: "the people who met in huge rallies to hurl their defiance from the shadow of the Red-flag-topped Brandenburger Tor, the people who turned out in bitter cold last December to vote a solid no to the Communists. . . . Without them, the West, for all its bold determination and its roaring C-54s, would have lost Berlin."[2]

The political corollary of friendship was a signal act of trust on the victors' part toward the former enemy: restoring self-government in West Berlin. On 14 May 1949—just two days after the Soviet lifted the blockade—the Western commandants granted city authorities broad autonomy over West Berlin's internal affairs.[3] Four months later, in September, the office of military government in the US sector dissolved. Although West Berlin would remain under tripartite occupation until 1994, the term "occupation" referred to the city's international status and not to Allied direction of its domestic affairs.

The dissolution of military government marked the natural end to the progressive recasting of German-American relations in Berlin. This paper examines how that recasting took place. In the process, it will examine a conspicuous success—fully unexpected in 1945—in the history of military administration of conquered areas.

Incorrigible Germans

As the war drew to a close, American occupation planners had detected few signs of democratic potential in postwar Germany and expected little good from most Germans. These planners found it easy to promulgate a negative policy of removing Nazis from positions of influence. But on whom could they call to make positive contributions to Germany's democratic reconstruction? The G5 section of Supreme Headquarters, Allied Expeditionary Force (SHAEF) flatly wrote off large segments of German society. In a paper prepared in April 1945, G5 officers "presupposed" that trade unionists, Social Democrats (*SPD*), liberals, and some former members of the Catholic Center Party were "reasonably" pro-Democratic. However, industrialists, big businessmen, and large landowners were suspect, as were conservative anti-Nazis who "were so generally imbued with German nationalism, militarism, and conservative traditionalism" as to be "unsuitable for all purposes." The political adviser to SHAEF, Ambassador Robert Murphy, agreed: "While many of the rightists and conservatives were anti-Nazi, they were at the same time strongly nationalistic. . . . Our aim is not only to destroy Nazism (negative) but to seek out and encourage elements which have been or may become truly democratic (positive)."[4]

For one official in the US Control Council Group, even Social Democrats and trade unionists were problematic. As he saw it, they elevated the desire for immediate social and economic reform above the obligation to pay reparations, demanded Germany be treated as a liberated rather than a conquered nation, and rejected territorial concessions by Germany beyond renunciation of Nazi conquests. In these respects, democratic socialists and union leaders would be more difficult to deal with than the communists who, as Moscow's loyal followers, eschewed irredentism.[5]

American officials did not expect the Germans to accept defeat. Instead, in American eyes, German nationalists would "bend every effort" to stir conflict between the Anglo-American Allies and the Soviet Union. In the words of the final report of SHAEF's Joint Intelligence Committee, German leaders were already at work "to gain for Germany the status of a co-belligerent against Russia." In hopes of fooling the West "into rebuilding Germany as a bulwark against the Russians, they would "take every opportunity of licking the Allies' boots to make us grudgingly acknowledge that they were 'correct.'" Murphy, in a blistering appraisal of the "non-Nazi" officer caste, reached the same conclusion: "Men like these are discussing how to swindle the United States into a meretricious 'friendship' with Germany and to embroil America in a war."[6]

Such profound distrust extended beyond German leaders to encompass the larger population. Accordingly, once American forces entered Berlin, US intelligence agencies cast surveillance nets over the entire city. The Berlin G2 "Civil Censorship" Division monitored German postal, telegraphic, and telephonic communications inside Berlin. By spring 1946, Civil Censorship was processing almost a quarter of a million pieces of mail a month. Between mid-March and mid-June, it had distributed nearly 5,000 extracts from mail and telephone intercepts to appropriate staff sections. Myriad G2 paid informants reported on political meetings, audience reactions to theater performances, workplace conversations, and complaints overheard from people standing in bread lines.

One of the chief uses of Civil Censorship surveillance and informant reports was to uncover the Berliners' views on life under occupation, their feelings toward the occupying powers, and their political mood.[7] The overall picture that emerged from these covert sources showed the Germans living up to their stereotypes, a people who, as one Office of Strategic Services informant described them, "ruthlessly kill and destroy, but when they are beaten . . . feel that somebody should 'help' them."[8] The average Berliner, in G2 eyes, was a "vicious, immoral creature" whose attitudes compounded "suppressed nationalism, hatreds, a feeling of insecurity, negative criticism and hunger" and who lost no chance to complain one day to the Americans about the Russians and the "next evening to seek out a Russian and pour out to him his grievances against the Americans while the Russian pours the Vodka." Such Berliners did "not comprehend the relationship between twelve years of Nazi rule and their present sufferings." They blamed the occupation for their low living standards and displayed no concern for other countries' losses and suffering.[9]

In October 1945, the Information Control Division branch in Berlin established an overt opinion research team employing German surveyors trained in Gallup techniques. They conducted numerous polls on political, social, and cultural issues and wrote public mood assessments. These publicly conducted polls reinforced the picture derived from the G2's covert intelligence. For example, a survey report of 26 January 1946 revealed that 77 percent of Berlin respondents (82 percent in the American sector) denied "any truth" to the statement that the German people were responsible for the war because they had ceded power to the Nazis. At the same time, virtually none of those questioned regarded a single Nuremberg defendant as innocent, demonstrating their readiness to assign guilt to the National Socialist leadership while dissociating themselves from all blame. The same survey showed that 53 percent of respondents (52 percent in the US sector) saw National Socialism not as a "bad idea" but as a "good idea badly executed"—astonishing for such a traditionally left-wing city and certainly not a vote for democracy.[10]

An earlier survey addressed the issue of compensating victims of religious or political persecution under National Socialism. Although 60 percent of the interview sample agreed to returning lost property (32 percent did not!), this form of restitution involved no public costs. By contrast, a mere 30 percent expressed willingness to pay higher taxes to compensate Nazi victims for financial loss or physical injury. Likewise, only 42 percent of the sample felt that people who were physically disabled due to Nazi treatment in concentration camps or jails should receive greater amenities than disabled Wehrmacht veterans. These and other public opinion poll results confirmed American preconceptions of "German character," cast doubt on German readiness to accept responsibility for Nazi crimes, and made it hard to identify Germany's democratic potential.[11]

America's *Soldateska*

Soldiers of the early US Berlin garrisons exacerbated imputed German negativism. Too often, their conduct ran the gamut from loutish to criminal. Such behavior gave Berliners another excuse to regard themselves as victims and to shun responsibility for their own situation. Moreover, poorly behaved troops sowed disrespect toward American political values.

The occupation was split between two largely uncoordinated elements. A small military government, officially termed the Office of Military Government, Berlin Sector (OMGBS), consisted of about 150 officials charged with supervising the German administration, ensuring public health and safety, and furthering US aims in the four-power control authority for Berlin, the Allied Kommandatura. The "tactical troops," initially numbering more than 30,000 until reduced to a stable strength of almost 6,000 by mid-1946, was the garrison force for the occupation.

Instead of ensuring public safety, many soldiers, including officers, devoted themselves to enjoying the victors' spoils. Freed from the deadly seriousness of combat, they indulged in acts of indiscipline and outlawry ranging from currency fraud, black marketing, and stealing requisitioned goods to violent drunkenness, rape, assault, and robbery. Often heavily inebriated, they assaulted Berliners with insults and physical abuse; even policemen became targets of brutal attacks. According to a July 1946 intelligence report sent to the de facto head of the US military government for Germany, Lieutenant General (LTG) Lucius Clay, the US troop crime rate in Berlin was nearly 13 times the rate for the Military District of Washington.[12] Given that many Germans were too afraid to report crimes or saw no point in it, the actual extent of crime was greater still. In addition to these criminal depredations, careless sexual conduct—particularly on the part of "low score" soldiers willfully impervious to sexual hygiene training—helped feed a venereal disease epidemic that ranked with typhus, typhoid fever, and tuberculosis as threats to Berlin's public health.[13]

Civil Censorship reports are filled with astonishing stories of American violence and pillage. In one intercepted letter, a resident of the Tempelhof district related the story of a student living on her floor "who was shot by the Americans last week. They stopped him in the evening . . . and demanded liquor. As he did not have any, they shot him twice." A second Templehof resident reported, "Young Schmidberger was killed by two Americans after he left his fiancé at 10:30." A Zehlendorf resident wrote, "Nearly every evening one heard the siren; . . . it is the signal for the Amis attacks. Some of them act like gangsters. . . . Here in our district they drag some into the woods, beat them up, and rob them." A resident of Steglitz wrote of two friends attacked by five Americans: "They were punched, thrown down and their heads knocked against a wall. Then they were kicked in the ribs." A female US Army employee reported feeling "very unhappy" about her work: "Having to deal with drunks all day long is the last straw. These continuous fights and often they attack us. Twice already I was almost raped."[14]

Since Berliners made no distinction between military government and tactical troops, the entire occupation was blackened in local eyes. Americans, as the deeply worried Berlin G2 quoted an "anti-Fascist" in February 1946, "are just Russians in pressed pants."[15] In the view of military government intelligence, German "disgust and disrespect" toward US forces undermined the public's willingness to cooperate with occupation authorities, and resentment over "marauding and ravages" could have led to "protective resistance." In this respect, US troop misconduct was considered perhaps the major security threat to the occupation.[16]

Added to the criminal indiscipline of marauding soldiers was an officially sanctioned indiscipline arising from authorized use of firearms as a normal means of guarding checkpoints and installations. When American soldiers first occupied the US sector of Berlin on 4 July 1945, weapons use against German civilians was limited to incidents requiring self-defense. When Soviet soldiers were in the US sector, where many came on looting sprees, sentries were ordered to avoid conflict and to employ no force or threat of force against them. This changed after 12 July 1945. New instructions—personally affirmed by the troop commander, Major General (MG) Floyd L. Parks—permitted US sentries to use whatever means, including firearms, they felt necessary to safeguard military personnel and property. There was no further requirement for self-defense, and the relative significance of guarded objects did not enter in the calculation.

Both Soviet soldiers and Berlin civilians began falling to American gunfire. The most prominent German victim was Leo Borchard, the first postwar conductor of the Berlin Philharmonic, who was shot dead on 23 August 1945 after his British driver misinterpreted a sentry's signal to halt at a checkpoint. The lesson drawn from the incident was not to stop such wanton firearms use but to mark checkpoints with conspicuous barriers rather than to rely on hand signals. In principle, as MG James M. Gavin stated in a November memorandum to Soviet LTG Dmitri I. Smirnov, doubts arising in cases of "resistance" to armed guards "are resolved in favor of the guard."[17]

Dilemmas of Occupation

Even if American soldiers had conducted themselves well, US occupation authorities would have still encountered serious problems in its relations with Berlin's population. Both the military government and tactical troops often seemed to perpetrate or countenance unfairness. American officials understood both this fact and the political difficulties associated with it. However, even with the best intentions, the very nature of the occupation made unfairness inevitable, for no occupation could function solely according to principles of either justice or efficiency. This was shown most clearly with requisitions (seen more as "confiscations" by affected Berliners), denazification, and American treatment of German leaders and officials.

Requisitions of offices, dwellings, and furnishings made the occupation a burden on "guilty" and "innocent" Berliners alike—particularly inasmuch as breakdowns in rent payments for requisitioned furniture left these obligations unpaid for two years from summer 1946.[18] On 30 September 1945, US forces controlled approximately 4,500 properties in the American sector. The US Army had supplanted an estimated one-quarter of the population of the choice district of Zeh-lendorf from its dwellings. Persons whose homes were designated for requisition had only 72 hours' notice to clear their dwellings of items they needed for survival. If they missed the deadline (due, for example, to being absent when the notice was delivered), they could be barred from further entry and could not gather their mattresses, sheets, or pots and pans. Public resentment over such procedures grew in proportion to their apparent senselessness. In contrast with British and French practices, US "nonfraternization" policies forbade billeting personnel with German families. Thus, Germans had to vacate entirely any residence selected for American use instead of merely sharing rooms.[19] To make matters worse, many evicted residents complained that some requisitioned dwellings were then left partially full or empty.[20]

Requistions, warned Zehlendorf's district mayor, were inflicting political wounds. One unhappy resident termed them a "war without weapons" that would turn Berliners toward Communism. According to a report prepared in the military government Information Control Section in November 1945, US Army confiscation of homes and belongings had disillusioned non-Nazis of every class with the occupation:

> Property owners whose homes are requisitioned find it difficult to understand why they are being penalized, claiming that there are still enough houses occupied by Nazi families to quarter all troops in the American sector. Actual victims of the Nazi regime, including former inmates of concentration camps and non-Aryans, are even more at a loss to understand why they should be put out of their homes by American troops. . . . In apartments where 5, 6 or 7 persons are crowded into the space formerly occupied by one or two, nerves are taut and complaints against American requisitioning the more violent. . . .'They cart away our furniture from our homes. Do you think we'll ever see it again? We aren't that naïve,' represents a fairly typical attitude.[21]

The Denazification Conundrum

Given case-by-case ambiguities, the difficulty of assessing extenuating evidence, and the sheer mass of cases to be processed, denazification posed severe difficulties for American administrators everywhere in the US zone of occupation. In Berlin, however, these general difficulties were compounded by harsh implementation that contrasted with the practices of the other three powers in the city and with American denazification procedures in West Germany.

The case of eminent surgeon, Dr. Ernst Sauerbruch, is illustrative of American rigorism in Berlin. Sauerbruch was no Nazi. His professional renown dated from pioneering advances in chest surgery toward the turn of the century. Since 1928 he had occupied posts as professor at the Berlin University and director of surgery of at Berlin's world-famous Charité Hospital where he built an international reputation in amputation and prosthesis. On 12 May 1945, Soviet city commandant Colonel General Nikolai Besarin summoned him to take office as director of public health in a municipal administration assembled for the task of ensuring survival in the shambles Europe's last great battle left.[22]

In late September 1949, US Commandant MG Gavin sent a letter to the Kommandatura requesting Sauerbruch's dismissal. Although never a party member and not regarded as a security threat, Sauerbruch had "prospered during the Nazi regime and occupied a position of prominence" through which he contributed to the Nazi Party's prestige. The Soviet representative agreed to Sauerbruch's dismissal as head of public health but resisted US demands that he also be removed as director of surgery at the Charité (located in the Soviet sector). In compromise, Sauerbruch was dismissed from both positions but permitted to remain at the Charité as a practicing surgeon.[23] The contrast between American and Soviet attitudes in this case could not have been more striking.

The core issue with denazification was the following: While individuals categorized as "active" Nazis, militarists, and Nazi supporters were to be expunged from public and private professions, employment of nominal, "nonactive" ex-Nazis in professional provisions was allowed under both American and quadripartite directives. The problem was that of determining who was a "nominal," as opposed to an "active," Nazi or Nazi supporter. As the Sauerbruch case illustrates, circumstances were rarely clear-cut, and Americans, as outsiders, were ill equipped to judge them. Moreover, virtually all "chargeable" individuals had exculpatory stories that required case-by-case examination, imposing crushing demands on time and judgment.

In the American zone in West Germany, denazification was first a military government responsibility carried out by the Public Safety Section "Special Branch," which made essentially mechanical determinations based on individuals' positions and ranks. The American zone denazification law of 5 March 1946 passed the responsibility to German authorities effective 1 June 1946. Once in German hands, denazification degenerated into assembly-line exoneration of ex-Nazis. Yet, while resulting in a farce, the devolution of responsibility had the political virtue of reducing the military government's direct involvement in an unpopular process.

In the American sector of Berlin, however, authority remained in the hands of the Special Branch. Seven-member German denazification commissions were established in each district to investigate appeals of Special Branch findings, but these boards could only make recommendations. Both initial determinations and final holdings were reserved to US authorities. This left the military government carrying the onus of negative decisions. It also made the process more cumbersome and time consuming. In a complaint sent to the military government in March 1948, the superintendent of the Protestant churches in Berlin, Dr. Otto Debelius, described the situation: "The final clearance would require an unmeasureable [sic] amount of time. . . . The files are raising [sic] up to the sky. . . . To settle even a favorable case, months are necessary. . . . Thousands of individuals torment themselves by waiting from day to day and despair and bitterness may be the issue to the last."[24]

If US denazifiers had restricted the scope of the purge by targeting only people in "leading" positions, they could have mitigated frictions. However, for reasons unknown to this author, the US sector denazification program treated people in "nonleading" positions with a severity practiced neither in the American zone of West Germany nor in the British, French, or Soviet sectors of Berlin. Thus, American denazification removed manual laborers, small shopkeepers, and nurses even when directives did not require, thereby inviting invidious comparisons with the other powers.[25]

US denazifiers could not control outcomes according to their intentions. Despite the rigor of American objectives, guilty parties frequently escaped punishment. Some individuals avoided sanctions first by omitting to register their party affiliations and then by successfully avoiding further attention; private employers frequently shut their eyes and employed whomever they pleased. German agencies and boards involved in denazification actions often had their own agendas. "Nominal" Nazis cleared for work under the category "employment discretionary with employer" could find German labor offices standing in the way of reinstatement. In the words of the military government liaison officer to the Tempelhof district, "Directives and decisions have been variously interpreted. . . . The present system allows German officers a good deal of opportunity for petty persecution or undesirable leniency when such is personally advantageous."[26]

Desirable members for the German denazification commissions were hard to recruit. Competent and objective persons did not want to perform such an unpleasant task that exposed them to pressure and slander. On the other hand, to cite the chief of the military government Security Review Board, "Competent people with prejudices are very anxious to serve."[27] Thus, although Germans were better qualified to assess evidence than Americans, they could not be counted on to remain objective in circumstances rife with favoritism and score-settling.

In the end, denazification satisfied neither those Germans who demanded thorough reckoning with former Nazis nor those advocating that "small" offenders be quickly rehabilitated. Neither did it contribute to a genuine reflection on Nazi crimes or to the moral regeneration of German public life. As Dr. Debelius put it:

> [accused parties] are trying to pretend that they did not make themselves guilty. . . . In consequence they are trying to pretend that their part in the Nazi movement was as insignificant as possible, often enough at the cost of truth. They have only one aim: to get out of the trouble by gaining a favorable sentence. If they have been successful, they feel themselves justified, having failed their aim, they go home angry and resentfully.
>
> There is no question of any . . . changing of mind. If a young man is liable to punishment who—by sincere idealism—has worked in the party for some time before he became aware of its actual character, it cannot be spoken of a moral substance of the proceeding. The whole action is only felt as a procedure of avenge [sic] allowing the cunning fellow to escape . . . and seizing only the fair and honest man. In this way nothing will be improved within the German people. On the contrary: morality will get undermined more and more, and the feeling of bitterness in our nation will still increase.[28]

Political Nonfraternization

Directives emanating from Washington and from the Office of the Military Government for Germany (OMGUS) severely complicated relationships with German authorities and party leaders. JCS 1067/8, the 10 May 1945 interdepartmental directive to the military governor, instructed US authorities to remain "just but firm and aloof" in conducting the occupation and strongly to "discourage fraternization with the German officials and population." Such a formulation was fully undifferentiated, prohibiting officials to get close even to individuals with proven credentials as democrats and antifascists.[29] Thus, German leaders who offered themselves as ready partners in the task of reconstruction had to be treated as carriers of infection.

The aloofness edict clashed with local realities. Parsimonious manning of military government, conjoined with a shortage of officers who were fluent in German and knowledgeable in German affairs dictated reliance on German officeholders to run local government. In addition, the Army relied on thousands of German employees to service the garrison. Such constant proximity, with both German officials and the Army's own work force, numbering about 20,000 people, made it extremely hard to maintain distance. Moreover, the restoration of Berlin's party life and electoral politics in 1946 (each, a success of American policy) heightened ideological competition, evoked sympathies and distastes, and drew US officials to take sides. Under such circumstances, aloofness became a fully artificial construct. By early 1946, US officials everywhere in the American zone of occupation were starting to take unauthorized leave of it.

Deputy Military Governor LTG Clay remained firmly opposed to military government involvement in German party affairs and insisted on limiting personal contact. In June 1946, having perceived a slackening of aloofness in Berlin and throughout the American zone, he issued instruction to local military governments reaffirming earlier strictures on relationships with German public figures. Remarking on the prestige that military government officials enjoyed, he stressed the importance of observing strict political neutrality and permitting no Germans to convey any impression to the German people that they enjoyed US favor. He decreed that military government personnel "must particularly avoid the formation of close individual friendships on a social entertainment basis." In an obvious reference to widespread, individual abandonment of aloofness, Clay concluded his instruction with an order to replace anyone who did not agree to its principles.[30]

OMGBS officials viewed with consternation Clay's prohibitions against "social entertainment." The Berlin branch chiefs for Civil Administration, Information Control, and Education and Religious Affairs all complained that the restriction would prevent them from fulfilling their duties. Information Control Chief Lieutenant Colonel Frederick N. Leonard wrote: "From time to time it is deemed appropriate to invite Germans to unofficial gatherings, not to 'entertain' them but, by means of showing confidence in them and their opinions, to encourage them to continue in this important reeducation of German thought and also to obtain information of value to the operation of Military Government generally."[31]

Clay had valid reasons for his attitude. He believed that all the occupying powers were fundamentally unpopular and that it would do no Germans any good to become identified with any of them. (Decades later, in reflecting on this view, he declared that he had been mistaken.)[32] However, there were two basic difficulties with his policy in Berlin. First, while neutrality was fully unproblematic in the western *Länder*, where the parties in competition were primarily Christian Democrats (*CDU*), Social Democrats (*SPD*) and Liberals (*FDP-LDP*), it denoted in Berlin the concession of material advantage to a political adversary, the Socialist Unity Party (*SED*), which received unabashed support from the Soviets. Second, the United States could not realize its goal of reorienting German society until it harnessed the full energies of German democrats. That presupposed engagement and dialogue, not "aloofness."

Soothing Friction: Discipline, Shootings, Requisitions

The lawful and correct treatment of the population of the US sector was key to achieving the minimal objective of the occupation: acquiescence to American authority. It was also a precondition for transforming the occupation's punitive countenance and winning Germans to active collaboration.

By mid-1946, an 80 percent reduction in troop numbers, compared with August 1945, diminished the number of incidents even if the rate remained high. Stepped-up enforcement of dress regulations and military courtesies, curfews, and restrictions on alcohol sales restored a semblance of order and improved US soldiers' public appearance.[33]

British, Soviet, and American troops joined with German police in staging massive sweeps to apprehend uniformed lawbreakers from all Allied nations. Court martial boards meted out exemplary punishments to edify the obtuse. In March 1946, the Allied Kommandatura authorized German police to use weapons against marauding troops, whether in self-defense or to protect others from injury. The regulation was heavily publicized in the US sector to "enhance military law and order."[34]

In October 1946, Berlin's "tactical" forces were removed from the military command structure, where they answered to theater headquarters in Frankfurt, and put directly under the OMGUS in Berlin. Shortly thereafter, in November, OMGUS moved to contain indiscriminate firearms use by sentries and military police (MPs). Clay's deputy, MG Frank A. Keating, reimposed the self-defense restriction, abandoned in mid-July 1945, with respect to using deadly force. At the same time, MPs were outfitted with nightsticks to enable them to subdue violators without resorting to using lethal weapons. (Beforehand, few appear to have grasped the importance of this. In Keating's words of exasperation, "It is unreasonable for us to assume that [MPs] can perform their mission merely by using a pistol.") Following these moves, security did not deteriorate while fatalities virtually ceased.[35]

Alongside troop misconduct, requisitions of dwelling space and furniture constituted major, daily irritants affecting relations between Berliners and US occupying authorities. Substantial reductions in the size of the Berlin garrison made it possible to "derequisition" confiscated items. (Indeed, derequisitioning became a political end—a means, in the eyes of one official, of selling to "the Germans our concept of democracy.") By spring 1948, more than 50 percent of the properties under requisition in September 1945 had been restored to German use, despite additional demand for housing for American families who began arriving in April 1946.[36] Purchasing new furniture from factories in Bavaria and, strangely, Czechoslovakia facilitated the return of home furnishings. Germans whose furniture remained in Army hands chose whether to receive rent or sell it outright. Claims procedures were established to reimburse owners for damages incurred by US personnel. Although mundane matters in comparison to the wider issues at stake in Berlin, all such measures worked to reduced thousands of individual frictions between American occupation authorities and the Berlin public.[37]

Ending Denazification

Denazification was unpopular in all regions of Germany. For American occupational authorities, the only clear solution to the problems of denazification would be capitulating to German views. Inevitably, this was the solution arrived at in Berlin as well as in all zones of occupation.

By early 1946, none of the occupying powers could ignore the economic and strategic advantages of having Germans on their side. Lenience toward small-time Nazis was one sure way to win countless German "friends." Indeed, within two years' time, this search for German friends resulted in what State Department analysts called "a race to end denazification."[38]

The Soviets and their *SED* allies were the first to offer open blandishments to "nominal" Nazis. In June 1946, the *SED* leadership proclaimed, "The SED believes the time has come to integrate simple members and fellow travelers [m*itläufer*] in the Nazi apparatus into the work of democratic reconstruction." On 16 August 1947, Soviet Military Governor Marshal Vasily D. Sokolovsky issued an order restoring full rights to all former Nazis who committed no crimes against peace and security. Military government intelligence reported highly favorable reactions to the Soviet move in both West Germany and Berlin where the "Russian order . . . has gone over big with public opinion." LTG Clay countered in October 1947 with an amendment to the US denazification law that permitted more people to be subsumed automatically under the "nominal" category, thus clearing them for employment with no further proceedings. In February 1948, the Soviet military administration stepped up the pace with an order to end Soviet zone denazification completely by 10 March.[39]

Clay consistently resisted both German and American pressures to end denazification, but he was faced with blatant Soviet attempts to curry German favor and with congressional critics who claimed that denazification was hindering Germany's economic recovery. In March he gave way to pressure from Washington and announced the intention to close out denazification by 1 June 1948. Accordingly, he issued instruction to OMGBS Director Colonel Frank Howley outlining specific steps to accelerate the process. The key element of Clay's plan was to screen case dockets for persons removed from "noninfluential" positions or "of minor Nazi affiliations" and to have such cases withdrawn from consideration and sanctions removed.[40] Clay proposed to have all "first appeals" finished up in Berlin "on or about" 1 May.

[40]The Soviet blockade started on 24 June 1948. The denazification issue receded from view in light of the larger historical drama that gripped Berlin. US sector denazification lingered on in the remaining employment categories still affected by it. In orders issued on 16 February and 6 April 1949, the Western Kommandatura placed responsibility for implementing allied denazification laws in the hands of West Berlin's government, amnestied individuals born before 1 January 1919, and amended previous law to reduce the number of people requiring denazification. In also gave West Berlin officials the authority to set punishments that were not to exceed punishments stipulated by Kommandatura law. On 25 July 1949, the Kommandatura conferred full responsibility for denazification to Berlin city authorities who were "requested" to submit German legislation as soon as possible to the Kommandatura so that Allied orders could be rescinded.[41] This step, which followed directly from being granted autonomy in May, ended American embarrassment, even if justice had not been done.

From Aloofness to Partnership

The drive to impose order on US troops, establish lawful relationships with Berlin's population, and assuage the frictions of occupation conformed to the "just but firm" doctrine of JCS 1067/8. It did not, however, redefine the American relationship with Berlin's political class. That a victor displays "correct" behavior toward the vanquished leaves their relative status untouched. For Americans to view Germans not as subjects but as partners required finding Germans broadly committed to American principles of democratic reconstruction.

To presume to build democratic structures in Germany while keeping German leaders at arm's length was pure contradiction. Nonetheless, it was not obvious where partners might be found. As already stated, US occupation planners in 1945 regarded virtually one-half of German society as "unsuitable for all purposes," and many Americans equated Germany with despotism. In US officials' eyes, each of Germany's reconstituted political parties had some flaw. The *CDU* and Liberals were viewed as nesting grounds for former Nazis seeking cover. Americans respected Soviet zone CDU leaders Jakob Kaiser and Ernst Lemmer for struggling to maintain their party's autonomy in East Germany but at the same time distrusted them as people especially amenable to the "eastern temptation"—a deal for German unification in trade for *CDU* backing of Soviet objectives in West Germany. Western zone *CDU* leader Konrad Adenauer posed no threat of succumbing to the eastern temptation but counted as an incorrigible reactionary who was hostile to American ideas for constitutional and social reform. While recognizing the *SPD's* democratic credentials, US officials regarded it as a bureaucratic machine, with little internal democracy, and distrusted the strident nationalism of its leader, Kurt Schumacher.[42]

The United States would have had no difficulty in rallying countless Germans under the banner of anti-communism. Such a course, however, appealed to the very extremism —and crypto-Nazi sentiment—Americans sought to eradicate. Writing in November 1947, one OMGBS civil affairs branch official pinpointed the American dilemma in an analysis that merits extensive quotation:

> As the basis for cooperation with the Russians becomes more difficult in Germany and elsewhere, and as American Military Government is compelled in self-defense to openly emphasize its anti-communist sentiments and policies, such emphasis naturally reawakens by association, not only the strongly ingrained anti-bolshevik propaganda of the Nazi days, but because of parallel associations, at the same time reopens the whole question of Hitler and his policies.
>
> The plain man on the street . . . remembers Hitler as an anti-bolshevik crusader and begins to see a posthumous justification for his policies in the attitude which the Western Powers, particularly America, . . . adopt toward the communists. Such sentiments can be verified by anyone taking the trouble to listen to the remarks of Germans standing in line while waiting to purchase some of the items on their meager diet. . . ."Oh yes, Hitler was a criminal and all that, but he was certainly more than right in his anti-communist conceptions." A careful observer can detect that the first part of the sentence does not carry much conviction. One has the feeling that the particular German making the statement does not want to reveal to the American with whom his is talking that in reality, he, the German, thinks much better of Hitler.[43]

The Americans sought political allies whose anticommunism came without nationalist or reactionary taint. More than that, Americans sought allies who were committed to destroying the social roots of German authoritarianism. In the eyes of military government officials, democratic reconstruction meant more than elections and parliamentarism. It presupposed, as well, radical reform of German civic institutions—above all, its schools and civil service. Their ideas on the substance of such reforms were colored by an underlying conviction that American models were right and in their applicability to German circumstances.

Berlin's unique environment yielded a singular case of German-American identity of views. From early 1946, a special relationship evolved in Berlin between US occupation authorities and the city's Social Democrats. The relationship evolved not through any plan but through a chain of experiences.

The party fusion struggle, a culminating chapter in decades of political warfare between Communists (*KPD*) and Social Democrats, marked the beginning of a progressive intertwining of Americans and the Berlin *SPD*. In February 1946, leaders of the *SPD* Central Committee—the Social Democrats' governing body for the Soviet zone of occupation and Berlin—surrendered to Soviet and *KPD* pressure to unite the two parties, a move that would end the existence of an independent SPD in East Germany. Party insurgents in West Berlin rejected forced unity and demanded that party members put the issue to a vote. Destitute of resources, they turned to Western military governments for assistance.

US military government and State Department personnel in West Berlin ignored the aloofness and neutrality precepts to which they were officially obligated. In March-April 1946, US military government and State Department personnel, in league with British colleagues, provided critical aid to antifusion forces. Some officials reached into their own pockets to share food and donate CARE packages to antifusion insurgents. At a time when most people lived with hunger pangs, these supplemental calories helped energize political action. Antifusionists received crucial supplies of paper and access to US-licensed newspapers and printing presses to fight a propaganda battle against Soviet-supported party functionaries.

On 31 March 1946, antifusionists held a party referendum in West Berlin under the protective hand of the Western allies. A resounding 82.6 percent of participating *SPD* members rejected union with the *KPD*. The *SPD* remained an independent party in Berlin and became the fulcrum of West Berlin's "front-line" anticommunism.[44] US officials in Berlin had contributed vitally to an outcome that would have far-reaching consequences in coming decades. In the process, they became directly acquainted with German democrats who had displayed not merely conviction but a willingness to act despite personal risk.

City elections in Berlin, held in October 1946, ushered in a new phase of German-American association in Berlin, witnessed by American advocacy of virtual autonomy for the city administration, the *Magistrat*. The *SPD* won 48.7 percent of the vote and became Berlin's dominant political force. The "Unity Socialists," the *SED*, took only 19.8 percent, coming in third behind the *CDU*. In December 1946, given the overwhelming strength of the pro-Western parties (*SPD*, *CDU*, *LDP*) in the City Assembly, the US military government proposed a radical step toward self-rule: All "legislative enactments" of the *Magistrat* would go into effect unless the Kommandatura expressly *disapproved* them. This meant, given the Kommandatura's unanimity rule, that German laws and ordinances could be blocked only if all four powers rejected them.

By contrast, the rule of "positive approval" required unanimous Kommandatura assent to legislation, thus giving each Kommandatura member a right of veto. None of the other three powers were willing to relinquish their veto at that time, and "positive approval" remained the requirement. The political significance of the American proposal lay in the fact that US authorities sided with German demands for early self-government and were prescribing control procedures for Berlin that were considerably more liberal than those employed in US-occupied West Germany.[45] The proposal testified more to the fact that US officials had discovered a political group they explicitly trusted to manage city affairs than to adherence to autonomy per se.

SPD leaders and military government officials in Berlin found themselves in agreement not only on democracy as a political form but also on substantive details of institutional change. Starting in 1947, the *Magistrat* undertook comprehensive reforms of education and public administration in Berlin. Although impetus to do so came from the occupying powers, German reform endeavors dated from the Weimar era and formed the basis of postwar debate. It was a notable coincidence that these German concepts, now put forward by the *SPD*, corresponded closely to reform ideas the US military government proposed. Indeed, nowhere else in Germany did German reformers adapt so much of the American model to German circumstances. Berlin and Bremen, for example, were the only German states to incorporate the military government's desire for a 12-year course of public schooling into their school reform.

SPD backing for Anglo-American measures in the Western zones of Germany reinforced its association with US policies and actions. By June 1947, the West German bizonal administration had been centralized in Frankfurt and equipped with executive and legislative powers. With this move setting up the forerunner for a German government, it was now clear that the Anglo-Americans were going to establish a separate Western state. Such a prospect disturbed many Germans because it wrote finish to hopes for reunification. West Berlin's *SPD* leadership, however, fully supported consolidating the bizonal agencies and sought to integrate Berlin into the new administration. Later in 1948, these leaders firmly supported founding a state in the West and played a prominent part in defeating the objections of those who feared abandonment of the eastern zone. In a July 1948 meeting of state minister presidents in Rüdesheim, *SPD* party leader Ernst Reuter countered such misgivings, declaring, "The political and economic consolidation of the West is a fundamental prerequisite for the . . . return of the East to our common motherland."[46]

Finally, the Berlin blockade greatly heightened the status of Berlin's *SPD* leadership. The part they played in defeating it was central and decisive. Instead of seeking negotiations, they mobilized public resistance against what Reuter termed "rotten compromise." Like Winston Churchill in wartime Britain, they bolstered public morale and stirred the Berliners' fighting spirit with appeals to collective sacrifice and righteous struggle. It is no happenstance that Reuter, who became West Berlin's mayor in December 1948, was Germany's best-known public figure in America at the end of the 1940s, lionized in one press article as "The Mayor Russia Hates" and praised in another as "indomitable . . . one of the few authentically big figures in Western Europe, a fearless, consistent foe of Communism who meets the enemy without flinching or compromise." When LTG Clay departed Berlin in May 1948, he visited Reuter's office to bid him farewell—the only time Clay ever broke protocol to pay such respect to a German politician.[47] That gesture, coming from a man who had once sought to enforce "aloofness," symbolized Clay's acceptance of Reuter as an equal and reflected the *SPD's* special position as the "American" party in Berlin.

Conclusion

When occupying powers voluntarily withdraw from exercising control over conquered territories, they have achieved a positive end to their mission. The US military government in Berlin terminated under particularly auspicious conditions. American officials had secured not only the cooperation of West Berlin's population in reestablishing orderly life in the city but also its willing and self-conscious association with American policies and aims. At the same time, West Berlin leaders had realized their own purpose of committing the United States to West Berlin's defense.

The American success, however, resulted only partially from US decisions and actions. American officials had the power to impose discipline on unruly soldiers, to reduce the burden of requisitions, and to give the occupation a more beneficent face through administrative enactments affecting US agencies and military personnel. But the most that could be attained by such measures was respect for US authority. The military government's wider success—in particular, winning the ideological struggle in Berlin—is traceable in large measure to favorable circumstances.

One such circumstance was the political party landscape in occupied Berlin. Americans did not create a political partner in the city; they found one who was already there. That partner—the Berlin *SPD*—belonged to a national party founded during the reign of Kaiser Wilhelm I. It had been a pillar of the Weimar republic and the dominant party in Prussia and in "red" Berlin. *SPD* members had served in parliaments, in national and state cabinets, and in all levels of civil service. (Indeed, all postwar parties in Berlin—the *CDU*, *LDP*, *KPD*, and *SPD*—stemmed from pre-Weimar formations and were well-rooted in German society. All had resumed activity before US forces arrived in Berlin.) The fact that Americans found West Berlin's *SPD* so ideal a partner owed to its own history and traditions, not to American inspiration. Its social reform concepts, democratic identity, and fierce anti-communism had been internally generated. Thus, US officials were working with an existing political force in Berlin rather than making it anew.

A second key circumstance was egregious Soviet mistakes. As Soviet denazification policies demonstrate, the Soviet Military Administration in Germany (*SMAD*) was clearly sensitive to German opinion. There is little evidence, moreover, of an orchestrated plan to "sovietize" the Soviet zone of occupation. Instead, up until the founding of the East German state in October 1949, the *SMAD* seemed to be struggling to keep the option open of securing Soviet aims in alliance with amenable Liberals and Christian Democrats. However, the Soviets could never capitalize on their possibilities. The coerced union between the *KPD* and *SPD* is only one example of the dysfunction of Soviet strong-arm methods. Operating independently of *SMAD*, the secret police applied accustomed Stalinist tactics without regard for political consequences and unknowingly violating legal principles. Despite attempts to compete for German favor, the Soviets came to be feared and detested. The corollary of this was that Berlin's population looked to the Western Allies for protection. In such a situation, any irritations with Americans became insignificant.

The third key circumstance was the imminent founding of a West German state. The strengthening of the bizonal administration in spring 1947 clearly presaged Germany's partition. In summer 1947, the Soviets launched a political offensive aimed at forging a common front with German non-Communists around the battle cry of national unity.

While Americans regarded such appeals to Nationalists and "susceptible" Conservatives as the chief political threat to their program, the imminence of partition only made Berliners more desperate for US protection.[48] The founding of a Western state would rob Berlin of its central importance and leave it an island in Soviet-occupied territory. Such a prospect intensified Berliners' desire to settle into an American embrace. The Soviet blockade of Berlin confirmed their dependency on the United States. Thus, although US officials had feared the Soviets would exploit the unity issue, the imminent division of Germany redounded to America's favor in Berlin.

The key talent US military government officials displayed in Berlin lay not in their ability to fashion democratic structures from a void but rather in their efforts to revitalize positive institutions and traditions. The Soviets often displayed the same such talent. In particular, restoring Berlin's cultural life owed greatly to Soviet efforts, but individual Soviet officers' good approaches were stultified by Stalinist contamination of the overall occupation. US officials had the decisive advantage of having grown up under conditions of liberal democracy. For them, respect for constitutional norms was second nature, not a tactic. Soviet officials had to work too hard to observe such norms, did not fully understand what they meant, and could not sustain them over time.

In sum, the shift of US-German relations in Berlin had much to do with given conditions and Soviet mistakes. Real frictions had divided US occupying forces from Berlin's public. The fact that both sides would end by seeing chiefly the positive aspects of each other owes to situational factors that proved favorable to the United States. If these factors had been absent, different outcomes are readily conceivable.

Notes

1. JCS 1067/8, Directive to the Commander-in-Chief of the United States Forces of Occupation Regarding the Military Government of Germany, 10 May 45, in US Department of State, *Documents on Germany 1944-1985* (Washington, DC: US Government Printing Office [GPO], 1985), 17-18.

2. *Time*, 16 May 49, 16.

3. Ibid., 262-64. The Office of US Military Government in Berlin was disbanded in September 1949. The British and French continued to call their political missions "military government," although these were neither "military" nor "government."

4. Memo, G5 for Ambassador Robert Murphy, Political Adviser [POLAD] to Supreme Headquarters, Allied Expeditionary Force (SHAEF), 24 Apr 45, Subject: Political Considerations for the Guidance of Military Government Officers in Making Appointments in Germany; Letter, Brigadier General (BG) Frank Sherry, Deputy Assistant Chief of Staff, G5, to Robert Murphy, 31 Mar 45; Letter, Robert Murphy to BG Frank Sherry, 4 May 1945, POLAD file 32/10, Bundesarchiv Koblenz (*BAK*).

5. Memo, Mortimer B. Wolf, Assistant Chief, Labor Relations Branch, US Group, Control Council for Assistant Direction, Manpower Division, 25 May 1945, Subject: Place of Émigré German Trade Unionists in the Post-War Labor Movement in Germany, POLAD TS file 32/48, *BAK*.

6. Political Intelligence Report, Joint Intelligence Committee (JIC), SHAEF, JIC SHAEF (45) 22 (Final), 14 May 1945, transmitted in Letter, POLAD to State Department, 18 May 1945, POLAD file 32/48, *BAK*; Letter, Robert Murphy to State Department, No. 359, 12 May 1945, POLAD file 32/73, *BAK*.

7. History Report, HQ, Berlin District, Report of Operations, 1 January-31 March 1946, Office of Military Government (OMGUS) file 5/35-3/11, Landesarchiv, Berlin (LAB), 37-43; History Report, HQ, Berlin District, Report of Operations, 1 April-30 June 1946, OMGUS file 5/35/12, LAB, 22-24.

8. Memo, [Kurt Riess for Alan Dulles], 5 Mar 45, Subject: Anti-Nazi Groups in Germany and Austria, POLAD file 729/45, *BAK*.

9. Report, G2, HQ, Berlin District, Intelligence Summary for Week Ending 8 December 1945; Report, G2, HQ, Berlin District, Intelligence Summary for Week Ending 5 January 1946; Report, G2, HQ, Berlin District, Intelligence Summary No. 45, 10-20 July 1945; Repor, G2, Intelligence Summary No. 47, 8-14 August 1946, author's files.

10. Opinion Survey, Information Services Control Section, Office of US Military Government, Berlin Sector (OMGBS), Subject: Survey of Attitudes Toward the Nürnberg trial, 24 Jan 46, OMGUS file 4/8-3/2, *BAK*.

11. Opinion Survey, Information Service Control Section, OMGBS, Subject: Survey of Attitudes Toward Restitution Problem, 4 Jan 46, OMGUS file 4/8-3/2, LAB.

12. Memo, Colonel (COL) T.J. Koenig, Office of Director of Intelligence [ODI] for the Deputy Military Governor (LTG Lucius Clay), 6 Jul 46, Subject: Comparative Figures on Troop Disorders, OMGUS, file 1945-46/42/12, *BAK*.

13. History Report, HQ, Berlin District, Report of Operations, 1 April-30 June 1946, OMGUS file 5/35-2/12, LAB, 87-89.

14. Postal Intercept, Civil Censorship No. BER/45/370, 5 Dec 45; Postal Intercept, Civil Censorship No.BER/45/374, 5 Dec 45, RG 260, Box 55, National Archives and Records Admini-

stration (NARA); Postal Intercept, US, Civil Censorship No. BER/1326; Postal Intercept, US Civil Censorship No BER/46/1658, 7 Mar 46, RG 260, Box 56, NARA.

15. Report, G2, HQ, Berlin District, Intelligence Summary for Week Ending 9 February 1946.

16. Memo, COL T.J. Koenig, ODI for Chief of Staff, Office of Deputy Military Governor, 4 Apr 46, Subject: Depredations of United States Military Personnel, OMGUS file 1945-46/42/14, *BAK*.

17. History Report, HQ, Berlin District and HQ, First Airborne Army, History and Report of Operations, 8 May-31December 1945, part 2, chapter 4, OMGUS file 5/35-3/8, LAB, 9-13, 17-19, 51, 56-57; Report, Information Services Control, HQ, Berlin District and HQ, First Airborne Army, Summary No. 15, 27 Aug 45, OMGUS file 5/242-3/13, LAB; Memo, MG James M. Gavin for LTG Dmitri I. Smirnov, [early Nov 45], Subject: Incidents Involving Red Army Personnel, OM-GUS file 1945-46/43/4, *BAK*.

18. Memo, COL Frank Howley, Director, OMGBS, for Commanding General, OMGUS, Subject: Payment for Requisitioned Furniture, 2 June 1948, Box 33, RG 260, NARA.

19. Memo, COL John Arrowsmith, District Engineer, Berlin District, for Chief of Staff, 24 Sep 46, Subject: Open Letter to Buergermeister of Zehlendorf, OMGUS file 4/135-2/9, LAB.

20. History Report, US HQ, Berlin District and HQ, First Airborne Army, History and Report of Operations, 8 May-31 December 1945, part 2, chapter 4, OMGUS file 5/35-3/9, LAB, 69-72; Letter, [illegible] to Mayor of Zehlendorf, 15 Aug 46; Letter, [anonymous] to Mayor of Zehlendorf, 25 Aug 46, OMGUS file 4/135-2/9, LAB. In one case, a German owner complained in March 1947 that her house had been requisitioned in September 1946 but was never occupied. Investigation confirmed her complaint. Letter, Frau Käthe Fichtner to COL Frank Howley, Director, OMGBS, 16 Mar 46; Memo, Major (MAJ) Lee Burnham, Military Government Liaison Officer, Zehlendorf, for COL Howley, 27 Mar 47, Subject: Letter From Frau Fichtner, OMGUS file 4/135-2/1, LAB.

21. Letter, Wittgenstein, Mayor of Zehlendorf, to COL Howley, 8 Feb 47, OMGUS file 4/135-2/1, LAB; Letter, [anonymous] to Mayor of Zehlendorf, 25 Aug 46, OMGUS file 1/135-2/9, LAB; History Report, Office of Military Government, Berlin District, Six Months Report, 4 Jan-3 Jul 46, vol. 8, 3, author's files.

22. Berlin *Senat*, *Quellen und Dokumente 1945-1951* (Berlin: Heinz Spitzing Verlag, 1964), 1:214-17; Wolfgang Leonhard, *Die Revolution Entlässt Ihre Kinder* (Cologne: Kiepenheuer & Witsch), 463-68.

23. Memo, MG James M Gavin, Commander, US HQ, Berlin District and HQ, First Airborne Army, for the Allied Kommandatura. Berlin, 29 Sep 45, Subject: Dismissal of Dr. Ernst F. Sauerbruch, OMGUS file 4/135-3/1, LAB; Minutes, Allied Kommandatura Berlin, 11 Oct 45, Ref: BK/M(45)14, OMGUS file 11/14-1/4, LAB.

24. Letter, Bishop Otto Debelius, Protestant Church Administration, Berlin-Brandenburg, to US Representative, Allied Kommandatura, 2 Mar 48, OMGUS file 4/10-3/30, LAB, hereafter cited as Letter from Debelius; Memo, Adoph J. Radosta, Chief, Security Review Board and Denazification Section, 16 Jun 47, Subject: History of Implementation of Directive No. 38, OMGUS file 4/38-3/7, LAB.

25. Memo, Adoph J. Radosta.

26. Memo, Eric C Wendelin, Office of High Commissioner, Berlin Element, for MG Maxwell C. Taylor, US Commandant, 29 Oct 49, Subject: Denazification and Nazi Activities,

OMGUS file 4/133-2/7, LAB; Memo, MAJ M.J. Kaspycki for Manpower Branch, 30 Oct 46, Subject: Interpretation and Application of Special Branch Decisions on Denazification Cases, OMGUS file 4/135-2/9, LAB.

27. Memo, Alfred J. Radosta for Chief Public Safety Officer, 27 Sep 46, Subject: Improvements in Review Procedure of Denazification Commissions in the US Sector of Berlin, OMGUS file 4/135-2/14, LAB.

28. Letter from Debelius.

29. JCS 1067/8, *Documents on Germany*, 17-18.

30. Message, Clay to Offices of Military Government (Bavaria, Hesse, Baden-Württemburg, Bremen, Berlin), 24 Jun 46, OMGUS file 1945-46/15/1, *BAK*.

31. Memo, LTC F.N. Leonard for the Director, Office of Military Government, Berlin District, 2 July 1946, Subject: Inviting Germans to Private Homes, OMGUS file 1945-46/15/1, *BAK*.

32. Clay oral history interview in Jean E. Smith, *Lucius Clay: An American Life* (New York: Henry Holt, 1990), 242.

33. History Report, HQ, Berlin District, Report of Operations, 1 April-30 June 1946, OMGUS file 5/35-2/12, LAB, 42-64.

34. History Report, HQ, Berlin District, Report of Operations, 1 Jan-31 Mar 46, OMGUS file 5/35-3/11, LAB, 71-76; History Report, HQ, Berlin District, Report of Operations, 1 April-30 June 1946, OMGUS file 5/35-5/12, LAB, 42-47.

35. Memo, MG Frank M. Keating for Chief of Staff, 20 Dec 46, Subject: Shooting at Anhalter Bahnhof; Memo, Commanding Officer, Berlin Command, for Provost Marshal, Berlin Command, 4 Dec 46, Subject: Shooting at Anhalter Bahnhof; Provost Marshal for Commanding Officer, Berlin Command, 6 Dec 46, Subject: Shooting at Anhalter Bahnhof, all in OMGUS file 17/162-1/10, *BAK*; Frank Howley, *Berlin Command* (NY: G.P. Putnum & Sons, 1950), 70-72.

36. Memo, Chief of Building, Housing, and Requisitioning Section for Chief of Economics Branch, OMGBS, 26 May 1948, Subject: 18 Months Report, OMGUS file 5/38-3/5, *BAK*.

37. Minutes, 9 Oct 46, Subject: Summary of the Third Monthly Meeting of US Sector BVK Buergermeisters and Chief of Staff With OMG, BD Officials, OMGUS file 4/135-2/9, LAB; History Report, HQ, Berlin Command, History of Activities, 1 November 1946-30 June 1947, OMGUS file 5/35-3/6, LAB.

38. Rpt, Office of Intelligence Research, State Department, OIR Report No. 4626, The Status of Denazification in Western Germany and Berlin, 15 Apr 48, RG 260, Box 30, NARA.

39. Leonhard, 550-53; Report, ODI, OMGUS, Weekly Intelligence Report No. 67, 23 Aug 47, OMGUS file 3/429-3/6, *BAK*, 25-29; Report, ODI, Weekly Intelligence Report No. 69, 6 Sep 47, OMGUS file 3/429-3/7, BAK, 34-37; Report, ODI, OMGUS, Weekly Intelligence Report No. 96, 13 Mar 48, BAK, L&D 7-9.

40. Memo, General Lucius Clay for COL Frank Howley, Director, OMGBS, Mar 48, Subject: Conclusion of the Denazification Program in the US Sector of Berlin, RG 260, Box 36, NARA.

41. Allied Kommandatura, Order BK/O(49)25, 16 Feb 49, Subject: Denazification; Allied Kommandatura, Order BK/0(49)72, 5 Apr 49, Subject: Denazification, OMGUS file 4/17-1/2, LAB; Allied Kommandatura, Order BK/O(49)159, 29 Jul 49, Subject: Denazification, OMGUS file 4/127-2/33, LAB.

42. For example, Report, Research Branch, Information Control Division, OMGUS, Special Report No. 4, Bureaucratic Trends in German Society, 7 Oct 47, RG , Box 130, NARA.

43. Report, Civil Affairs and Political Affairs Branch, OMGBS, Weekly Report, 7-13 Nov 47, OMGUS file 5/38/1/29, LAB.

44. Harold Hurwitz, *Zwangsvereinigung und Widerstand der Sozialdemokraten in der Sowjetischen Besatzungszone* (Cologne: Verlag Wissenschaft und Politik, 1990), 25-49, 141-60. The only high-level encouragement US officials received for their actions was a brief message from the Department of State calling on them to safeguard the personal safety of *SPD* members. Message, Secretary of State (Byrnes) to Political Adviser for Germany (Murphy), 13 Mar 46, US Department of State, *Foreign Relations of the United States*, 1946 (Washington, DC: GPO, 1969), 5:709.

45. Allied Kommandatura, Report BK/R(46)436, 30 Dec 46, Subject: Approval of Enactments of the Berlin City Council, OMGUS file 11/148-2/10, LAB; Minutes, Allied Kommandatura Deputy Commandants, BKD/M(47)1, 3 Jan 47, OMGUS file 11/149-1/2, LAB; Minutes, Allied Kommandatura Commandants, BKC/M(47)1, 7 Jan 47, OMGUS file 11/148-3/9, LAB; Message, Steel No. 1577 to Foreign Office, 7 Dec 46, FO 371/55906, Public Record Office (PRO), London; Letter, Political Division, Control Commission for Germany (British Element) to Foreign Office, 31 Mar 47, FO1049/838, PRO.

46. Willy Brandt and Richard Löwenthal, *Ernst Reuter: ein Leben für die Freiheit* (Munich: Kindler Verlag, 1957), 468-83.

47. Willy Brandt, *Mein Weg nach Berlin* (Munich: Kindler Verlag, 1960), 239-44; Brandt and Löwenthal, 428, 432-35; Smith, 554-55; James P. O'Donnell, "The Mayor Russia Hates," *Saturday Evening Post*, 5 February 1949, 26-27, 108-10; *Time*, 18 September 1950, 16.

48. See William Stivers, "*Amerikanische Sichten auf die Sowjetisierung Ostdeutschlands 1945-1949*," *Sowjetisierung und Eigenständigkeit in der SBZ/DDR , 1945-1953*, Michael Lemke, ed. (Cologne: Böhlau Verlag, 1999), 295-304.

Ps, Gs, and UW—Korea Style

Richard L. Kiper

Those who are familiar with the history of Army special operations will recognize the terms OSS, SOE, Detachment 101, and Jedburgh—all terms are associated with unconventional warfare (UW) conducted during World War II.[1] Few who are familiar with the foregoing terms, however, have heard of Donkeys; the Far East Command Liaison Group (FEC/LG); the 8086 Army Unit (AU); 8240 AU; the Combined Command for Reconnaissance Activities, Korea (CCRAK); or the Joint Advisory Commission, Korea (JACK)—terms associated with UW during the Korean war.

The military legacy of Korea has been Task Force Smith, Inchon, the Yalu River, Chosin Reservoir, Heartbreak Ridge, and the 38th parallel. Yet, while conventional soldiers were fighting initially for survival and finally to reestablish a free South Korea, guerrillas and partisans—aided by a few American soldiers—were conducting an active UW campaign behind the lines of North Korean (NK) forces and the Chinese Communist Forces (CCF).[2] Although the 50th anniversary of the Korean war has given rise to several works that examine the previously unrecognized role of partisan operations in that conflict, UW remains a little-known story of the Korean war.

During World War II, the Office of Strategic Services (OSS) provided the United States with the ability to perform UW. But three weeks after World War II ended, President Harry S. Truman disbanded the OSS, and the American military capability to perform unconventional operations disappeared.[3] Not until the National Security Act of 1947 created the Central Intelligence Agency (CIA) did the US government formally acknowledge the need for a UW capability. National Security Council (NSC) Directive 10/2, *National Security Council Directive on Office of Special Projects*, 18 June 1948, assigned the CIA responsibility to "conduct covert operations," to include "direct action, including sabotage . . . assistance to underground movements . . . [and] guerrillas."

NSC Directive 10/2 also directed the Joint Chiefs of Staff to assist the CIA during "wartime covert operations." The Joint Chiefs implemented the military's portion of 10/2 through a 1 March 1949 memorandum, "Study on Guerilla Warfare," which stated the Army "shall be assigned primary responsibility for all other guerrilla warfare functions."[4] But not until September 1950 when Secretary of the Army Frank Pace forced the Army to activate the Office of the Chief of Psychological Warfare under Brigadier General Robert A. McClure was there a branch of the Army G3 section responsible for UW.[5]

General (GEN) Douglas MacArthur, commander, US Far Eastern Command (FECOM) in 1950, had a long-standing antipathy toward the OSS during World War II. It is therefore not surprising that when war came to the Korean peninsula on 22 June 1950 that the CIA (successor to the OSS) had only six personnel in Japan to plan and conduct UW operations.[6] The FECOM G2, Major General Charles Willoughby, had not detected any basis for conducting UW operations in Korea, although he had received unconfirmed reports of guerrilla resistance.

In fact, after United Nations (UN) forces landed at Inchon on 15 September 1950 and advanced north, Korean guerrillas rose up behind the UN advance and supplanted the communist North Korean government officials who had been in control since 1945. But after China entered the war, the UN forces were forced to withdraw from North Korea, leaving the Korean partisans in dire straits. The partisans soon withdrew to Hwanghae province on Korea's west coast. From there many were able to flee to nearby islands; others went into hiding.

Not until FECOM's Army component, the Eighth US Army (EUSA), received a message from Navy Task Force 95.7 on 8 January 1951 that there were 10,000 partisans in Hwanghae province were the reports of guerrilla resistance confirmed. The intelligence regarding the existence of such a large body of partisans was passed immediately to Colonel (COL) John McGee, the officer in the EUSA G3 responsible for UW. One week later, EUSA created within its G3's Miscellaneous Division, the Attrition Section that was responsible for partisan operations. By 23 January McGee had produced "Operational Plan Number One" for employing partisans to support an anticipated UN counteroffensive.

McGee's plan called for the establishment of three partisan units: William Able Base, soon renamed Leopard, that would operate off the west coast of Korea, Kirkland that would operate off the east coast, and Baker Section that would conduct airborne operations throughout North Korea. The plan included a fourth unit, Task Force Redwing, which was actually a company of Republic of Korea marines that was organized to conduct raids and sabotage. McGee's Attrition Section was to command all the partisan units.[7] Thus began US Army UW operations against NK forces and CCF.

Immediately after McGee received the report of a potential partisan force on the islands off the west coast in January 1951, he sent Major (MAJ) William Burke to assess the situation and provide the force with weapons and ammunition. Burke learned that partisans occupied five islands, with the largest group being on the island of Paengnyong-do, which is just south of the 38th parallel. On the basis of Burke's report, McGee quickly revised Operational Plan Number One. Among the revisions was a provision that American officers would command each partisan base. The Americans would train and equip the partisan forces and deploy them in accordance with EUSA's orders.[8] After making his report, Burke quickly assembled a staff and returned to Paengnyong-do in February to establish a partisan training program.

Burke's new mission was to prepare the partisans to conduct guerrilla operations in conjunction with a planned UN counterattack that would force the NK army and CCF to withdraw at least to the 39th parallel. He moved quickly to establish training bases on Paengnyong-do, Taechong-do, Sok-to, and Cho-do.[9] By March the training bases were ready.

The partisans had organized themselves into bands whose leader was usually a prominent individual from the area that was home to that particular band. The bands referred to themselves as "donkeys." Three primary theories exist for that name, none of which former partisans can agree upon as **the** reason. One theory is that it originates from the Korean word "dong-li," which means "liberty." Another theory is that it refers to the traits of a donkey: mean, patient, and sturdy. A third theory is that the partisans thought they looked as if they were riding donkeys when operating the crank-driven generator for the AN/GRC-9 radio.[10] Whatever the origin, the name was a source of pride. So, too, would be their accomplishments.

Leopard Activities

On 3 March 1951, Donkey 1, led by former merchant Chang Jae Hwa, became the first donkey unit to return to North Korea's mainland. Chang and 37 partisans moved to the vicinity of Sari-won and Hwang-ju to obtain information about enemy movements on the main highway leading south from Pyongyang. When the partisans returned to the island base, Chang reported 280 enemy soldiers killed, and railroad and telephone links were cut.[11] On 5 March, Donkey 4 (known as the "White Tigers") landed on the mainland, followed by Donkey 7 on 27 March, Donkey 11 on 14 April, and Donkey 3 on 27 May.[12] Most donkey units had one or more American advisers, but existing records indicate that the Americans only occasionally accompanied the partisans on operations.[13]

One such operation was launched from Wollae-do, 2 miles off the NK coast, on 13 July 1952. An NK 76-millimeter gun was harassing the partisan base on Wollae-do as well as ships operating in coastal waters. Pak Chol, leader of Donkey 4, persuaded the US adviser on Paengnyong-do, First Lieutenant (1LT) Ben S. Malcom, that the gun had to be eliminated. After four months of intense training, Pak, Malcom, and 118 partisans boarded four junks and set sail for the mainland.

At 0430, according to plan, the US Navy began a 30-minute barrage of the objective. At 0500, Donkey 4 began its attack. With Navy air support, the partisans gained the top of the bunker that housed the gun; from there, they threw grenades through the apertures. Eventually they forced open the door leading into the bunker. Close-quarters fighting ensued, and several partisans were killed. Finally, Donkey 4 overcame all resistance and, using C-3 explosives, destroyed the gun and its bunker. When Navy aircraft reported that enemy reinforcements were moving in rapidly, the partisans began a wild run to the beach. Naval gunfire was invaluable as it covered the withdrawal. Soon Pak, Malcom, the partisan force, and 10 refugees reached Wollae-do.[14]

The mission was a success. Sustaining losses of six partisans killed and seven wounded, Donkey 4 had destroyed a hardened enemy position, killed approximately 60 enemy soldiers, and garnered an abundant haul of intelligence. Also important was that the partisan advisers' training techniques and skills had been proven effective. By accompanying the raiders, Malcom had gained great "face" with the Koreans. The raid also demonstrated that the North Koreans were not invulnerable.[15]

Baker Activities

Although the CIA began parachuting agents into North Korea shortly after the war began, Baker Section did not conduct its first airborne operation until 15 March 1951.[16] That night the Special Air Mission Detachment, 21st Troop Carrier Squadron dropped four Americans and 20 Koreans near Hyon-ni, 30 miles inland from the Sea of Japan, where the partisans were to destroy railroad tunnels. The Americans—three corporals and one private first class—were from the 4th Ranger Company and had volunteered for a classified mission.

The mission, code-named Operation VIRGINIA, was a disaster. The team missed the drop zone, and a blizzard delayed the team's arrival at its primary objective. Finding the tunnel to be too heavily defended, the team slowly moved east to attack another tunnel. After the attack, because of heavy cloud cover and cold so severe that it caused the team's radio batteries not to function, the team was unable to contact friendly units for two weeks.

When the team was able to make radio contact, the Navy dispatched three helicopters to rescue the team. One helicopter was shot down as it approached the pickup zone. The remaining two helicopters managed to hoist three Americans out, but heavy enemy fire prevented further evacuations. The pilot of the downed helicopter, the remaining Ranger, and seven Koreans escaped the site. The two Americans were captured after they had evaded the enemy for 10 days. They would not be released until 6 September 1953. Five of the seven Korean partisans returned to friendly lines on foot.

By the end of the war, Baker Section had conducted 19 airborne operations involving 389 partisans. Including the five returning partisans who returned from Operation VIRGINIA, only 10 of the 389 partisans returned. One American soldier and one British soldier were never heard from. Tangible results of Baker Section's airborne insertions were nil. A 1956 study concluded, "These decisions to use partisans against enemy supply routes in airborne operations appear to have been futile and callous."[17]

Kirkland Activities

Kirkland, the third partisan force, was organized in April 1951. Jurisdictional disputes between the Army and the CIA led to Kirkland's area of operations being limited to the area from Wonson south. The CIA conducted all operations north of Wonson. McGee transferred 1LT William S. Harrison from Donkey 4 to command Kirkland. Initially, one other US officer and two US enlisted soldiers assisted Harrison. Based on the island of Nam-do, Kirkland had the initial mission, as did Leopard, of supporting a major UN counteroffensive. When the UN did not mount the counteroffensive, Kirkland's mission changed to conducting coastal raids, collecting intelligence, and identifying targets for Navy air operations and naval gunfire. The scarcity of islands off Korea's east coast forced Kirkland to become a secondary partisan area. During the war, slightly more than 1 percent of partisan operations occurred along the east coast. By January 1952 only 11 Americans and 195 partisans had been assigned to Kirkland's region. Seventeen months later, Kirkland's personnel strength peaked at 4,844 partisans and 32 American advisers. Soon afterward, an increase in enemy troops along the east coast and the pending armistice led the UN to evacuate the partisans to islands south of the 38th parallel.[18]

Reorganizations

At the same time the Army's UW operations began, there also began a bewildering series of command changes, reorganizations, and redesignations as FECOM sought to establish the responsibility for UW. Fortunately for the Americans who worked closely with the partisan groups, the successive UW reorganizations had little direct impact on partisan operations.

Although the Attrition Section was established in January 1951 as part of the FECOM G3's Miscellaneous Division, an operational organization, the Attrition Section received its operational guidance from the FECOM G2 through a subsection known as the Far East Command Liaison Group (FEC/LG). On 11 April 1951, Lieutenant General

(LTG) Matthew Ridgway replaced MacArthur as commander of FECOM, and LTG James Van Fleet replaced Ridgway at EUSA. On 5 May, Van Fleet redesignated the Attrition Section as the Miscellaneous Group, 8086 Army Unit (AU), "to develop and direct partisan warfare."[19] Partisan operations were now the responsibility of an Army unit, not of a staff section.

On 26 July, Ridgway designated the FEC/LG as FEC/LG, 8240 AU. He also activated the Far East Command Liaison Detachment (Korea) [FEC/LD(K)], 8240 AU, in Korea. Initially, the FEC/LD(K) was responsible only for intelligence gathering; partisan operations remained the EUSA 8086 AU's responsibility.[20]

That arrangement changed dramatically on 10 December 1951 when, in an attempt to resolve jurisdictional disputes and to deconflict ongoing UW operations, FECOM created another organization, the Combined Command for Reconnaissance Activities, Korea (CCRAK), 8240 AU. The CCRAK, under command of the FEC/LG, assumed total control of all partisan operations.[21] The FEC/LG was based in Tokyo, and the CCRAK was based in Seoul. While EUSA retained some staff, administrative, and logistics functions to support guerrilla operations, all covert activities were to be the responsibility of one command at the theater level, at least on paper.[22] EUSA abolished the 8086 AU, but the FEC/LD(K) took over several of the 8086 AU's functions. Remaining under the FECOM G2's operational control, the FEC/LD (K) now had two sections, an intelligence section and a guerrilla section that controlled partisan operations.

The reason why there were jurisdictional disputes and conflicting UW operations was that while the US Army had been establishing a structure for managing partisan operations, the US Air Force and the CIA had been doing the same. In July 1950, one month after North Korea invaded South Korea, Hans Tofte, an OSS veteran, had arrived at CIA headquarters in Tokyo to take charge of the agency's covert operations in Korea in accordance with NSC Directive 10/2. Tofte began to recruit, train, and insert agents who would gather intelligence behind enemy lines. In July 1951, the CIA created an operational arm known as the Joint Advisory Commission, Korea (JACK) to insert agents.

In early 1951, the Air Force had created Special Activities Unit Number One, whose mission was to conduct guerrilla operations, but in March that portion of its mission was deleted. The Air Force allowed the CIA to use the Special Air Mission Detachment, 21st Troop Carrier Squadron, and aircraft from the 581st Air Resupply and Communications Wing to parachute agents into North Korea. The Air Force also operated a fleet of boats to insert agents into the north.[23]

At one time, therefore, three autonomous agencies planned and conducted guerrilla operations with no centralized control. After the Air Force relinquished any pretense to advising guerrillas in March 1951, the major issue over control of UW was between the Army and the CIA. Coordination between the two agencies was not improved by the bitterness that resounded between Tofte and FECOM G2's Willoughby.[24]

When Ridgway directed the creation of the CCRAK, he determined that to enhance coordination and reduce conflict the commander would be an Army officer and the deputy commander would be from the CIA. Unfortunately, although the CIA's JACK came under the operational control of the CCRAK, the orders that created the CCRAK did not place JACK under the CCRAK's command. Furthermore, CIA officers in Korea had no confidence in the FECOM G2 staff's ability to "command" operations. So while creating the CCRAK appeared to alleviate the bureaucratic bickering between the Army and the CIA, the reality was otherwise.[25]

By early 1952 it became apparent to the partisans who had believed they were to support a UN counteroffensive that they existed only to provide intelligence. Their perception changed on 1 October 1952 when the United States activated Army Forces, Far East (AFFE) as the theater Army component command. GEN Mark Clark, who had replaced Ridgway as FECOM commander, then removed the CCRAK from the FEC/LG's jurisdiction, renamed it AU 8242, placed it directly under AFFE, and gave it operational control over the FEC/LD(K). The FEC/LG remained a part of the FECOM G2 but provided administrative and logistics support to the CCRAK. Simultaneously, Clark directed that partisan strength be increased from 10,000 men to 20,000 by March 1953 and to 40,000 by 15 July 1953. On 10 May 1953, FEC/LD(K) Operation Plan Partisan Operations (K), phase IIA, directed that partisan activity be increased. FECOM also began drafting plans for a general offensive.[26]

Another organizational change occurred on 21 November 1952 when the guerrilla section of the FEC/LD(K) became the United Nations Partisan Forces, Korea (UNPFK). Of the guerrilla section's partisan units, Leopard, Wolfpack (created from part of Leopard on 1 January 1952), and Scannon (renamed from Kirkland in September 1952) became partisan infantry regiments. Baker Section became the 1st Partisan Airborne Infantry Regiment. In December, in a major shift in responsibility for guerrilla operations, Clark ordered that the FEC/LG become a support group for partisan operations and that the operations be returned to EUSA's control.[27]

In April 1953, FECOM formed two additional partisan infantry regiments. On 16 August 1953, FECOM, in cooperation with the Republic of Korea (ROK) government, established the 8250 ROK AU to provide administrative support to partisans. The last organizational change occurred in fall 1953. On 23 September, UNPFK became the United Nations Partisan Infantry, Korea. The CCRAK was abolished and was reestablished in Japan as the Combined Command for Reconnaissance Activities, Far East, 8177 AU. Simultaneously, the AFFE activated the AFFE Coordinating Detachment, 8078 AU in Korea to represent the AFFE's UW interests.[28]

Belated Doctrine

These organizational changes and shifts in responsibility for UW occurred during less than three years. Bureaucratic rivalries contributed significantly to the constantly changing landscape of lines and boxes on organization charts. Much of the flux resulted from the lack of Army doctrine to implement NSC Directive 10/2. To remedy the lack of doctrine, the Army began to draft two manuals. Field Manual (FM) 31-20, *Operations Against Guerilla Forces*, acquainted commanders with the "organization and tactics of guerillas" and provided "a guide for combating and destroying guerillas." FM 31-21, *Organization and Conduct of Guerilla Warfare*, addressed "organizing, training, commanding, and exploiting guerilla forces in war." Unfortunately, neither was published until 1951 and the latter not until October of that year.[29]

Retired COL Ben Malcom, who was the adviser to Donkey 4, made clear how this lack of doctrinal guidance affected those charged with executing the mission: "We were sent to conduct partisan operations with no knowledge of the history of these operations and no training in how best to implement them." He continued, "To my knowledge not a single copy of FM 31-21 ever filtered down to operational level."[30] The officers and enlisted men detailed to advise the partisan groups were on their own.

The only "doctrine" available to partisans before the Americans' arrival was the principle of war "surprise." Although the principle was not codified, as partisan leader Pak Chol stated, "Surprise is the whole of guerrilla warfare." Pak and other leaders knew that because they lacked training and equipment they could not stand against Regular Army units. All operations had to be planned to strike the enemy when it was least expected. No school prepared the partisans with studies of tactics; they learned from experience. "We guerrillas had no theory, but we had experience," said Pak. "In the experience we found the theory."[31] But experience is of little use without transportation, communications, weapons, ammunition, and training.

Compounding the problems resulting from the lack of doctrine and in-place organizations was the fact that, as retired COL Al Paddock put it, the Army's "unconventional warfare capability was non-existent."[32] After World War II, soldiers with UW experience who remained in the Army had been assigned to conventional units. The burden of providing trainers for the growing partisan force fell to McGee and his replacement, Lieutenant Colonel Jay Vanderpool (who had World War II experience with Filipino guerrillas), and soldiers such as 1LT Harrison (who had advised a South Korean guerrilla battalion) and a few Rangers who had been recruited when the Army disbanded all its Ranger companies in August 1951. Competing with the Army for the few available soldiers who had OSS experience was the CIA, which recruited officers such as MAJ John K. Singlaub who had served with the OSS in France and China. The shortage of experienced personnel was the reason that infantry officers, such as Malcom, with no language or UW experience and with no training to prepare them, were pressed into the role of UW adviser.[33]

Conclusion

What to make of the partisan, guerrilla, UW campaign of the Korean war? Did its operations have a material effect on the war? Between March 1951 and the armistice on 27 July 1953, partisans reported 4,445 combat actions and 69,084 enemy casualties. While these figures are impressive, they cannot be verified. Furthermore, because the CCF had an almost inexhaustible manpower pool, the number of casualties the partisans inflicted had virtually no effect on the outcome. The UW campaign's airborne operations, other than those the CIA conducted to gather intelligence, were complete failures. Until the beginning of truce talks, partisan activity did tie down enemy forces. Once the lines stabilized, however, the CCF and NKs were able to shift their forces to the coastal areas. The subsequent overwhelming number of enemy soldiers in those areas rendered partisan activity inconsequential.[34]

The operational ineffectiveness of partisan operations can be blamed on a number of factors:

- The lack of experienced guerrilla warfare personnel in the US Army as a whole.

- The inability of the Army and the CIA to work together consistently toward a common goal.

- The lack of understanding at FECOM of what partisans could do.

- The lack of US doctrine on UW.

The results of these shortcomings were:

- Haphazard mechanisms to identify soldiers with OSS experience.

- Assigning soldiers to a foreign culture that they did not understand.

- A lack of training, other than perhaps basic infantry training, to prepare them to organize and train partisan forces.

- A constantly changing command structure that only confused UW responsibilities.

- A rotation policy that allowed soldiers who gained in-theater UW experience to leave just when they could become most effective.

Not until 14 November 1986, when the US Congress passed the Nunn-Cohen Amendment to the Defense Reorganization Act, were many of the problems listed here resolved.[35] Nevertheless, the little-known story of UW during the Korea war and the courage of the Korean partisans, guerrillas, and their American advisers remain a notable chapter in the history of Army special operations.

Notes

1. The Office of Strategic Services (OSS), under the Joint Chiefs of Staff, was responsible for conducting unconventional warfare (UW) in both the European and Pacific theaters. The Special Operations Executive was the British equivalent. Detachment 101 conducted guerrilla operations for the OSS in Burma. Jedburgh teams coordinated French resistance to support Allied ground operations.

2. The *Dictionary of U.S. Army Terms* for 1950 defined partisan warfare as "activity carried on against an enemy by people who are devoted adherents to a cause, but who are not members of organized and recognized military forces." The dictionary defines guerrilla warfare as "operations carried on by small independent forces generally in the rear of an enemy." It does not define either "UW" or "special operations." In practice, guerrilla and partisan often were used interchangeably.

3. The same is true for Ranger and psychological warfare capabilities.

4. NSC 10/2, "National Security Council Directive on Office of Special Projects," <http://www.state.gov//www/about_state/history/intel/290_300 html>; "Memorandum for Record: Study on Guerrilla Warfare," 1 March 1949, National Archive Record Group 319.

5. Alfred H. Paddock, *U.S. Army Special Warfare: Its Origins* (Lawrence, KS: University Press of Kansas, 2002), 68, 93.

6. *The Clandestine Cold War in Asia, 1945-65: Western Intelligence, Propaganda and Special Operations*, Richard J. Aldrich, et al., eds. (London: Frank Cass, 2000), 22-23; John Prados, *Presidents' Secret Wars: CIA and Pentagon Covert Operations Since World War II* (New York: William Morrow and Company, 1986), 68.

7. Message, CTG 95.7, to Eighth US Army Korea, 080135Z Jan 51; Rod Paschall, "Special Operations in Korea," *Conflict* (1987), 158; Frederick W. Cleaver, et al., *UN Partisan Warfare in Korea, 1951-1954* (Chevy Chase, MD: The Johns Hopkins University Operations Research Office, 1956), 30, 32, 39; Ben S. Malcom, *White Tigers: My Secret War in North Korea* (Washington: Brassey's, 1996), 19. During World War II, McGee had been captured by the Japanese in the Philippines, had escaped, and then fought with Filipino guerrillas.

8. Ed Evanhoe, *Dark Moon: Eighth Army Special Operations in the Korean War* (Annapolis, MD: Naval Institute Press, 1995), 38, 40.

9. William Breuer, *Shadow Warriors: The Covert War in Korea* (New York: John Wiley & Sons, 1996), 161; Cleaver, et al., 32.

10. Evanhoe, 41; AFFE MHD 8086 AU, *UN Partisan Forces in the Korean Conflict*, 21, 94-94; Malcom, 56. Donkey 13 leader Mr. Kim Chang Song, provides the generator version as the reason for the name "donkey."

11. Ibid.; Armed Forces Far East (AFFE) Military History Detachment (MHD) 8086 Army Unit (AU), 47. Although Donkey 1 was the first partisan unit inserted behind enemy lines, the CIA had been inserting agents and using stay-behind agents. Known as Operation BLUEBELL, agents were to gather intelligence as opposed to conducing combat operations. Central Intelligence Agency (CIA), *CIA in Korea, 1946-1965* (Washington, DC: CIA, 1973), vol. 1, 100; CIA, vol. 3, 97; Prados, 69. The Tactical Liaison Office, a section of the FEC/ LG, recruited agents as line crossers to gather intelligence immediately behind enemy lines. The 25-man Korean teams, usually controlled by one American officer and two enlisted men, were attached to each front-line US division. Garth Stevens, et al., *Intelligence Information by Partisans for Armor* (Fort Knox KY: The Armored School, 1952), vol. 1, 19.

12. AFFE MHD 8086 AU, 47, 77, 99, 101, 117, 119.

13. Cleaver, et al., 13.

14. Malcom, 83-107.

15. Ibid,, 106-107.

16. The code name for clandestine airborne operations was AVIARY. Douglas C. Dillard, *Operation Aviary: Airborne Special Operations-Korea, 1950-1953* (Victoria, BC: Trafford, 2003), 4.

17. The CIA's first insertion of an intelligence team was on 9 December 1950. Stevens, et al., 1:10; Evanhoe, 50-51; Robert W. Black, *Rangers in Korea* (New York: Ballantine Books, 1989), 85; John W. Thornton, *Believed to be Alive* (Middlebury, VT: Paul S. Eriksson, 1981), 70-80, 100, 255; Michael E. Haas, *Apollo's Warriors: US Air Force Special Operations During the Cold War* (Maxwell AFB, AL: Air University Press, 1997), 44; Cleaver, et al., 52, 94; Lawrence V. Schuetta, *Guerrilla Warfare and Airpower in Korea, 1950-1953* (Maxwell Air Force Base, AL: Air University, 1964), 146-49. Some sources say 19 partisans were on Operation VIRGINIA.

18. Cleaver, et al., 32, 41, 82, 114, 117, 132, 158. In July 1951, 1LT Joseph Ulatoski replaced Harrison as commander of Kirkland Forward when Harrison returned to the United States. MAJ A.J. Coccumelli became commander of the entire Kirkland area of operations.

19. Headquarters, Eighth US Army, Table of Distribution 80-8086, Miscellaneous Group, 8086 Army Unit, undated, Record Group 319, National Archives, as quoted in Paddock, 104.

20. Cleaver, et al., 34-37.

21. Ibid., 37-39.

22. Ibid., 39.

23. Schuetta, 73-74, 77-78. The 581st also had H-19 helicopters that were used to insert agents. B Flight, 6167 Operations Squadron, eventually assumed the Special Air Mission Detachment's UW support missions. Haas, 66-75.

24. "National Security Council Directive on Office of Special Projects," NSC 10/2, 18 June 1948, National Archives and Records Administration, RG 273; Michael E. Haas, *In the Devil's Shadow: UN Special Operations During the Korean War* (Annapolis, MD: Naval Institute Press, 2000), ix, 40, 177-79; Paddock, 106.

25. Malcom, 27; Haas, *In the Devil's Shadow*, 41-42.

26. Cleaver, et al., 62-64, 66, 156, 162-65.

27. Haas, *In the Devil's Shadow*, 42; Headquarters and Service Command, FEC, General Order 21, 3 October 1952; Cleaver, et al., 67-68, 155-56. "United Nations Partisan Forces-Korea, 8240th AU (FEC/LD) Partisan Operations," <http://www.korean-war.com/SpecOpsRosters/UNPIK PART htm>.

28. Cleaver, et al., 112, 157; Harry G. Summers, *Korean War Almanac* (New York: Facts on File, 1990), 112.

29. Department of the Army Field Manual (FM) 31-20, *Operations Against Guerilla Forces* (Washington, DC: US Government Printing Office [GPO], February 1951), 1; FM 31-21, *Organization and Conduct of Guerilla Warfare* (Washington, DC: GPO, October 1951), 1.

30. Malcom, 40-41.

31. AFFE MHD 8086 AU, *UN Partisan Forces in the Korean Conflict, 1951-1952: A Study of Their Characteristics and Operations* (Tokyo: 8086 Army Unit, 1954), 66-67.

32. Paddock, 65.

33. Haas, *In the Devil's Shadow*, 37, 62-63, 65.

34. Stevens, et al., vol. 1, 13; Cleaver, et al., 16. In 1985, COL Glenn Muggleberg, former commander of UN Partisan Infantry, Korea, commented on the partisan reports. "The partisan reports were about as accurate as our own," he said. US Army Military History Institute Oral History Project 85-S, 15 November 1985.

35. Public Law 99-661 created the Office of the Assistant Secretary of Defense (Special Operations/Low-Intensity Conflict), established the unified US Special Operations Command, and dramatically increased funding for special operations. On 1 December 1989, the Army activated the Army Special Operations Command as a major Army command to command all Army special operations forces in the continental United States and to train all Army special operations soldiers.

Special Forces in Afghanistan: Oct 01-Mar 02

Richard W. Stewart

During combat operations in Northern Afghanistan as part of Operation ENDURING FREEDOM, Army Special Forces (SF) were asked to accomplish miracles. With little to no preparation, Army teams were to land by helicopter deep in hostile territory, contact members of the Northern Alliance, coordinate their activities in a series of offensives, bring the entire might of US air power to bear on Taliban and al-Qaeda forces, and change the government of Afghanistan so that Afghanistan was no longer a safe haven for terrorists. They accomplished all of this, and more, in the space of a few months. How? That is the question I will attempt to answer, although obviously the information at the moment is too sketchy for anything definitive.

Major Players

Task Force Dagger: K2, Uzbekistan, and Bagram AB, Afghanistan

    5th SFG (A)
    B/2/160th SOAR
    Air Force Special Opera ions

Northern Alliance Forces

Task Force K-Bar: Kandahar and Bagram AB, Afghanistan

Task Force 64: Kandahar

Coalition Joint Task Force Mountain: Karshi Khanabad, Uzbekistan, and then Bagram AB, Afghanistan

Coali ion Forces Land Component Command (CFLCC): Camp Doha, KU

Joint Combined Forces Special Operations Component Command (JCFSOCC)

Central Command: Tampa, FL

Task Force Bowie: Bagram AB, Afghanistan

These were some of the major units or headquarters involved in operations in Afghanistan in late 2001, early 2002. I will focus on Task Force (TF) Dagger because, initially, it carried most of the burden for US combat operations in the region. I was assigned to this TF for three months in early 2002 and can speak knowledgably about its operations.

TF Dagger, built around the 5th Special Forces Group (SFG) (A), was tasked to conduct special operations in support of a number of Northern Alliance commanders to gain their active assistance in overthrowing the Taliban regime. The three first contacts were with General (GEN) Abdul Rashid Dostum, GEN Mohammed Daoud, and GEN Mohammed Fahim Khan. It was important for SF to establish contact early with each of these leaders, provide them with the air support they needed, and work with them to establish a foothold in the northern part of Afghanistan before the winter came.

Task Force Dagger

Task Force Dagger: K2, Uzbekistan, and Bagram AB, Afghanistan

    5th SFG (A)
    B/2/160th SOAR
    Air Force Special Opera ions

TF Dagger JSOTF Headquarters, Uzbekistan

Karshi Kanabad (K2) Airfield, Uzbekistan

MH-47 Chinooks and MH-60 Black Hawks at K2

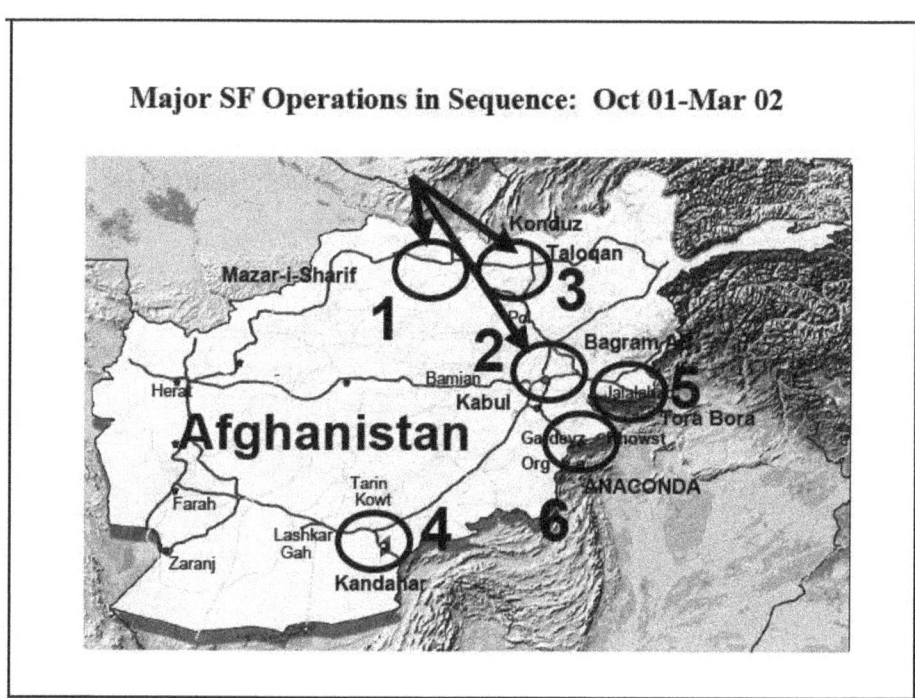

The concept of the operation was to land teams in the Mazar-i-Sharif and Konduz-Taloqan areas, followed by insertions into the Bagram-Kabul area before moving on to the Tora Bora mountains region, a known al-Qaeda training site. Finally, the mission was to liberate Kandahar, the center of the Taliban movement. The SF teams were to coordinate the various Northern Alliance factions' operations and ensure that they worked together, in conjunction with US air power, to break the stalemate and defeat the Taliban and its terrorist allies.

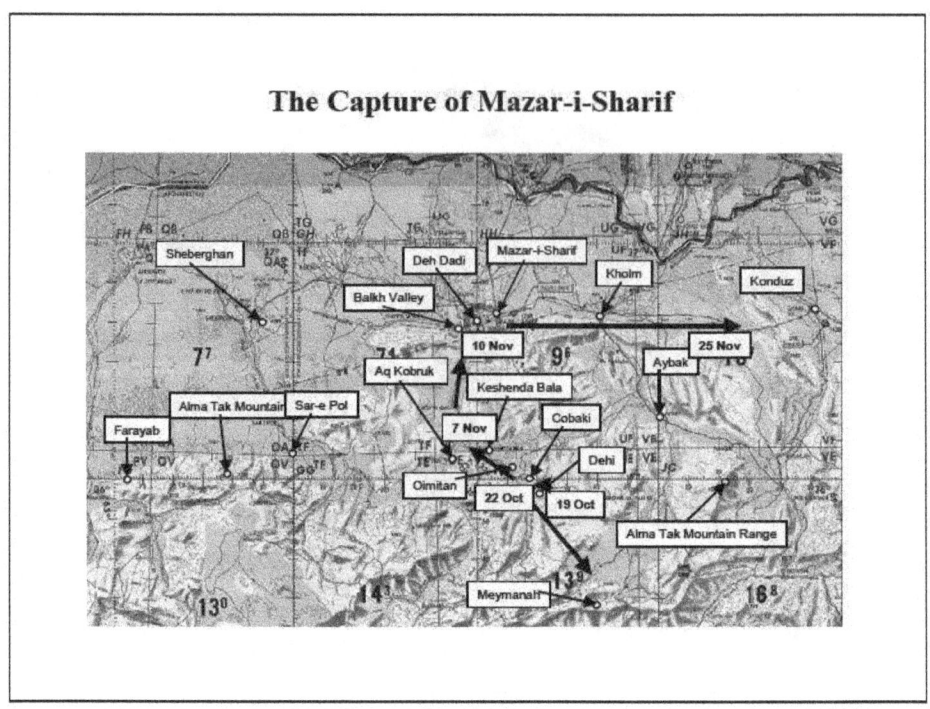

The Capture of Mazar-i-Sharif

Working out of an abandoned Soviet air base in Uzbekistan, TF Dagger launched its first teams into Afghanistan in mid-October. The first 12-man SF team, radio call sign Tiger, infiltrated into northern Afghanistan to the south of Mazar-i-Sharif via helicopter on 19 October 2001. These insertions and the ones that followed were all at night, flying into mountains up to 18,000 feet high, with clouds and sandstorms limiting visibility. The insertion alone was highly dangerous.

After a 2 ½-hour hazardous journey through high mountains and extremely poor weather, team Tiger reached its landing zone south of the city of Mazar-i-Sharif where it linked up with the local warlord, GEN Dostum.

General Abdul Rashid Dostum

The team then split into two elements to better assist GEN Dostum's scattered forces.

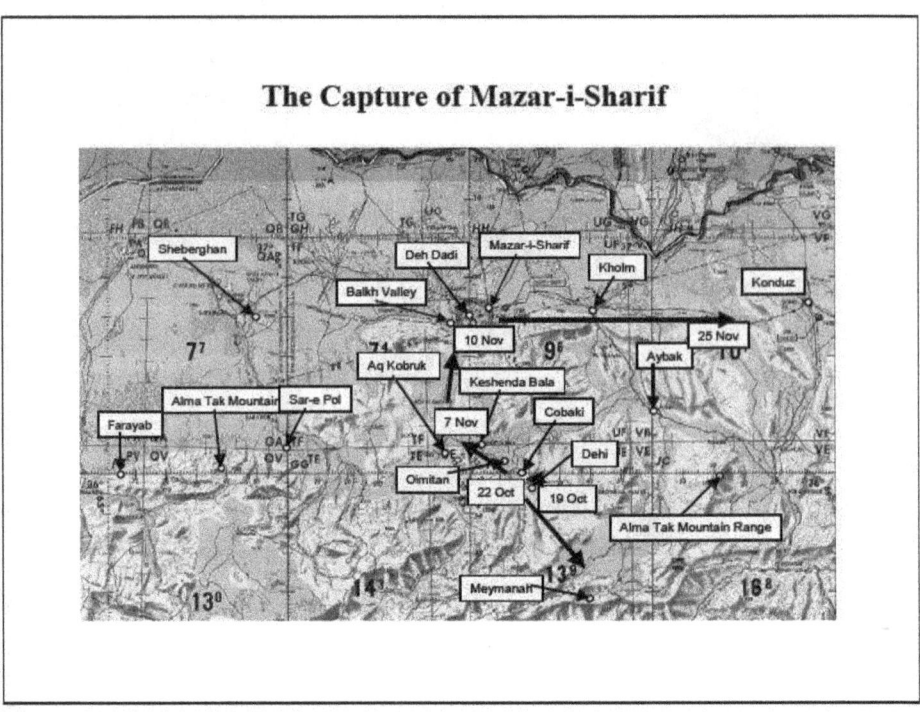

The Capture of Mazar-i-Sharif

From 19-24 October, the team operated as a split team. The Alpha element rode on horseback north into the mountains near Keshenda Bala along with GEN Dostum to help him plan the attack on Mazar-i-Sharif. The Bravo element moved south into the nearby Alma Tak Mountains to attack the Taliban in the southern Darya Suf Valley.

Team Alpha quickly began helping Dostum directly by calling in close air support (CAS) from US B-1 and B-52 bombers and F-14, -15, -16, and -18 fighter bombers. At first, however, the team was not permitted to move forward close enough to the Taliban positions to be most effective. Dostum was afraid team members would be killed or captured. On several occasions, he told the Tiger leader "500 of my men [Northern Alliance troops] can be killed, but not one American can even be injured or you will leave." The SF had to call in CAS from a distance of 8 to 10 kilometers (km) away from the targets, looking across the Darya Suf Gorge. Weather conditions made visibility extremely hazy, even with binoculars and spotting scopes. Eventually this barrier was broken when it became obvious the team could take care of itself. The Tiger element was soon able to choose observation post (OP) locations at its discretion, regardless of the element of danger as Dostum began his move north to Mazar-i-Sharif.

SF on Horseback

The massive CAS the SF brought down had a huge and immediate psychological effect on the Taliban, causing panic and fear and a correspondingly positive effect on GEN Dostum's men. Starting on 22 October, the Tiger element, traveling on horseback in support of Dostum's cavalry, decisively demonstrated to the Afghans the US commitment to their cause. From an OP near the villages of Cobaki and Oimitan, it began systematically calling in CAS missions. In one 18-hour period, CAS destroyed more than 20 armored vehicles and 20 support vehicles. The Taliban began to reinforce its troops heavily, sending reserves into the area from Sholgerah, Mazar-i-Sharif, and Kholm. All that did was provide more targets for the CAS teams. Numerous key command posts, armored vehicles, troop concentrations, and antiaircraft artillery pieces were destroyed.

Meanwhile, the Bravo element, also on horseback, moved to the Alma Tak Mountain range to link up with one of Dostum's subordinate commanders. The mission was to engage Taliban units in the southern Darya Suf Valley, preventing them from mounting a coordinated counterattack against Dostum and denying the Taliban the ability to resupply its forces. Bravo element would continue to interdict and destroy Taliban forces from these mountains until 7 November, destroying more than 65 enemy vehicles, 12 command bunker positions, and a large enemy ammunition storage bunker.

The two Tiger elements' airstrikes caused a crumbling effect, breaking the Taliban defensive positions wide open. Many Taliban vehicles and troops were killed, and those who were not killed fled for their lives north to Mazar-i Sharif. Very few Taliban reached the city without being killed or captured. GEN Dostum's forces were able to continue to conduct cavalry attacks into the Darya Suf and Balkh Valleys. During these attacks, the

SF was in the forefront of the action, on horseback, even though only one member of the team had ever ridden a horse extensively. Dostum continued to pursue the Taliban toward Mazar-i-Sharif.

The SF was a critical element of support to the Northern Alliance troops in their assault through the pass just south of Mazar-i-Sharif. This was a natural chokepoint, and the enemy was there in force. Moving over treacherous terrain on horseback and on foot, the SF moved into a forward mountain OP and, on 9 November, engaged Taliban defenses on the north side of the pass with CAS. The CAS efforts destroyed several vehicles, a number of antiaircraft guns, and numerous troop concentrations. Coming under direct effective enemy BM-21 multiple rocket launcher fire on two separate occasions, the SF continued to engage Taliban forces with B-52 strikes. The B-52 strikes broke the Taliban's back, and it began retreating to Mazar-i-Sharif.

SF at the Fall of Mazar-i-Sharif

With the way to victory opened up to him by SF, GEN Dostum and his subordinate commanders quickly secured the city of Mazar-i-Sharif on 10 November. Riding with Dostum into the heart of the city, the SF team watched as local Afghan citizens lined the streets, cheering and bringing gifts to GEN Dostum. This triumphal progress into the city ended at the medieval fortress of Quali-Jangi where Dostum established his headquarters (HQ).

The Fortress of Quali-Jangi

This was GEN Dostum's former HQ when he was in command of the city before the Taliban came to power. The capture of Mazar-i-Sharif was the first major victory by US forces in the war in Afghanistan. The United States now had a strategic foothold and an airport in northern Afghanistan.

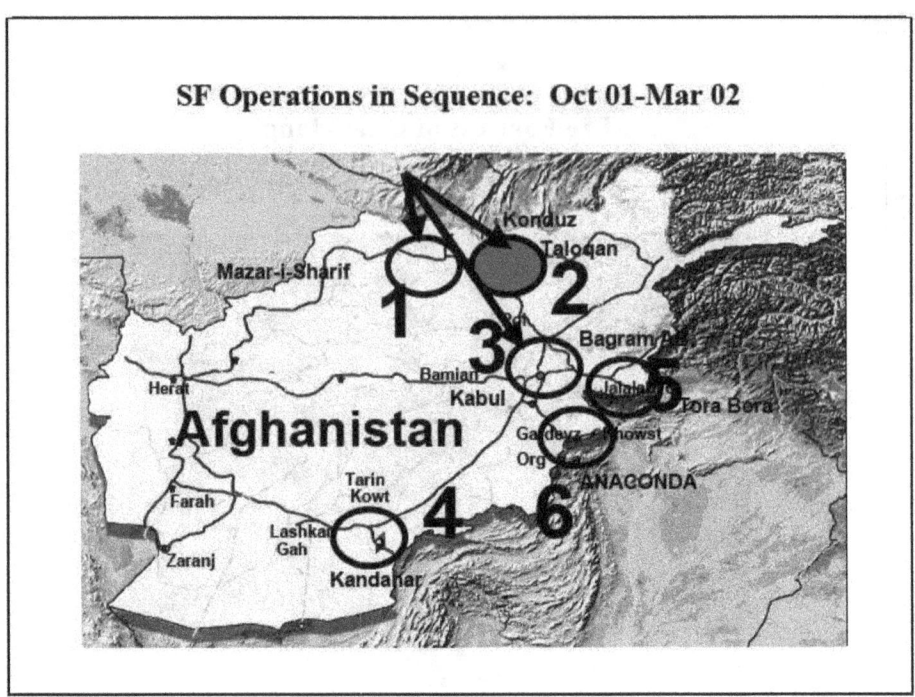

Now the targets shifted to the area to the east of Mazar-i-Sharif to the Taloqan-Konduz area.

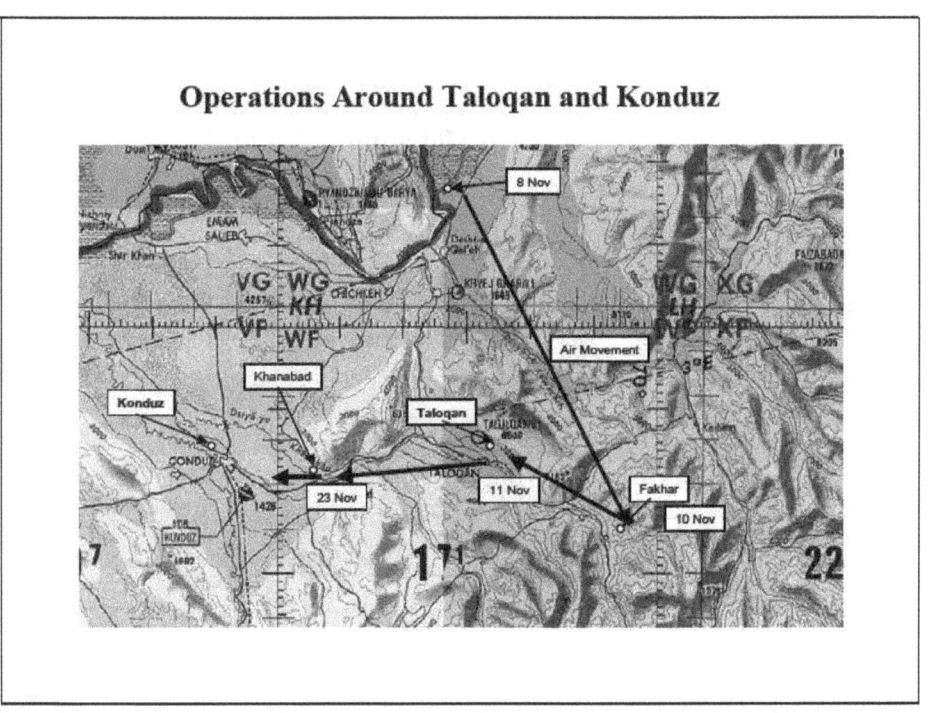

Operations Around Taloqan and Konduz

SF teams had infiltrated into the area on 8 November and moved quickly to link up with GEN Daoud, a prominent Northern Alliance warlord.

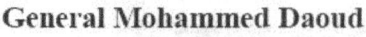

Soon the SF soldiers were overlooking enemy positions near the city of Taloqan. They began setting up their OPs to call in CAS.

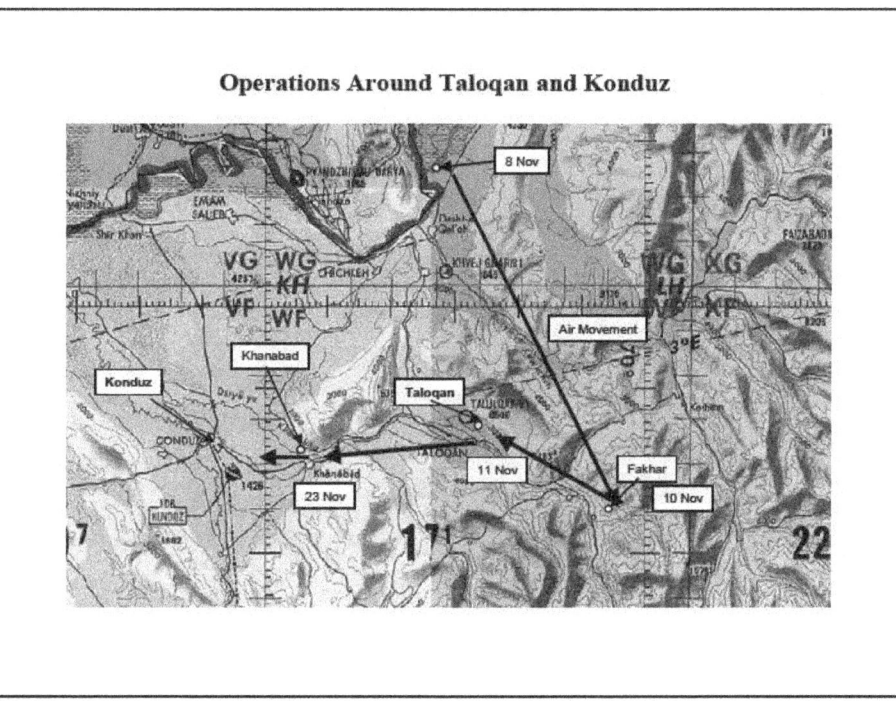

However, before the SF soldiers could call in the first mission against Taliban positions, GEN Daoud started his offensive, and his front lines quickly moved past the line of sight of the OP. By the end of that night, Taloqan fell with little resistance. A major victory had occurred almost without a fight, based solely, it seems, on Dostum's new confidence in US support and air power.

After the fall of Taloqan on 13 November 2001, SF continued its primary mission of assisting Daoud's combat operations with CAS as Daoud began moving west toward the city of Konduz. To accommodate both CAS operations and team sustainment, the SF team split into three teams. On any given day, one CAS team would be on or forward of the front lines at an OP calling CAS, while another was recovering from its CAS operations the previous day. The third element was preparing for its CAS operations the next day. Thus, the team established a one day on, two days off rotation cycle, maintaining 24-hour-a-day airstrikes on enemy positions blocking the advance to Konduz.

Up to this point, GEN Daoud had met very little Taliban resistance. Taloqan had fallen without a fight. But on 13 November, Daoud met his first heavy resistance when one of his commanders attacked enemy positions without orders, triggering a Taliban counterattack. While receiving both direct heavy weapons fire and indirect tank fire, the SF CAS team for that day repositioned to a different OP, called in CAS on the Taliban, and helped Daoud repel the attack. This marked increase in Taliban resistance, however, altered Daoud's plan of attack. Instead of trying to blitz through the Taliban all the way to Konduz, Daoud entrenched his forces and decided to use heavy US air attacks to weaken the Taliban, setting the conditions for a successful attack or forcing the Taliban into surrendering.

SF at Konduz Calling in Close Air Support

For the next 10 days, SF called in CAS to pound Taliban entrenched positions in and around Khanabad and Konduz. Over the course of these CAS operations, the SF teams destroyed 12 tanks, 51 cargo trucks, 44 bunker complexes, and numerous other vehicles and supply dumps while inflicting losses on the Taliban and al-Qaeda of around 2,000 killed or wounded.

By the end of 11 days of intense CAS bombing, GEN Daoud captured the nearby city of Khanabad and was prepared to move on Konduz. He then opened up negotiations with Taliban leaders in Konduz, and they, seeing that their position was hopeless, agreed to surrender on 23 November. Konduz, the last Taliban stronghold in northern Afghanistan, was under Northern Alliance control.

No one was prepared, however, for the Taliban forces' wholesale surrender. More than 3,500 Taliban troops surrendered in the Konduz area faced with the threat of the combination of Northern Alliance ground forces and American air power concentrated on the ground by SF. Many of these forces were moved quickly, but without fully disarming them, to join GEN Dostum's prisoners in the Quali-Jangi prison in Mazar-i-Sharif.

During these two campaigns with the Northern Alliance forces, SF troops effectively liberated the six northern provinces including the key cities of Mazar-i-Sharif, Meymanah, Sare pol, Sheberghan, Heyraton, Auybak, Konduz, and more than 50 other towns and cities. To accomplish this, the SF had traveled by horse, all-terrain vehicles, pickup trucks, and on foot along hazardous mountain trails, often at night and in extreme weather through 100 miles of mountains, gorges, hills, and valleys. The SF accomplished all of this without any friendly US casualties and while inflicting thousands of casualties on the enemy and destroying its defensive positions.

The thousands of prisoners taken in this operation created a crisis in US operations, and it revolved around the fortress of Quali-Jangi.

The Fortress of Quali-Jangi

During interrogation operations in this fortress, some 600 poorly supervised al-Qaeda and Taliban detainees took over the prison compound. Two US intelligence officers were trapped and required immediate evacuation. SF personnel immediately responded by organizing a team of US and British SF to infiltrate the facility and bring back those the enemy forces held. As they neared the facility, the volume of enemy fire increased to include rocket-propelled grenade (RPG) rounds exploding in the team's immediate vicinity. The SF team requested CAS, even though it would be in the "danger close" range, and the risk was that bomb fragments would hit them even if the bombs were accurate. Throughout the next three days the team exchanged fire and used laser designator devices to illuminate enemy positions for airstrikes and for night attacks from circling AC-130 Spectre gunships. It was during this time that they received notification that Mike Spann, a missing intelligence officer, had fallen into prisoners' hands and was killed.

SF at Quali-Jangi

After five days of consistently engaging the enemy with fire and maneuver, during which time five US and British soldiers were medically evacuated for severe wounds received by exploding munitions, the battle came to an end by flooding the lower level of the facility where the prisoners were hiding. Out of the more than 600 prisoners at the facility, approximately 500 were killed while the remaining few surrendered.

10th Mountain QRF at Quali-Jangi

During this crisis, the first major element of US troops arrived from the 1-87th, 10th Mountain Division, assigned to provide base security initially at K2. They assisted the SF in perimeter security and in taking charge of and finally disarming the prisoners taken at Quali-Jangi and other nearby battles.

With winter closing in, it seemed as if the SF had accomplished all it could hope to in Afghanistan until spring. It was wrong. Let us now turn to the situation north of Kabul.

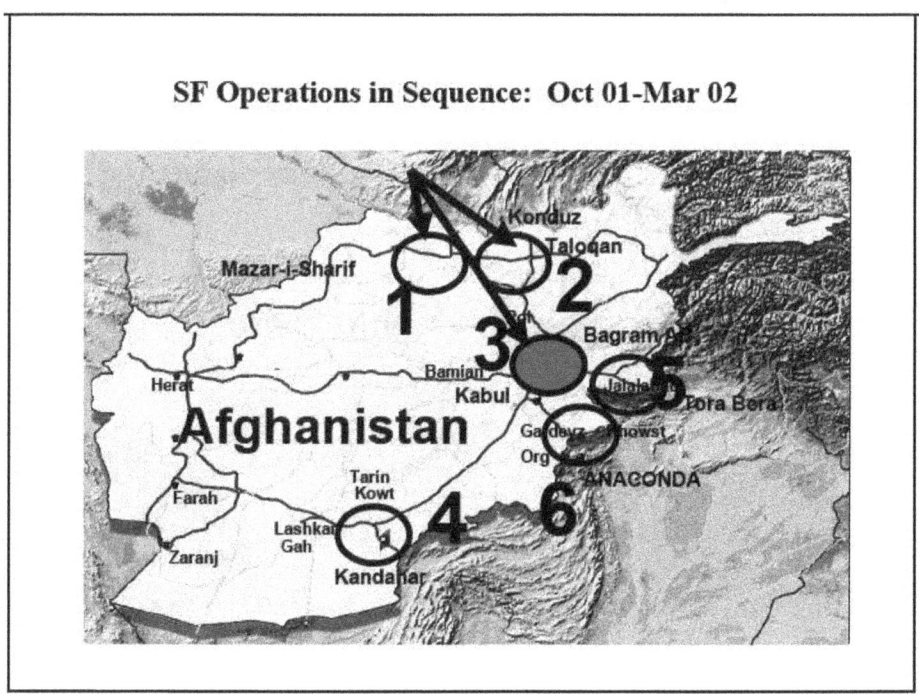

The Capture of Kabul

The situation near the capital city, Kabul, looked intractable. Northern Alliance forces north of Kabul near Bagram, an old Soviet air base, had been in a stationary position against the Taliban for close to five years. The Taliban could not penetrate the defensive minefields near the base nor attack into the rich Panjshir Valley. The valley was the home of Ahmed Shah Masood, the revered leader of the Northern Alliance that al-Qaeda agents assassinated on 9 September 2001, just days before they attacked America on 11 September.

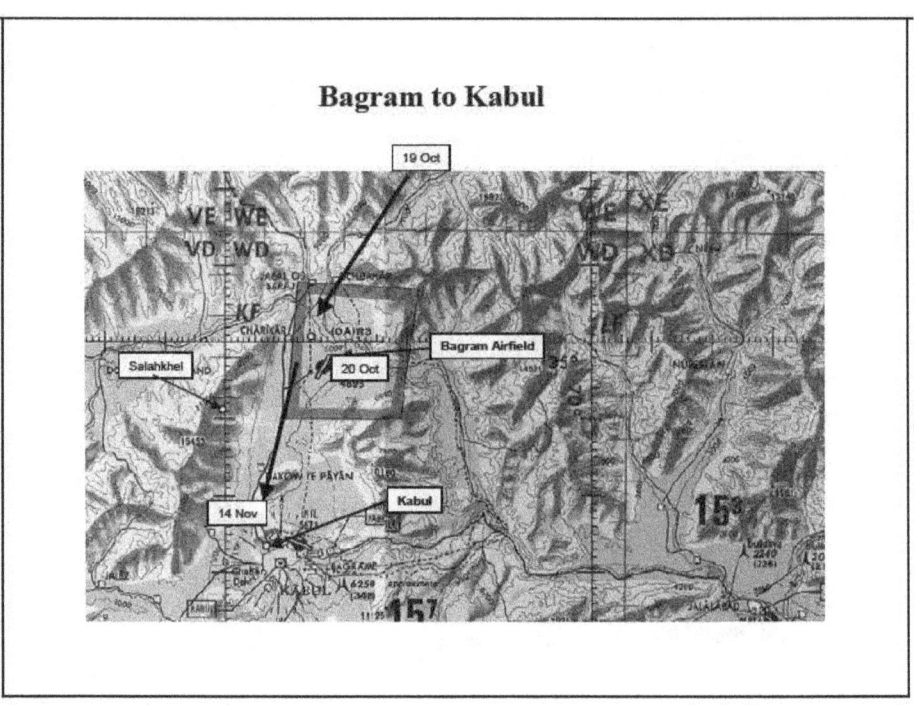

SF teams infiltrated into northeastern Afghanistan to assist the Northern Alliance forces, now under the overall command of GEN Fahim Khan and GEN Bismullah Khan, on 19 October 2001.

Fahim Khan   **Bismullah Khan**

CAS at Bagram: 20 Oct-14 Nov

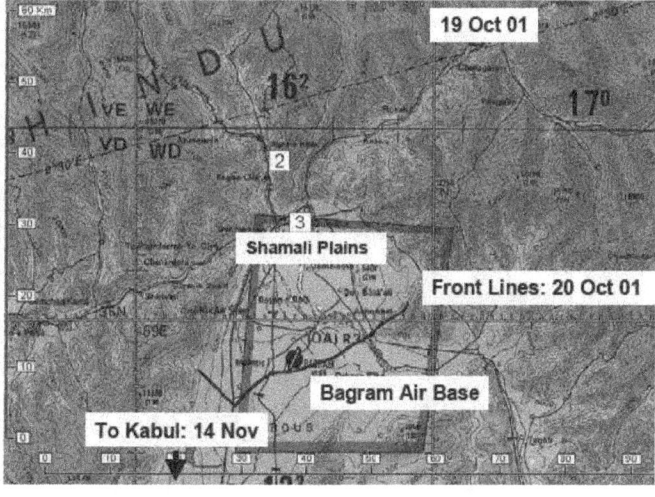

The next day, the team linked up with the alliance commanders at Bagram and began looking for vantage points in the valley to call in CAS. The team members noticed an ideal position and established an OP in the old air traffic control tower for the airfield. From this position, they immediately began calling in airstrikes on the entrenched enemy. From 21 October through 14 November 2001, SF teams directed 25 continuous days of CAS missions against the dug-in enemy. The constant air attacks degraded Taliban and al-Qaeda command and control, killed hundreds of entrenched front-line troops, and disrupted support elements. GEN Khan was encouraged to begin thinking about an immediate move against Kabul while the enemy was in disarray.

The Afghanis had originally planned a multiple-day, five-phased operation to attack Kabul. However, the Taliban and al-Qaeda forces were so weakened by airstrikes that when the attack was launched on 13 November, they crumbled. By noon on the first day of the offensive, the operation had achieved all of its phase three objectives. Twenty-four hours later, to the surprise of the world press and the delight of the Northern Alliance, GEN Khan's ground forces liberated Kabul. The Taliban and al-Qaeda fled in disarray toward Kandahar and into the nearby Tora Bora Mountains.

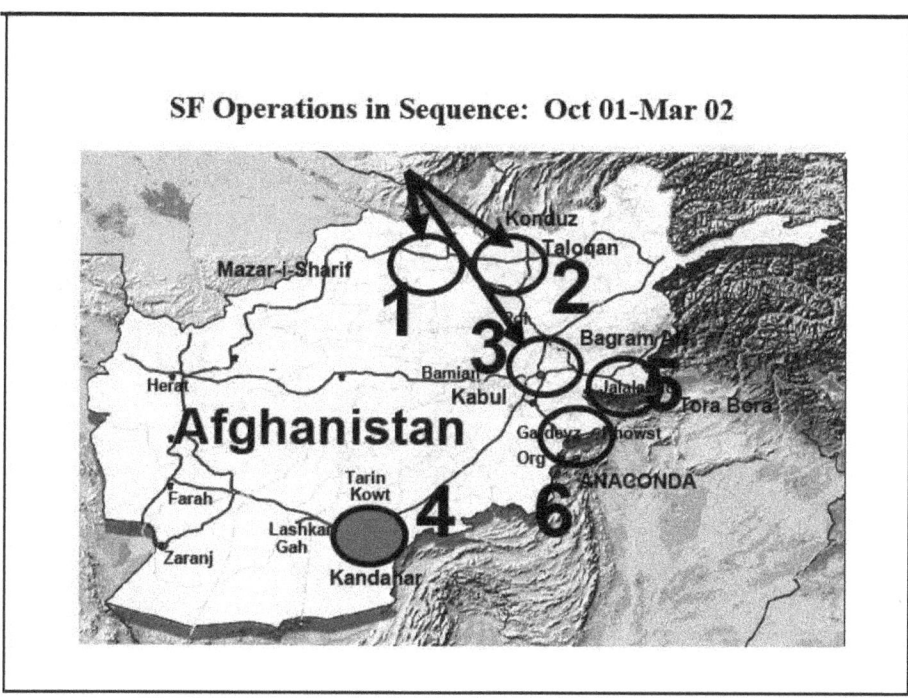

Special Forces: Two Approaches to Kandahar

Kandahar was to be the next objective. It was also suspected that it would be the hardest to take. The populous southern city was a long way from the Northern Alliance's region of control, was of a different ethnic makeup—Pashtuns, not Tajiks—and was the spiritual and political center of the Taliban movement. There was little or no opposition force in the area to work with. It seemed as if its capture would take months and might have to be delayed until spring. Still, two separate SF elements infiltrated the region and approached the city from the north and south with their supported host nation commanders picking up support along the way.

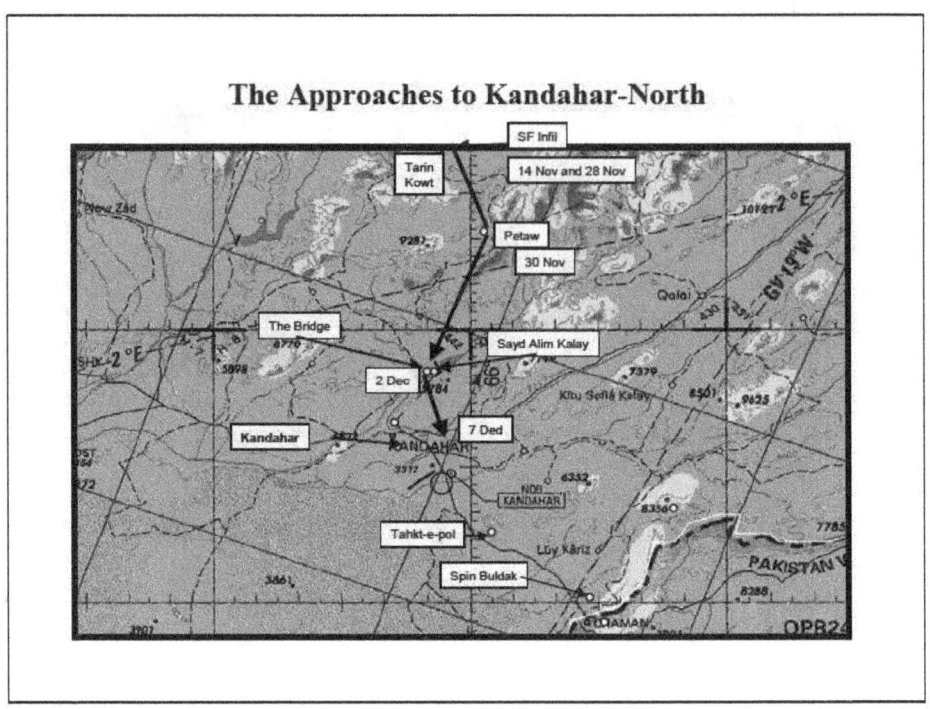

The first SF team was inserted north of Kandahar on 14 November. There it linked up with Hamid Karzai and a small number of his followers.

Hamid Karzai

Karzai was a charismatic Pashtun tribal leader from that area, and it was vital that the United States support his attempts to establish an anti-Taliban front in the region.

The SF team was almost immediately drawn into operations when, on 16 November, Taliban forces moved about 500 soldiers to crush Karzai. He deployed his handful of men near the village of Tarin Kowt but relied heavily on his new US allies to provide CAS. As US planes pounded the approaching Taliban, guided by SF teams on the ground, the Afghan opposition fighters rallied and repulsed the Taliban attack. The Taliban, stunned by an attack for which it had no defense, retreated in disarray.

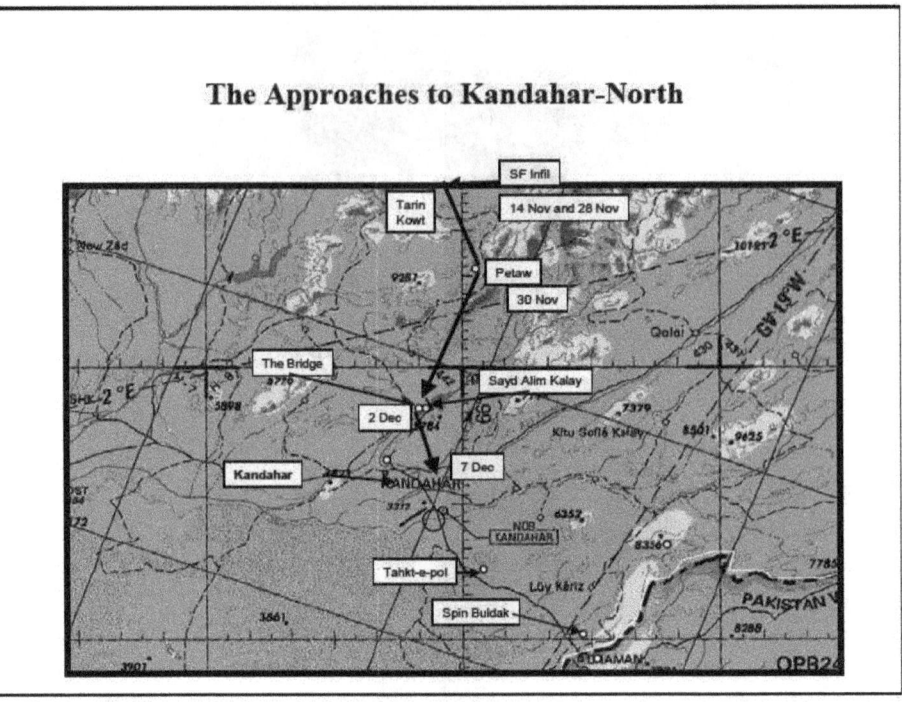

Having gained a breathing space, the SF team began working closer with Karzai's small force to equip, train, and prepare it for the move south. Feeling that time was wasting, Karzai agreed to move toward Kandahar as soon as possible. This action would show the Taliban that he was serious and a force to be reckoned with. Accordingly, Karzai's small Afghan force, initially little more than 35 "well-meaning" supporters—a force that would eventually grow to an "armed mob" of almost 800 men—moved southeast around 30 November from Tarin Khowt through narrow passes, along what was virtually a goat path, toward the village of Petaw.

Karzai's men spent a few days resting at Petaw while the SF brought in some weapons, food, and clothing for the growing army. Then, on 2 December, the "army" moved south to the village of Sayd Alim Kalay where there was a critical bridge over a dry riverbed. By this time Karzai had been notified that he had been selected as head of the interim government of Afghanistan, making speed of movement to Kandahar important.

Karzai's forces quickly routed the small force of Taliban soldiers holding the village, but they could not take the well-defended bridge. For the next two days, despite the steady drone of CAS missions, the Taliban successfully defended the crossing. It even launched occasional attacks through the dry riverbed in an attempt to gain a foothold on the friendly side of the bridge. Each time they attempted it, the alert SF team would bring in more CAS missions and, in conjunction with Karzai's soldiers, drive them back.

The morning of 4 December the force began to prepare for an all-out attack to take the bridge. After final coordination with the Afghans, the combined force of SF soldiers and Afghan irregulars mounted up on their Toyota pickup trucks and drove to battle. Each pickup was packed with a motley crew of Afghan warriors with a variety of weapons such as machine guns, AK-47s, and RPGs hanging out of the back. Some crew-served weapons were mounted on the vehicles, making the convoy look like a combination of a traveling circus and a Somali war party.

The SF team directed CAS on the enemy-held ridge opposite them, but the enemy directed heavy and accurate fire on the attacking force. Next, the Taliban tried a flanking counterattack. One SF leader observed it attempting to cross the dry riverbed, and he alerted an Afghan/SF quick-reaction force (QRF). The Afghans laid down a base of fire and prevented the Taliban from moving. Three times the Taliban tried to cross, but each time the fire from Karzai's forces turned it back. Meanwhile, the SF team on the ridge continued to call down CAS onto the enemy positions. One SF soldier was wounded, but the Taliban failed to dislodge the combined SF/Afghan force, and the Taliban began to withdraw. Karzai dug in his forces that night to avoid the confusion of a night operation and next morning moved over the intact bridge without a problem.

The next day, 5 December, the US effort suffered a horrible setback. While observing from the ridgeline near the bridge and calling in CAS, a stray 2,000-pound joint direct-attack munition (JDAM) bomb landed in the middle of the SF observation party. They were blown off their feet. Three Americans were killed and dozens wounded along with many of their Afghan allies. They called for a medical evacuation (medevac) and patched up the survivors as they waited. The same helicopters that came in to evacuate the wounded also brought in another SF team to fill in for the broken team. The mission had to go on despite the dead and wounded.

Hamid Karzai and SF Team

As the SF team was recovering from the bomb accident, Karzai's negotiators finalized an agreement for the Taliban forces to surrender across the river and for the surrender of the entire city of Kandahar. On 6 December, the force moved again toward the open city.

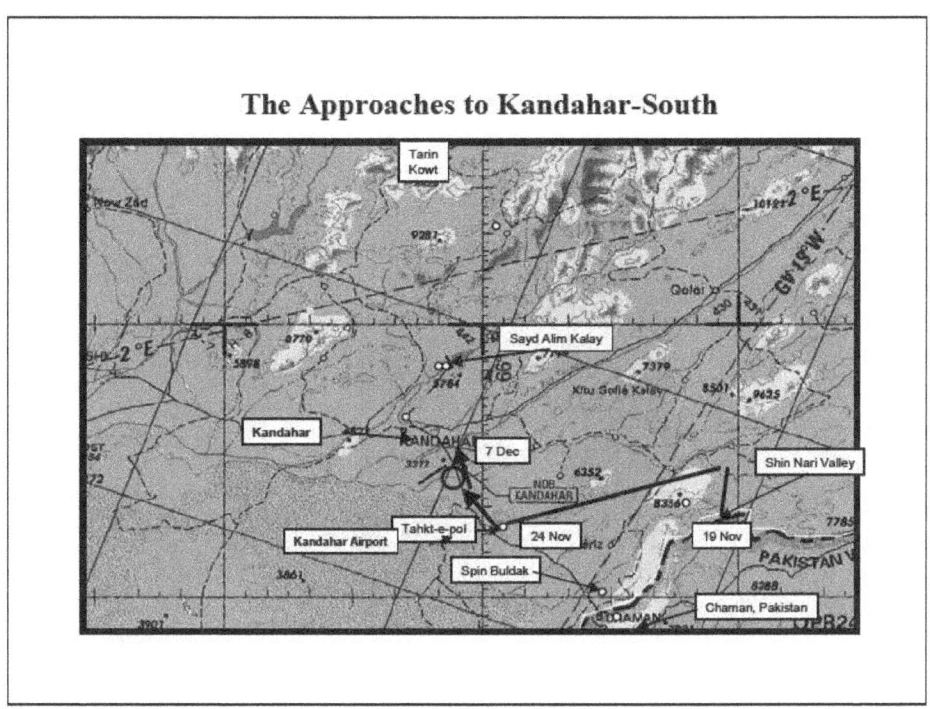

While Karzai and his SF element were making their way toward Kandahar, another team had linked up in the south with a different opposition group commander and was also advancing on the city.

On the night of 18 Nov, an SF team infiltrated into southern Afghanistan into the Shin Narai Valley. The team quickly linked up with an anti-Taliban leader, Gul Sharzai, a former governor of Kandahar.

Gul Sharzai

The Afghans, heavily outnumbered by the local Taliban, were very glad to see the team, and they moved quickly to provide weapons and food to support Sharzai's force of close to 800 tribesmen.

During the night of 21 November, Sharzai sent a delegation led by his brother out of the valley to meet with the local Taliban representative to negotiate the Taliban's surrender and ensure safe passage out of the valley for his forces. Unfortunately, the mission did not go well, and the "truce party" came under small-arms fire. There were no casualties, but Sharzai was forced to change his movement plans to avoid an early, and disruptive, battle.

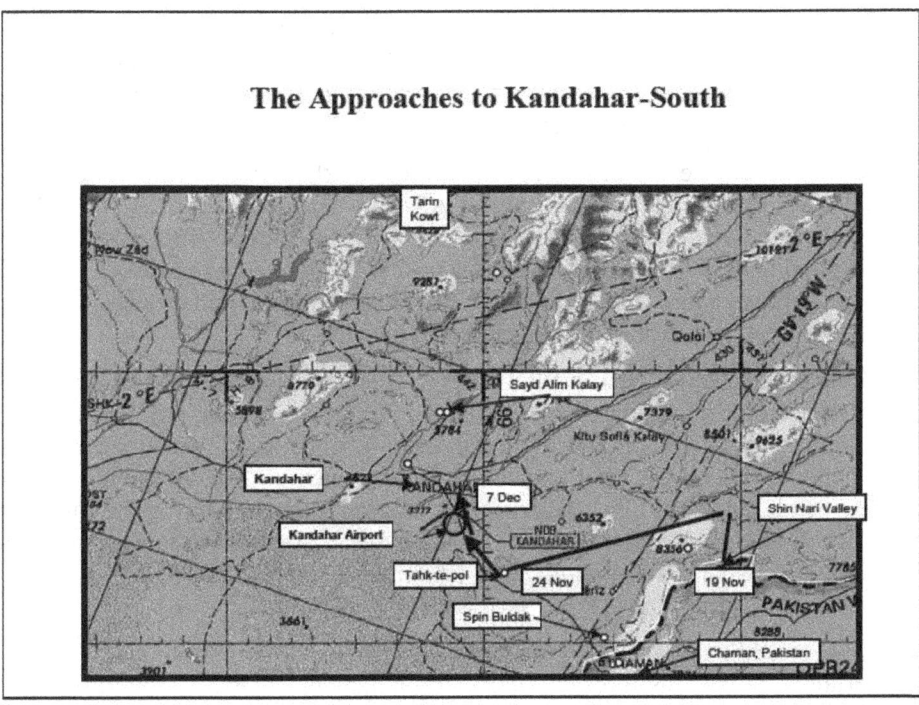

The Approaches to Kandahar-South

To avoid this battle, Sharzai decided to move north from the Shin Narai Valley and then west through the Arghastan wadi district to Tahk-te-pol located on Highway 4 south of the Kandahar Airport. That way the force would avoid any major Taliban emplacements that could slow down its movement. The prize was Kandahar, where Sharzai was determined to be made governor, and intermediate firefights might only disrupt the force.

On the morning of 22 November, the group departed the valley. The movement took the entire day and progress was slow. The convoy consisted of more than 100 vehicles of many different types, including pickups, transport trucks, and tractors pulling trailers. The movement to Tahk-te-pol took two and one-half days and was virtually unopposed until the second night. At that time the group moved into a small bowl-shaped valley just east of Highway 4 approximately 6 km from Tahk-te-pol. Sharzai decided to send a delegation into the town to negotiate for the local Taliban's surrender. The SF moved two CAS teams forward with the Afghan commander, covering the town from a ridge overlooking the negotiations. The Taliban suddenly ambushed the small security force. Immediately, the SF requested CAS and used the aircraft to break up the ambush and allow the forward friendly elements time to withdraw to the main body located in the valley. The Taliban moved its vehicles from Highway 4 behind several ridgelines to the immediate north of the main body where it began to attack Sharzai's men with machine guns and RPGs. The SF moved a CAS team to engage the vehicles and successfully eliminated the threat. Almost immediately the Taliban retreated and shortly thereafter abandoned the entire Tahk-te-pol area. It only took a few CAS missions to knock much of the fight out of it.

The next morning, Sharzai's forces entered Tahk-te-pol with very little resistance, severing the main highway between Kandahar and Chaman, Pakistan. Sharzai established 360-degree security around his force with checkpoints north and south along the highway. From the northern checkpoint, one could almost see the major airport at Kandahar.

On 25 November, the friendly checkpoint to the north started to receive indirect fire from the airport. The SF team sent a small CAS team forward with a 100-man friendly Afghan element to secure the ridgeline and eliminate the indirect-fire threat. This was accomplished without incident, and during the next week, the team rotated a CAS team to the ridgeline 24 hours a day. The team could overlook the airport and direct CAS onto the enemy forces operating between the ridgeline and the airfield.

The Taliban launched regular artillery and rocket attacks against the SF and Afghan security elements on the ridgeline and against the village of Tahk-te-pol. The airport appeared to be heavily defended, and the defenders had antiaircraft artillery and missiles. The team conducted CAS around the clock to destroy enemy forces at the airport and to prepare for the all-out assault on the airfield by Sharzai's forces. During the same week, Taliban forces began to move north from Spin Bolduc, a small town to the south, along Highway 4 to defensive positions in a large wadi approximately 5 km from the southern element of Sharzai's army, but they never posed much of a threat.

By early December, Sharzai had positioned his troops for an all-out attack on the airport. The Taliban probed his forces by launching a number of small counterattacks from the west using a series of canals to mask its movement. However, Sharzai's men, supported by US CAS, were able to repel the attacks and take a number of emplacements around the canals.

Finally, on 7 December, Sharzai began his assault on the airfield. His forces moved carefully to the entrance of the airfield but ran into no resistance. Then suddenly, Sharzai received a satellite phone call informing him that the Taliban had evacuated Kandahar. He immediately gathered his personal security force and, along with an SF element, sped into the city to gain control of the governor's mansion and solidify his position within the city. The rest of the SF elements followed the next day and moved into the governor's mansion with Sharzai. The city had fallen without a shot, and Karzai confirmed Sharzai as governor.

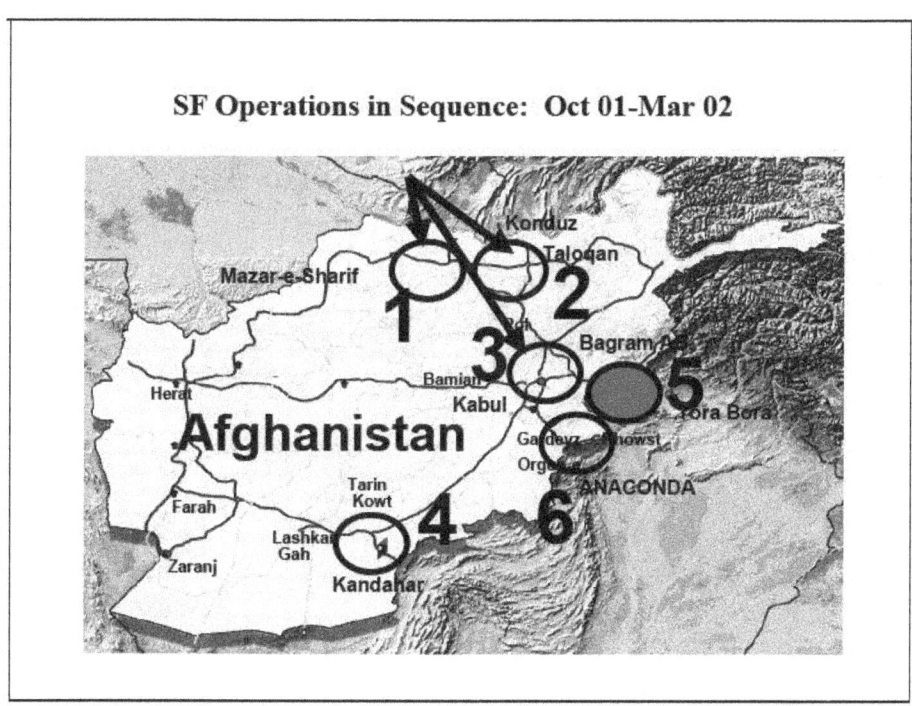

Tora Bora

While SF were operating around Kandahar, they were also pursuing enemy forces in the area near Jalalabad. After the fall of Kabul, al-Qaeda and Taliban forces had retreated into major strongholds in the Tora Bora Mountains south of Jalalabad near the Pakistani border.

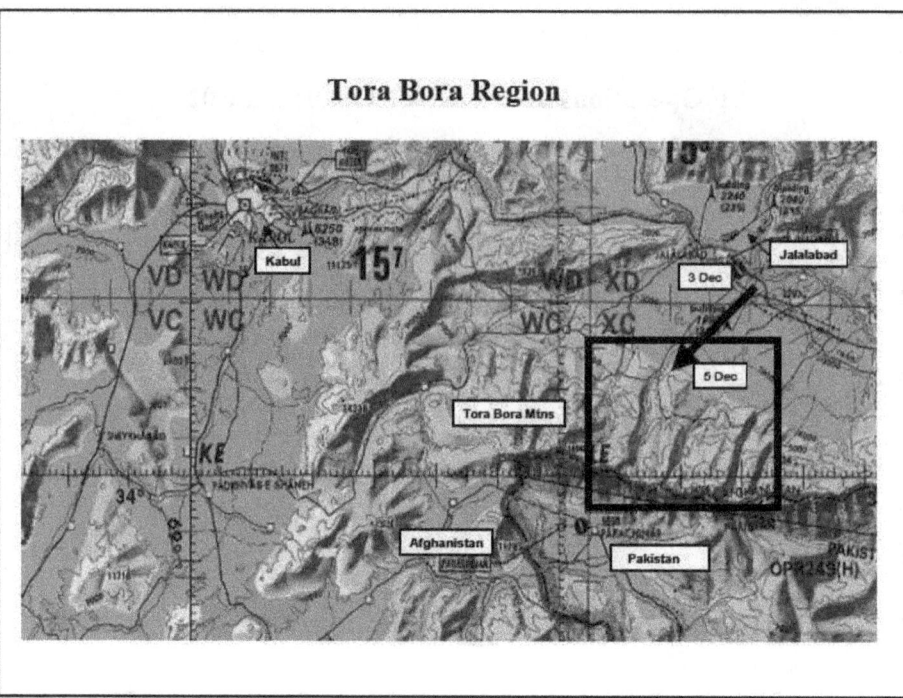

Tora Bora Region

This is some of the most rugged terrain in the world, and terrorists had controlled the area for years. In addition to being intimately familiar with the area, they had dug extensive fortifications and stockpiled weapons and ammunition to fight a protracted defense. With large numbers of fanatical al-Qaeda troops dug into extensive fortified positions and supplied with vast stocks of weapons and ammunition, Tora Bora was going to be a very tough nut to crack.

Approaches Into the Tora Bora Mountains

To make matters worse, the local anti-Taliban forces were even more disorganized than they were in other areas. They were divided into mutually hostile factions, and they deeply distrusted the United States.

TF Dagger directed several SF teams to go the Tora Bora region; meet with the local Afghan anti-Taliban commander, Hazrat Ali; and coordinate his attacks on the caves with US air power.

Hazrat Ali

Hazrat Ali's forces were a heterogeneous mixture of Northern Alliance soldiers whose loyalty was to Ali but whose fighting qualities were somewhat mixed. Yet, because of the US policy that local forces were primarily to conduct ground operations, it was necessary to give them guidance and direction but not to lead them into combat directly. The plan was to send the Afghan forces up into the Tora Bora, into essentially a box canyon, and assault al-Qaeda positions on the high ground. The latest intelligence even placed senior al-Qaeda leaders, possibly even Osama bin Laden, in that area.

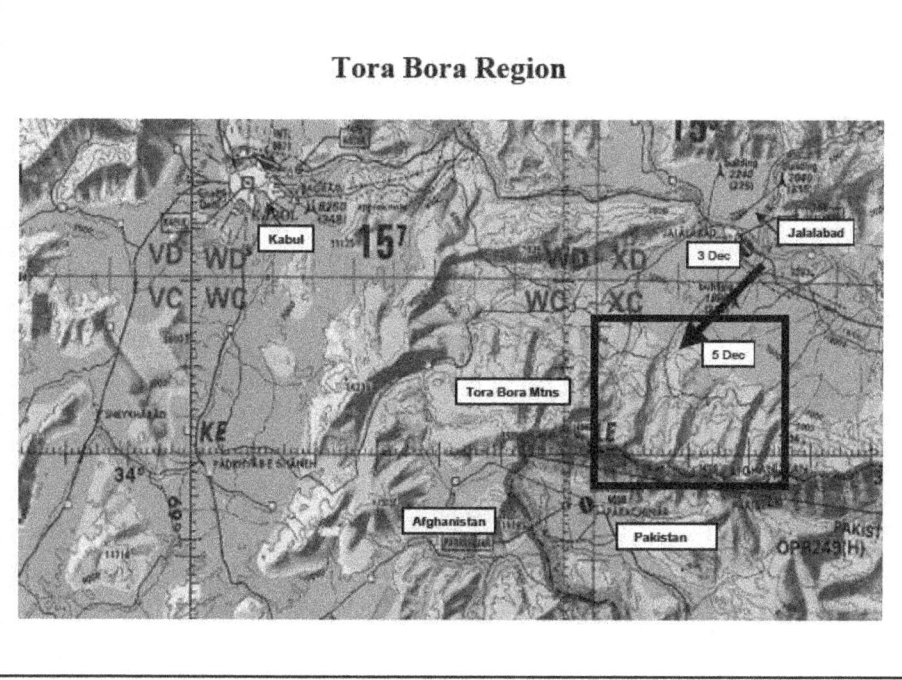

Tora Bora Region

The SF teams moved south out of Jalalabad and set up an OP along the high ground near the canyon the al-Qaeda held. A small Afghan security element guarded them to ensure that while they were calling down airstrikes an enemy counterattack did not disrupt their activities. The movement down into the Tora Bora Mountains was slow and hazardous. After a short movement by the ubiquitous pickup truck, the teams were forced to unload and move forward by foot with burros carrying their packs. They moved into mountains where the altitude varied from 8,000 to 10,000 feet, the terrain was rocky, and the pathways were extremely narrow.

The SF team set up an OP on the western ridgeline and immediately began calling down airstrikes, forcing the al-Qaeda to concentrate into a small canyon. They then moved to set up another, smaller, OP on the eastern side of the ridgeline, allowing them to directly observe the canyon concentration. Then, for 17 straight hours, the SF team rained fire onto enemy positions just in front of the advancing Afghani forces. At night, as enemy troops lit campfires to keep warm, the team used thermal imagers and brought in more bombs and fire missions from AC-130 Spectre gunships' 105mm howitzer 40mm cannon.

The enemy fought stubbornly. Each day, Ali's forces would take advantage of US air power and advance up the mountain, and each evening they would fall back. The ground would have to be taken again the next day. This went on for eight days and nights, as the enemy pocket grew smaller and smaller. By the time the Tora Bora fighting slowly ground to a halt in mid-December, SF teams had called in hundreds of airstrikes, dropping thousands of tons of munitions and killing hundreds of enemy troops. A few al-Qaeda were captured, but most of them fought to the death or slipped away into the relative safety of nearby Pakistan.

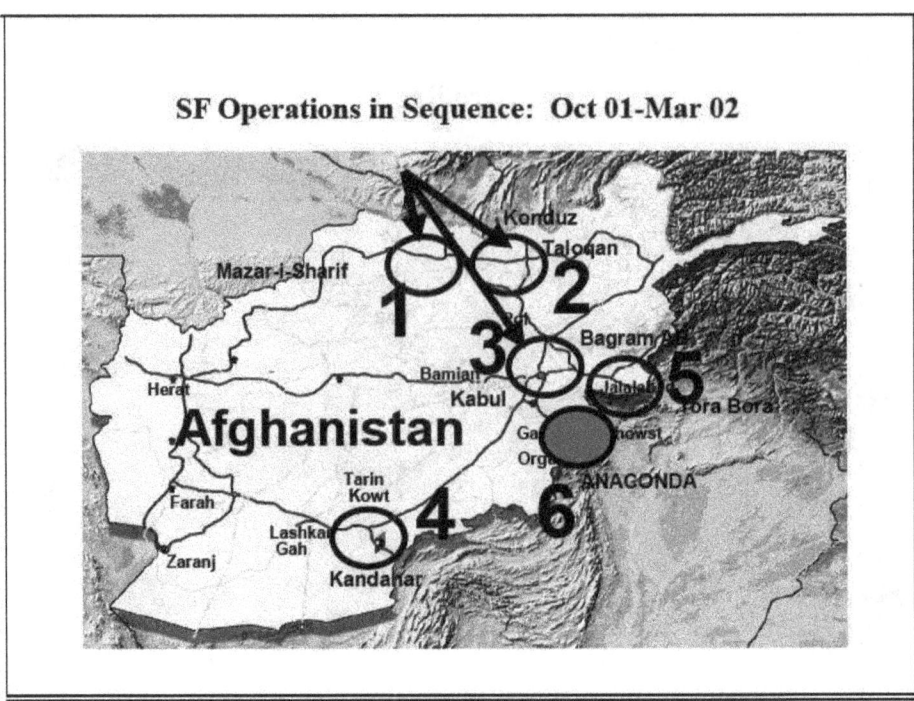

Special Operations Forces in Operation ANACONDA

With the capture of Kabul and Khandahar and the destruction of organized resistance at Tora Bora, Afghanistan was now, in effect, liberated. It had taken less than 60 days of concentrated military operations and only a few hundred soldiers to seize the country from the Taliban and its terrorist allies. Attention now turned to locating and destroying other, hidden al-Qaeda and Taliban forces. This was easier said than done. Afghanistan is the size of Texas and has hundreds of square miles of virtually impenetrable mountains and valleys. Plus, there was the problem of what to do with them once you found them. Afghanistan had no army. US forces were still only in the few hundreds on the ground. The attack on the Tora Bora caves complex in December 2001, while successful to the degree of destroying an enemy strongpoint and clearing hundreds of caves, was not successful enough. Hundreds of al-Qaeda soldiers slipped away into Pakistan despite Pakistan's token attempt to "seal" its border.

Thus, the incomplete result of battle forced US intelligence to look for the next concentrations of enemy forces. The focus began slowly to shift toward the nearby Paktia province to the south and west of the Tora Bora Mountains. In particular, the Gardez-Khowst-Urgun-e triangle seemed to hold promise of enemy activity. This region became the new focus of US intelligence and special operations assets in Afghanistan. The attempt to deal with this concentration of enemy forces came to be code named Operation ANACONDA.

Operation ANACONDA
The Shah-i-Kowt Valley

2-14 March 2002

Anaconda: Area of Operations

This is a rough timeline for Operation ANACONDA. In essence, it was an SF-conceived operation during which it led several ad hoc bodies of Afghan Military Forces, or AMF, to attack a major concentration of between 200 and 500 terrorists in the Shah-i-Khot Valley from 2-14 March 2002. At the time I was at the HQ of TF Dagger located forward at Bagram Air Base, Afghanistan.

Let's now briefly look at the area of interest and area of operations for ANACONDA. The Shah-i-Khot Valley south of Gardez is a valley just to the west of a major mountain range south of Kabul near the Pakistani border in Paktia province to the southwest of the Tora Bora Mountains.

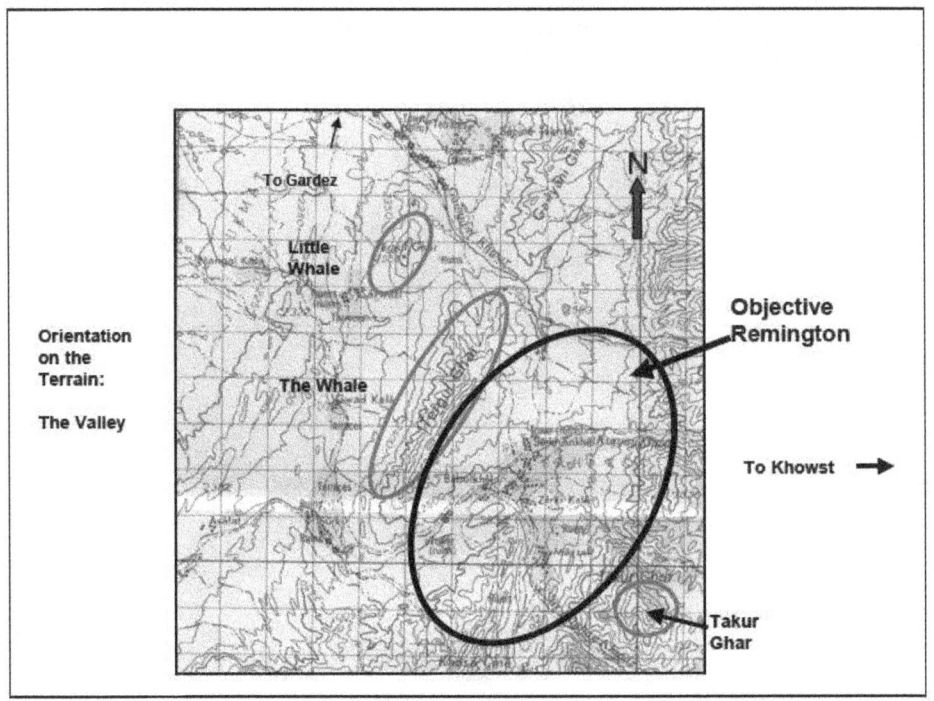

Looking into the valley we can see some key terrain. To the west of the valley is a major ridgeline known as Terghul Ghar, nicknamed the "Whale" by US troops. To the northwest of the valley, along the entrance to the northern end of the valley, is a small ridgeline called little Terghul Ghar, or the "Little Whale." Both are important pieces of terrain because they cover the best approaches to the valley. In the center of the Shah-i-Khot Valley are the three main villages of Serkhankhel, Babulkhel, and Marzak. These villages comprised Objective Remington during Operation ANACONDA. Much of the valley is at approximately 8,000 feet elevation with the surrounding peaks exceeding 11,000 feet. A three-dimensional map helps you appreciate the terrain.

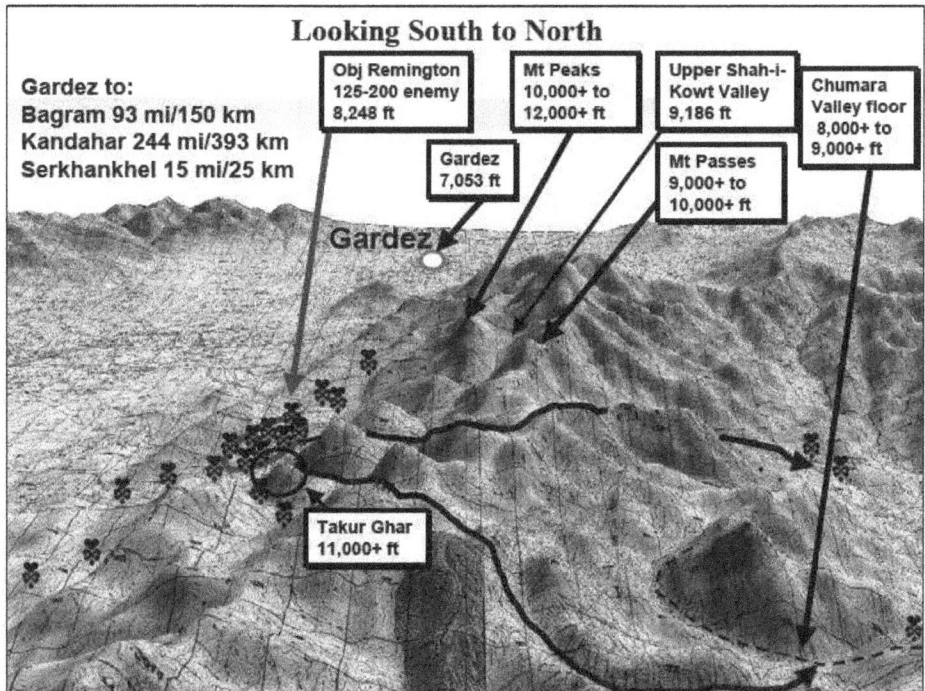

To the east of the valley is a major mountain range pierced by only a few main routes running through the valleys at their base (and dozens of smaller goat paths as well!). At the southern end of this mountain range with excellent observation over the valley and a number of exit routes is a mountain peak called Takur Ghar, the site of the sea, air, land team (SEAL)/Ranger firefight on 3-4 March. It is formidable terrain that makes the area difficult, nearly impossible, to isolate.

The first real confirmation of enemy forces in strength in the Shah-i-Khot Valley did not come from air reconnaissance or other sophisticated collection means but, rather, through the efforts of an SF team on the ground with the radio call sign of Texas 14. Working closely with local Afghan forces, Texas 14 tried to conduct a reconnaissance of the valley in late January, only to be turned back after its own Afghan security forces warned it of a major enemy concentration there.

After Texas 14 reported this contact, US intelligence assets began to focus correspondingly on that area. All these assets began to clarify a picture of a major concentration, initially perhaps as many as 150 to 200 foreign fighters in the area. That number would grow to estimates as high as 800 to 1,000 enemy forces.

Initially, TF Dagger considered the option of attacking into the valley using only SF teams leading Afghan military forces trained by them. However, as the number of enemy projected to be in the valley began to climb, the special operations forces planners asked for, and received, additional US conventional units from the 10th Mountain Division and 101st Airborne Division. The plan quickly grew in scope and size. By mid-February, six SF operational detachments, three SF command and control elements, three other special operations TFs, and a US infantry brigade of three battalions were involved.

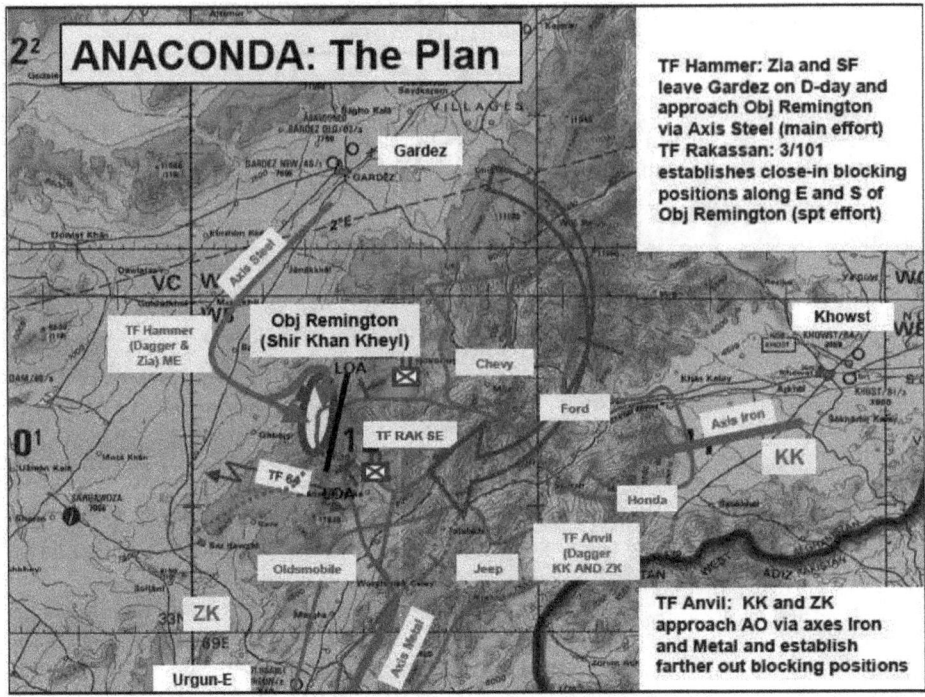

The essence of the ANACONDA plan was to establish an outer ring of blocking positions (BPs) around the valley using SF and Afghan forces (called TF Anvil), then air assault an inner ring of BPs along the eastern inside portion of the valley (TF Rakassan), and finally conduct a main attack with SF and Afghan forces into the southern end of the valley while blocking in the north (TF Hammer). The goal was to hit the enemy hard enough to kill or capture as many al-Qaeda as possible in the valley and squeeze the others out of the valley and get them running into the BPs where they would be eliminated. Those who escaped the trap would be tracked using reconnaissance assets as they moved along the various "ratlines" through safe houses and refuges.

Looking closer at the forces in the valley, we see that at D-1 the two elements of TF Anvil would move from Khowst and Urgun-e. From Khowst would come Kamil Khan's forces, approximately 300 strong, along Axis Iron. Zakim Khan would come from Urgun-e with another 200 or so troops along Axis Metal. They would establish BPs from north to south code named Chevy, Ford, Honda, Jeep, Dodge, and Oldsmobile.

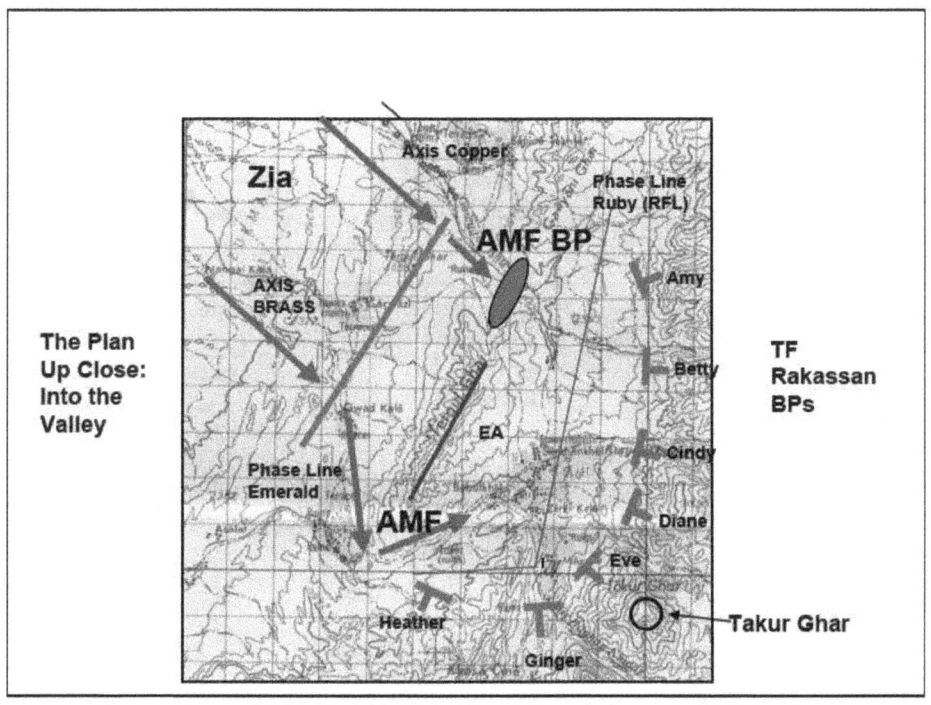

TF Hammer was the main effort. TF Hammer forces would depart Gardez just before H-hour on D-day and drive southwest along route Steel. The force would then divide into two elements and approach the valley along routes Brass and Copper.

One element would proceed along Axis Brass to establish a BP just north of Objective Remington. The other element would move along Axis Copper to Phase Line (PL) Emerald where it would await airstrikes before assaulting and clearing the three villages on the objective: Babul-kheyl, Marzak, and Sher-khan-kheyl. TF Rakassan would establish BPs at Amy, Betty, Cindy, Diane, Eve, Ginger, and Heather.

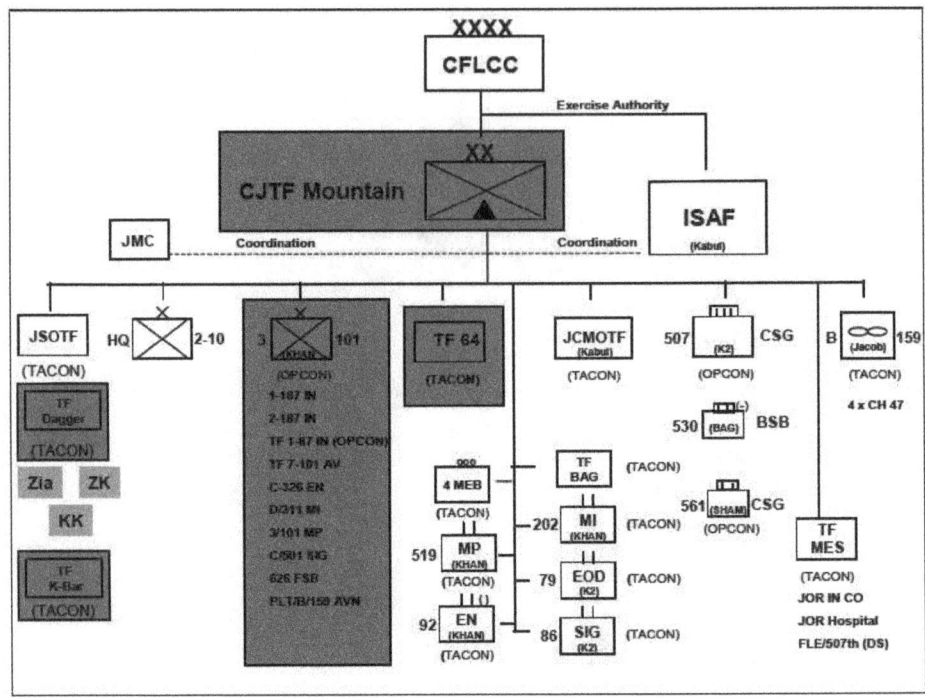

Here are the forces that were part of Combined Joint Task Force (CJTF) Mountain, in command of the operation (darker shading). Here you see TF Dagger forces and, supporting the attack, elements of TF Rakassan, two battalions (-) air assaulting just inside the valley on D-day—2-187 Infantry (-), 3d Bde, 101st Airborne (Air Assault) and 1st Battalion 87th (-) Infantry, 2d Brigade, 10th Mountain Division—with the 1-187th Infantry in reserve. To the south, TF 64 (Australian SF) would conduct special reconnaissance (SR). TF K-Bar (another special operations element) would conduct SR to the east of Objective Remington. All of the SR elements were to spot enemy forces moving out of the valley and assist in bringing in airstrikes to neutralize them.

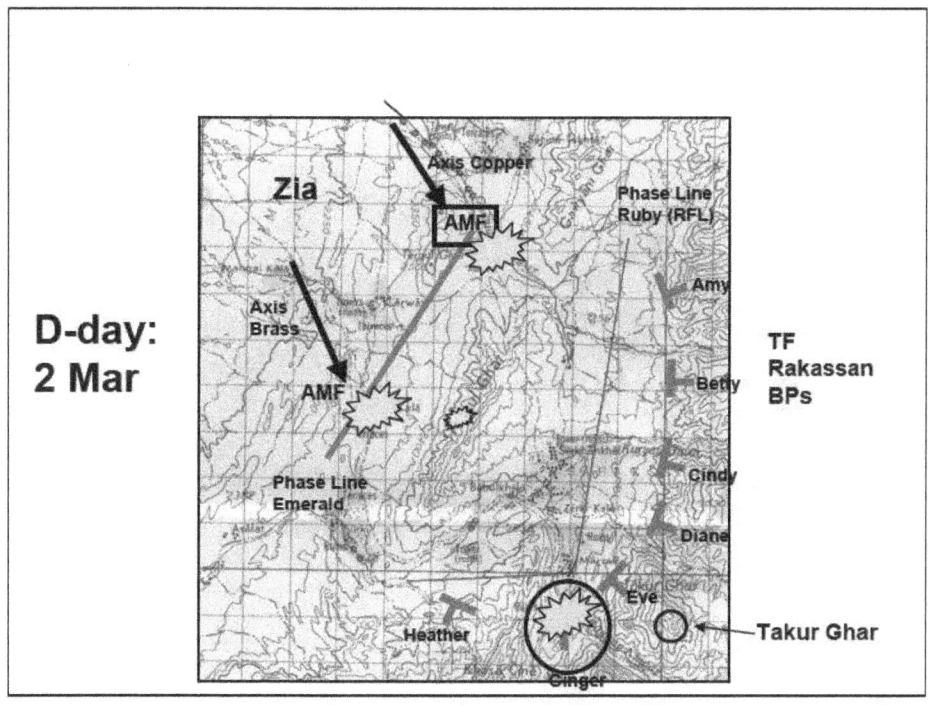

D-day for the operation was planned for 28 February, but bad weather forced a delay to 2 March. On D-1 (1 March), the TF Anvil elements moved out from Urgun and Khowst, and established the external Afghan BPs.

On 2 March, D-day, TF Hammer crossed the line of departure at 1930Z (2400 local time) and hit the first checkpoint on time. Almost immediately after, however, things began to go wrong. One of the large "Jinga" trucks tipped over, halting the convoy.

A Typical "Jinga" Truck

When the troops and equipment were cross-loaded and the truck moved out again, another got stuck in the mud. It did not extricate itself for several hours. Many of the large trucks got stuck and had to be abandoned. Others were only driven out of the mud by throwing hundreds of combat rations (MREs) under the wheels for traction. Many of the soldiers had to move the remaining distance to PL Emerald on foot.

As the troops approached their attack position on PL Emerald where they were to await the supporting airstrikes, they were suddenly attacked. Suspected mortar hit the lead SF vehicle in the north, wounding three Americans and killing one. Subsequent investigation discovered that the vehicle was hit by friendly fire from a circling AC-130. Two of Zia's men were also killed and 12 to 15 were wounded. With the whole northern force being around 40 strong, almost half the force was now out of action. The wounded were medevaced, but it took one to two hours to accomplish this and another hour to bring additional AMF forces out of the southern part of the TF to provide security for the remnants of the northern element on little Terghul Ghar. This was complicated because the southern element was also under attack by enemy mortars and artillery.

The deadly rounds and subsequent halt as the situation was reevaluated were fatal to the momentum of the attack. It was obvious that the enemy could observe all friendly movements. The airstrikes also were poorly coordinated and far from impressive. Expecting a hail of bombs, Zia's men watched as only a handful of bombs hit enemy positions on Terghul Ghar, causing no slackening in enemy mortar and artillery fire. GEN Zia and his men initially held up well, but after hours of bombardment with no way to answer back and ineffective or nonexistent CAS, their morale began to suffer. TF Hammer received only one additional CAS mission and one Apache fire support mission throughout that long day.

CH-47s at Bagram AB in Support of ANACONDA

Meanwhile, TF Rakassan had air assaulted its first lift onto the landing zones, but it immediately began taking fire. A sudden rainstorm prevented the second lift from being launched for several hours. Thus, the positions were at half-strength for some time. Enemy mortars were particularly effective against the 10th Mountain Division's 1-87th Infantry soldiers at BP Ginger. Calls for in-contact CAS from these troops began to drain off the limited air power available to the operation and further limited support to the now-bogged-down "main effort."

Meanwhile Zia's men suffered more wounded and needed medevac. Morale, although steady, was beginning to suffer. The pinned-down troops stood up to the fire for many hours, but as darkness approached, their position became untenable. The SF commander, in consultation with Commander Zia and the TF Dagger commander, determined that it was time to fall back, regroup, and come back to fight another day. As darkness began to fall, Zia's weary men loaded up on what trucks they had and returned to Gardez.

As Zia's forces pulled back, the main effort shifted to the US units.

101st Airborne and 10th Mountain During ANACONDA

The situation in the valley was somewhat stable by this point. The second lift had brought in additional troops. Five AH-64 Apache helicopters had acquitted themselves well in the fight, flying dozens of hazardous missions into the valley. They attacked enemy troop concentrations, operations, and firing positions and had, as a result, taken heavy ground fire themselves. By the end of the day only one undamaged Apache was flying. With CAS still poorly coordinated and slow and no available artillery support, the Apaches were the one bright spot of fire support during a long day. After hours of bombardment and more than 20 wounded, the 1-87th Infantry soldiers trapped in BP Ginger were pulled out at nightfall, leaving a major exit from the valley wide open. It was never effectively closed.

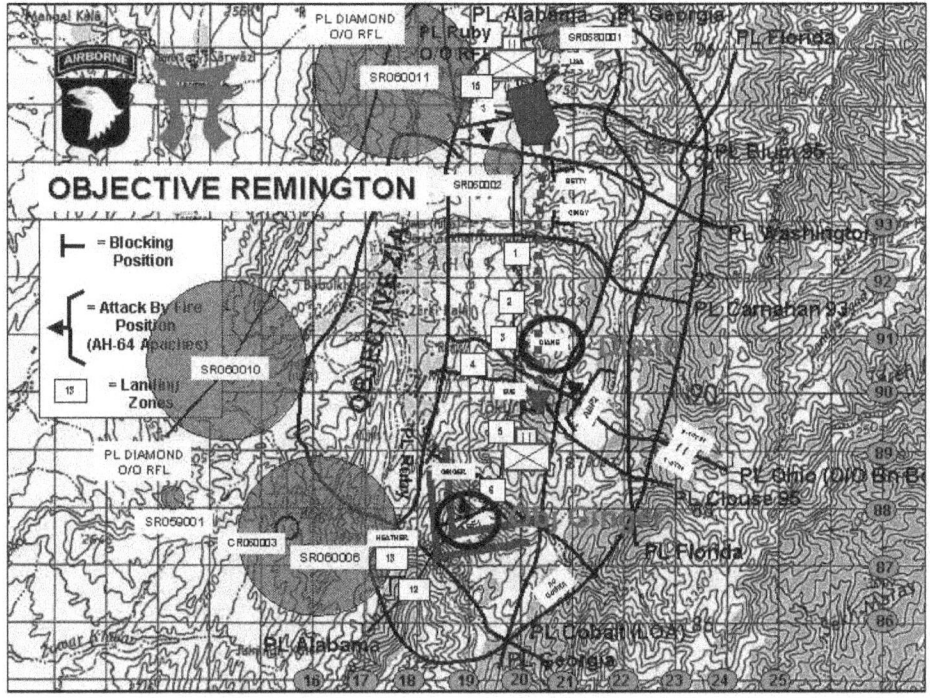

The night of 2 and 3 March TF Rakassan prepared a new plan to seize the high ground to the east and seal off the valley. This operation began in the early hours of 4 March, but the going was slow. The terrain was broken, and the altitude quickly exhausted anyone who was not acclimated to it. Still, by the end of the day, advanced elements of TF Rakassan had already pushed down as far as BP Diane. Nearly simultaneously, it sent a small reconnaissance element onto the northern portion of the Little Whale to watch enemy movements.

Most of the attention on the battlefield on 3 to 4 March, however, was focused on a firefight on Takur Ghar, a mountain to the southeast of the valley. There had been a botched attempt to insert an SR team on an enemy-held mountain, and a Navy SEAL had fallen out of a helicopter and left to face certain death or capture.

Takur Ghar

A small SEAL force was quickly inserted, but it was driven off and a Ranger QRF was inserted on the mountain. During the nearly 20 hours of the unfolding drama came reports of two helicopters lost, six dead, one missing, and many wounded. Special operations forces operate in a high-risk environment, and missions occasionally go wrong with fatal results. All the men were finally rescued but at the final cost of seven dead.

KIA at Takur Ghar

Neil Roberts—SEAL
John Chapman—AF
Marc Anderson—Ranger
Bradley Crose—Ranger
Mathew Commons—Ranger
Jason Cunningham—AF PJ
Philip Svitak—Avn Gunner

Memorial

Over the next few days TF Rakassan continued to move slowly down the ridgeline from BP Diane to BP Ginger, clearing all the caves and potential enemy positions along the way. Due to the enemy strength in the valley, it became apparent that more than Zia's attenuated forces, by now around 200 strong, would be needed to clear Objective Remington.

Gul Haidar's Armor and Mech Force

Afghan Defense Minister Fahim Khan was contacted. He selected one of his best generals, Gul Haidar, to lead a mixture of Afghan infantry, motorized infantry, and tanks—about 700 soldiers in all—down from Kabul to join the fight.

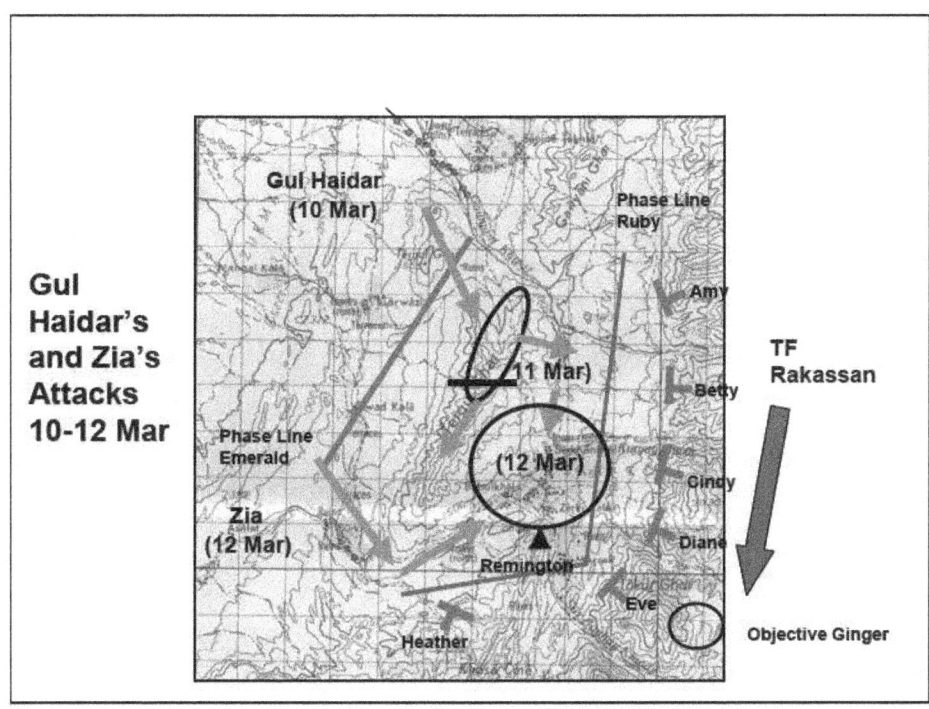

By 10 March, all of Gul Haidar's elements were in place, and after a quick reconnaissance of the area, Haidar seized the northern half of the Whale. The following day, they moved to the northern portion of the valley for an attack on the 12th.

On 12 March, part of Gul Haidar's force attacked straight down through the valley and moved quickly to clear the villages of Serkhankhiel and Babukhiel. Another element moved from north to south along Terghul Ghar, clearing the ridge, killing at least two enemy soldiers, and discovering many bodies and body parts. Simultaneously, Commander Zia sent his reconstituted force into the valley from the south and began clearing the village of Marzak. The three villages were quickly cleared; the enemy had fled.

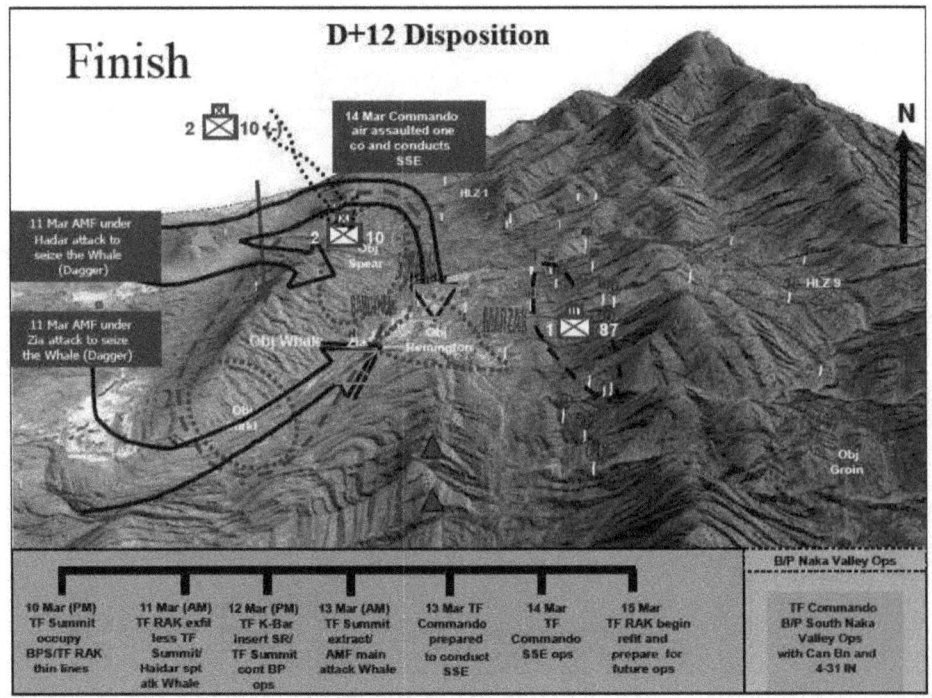

To help clear the valley, simultaneously with Gul Haidar's and Zia's attacks, CJTF Mountain launched TF Commando, 2d Brigade (-), 10th Mountain Division (brigade HQ with 4-31st Infantry), onto the Whale, subsequently into the area known as the "groin," and then to the Naka Valley to pursue fleeing al-Qaeda. Only two wounded prisoners were taken. The entire operation, including the suboperation of Operation HARPOON with TF Commando, was declared over on 19 March.

For the first time in the war, the al-Qaeda had indeed stood and fought. It had well-camouflaged, dug-in fighting positions with overhead cover and large stocks of food and ammunition. It had excellent forward OPs that provided early warning and observation for placing well-targeted mortar and artillery onto any enemy coming into the valley. But despite an initial ground force setback, poor air support, and a crippling lack of artillery, US and Afghan forces killed or drove out all the al-Qaeda in the valley. Estimates of enemy dead varied; at least100 to 200 were killed, perhaps as many as 1,000. More probably fled the area into the surrounding hills and then to safe havens in Pakistan's tribal regions. Still, the enemy was located, forced into a losing battle, and killed or forced to flee without its large equipment or stockpiles of supplies. In a guerrilla war, that counts for much.

> **Conclusions/Thoughts**
>
> **SF, with close air support and key ground allies, <u>can</u> be decisive out of all proportion to numbers.**
>
> **You do not gain without risk.**
>
> **Artillery: <u>do not</u> leave home without it! (Air power, especially slow and inaccurate, against a dug-in, wily foe, is not enough.)**
>
> **The conditions in Afghanistan were unique, and the "lessons" learned should be applied carefully to dramatically different countries and situations. (One size does <u>not</u> fit all!)**
>
> **Well-trained, disciplined professionals can operate <u>well</u> in a fluid environment. (You do not create these people overnight.)**

In conclusion, I think we can see that US Army Special Forces, operating closely with allied Afghan units, were decisive in defeating the Taliban and its al-Qaeda allies and liberating Afghanistan. Their high level of training and dedication to duty overcame all obstacles and delivered a heavy blow against terrorism. In this type of mission, SF was clearly the force of choice to achieve dramatic results with only a handful of men. Too much should not be drawn from the Taliban's easy collapse. We had heavy assistance from our Northern Alliance allies who had their own political aims in mind. These circumstances are so unique that one should be leery of applying a "new model" of warfare wholesale without considering all the unique elements of any other situation. However, special operations forces are true professionals. Operating with a minimum amount of support and guidance in a highly fluid political and military environment, they showed that they can be a valuable combat multiplier.

To Succeed Where Others Have Failed: Forming and Training the Afghan National Army, 2003[1]

Lieutenant Colonel Kevin W. Farrell

The insolence of the Afghan, however, is not the frustrated insolence of urbanized, dehumanized man in western society, but insolence without arrogance, the insolence of harsh freedoms set against a backdrop of rough mountains and deserts, the insolence of equality felt and practiced (with an occasional touch of superiority), the insolence of bravery past and bravery anticipated.[2]

—Louis Dupree

The quotation above from the preeminent scholar of Afghanistan is useful because it intimates very well the diverse challenges combatants as well as "nation builders" will encounter in Afghanistan. Beyond simply overcoming the harsh and inaccessible nature of the terrain and devastated national infrastructure, any occupier or would-be ally must address and attempt to understand native Afghans' character. Without a solid grasp of the unique cultural, religious, and ethnic situation in Afghanistan, an outside power has little hope of making significant and lasting improvements for this troubled nation. To have any chance of being successful, any effort to build and train an indigenous, effective, and legitimate Afghan National Army must consider the unique situation that is Afghanistan today. With a long and turbulent history, the region that comprises the current borders of one of the poorest nations on earth has never been easily pacified internally or externally. This short paper is based on a presentation the author gave that provided an overview of the allied effort to create and train an indigenous Afghan National Army that was current as of mid-2003.

The issue of how best to build an indigenous army that is loyal to the nation of Afghanistan and not bound strictly to a single warlord or ethnic group's command is challenging indeed. Before the current involvement of the United States and its allies in Afghanistan, two other great powers of the modern era—the United Kingdom and the Soviet Union—tried not only to conquer the nation but also to create for it a national army that was allied with the interests of the invading power. Although a detailed discussion of their efforts is beyond the scope of this paper, it is worth pointing out that what the United States is attempting to do now has been tried before. The British and Soviets sought different political end states for the Afghanistan they attempted to subdue, but it is worth remembering that they also tried to co-opt native forces to support a nation and its government that was amenable to the host nation.

In their three wars in Afghanistan during the 19th and early 20th centuries, the British experienced an astonishingly preindustrial Afghanistan wracked with tribal factionalism.[3] The British involvement in the region was based primarily on issues related to protecting and maintaining the British Empire; in particular, the "Jewel in the Crown" of the Empire, India.[4] Although the relevance of the British experience is difficult for many modern observers to discern and there are different reasons for involvement there, many of the challenges the British faced in Afghanistan remain challenges the United States and its allies face today. With a finite amount of resources; tenuous logistics support; inhospitable terrain; and an alien, diverse, indigenous population, the British tried repeatedly over a lengthy period to reform Afghanistan and mold it into a nation that would further British goals in the region. In perhaps the most notable exception in British imperial history, Great Britain failed.

Six decades after the last British combat in Afghanistan in May 1919, the Soviets would find themselves mired in a protracted war. Although this was not the first Soviet invasion of its southern neighbor, the size and cost of the 1979 invasion dwarfed the previous incursions, relegating them to relative obscurity.[5] With surprisingly few casualties, the Soviets secured Kabul and the major Afghan cities within days of launching their Christmas Eve invasion in 1979. In a description that is reminiscent of the current involvement of US and allied forces in Afghanistan today, control of most of the countryside of Afghanistan eluded the Soviets and Afghan allies even at the peak of the Soviet military involvement.[6] Apart from rocket attacks or seizing key facilities, the struggle for the Soviets in Afghanistan was gaining control of the fiercely independent rural population. Key cities and outposts often had to be resupplied by air because most logistics routes were frequently targeted for ambushes.

The Soviet strategy was to concentrate on securing the key cities of Kabul, Kandahar, Heart, and the highways linking them to the Salang Pass and the Soviet Union. They sought to carry the war to the opponents of the Soviet-backed regime, the Democratic Republic of Afghanistan (DRA).[7] Although most of the Soviet military effort was focused on these objectives and the fighting that therefore followed occurred in mountainous and remote regions rather than urban areas, there were major exceptions. Most notable was the largest rebel attack of the war in 1985 when more than 5,000 Mujahideen attacked the DRA garrison at Khost and fierce guerilla street fighting in Kandahar, again in 1985.[8] The Soviet tactic was to remove the opposition from its base of support. This in turn often meant that the civilian population bore the brunt of Soviet operations, either indirectly or on purpose.

The end result of the Soviet strategy was the death of tens of thousands of civilians and the mass exodus of millions, both within Afghanistan and to neighboring Pakistan and Iran. What is telling from the Soviet experience, however, is that similar to the United States' experience in Vietnam, the Soviets developed effective tactics to deal with the Mujahideen. Throughout both superpowers' wars, it proved impossible for the resistance to make concerted and extended stands against its far-better-equipped, better-supplied enemies. Without much difficulty, the Soviets maintained solid control of the key cities of Afghanistan—Kabul, Heart, and Khost—and held them throughout the Soviet-Afghan war of 1979-1988.[9] The overwhelming majority of combat occurred in what military professionals term "complex terrain," defiles, mountains, valleys, and urban areas. Very little combat other than terrorist actions occurred in the few actual cities of Afghanistan. Combating the Mujahideen for the Soviets or the remnants of al-Qaeda for the Americans could only be a part of a long-term strategy for creating a new Afghanistan. Finding and killing enemy combatants was and is essential to long-term success. The other, and arguably more essential, challenge was for the Soviet Union and is for the United States to create an indigenous national army capable of executing the will of the Afghan government.

Despite their determined efforts to enable the DRA (after 1987, the Republic of Afghanistan) to become a nationally accepted and legitimate government (regardless of its international standing as a puppet state), the Soviets never succeeded, and most of the country and its population remained outside the control of the Soviet army and the DRA. Military tactics might have worked at the local level, but the Soviet strategy, despite significant effort and improvement throughout the war, failed completely in the end.[10] It remains unclear as of this writing the degree to which the United States and its coalition partners have investigated the recent Soviet experience in Afghanistan. Once the Soviet Union withdrew its forces and the nation itself subsequently ceased to exist, the United States paid little attention to Afghanistan throughout the 1990s. Within a dozen years of the Soviet withdrawal, however, Afghanistan would be the staging area for the deadliest foreign attack on American soil in the history of the United States. The initial justification for deploying American forces into Afghanistan was to destroy the organizations responsible for the attacks of 11 September 2001, the Taliban and al-Qaeda. Over time the basic mission would expand to include the current corollary mission of creating a stable Afghanistan with an internationally recognized, democratically elected government. A key, if not **the** key, implied task to accomplishing this is creating an Afghan army loyal to the national government.

As far as the goal of the United States and its allies to build an Afghan National Army that is genuinely a national, legitimate force composed of professional soldiers that proportionately represent the Afghans' ethnic makeup, it bears pointing out that the Soviet Union attempted to create a force that was similar in many ways. Before the invasion of 1979, the Soviets committed significant numbers of military advisers and many millions of dollars in an attempt to build an effective and stable Afghan army, loyal to the Afghan government and therefore an extension of Soviet interests in the region. This initial attempt failed miserably, and most of the Afghan army "melted away" from an initial estimated strength of 80,000 men to much less than half of that within a year of the Soviet invasion.

Despite initial setbacks, the Soviets rightly recognized that to carry out their long-term political goals in the region—creating and maintaining an effective national army of Afghans that was loyal and responsive to the DRA—would be crucial to their overall success. Addressing issues of equitable pay, promotions based on merit, effective leadership, and realistic training, the Soviets succeeded in expanding the DRA army to more than 40,000 men by the mid-1980s. But in the end, without massive assistance from the Soviet Union, this force could not function independently and did not survive for more than a few years after the Soviets withdrew from Afghanistan in 1988.[11] Space here does not allow a detailed investigation of the Soviet attempt to form and train an Afghan National Army, but it is worth remembering that the Soviets understood the crucial importance of an effective Afghan National Army to their overall strategic goals in the region, They dedicated enormous resources to this task and yet, in the end, failed utterly in creating an effective Afghan army. Obviously, many differences exist between the former Soviet and current American situation, so this historical example is only of limited utility. For the United States and its allies to ignore the Soviet and British experiences in this inhospitable region would be a mistake.

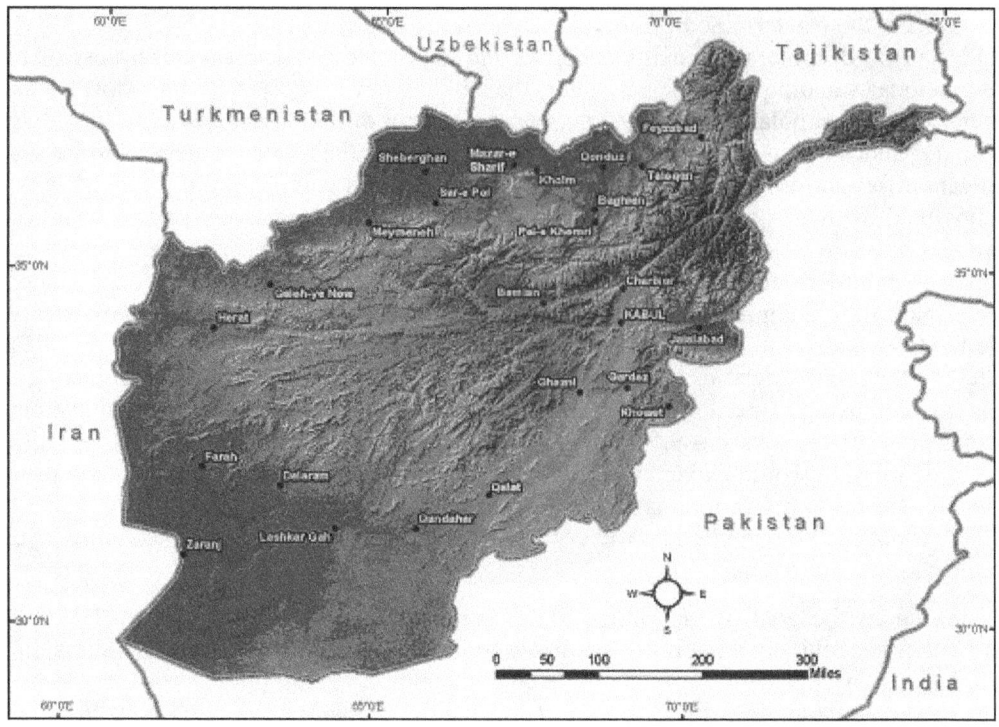

The current boundaries and major cities of Afghanistan.

Despite the daunting challenges the United States and its allies face in trying to build Afghanistan and its army, President George W. Bush and key members of his administration have stated publicly and repeatedly that they are determined to build a new Afghanistan that will join the international community, ideally as a functioning democracy but more importantly as a nation that will no longer be a haven to terrorist organizations. It is not the purpose of this paper to question the validity of that decision but instead to explain briefly how it is being conducted and some of the issues related to its execution.

To Succeed Where Others Have Failed: Forming and Training the Afghan National Army

At the end of the Bonn II Summit on 2 December 2002, President Hamid Karzai stated resolutely, "The Afghan National Army shall be established."[12] With the full backing of President Bush and US Secretary of Defense Donald Rumsfeld, an initiative that had been under way furtively and intermittently was now an official goal of the Transitional Islamic State of Afghanistan and its allies.

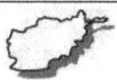 **Geneva–Lead Nations**

	Germany	Police
	Italy	Judiciary
	Japan	DDR
	United Kingdom	Counternarcotics
	United States	Afghan National Army
	Norway	Border Police?

At a subsequent meeting in Geneva, signatories to the Bonn II agreement assigned five nations primary responsibility for reconstruction missions: Germany, police; Italy, judiciary; Japan, demobilization, deactivation, and reintegration (DDR); UK, counternarcotics; United States, forming and training the Afghan National Army; and Norway, border police. Currently, the United States also has overall responsibility for the border police, but it is planned that eventually Norway is likely, with other Scandinavian countries, to take over this task.

Bonn II Principles

- Four major commands
- Will not <u>exceed</u> 70,000
- Subordinate to the command of legitimate civilian authorities
- Based on individual merit
- Balance among different ethnic groups
- Establishment of trust among all citizens

"The process of building the ANA
—including recruitment, training, and equipping—
will take several years to complete."

The Bonn II agreement of December 2002 established the fundamental outline for the future Afghan National Army (ANA). Ultimately, Afghanistan would possess an army of four major commands that would not exceed 70,000 troops in its final form. It was also agreed that the armed forces of Afghanistan must be subordinate to the legitimate government and that it would recognize, with the president of Afghanistan as commander in chief of the army, a situation uncommon in the history of Afghanistan. Selection of soldiers at all ranks was to be based on individual merit and not patronage, connection, or ethnicity. Officers, noncommissioned officers (NCOs), and soldiers would be recruited and trained extensively and properly.

As a whole, the army's ethnic makeup had to reflect the ethnic proportions at the national level. The ethnic balance should be represented down to battalion level. This would further another requirement of the Bonn II Agreement, that citizens of Afghanistan of all ethnicities would trust the army and regard it as their own. Frequently, throughout the history of Afghanistan, armies were comprised of members of individual tribes or ethic groups who would act rapaciously toward civilians who happened to be in the same area.

The participants at the Bonn II Summit also recognized, perhaps with intentional understatement, that "The process . . . will take several years to complete." This is a key point because despite internal and external political pressures and expectations, building an Afghan army that is professional, robust in structure, ethnically balanced, and loyal to the national government will require a multilayered, multinational process. The fact that this effort is being undertaken in an environment with a nonexistent national infrastructure in a country wracked by crushing poverty and devastated by more than two decades of war makes the challenge great indeed.

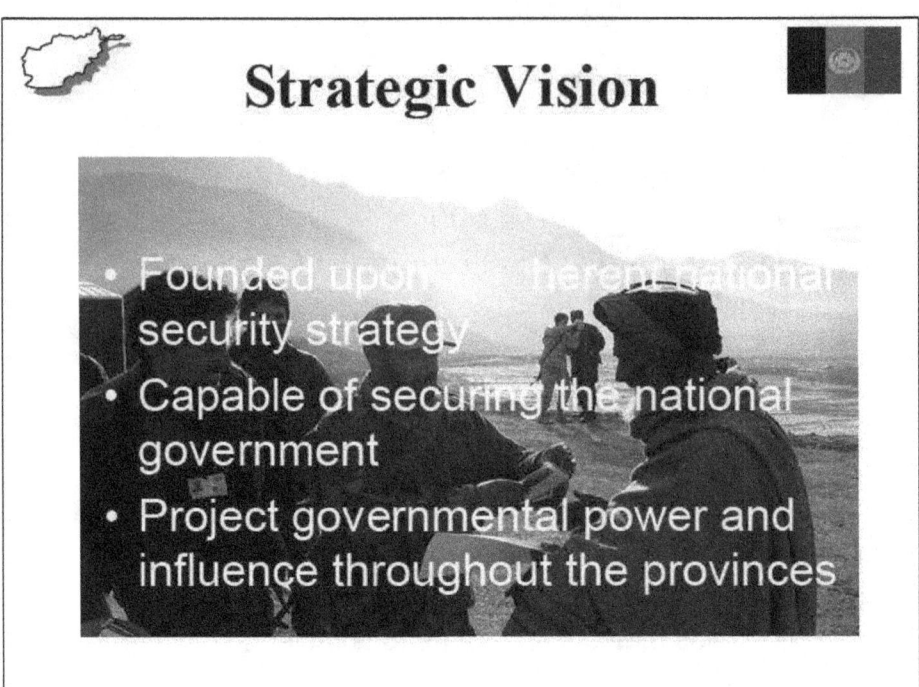

Over time the agency charged with assisting the Transitional Islamic State of Afghanistan in carrying out the mission of forming and training the Afghan National Army —the Office of Military Cooperation, Afghanistan—refined the strategic vision for the Afghan National Army. To be successful, the Afghan National Army must function as part of an integrated national military and government operating under a coherent national security strategy. The army must be able to defend the national government without assistance from an outside power, and it must be able to exercise the national government's will and power throughout the nation.

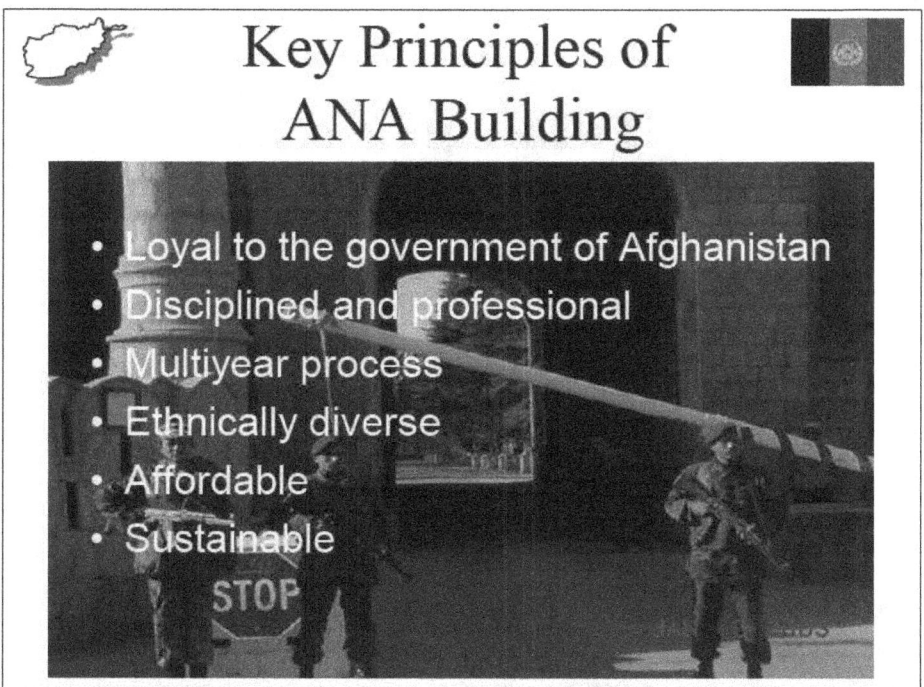

From this broad national security strategy, the Office of Military Cooperation, Afghanistan, derived key principles for building the Afghan National Army (ANA). Loyalty to the government is an obvious requirement, but it has proved to be a rarity historically. The other principles are not surprising: the army must be disciplined and professional, it will take years to develop, and ethnic balance must be maintained. Also not immediately obvious is that the ANA must be affordable to US and coalition forces in the short to medium terms and be affordable to the Afghan government. As for sustainability, this means that not only in terms of equipment maintenance and supply that the army can be maintained indefinitely but also that its educational institutions and training facilities must be properly structured and run. Crucial to all of these principles is and always will be recruiting and retaining good quality officers and soldiers.

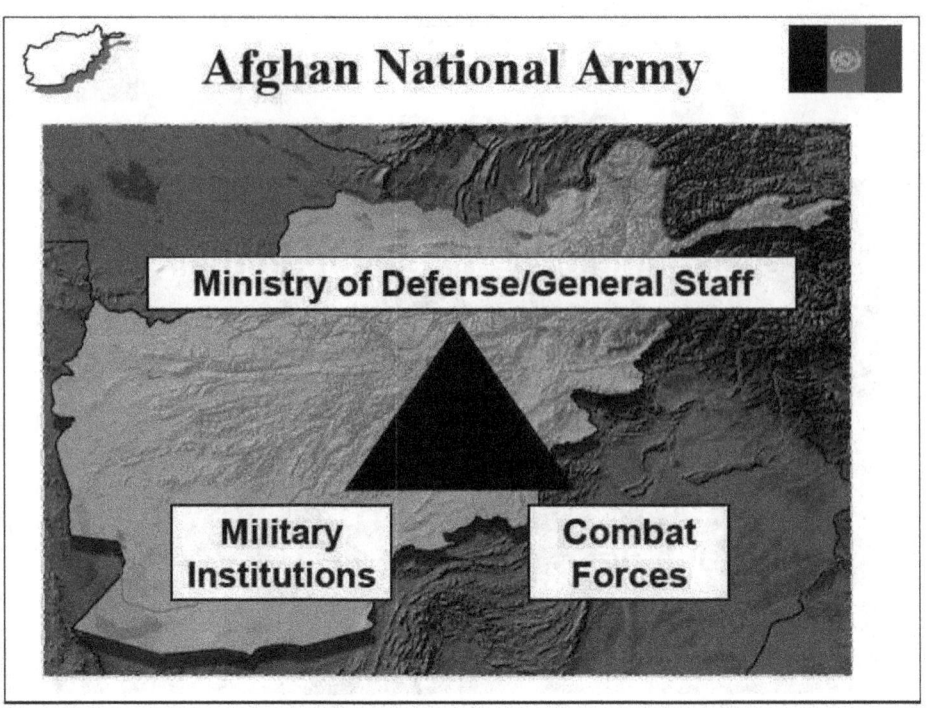

The Afghan National Army will have three elements. The Ministry of Defense and the General Staff provide, or eventually will provide, the overarching strategy and direction for the military institutions that support, sustain, train, and educate the combat forces and for the combat forces themselves.

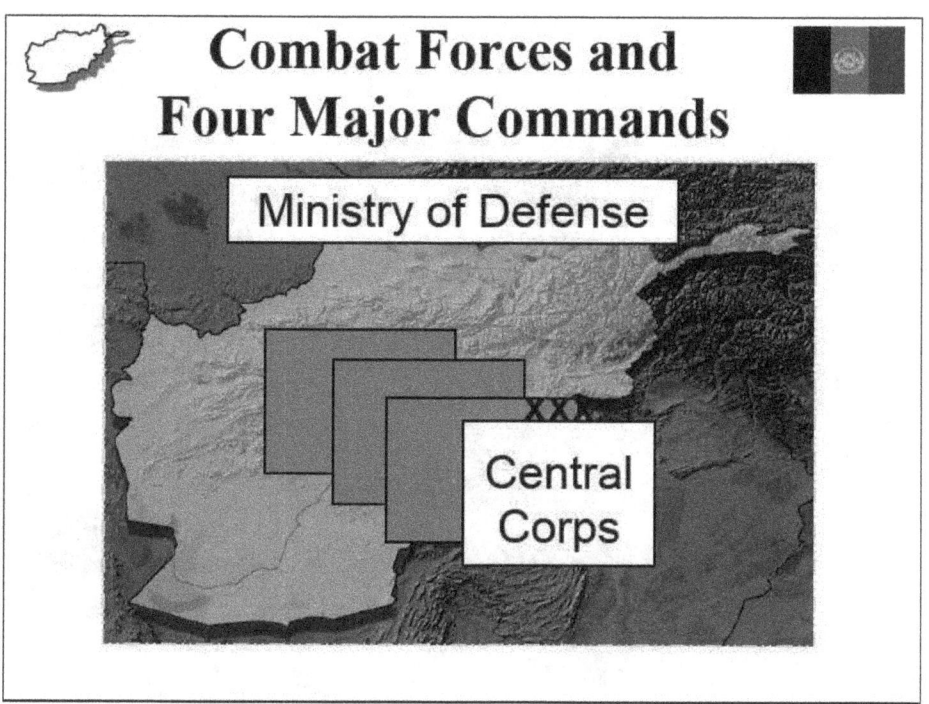

Currently, only one of the planned four major commands exists. The Central Corps contains the Afghan National Army's only combat forces. This unit's size fluctuates between 4,000 to 5,000, depending on retention.

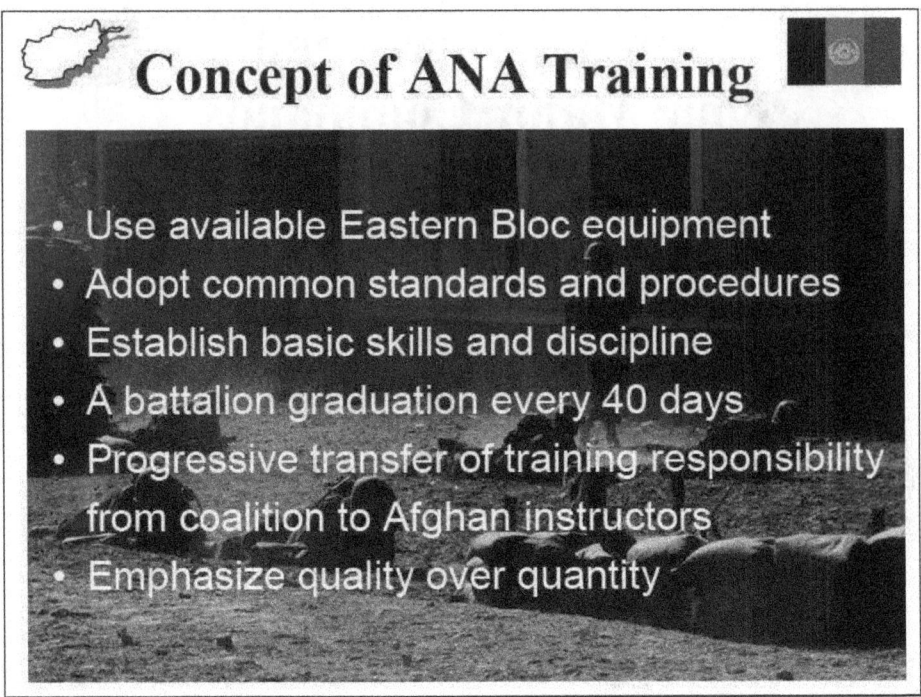

The general concept for training the Afghan National Army (ANA) is to use Eastern bloc military equipment wherever possible due to the native Afghans' familiarity with such equipment. Furthermore, the relative ease of maintenance, simplicity, and ruggedness, not to mention equipment availability, argue for its employment. A consequence of such a policy makes the ANA depend on donor support from foreign powers that possess such equipment and technical support.

Adopting and maintaining common standards and procedures throughout the army is essential to creating a professional army. At all levels advisers and trainers will establish and continue to reinforce basic skills and discipline. The goal is to graduate a battalion every 35 days. A vital aspect of the plan is to place "embedded training teams" of approximately 10 men to remain with each graduated battalion to train, mentor, and advise the command team. This, in turn, will allow standards and unit cohesion to remain at high levels.

The United States and its partners are achieving a progressive transfer of training responsibility from coalition to Afghan instructors. This training occurs at the Kabul Military Training Center with the Basic Training Course. At all times, selection and training strive to maintain quality soldiers and officers, not merely chase numbers. Embedded trainers are therefore a crucial aspect of this process.

Basic Training

- 10-week course
  - 12 weeks for officer candidates
  - NCOs selected at week four
- Common syllabus and standards
- 700 per basic training cycle
- Progressive transfer of training responsibility from coalition to Afghan instructors

Basic training is a 12-week course. Officer candidates report two weeks before enlisted men. Coalition partners use a common approach to ensure one set of standards. The battalions trained have all been infantry battalions, except for the first specialized unit, a T-62-equipped tank battalion. Soldiers in each course beyond the number needed for a specific battalion are distributed to other units in the Central Corps to bring the other units up to full strength. For basic training, the Afghan cadre at the Kabul Military Training City (KMTC) has assumed almost complete responsibility for training.

As of this writing, five countries have participated in Afghan National Army (ANA) training. The British and Turkish armies taught the first two battalions. Currently the US Army provides most of the training. The French army and the German army have contributed significantly to this training mission as well. Other countries will join the process in the months ahead.

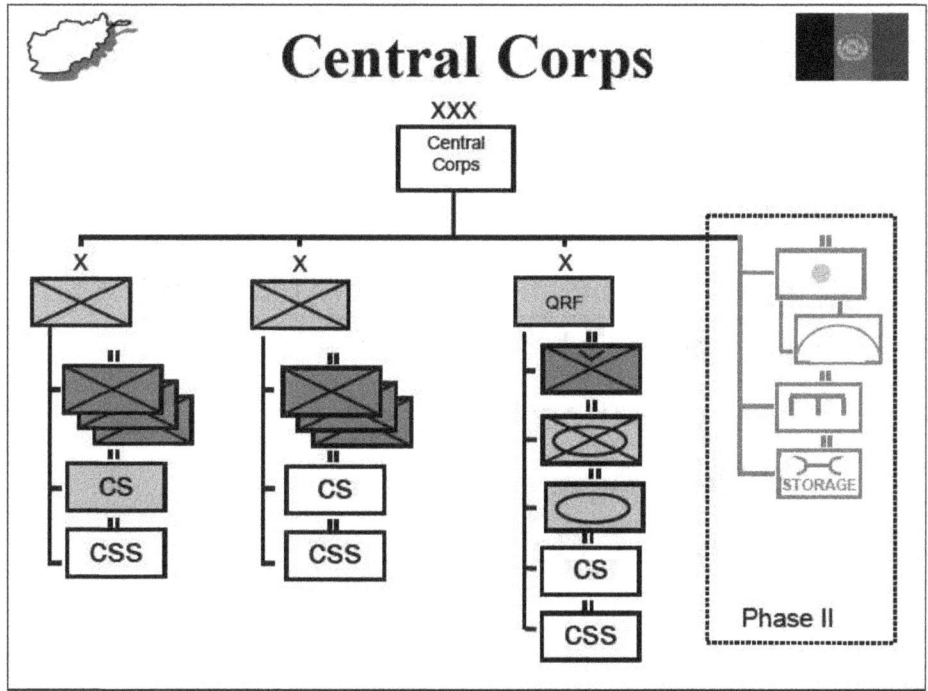

As of this presentation, seven of 15 battalions in Central Corps—the seven infantry battalions mentioned—have graduated. On this graphic, the units trained are shaded darker gray. Those in training are lighter gray, while those in white are planned.

The three brigade headquarters are scheduled to begin a combined US-Afghan Staff Training Course after the Afghan Ministry of Defense revises its senior officer selection and command processes. These officers should have finished their course in early June 2003 and assumed operational command of their brigades. Two of the brigade staffs have already completed an Afghan staff course.

 **Military Institutions**

- KMTC/Individual Training Center
- Officer and NCO Schools
- Major Collective Training Center
- Military High School
- Maintenance Facilities
- Military Academy
- Technical College

As well as training the combat forces, a crucial component of forming the Afghan National Army is rebuilding Afghanistan's military institutions. The institutions listed in the graphic above the line are organizations the United States and its allies are actively rejuvenating. The institutions below the line, which provide the officer corps' long-term educational needs, remain under consideration.

Key Tasks for MOD Reorganization

- Develop a national military strategy
- Develop doctrine and policies
- Organize, train, equip, and sustain the ANA

Perhaps the most challenging and most crucial aspect of forming and training the Afghan National Army (ANA) is reforming the organization charged with commanding it—the Afghan Ministry of Defense (MOD). Key tasks for the MOD reorganization are developing the national military strategy, assisting in developing the right doctrine and policies of the new Army, and ensuring the MOD and General Staff are properly structured and manned to progressively take over the functions of running the Army.

 **MOD/General Staff Program**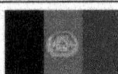

MOD structural reform and development of—

- Resource management for equipment, facilities, and personnel compensation
- Personnel management that ensures merit-based selection, promotion, and training
- Training and range management oversight
- Logistics and facilities management
- Command, control, and communications at tactical and strategic levels

The program delineated above demonstrates how the Office of Military Cooperation, Afghanistan, intends to carry out the reform of the Ministry of Defense (MOD). This remains the biggest challenge of all.

Notes

1. The information and opinions contained within this paper are solely the opinion of the author and do not reflect the official position of the US government, the US Army or any official organization of the US government. The author was privileged to be attached to the Office of Military Cooperation, Afghanistan (OMC-A) in Kabul, Afghanistan, while assigned to Combined Joint Multinational Task Force 180, headquartered at Bagram Air Base, Afghanistan for several months during spring 2003. Special credit is due to the Chief of the Afghan National Army Design Team, Colonel Timothy R. Reese, under whom I served and from whom I received much of the information contained in this paper. The author presented this to the assembled participants of the first annual TRADOC Military History Symposium held 5-7 August 2003. Any misrepresentations presented here are strictly the author's. The information contained herein was current as of 1 June 2003. It is quite likely that programs and policies addressed will change considerably as the United States' involvement in Afghanistan continues to evolve.

2. Louis Dupree, *Afghanistan* (Princeton: Princeton University Press, 1973), xvii. Although now some three decades old, Dupree's work remains the single most important volume on the history and culture of Afghanistan and should be the starting point for anyone trying to understand the region.

3. For a superb account of how parts of Afghanistan, especially the capital city of Kabul, did modernize relatively quickly, see Dupree, Part IV, "The Present," 415-666.

4. For a colorful but scholarly analysis of the relationship between expanding Empire and the British Army, see *The Cambridge Illustrated History of the British Empire*, P.J Marshall, ed., (Cambridge: Cambridge University Press, 1996). The work also provides a concise explanation of how international politics, competition for colonies, and domestic pressures all interacted with substantive effect on the size and nature of the British Empire.

5. Thomas T. Hammond, *Red Flag Over Afghanistan: The Communist Coup, the Soviet Invasion, and the Consequences* (Boulder, CO: Westview Press, 1984), 9. The three previous invasions or incursions took place in 1925, 1929, and 1930.

6. David C. Isby, *War in a Distant Country: Afghanistan: Invasion and Resistance* (London: Arms and Armour Press, 1989), 56.

7. Robert F. Bauman, *Russian-Soviet Unconventional Wars in the Caucasus, Central Asia, and Afghanistan*, Leavenworth Paper Number 20 (Fort Leavenworth, KS: Combat Studies Institute, 1993), 136.

8. Ibid., 145.

9. The official Soviet withdrawal from Afghanistan began in May 1988, but significant Soviet involvement—and casualties—in Afghanistan began well before the December 1979 invasion and continued well into 1989.

10. A superb and concise analysis of the Soviet-Afghan war can be found in Bauman, chapter 4, "The Soviet-Afghan War," 129-210. This should be required reading for anyone interested in understanding the Soviet experience or involved with current US operations there today.

11. For a concise analysis, see Baumann, "Building the DRA Army and Regime," 165-169.

12. Office of Military Cooperation—Afghanistan.

US Army Center of Military History
Occupations: Then and Now

Dr. Richard W. Stewart
Chief, Histories Division
7 August 2003

As the planning for Operation IRAQI FREEDOM (OIF) was under way, we at the Center for Military History were asked to draw upon historical examples to develop numerical considerations that might apply to occupation forces. Along the way, some additional questions and considerations arose. The material that follows represents my personal opinion as a historian, derived from appropriate sources and enriched by my colleagues' counsel and advice. It does not represent an official position of either the US Army or the Department of Defense. It is sort of our best advice at the time, late 2002 and early 2003, as to how big a job occupations have been in the past and how big it might be in a country like Iraq. I will also end with some **very** tentative points on the occupation so far in Iraq—how it is playing out.

> **US Army Center of Military History**
>
> **Occupation Questions**
>
> - What is an occupation force?
> - How big should it be?
> - What has been our historical experience with occupations?
> - How many forces would be needed to occupy Afghanistan? Iraq?
> - How long has it taken in the past to restore basic services? A functioning economy? A government? (In other words, when can we leave?)

As we gathered material on occupations, we had to pose some questions to help guide our answers.

- What do we mean by occupation? At what moment in time do we say military operations are over and an occupation has begun? Sometimes this is clear; sometimes not.
- What has our experience been in the past, and how many troops has it taken to run an occupation? What missions are included in the word "occupation"?
- What would it take if we had to occupy Afghanistan? Iraq?
- How long does it take to get a country up on its feet in terms of basic services—food, water, sanitation, electricity—and, longer term, on its economic feet or with a functioning government? Bottom line: How long has it taken us in the past to work ourselves out of a job—always the Army civil affairs (CA) goal?

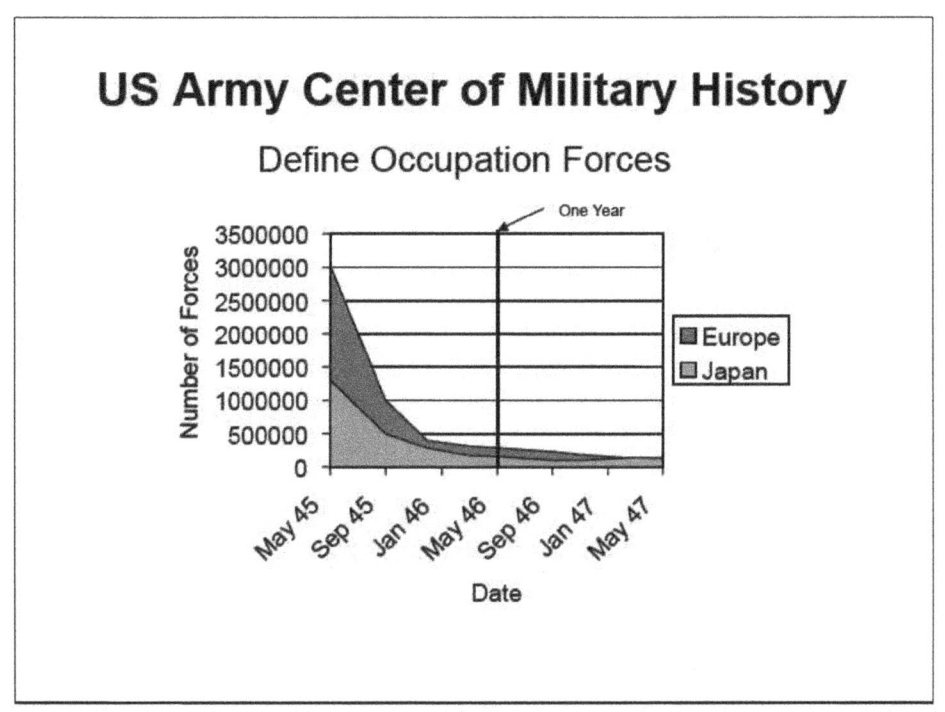

We had to pick a moment in time to say that war is over, now it's an occupation. So occupation forces are the residual that must remain to accomplish national purpose after warfighting has ceased. For the purpose of this study, in most cases, we defined occupation forces as those remaining **six months** after hostilities had ceased. In the case of World War II we allowed ourselves a year since it took so much longer in that case to redeploy huge masses of no longer necessary military manpower back from overseas.

US Army Center of Military History

How Large Does an Occupation Force Need to Be?

It depends on—

- Scope of mission
- Demographics of country
- Socioeconomic conditions
- Strategic circumstances

US Army Center of Military History
Collateral Missions

Law and Order

External Defense

Occupation Per Se

Humanitarian Relief

Nation Building

The manpower required for an occupation force depends, of course, upon the missions expected of it. Occupation per se is enforcing the instrument that ends hostilities, be it a treaty, an accord, a cease-fire, or some other arrangement. Occupation seldom occurs without some mix of such additional missions as external defense against third parties, enforcing law and order, humanitarian relief, and nation building or rebuilding.

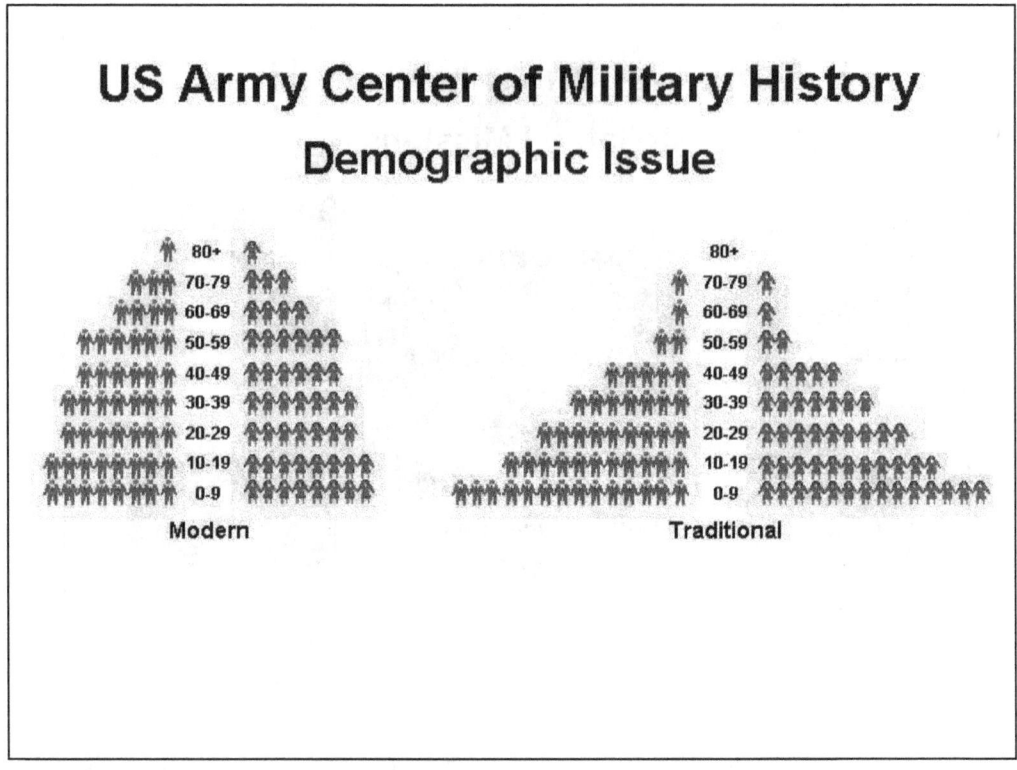

There necessarily is a numerical relationship between the size of an occupation force and the size and nature of the population in the territory to be occupied. Demographics matter, particularly the numbers of young adult males—and the numbers of young adult males who are underemployed. A modern demographic pyramid features low birth rates, low death rates, and relatively equivalent age cohorts through people in their 60s. A traditional demographic pyramid features high birth rates and high death rates, thus much greater proportions of young people. This affects the youthful manpower available for mobilization in wartime and for employment—or unemployment—in peacetime.

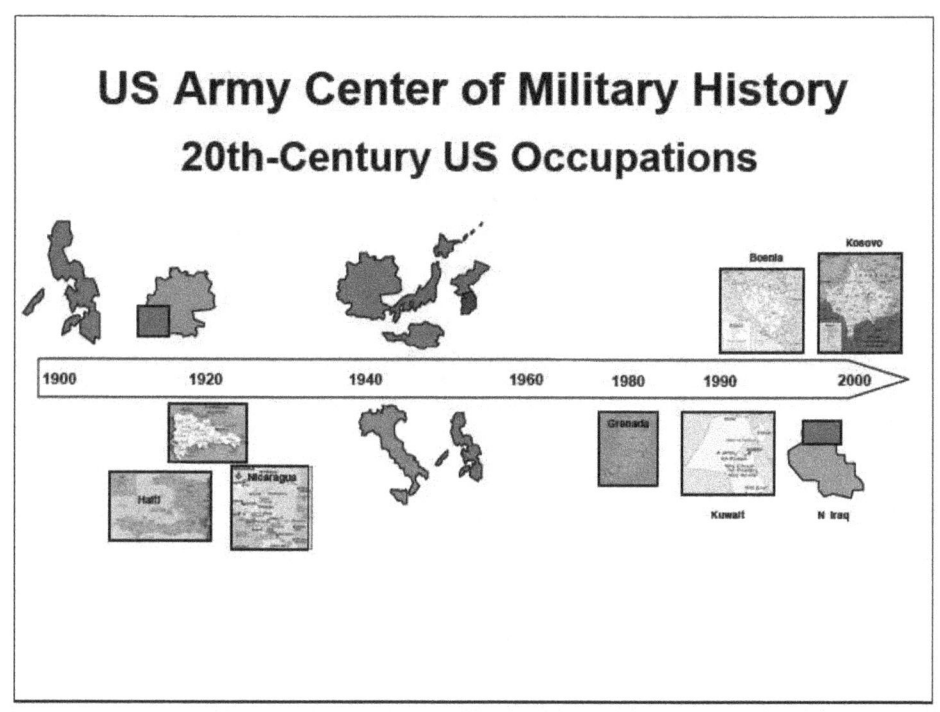

Our sample included 16 operations spread broadly through the 20th century. Of these, those depicted above the line were occupations proper, wherein an adversary was defeated in battle and US forces then occupied the territory—in all or part. Those depicted below the line were not quite so clear cut but nevertheless sufficiently resembled occupations to be useful for our purposes here.

US Army Center of Military History
The Philippine Experience (1898-1946): Occupation/Empire

- Population: 7.6 million
- US Forces: 23,000 (.03%) (1903)
- (Total Regular US Army (1903) 75,000)
- Philippine Forces:
    - Constabulary, 1901: 2,000
    - Scouts, 1901: 5,000
    - Army, 1935: 120,000
- Missions:
    - Occupation
    - Law and Order
    - Nation Building
    - External Defense
    - Rebuilding to Independence

Our initial missions were occupation, law and order, and nation building. A relatively small number of US forces were involved due to the rapid buildup of a Philippine force of scouts and constabulary. It was a small number, but given the size of the regular force at that time, it was a huge percentage—almost 30 percent—of the entire Regular Army. (Some of these were volunteer units and not in the regular establishment.) After World War I, the mission for US forces (about 5,000) was almost entirely external defense with most of the law and order duties performed by the constabulary (another 5,000) and the scouts (5,000), despite the population doubling to about 13 million. The mission accelerated after 1935 as we attempted to build a Philippine army to defend the islands, with some US units, against the growing Japanese threat.

US Army Center of Military History
The Japan Experience (1945-52)

Population: 83,199,600
US Forces: 92,538

Military/Population Ratio: 0.1%
Missions:
   Occupation   1945-47
   External Defense   1950 →

The best experience with respect to manpower required in an occupation setting would be Japan before the Korean war. Japan was a well-organized, homogenous society with a great deal of internal social discipline. External threats seemed minimal, the worst humanitarian crises had passed, the population was dutifully engaged in national reconstruction, and resistance to the American overseers was virtually nonexistent. Emperor Hirohito had directed cooperation with General Douglas MacArthur upon Japan's surrender, and Japan did so. Americans fielded only one soldier per 1,000 Japanese to occupy Japan. But then, except for some higher-level government restructuring, we did very little in the nation-building mission.

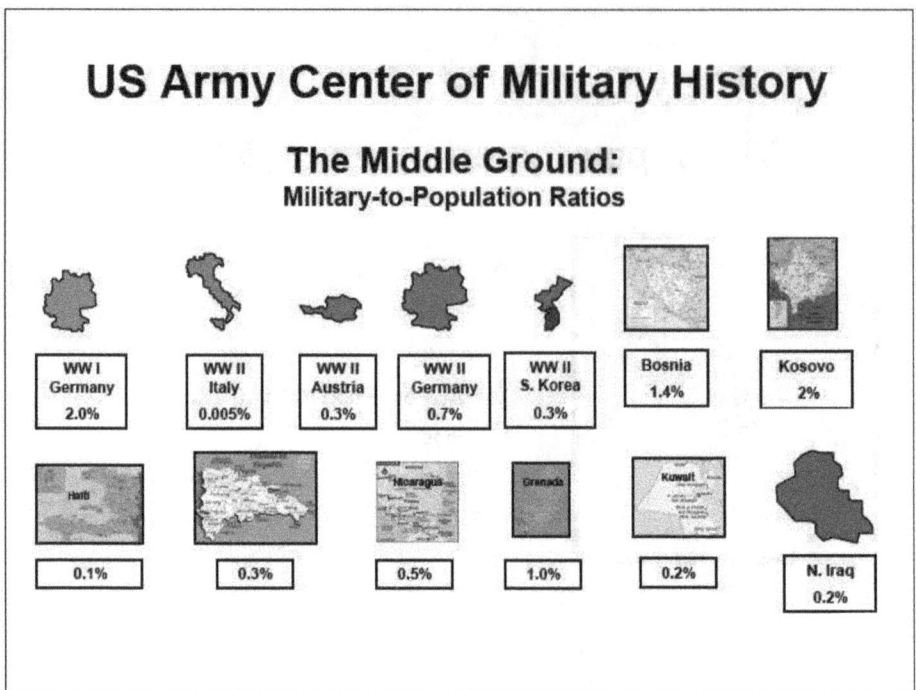

The rest of our occupation experiences came in somewhere between the 9.2-percent military-to-population ratio of Vietnam, 1969 and the .1 percent of Japan, 1950. A median seems to be about .5 percent. Thus, if we had to field appreciably more than one soldier per 200 in the occupied population we should probably ask ourselves why we needed so many, and if we had to field appreciably less we would ask why we had to field so few.

US Army Center of Military History

21st-Century Possibilities
(Briefed **Before** Operation IF)

Afghanistan	Iraq Proper
	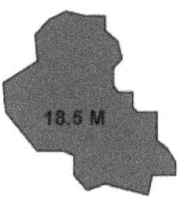
± 29 M	18.5 M
Tribal . . . With Law and Order, Nation Building, and Humanitarian Relief Issues	National . . . With Robust Infrastructure, Oil Wealth, and Modernized, in Part
Therefore: 300K(+)	Therefore: 100K(-) (.5%)

One projects past experiences into the future at great risk. With respect to decision making, historical analysis is only one leg on a three-legged stool, with a second being contemporary analysis or war gaming, and the third detailed appreciations of current capabilities—no one starts with a blank sheet of paper. That having been said, Afghanistan presents difficulties at least as complex as those of the 1902 Philippines, with tribal organization and huge law and order, nation-building, and humanitarian relief issues. An occupation wherein we and our allies directly and effectively steered the course of events would require more than 300,000 soldiers if historical models applied. We have intervened in Afghanistan, but neither we nor our allies seem to have any intention of occupying it. The course of future events in Afghanistan, given our historical models, will be one that we may influence but will not control. Iraq is more properly a nation state with robust infrastructure, oil wealth, a nascent middle class, and appreciable social discipline. A traditional occupation of Iraq would require lower percentages of manpower from the United States and its allies, perhaps 100,000 soldiers over a number of years or about .5 percent. This estimate is low compared with Kosovo or Bosnia but higher than Japan and about on a par with most past occupations.

US Army Center of Military History
Restoration of Basic Services/Economy

	GE	Japan	Korea	Italy	Bosnia
• Public Order	2 yrs	Immed.	1 yr	?	?
• Food	4 yrs	3 yrs	2 yrs	6 mos	1 yr
• Water/Sanitation	1 yr	Immed.	?	8 mos	6 mos
• Electricity	1-3 yrs	Immed.	3 yrs	2-6 mos	spotty
• Local Government	2-4 yrs	2 yrs	3 yrs	2 yrs	?
• Economic Recovery	4 yrs	5 yrs	10 yrs	5 yrs	?

Having determined numbers, crude though they are, we let the project drop a bit until after OIF, when we readdressed occupations from the perspective of how long these things take. We had no sooner occupied Iraq than the world press—whose chorus during the operation was "Are we there yet? Are we there yet?"—took up the hue and cry, "Well, what's the problem? What's taking so long to get water and electricity to everybody?" So we decided to look at how long some key events had taken in the past to resolve. Obviously rough, each country had services on line in different places at different times. Look at Italy: southern occupied for years before northern. Water in Rome in three months for some but eight before the city was up to prewar levels. Naples? If you have ever been to Naples I think you will wonder if the sanitation issue was **ever** addressed.

US Army Center of Military History

Occupation of Iraq

- Planning: Garner TF (Orha)
  352d CA Command
- Humanitarian Relief
- Coalition Provisional Authority (CPA)
- Public Order
- Water, Electricity, and Fuel
- Civil Administration

Planning: false assumptions. The Office of Reconstruction and Humanitarian Assistance and 352 not really involved in planning civil administration. Humanitarian relief: public order was the conventional force mission—regime collapse and, I believe, an insufficient number of troops on hand led to looting and a collapse of public order that should have been predicted. Water is always a problem. Electricity: Baghdad was always given more power. Thirty percent of the country was without electricity. Guess what? Thirty percent of the country has never had enough electricity! And the locals are stealing wire, and sabotage continues. Fuel: siphoned off by smugglers. Long-term civil administration problem: those who clamor most want to grab power faster before a popular and representative system is in place. And they seem to get the press.

> # US Army Center of Military History
> ## Conclusions
>
> - Successful occupations take time and resources!
>
> - The most <u>essential</u> task is public security—everything else flows from that.
>
> - Public security starts with numbers on the ground but in the long run relies on establishing local, host nation police and constabulary army.
>
> - Planning for occupation of Iraq seems to have been based on optimistic or wrong assumptions.
>
> - A 200,000 initial occupation force does not seem to be "wildly off the mark," but 100,000 for long term still seems about right.

Surprise . . . these things take time. The ignorance of the press continues to astound me: "Why haven't we completely rebuilt the country yet?"

Public security is key. Without it, nothing happens. You are building your house on sand without public order.

See Paul D. Wolfowitz's apology in the paper last July 2003. Oops! They had been told—willful blindness!

General Eric K. Shinseki looks a whole lot more prescient and intelligent that does the current civilian Department of Defense command group.

"The Small Change of Soldiering" and American Military Experience

Roger Spiller

"Armed diplomacy," the term this conference used as an organizing theme, defines a class of military operations with certain characteristics. Roughly speaking, these fall under the heading of "the small change of soldiering," to use John Keegan's now-famous phrase.[1] Finer-gauged definitions are unnecessary. No doubt soldiers have always understood: when they were charged with a mission that did not look familiar, that diverged from the agreed-upon business of fighting wars, they entered this unorthodox realm of soldiering. This might include interventions and invasions, punitive expeditions, constabulary operations, occupations, peacekeeping, or even colonial or imperial warfare.

The first of the case studies presented here, by Irving Levinson, considers America's occupation of Mexico as a classic "stability operation." Next, J.G. Dawson considers the US Army's role in the Reconstruction of the South after the Civil War as an important early case of "nation building." For Robert Wooster, the Army's operations on the frontier after the Civil War amounted to a very different sort of occupation and, in many ways, one of the most complex in American history. The volume concludes with surveys of recent American operations in Somalia, Afghanistan, and Iraq. The scope of these and other cases collected here is vast, reaching across the past century and a half of the American military experience up to the present campaigns in Afghanistan and Iraq. Seen together, these studies contribute to the body of professional knowledge American soldiers are most likely to require in the foreseeable future.

Apart from their unorthodox nature, what all the campaigns considered in this volume have in common is that they were in some way *limited*. None approached, or was intended to approach, the intensity of total war seen in the two world wars of the 20th century. Something a good deal less than the United States' national survival was at stake. Instead, their limitations determined their fundamental character. In each case study, America's aims and methods were bounded in some way by the immediate situation, usually by the immediate cause that gave rise to the operation. These less-than-vital circumstances in turn framed the mission of the forces deployed, although hard—and repeated—experience has shown how missions often take on an elastic quality as the shapes and purposes of these struggles evolve. American operations in Somalia, the United Nations Operation in Somalia (UNISOM) II, is a case in point. What began as a humanitarian relief mission metastasized over time into an altogether different kind of operation with a tragic result for American policy, American forces, and not least, the people of Somalia.

Such operations are limited in other respects, too. For instance, they are always confined geographically. A limited mission and a limited operational area both require a fine sense of discrimination about the number and kind of troops that should be employed. Having too many troops or having the wrong kind of troops could be just as bad as not having enough. Too, no matter how small a given area of operations, expeditionary forces are never strong enough to cover it entirely, even if it were desirable to do so. The Army's pacification campaigns in the Philippines were typical in this respect. The Army put its formations and detachments where they would challenge the most intractable problems. Troublesome provinces such as Batangas received a large share of attention while others were left to their own devices. Unable to dominate an entire territory or region by physical means, statesmen and commanders are always forced to discriminate, to decide where limited assets could advance their mission, to calculate where politics might substitute for combat power, or to risk dissipating their power and failing altogether.

And American statesmen and commanders did fail. One might be misled to think that because vital national interests are not immediately in danger, a limited operation's failure may be of only limited importance. But the military dimensions of an operation may not be a mirror image of its larger, long-term political importance. The United States' relatively small-scale intervention in the Russian Civil War did much to poison American relations with the USSR during its formative history and for most of the century thereafter. History does not obey a rule of proportionality. Small events may produce great effects. As colonial soldiers have long understood, a politically charged tactical defeat can have strategic consequences.

Next, limited operations do not conduce to a leisurely pace. American political and military authorities have usually set these campaigns in motion with one eye on the clock. The role of the United States is usually *reactive*, and this suffuses the campaign with the sense that American forces must move quickly if they hope to take the initiative and control the situation. Very seldom is the American public consulted beforehand. Provided the cost in lives, treasure, and time does not outrun the American government's justifications, the public's sufferance can be assumed but, warily, not for too long. So, forces engaged in limited operations almost always feel undermanned and out of time. And for troops trained only in orthodox soldiering, mission, enemy, terrain, troops, and time available always feels out of whack in these operations. As one soldier said of his role in stability operations in Panama, "I didn't sign up for this bullshit."[2]

Nowhere is the departure from "real soldiering" more keenly felt than in the imbalance of combat power between the forces engaged. In limited operations, American forces have rarely faced opponents whose orders of battle approached their own, even—with notable exceptions—in a momentary, tactical sense. The lack of parity between forces works its own important influence on the greater character of the operation. The Americans' abundance of combat power has naturally led to frustration over policies that prevent its wholehearted use. Often, on the other side, the very lack of combat power will drive opponents toward the more inventive, less orthodox methods that have become so familiar in 20th-century warfare. From time to time, in cases of what one might term the "Custer syndrome," the overconfidence bred by such abundant combat power has been met with dramatic and wholly unexpected American defeats.

It is no wonder, then, that soldiers throughout history have never been particularly fond of limited warfare. Given a choice in theory that is never available in practice, soldiers would prefer to meet their own kind in battles where there was no ambiguity about ends, ways, and means. Perhaps it is this preference, or prejudice, that has worked against advancing military theories of unorthodox operations, a deficiency that has extended even to simple doctrines and methods until quite recently. While modern orthodox warfare has given rise to a vast professional literature to guide every facet of strategic planning, campaign design, and operational execution, the same cannot be said of more limited operations.[3]

Perhaps that is because these operations are seen as too much affairs of the moment, too much accidents of history than any well-planned, deliberate orthodox operation could be. Thus, so the argument runs, it is impossible for military theory and doctrine to anticipate these operations in any useful way. We must concede the initiative to reality and realize that improvisation is more important than knowledge in such operations.[4] Of course, this is an argument for ignoring experience—one's own as well as others'.

One might expect such opinions from armies with no experience, seeking to rationalize their ignorance. On the contrary, officers in mature armies with long experience of colonial and expeditionary warfare such as the French were quick to say, "adaptability in the face of each new situation, not the application of some pat formula of the Ecole de Guerre, made for success in the colonies."[5] The ambiguous character of these operations was supposed to create bold, innovative military leaders who could reinvigorate the staid practices of the orthodox army when they finally returned home. The common view among expeditionary soldiers that this kind of soldiering was beyond the reach of codification certainly worked against any but the most informal, ass-in-the-saddle doctrines.[6]

Indeed, only a forgiving definition of doctrine could be applied to the nostrums that were handed down like saddle blankets from soldier to soldier on the American frontier after the Civil War.[7] And while it is certainly true, as Andrew Birtle has observed, that doctrine in the modern sense did not exist in the 19th-century Army, the differences between the state of the military art as it existed for orthodox operations and the state of the art for unorthodox operations were difficult to ignore.[8] The difference in the two bodies of knowledge was the sign of a preference being enacted by an increasingly professional officer corps. Choices were being made about what was most important to learn and what could be dealt with informally. The distance between these two bodies of corporate knowledge has persisted throughout the 20th century and into the 21st. As a consequence, the US Army still greets unorthodox campaigning as if it were a new day where improvisation and hoping for the best overrule experience.

Yet, there is no intrinsic reason why this should be so. The US Army's experience alone is sufficient to inform the creation of an "American school" of limited warfare.[9] Hardly a year has passed in the last two centuries in which American soldiers have not been engaged in such missions, with very little time out for the world wars. And with the advent of the Cold War, not only the frequency of contingencies intensified, so did their scope of consequence. Between 1945 and 1976, arguably the most dangerous period of the Cold War, the United States employed its Armed Forces in support of its foreign policy 215 times.[10] Behind every one of these operations lay the possibility that it might escape its limitations and spin toward a confrontation between the Superpowers. After a period of relative quiescence during the 1980s, the pace of American contingency operations surged again. During the dozen years of the Bush and Clinton administrations, the United States employed its Armed Forces in contingency operations grand and small on more than 1,000 occasions.[11] What have we learned from all of this experience?

A collective look at the military operations discussed in this volume suggests we still have much to learn about unorthodox conflict, if only because we have forgotten so much. Notwithstanding their wide variety of intent, type, scope, and result, certain shortcomings still seem to appear with depressing regularity.

These shortcomings are evident from the very beginning of such operations and do much to set the course for how they will play out. In no case cited in this volume will one see an instance in which the principal actors took heed of the nation's hard-won experience, studied the problem at hand with any discipline, or allowed their actions to be shaped in any way by the body of knowledge available to them. How American policy is framed and how the Army's mission is defined exercise a critical influence over all subsequent action. But the translation of policy into a military mission has always been fraught with difficulty. It has been so difficult that Army leaders often relented in the face of presidential insistence, as Secretary of War Newton Baker did when he received President Woodrow Wilson's less than exact guidance for intervening in the Russian Civil War.[12] All too often, Army generals have adopted a dog-in-the-manger attitude when confronted by a willful president, preferring to comfort themselves with the illusion that their role is only to follow orders so they can be held blameless if the mission goes awry.

The traditional lack of collaboration between American policy makers and soldiers tends to create a false picture of what might be expected from the mission about to be launched. All parties, civil and military, have tended to overestimate how much of any given problem military force can solve. One repeatedly sees the assumption that policy makers and soldiers alike make that exercising sufficient force alone would obviate the need for expertly understanding the problem before them. Experience indicates quite the opposite. If anything, it is possible to hypothesize that the political dimension of these operations is always miscalculated. From the Mexican War to the Philippines, to Russia, Germany, Vietnam, Panama, Bosnia and beyond, missions guiding American action have fallen short on this very score. A misshapen strategy thus passes its deficiency of vision down the echelons until the price is paid in the field.

Yet, armed with even the best-framed mission—one that provides expert, professional guidance for execution—soldiers will be forced to improvise. Missions always change simply because the situations that gave rise to them change. Furthermore, as a kind of military codicil to Werner Heisenberg's principle of uncertainty, one may assume that as soon as American soldiers enter the operational environment, the character of the experiment is unavoidably altered.[13] This may be the reason another rule seems appropriate for these kinds of operations: *missions never contract.*[14]

Uncertain policies, inadequately framed missions, a long-standing professional bias against unconventional operations, all these virtually guarantee that soldiers will be assigned to execute these missions with little doctrine to guide them and less training to protect them. The usual disparity of force evident at the onset of a mission naturally breeds confidence, but the opposition is not required to comply with expectations. In several of the cases discussed here, planning assumed—wrongly—a compliant noncombatant population. A wrong-headed assumption on such a question spells the distance between a short, uneventful operation and an all-out resistance movement.[15]

The haste to respond and the focus on immediate action militate against "what happens next" planning. As if the presence of combat power alone will render all other questions moot, intervening forces are usually caught off guard as the operation changes shape and gradually demilitarizes (or remilitarizes) itself. This is usually the phase when the occupying power learns that the noncombatant population's initial reaction was less approval than grudging acquiescence. Depending on the depth of popular resistance, the opposition to the intervening power may reconstitute itself, as indeed it did during the Philippine Insurrection.[16] If modern military planners are unable to look beyond the first shots, the old problem of enemy reconstitution will seem wholly new. At that point, execution defaults to improvisation that, in fact, is not so much a plan as the absence of a plan.

Ten of the cases collected in this volume show unprepared American soldiers confronted by the complex challenges of occupation duty. Faced with this unattractive prospect, American political and military leaders rarely took their thinking beyond the point of settling old scores and stabilizing the country long enough to depart. Yet, the American experience with occupation operations is so extensive that one can easily discern recurring themes—installing temporary government, controlling the population in general, suppressing residual resistance, resettling displaced noncombatants, rejuvenating supply and distribution systems, repairing infrastructure, and institutional reform. With the one exception of the American occupation of Germany after World War II, in preparation for which the Army had very wisely established a School of Military Government two years earlier, American soldiers have suffered the disadvantages of ignorance time and again, plunging into operations where they were forced to learn as they ran.[17] Abundant knowledge offers no guidance simply by existing. Ideas are like orphans: unless adopted, they will not serve their rightful function.

If the Army will not consult the wisdom of its own experience, the question is why not? If actions are not informed by fact, what remains other than passion, prejudice, or wishful thinking? During the conference's session on irregular warfare, one of the participants spoke with some heat of "an incredible resistance to lessons learned" after the Vietnam war and reminded everyone of the old saying that the war did not really last eight years but one year eight times. The late Douglas Pike, an eminent scholar of the Vietnam war, believed that this resistance to knowledge permeated every level of the American politico-military system. To describe this phenomenon, Pike used a term coined by Aldus Huxley—*vincible ignorance*: a state of mind in which one does not know and understands he does not know *and does not believe it makes any difference*. Pike's characterization of how vincible ignorance works in action is worth recounting:

> We first committed ourselves to the war and then began to think about it comprehensively. The highest level leadership did not initially sit down and address in detailed and extended fashion its strategic position, did not discuss and analyze enemy strengths, weaknesses, and probable strategies, did not wrangle and argue and finally hammer out a fully articulated strategy.
>
> There was in this behavior a sense of enormous self-confidence, indeed a kind of unconscious arrogance on the part of the Americans.[18]

As Pike goes on to explain, this is not to say that no one in the system understood the situation and what answers were required. On the contrary, the United States had experts aplenty willing to put their knowledge to work. "The villain in the piece," he writes, was not so much particular people but the system itself.[19] The system somehow arrested the necessary translation of knowledge into action.

Certain institutions seem to be especially susceptible to these misfires, as if the institution subordinates all its functions to its own survival. Where an organizational hierarchy manages knowledge by subordinating it to process, the potency of the knowledge the institution possesses is inevitably dissipated. With all operations reduced to routine, knowledge counts for less and less until its acuity—its capacity for effecting change—simply disappears.

We have in two recent tragedies a nonmilitary variant of Pike's vincible ignorance. A comparison of the United States' two space shuttle disasters reveals virtually identical institutional shortcomings. In both cases, accident investigators assigned a greater weight of responsibility to the National Aeronautics and Space Administration's (NASA's) "institutional culture" than the immediate technical reasons for the crashes. The management of expert knowledge, which existed in abundance at all organizational levels, nevertheless worked against its critical influence over the larger policy-level decisions made within the agency.[20] After the *Challenger* disaster in 1983, both a presidential commission and a congressional investigation recommended corrective reforms in how NASA managed its critical knowledge. The recently released Columbia Accident Investigation Board report identifies the same deficiencies in the agency's organizational culture—17 years later.[21]

In 1944, British military historian and theorist B.H. Liddell Hart published a brief meditation on his professional life titled *Why Don't We Learn From History?* Considering the experience he and his countrymen were living through at the moment, Liddell Hart's answer was quite optimistic. World War II had reached its apogee when he was writing. The war had grown to truly global proportions. To many at the time, the war seemed the tragic result of civilization's failure to heed the lessons of World War I.

Liddell Hart's optimism was all the more remarkable because he had personal reasons for doubting the value of knowledge as a guiding force in contemporary public action. He had been intimately involved in his nation's debates over foreign and military policy for nearly two decades. Immediately before the war, he had served as an adviser to the Secretary of State for War in the ill-fated Chamberlain government, which had added the word "appeasement" to every politician's lexicon of nightmares. His reputation suffered when the government fell, and he spent the war in a kind of intellectual exile. He claimed his faith in the power of experience to inform reason was undeterred. Liddell Hart was putting on a brave face, however; he surely knew better by then, if not long before. And he seemed to admit as much later, wondering whether there was "a practical way of combining progress toward the attainment of truth [that is, knowledge] with progress toward its acceptance."[22] In some modern armies, this process might be manifested as doctrine.

For those who have direct experience of military planning and active service in limited operations—as quite a few of those attending this conference did—Liddell Hart's optimism seems closer to denial than reality. Very likely, every one of them could recount an episode in their own experience in which "prerational" thinking suppressed informed professional judgment.[23] In my own experience, the answer to Liddell Hart's question comes down to two reasons: ignorance and the kind of arrogance Douglas Pike described so well. The first of these is certainly correctable. The second is, finally and regrettably, as close to a historical constant as anyone is ever likely to isolate. For a modern army with much to do, the only possible corrective is to learn how to learn from itself.

Notes

1. John Keegan, *The Face of Battle* (New York: Viking Press, 1976), 16. "For there is a fundamental difference between the sort of sporadic, small-scale fighting which is the small change of soldiering and the sort we characterize as battle."

2. Author's conference notes. Oral interview with Dr. Lawrence Yates during general discussion on "Intervention and Peacekeeping in Panama and Bosnia."

3. The exceptions are few and important. The classic study of these forms of operation is Colonel C.E. Callwell, *Small Wars: A Tactical Textbook for Imperial Soldiers* (London: Grenhill Books, 1990; orig. London: Her Majesty's Stationery Office, 1899); Frank Kitson, *Low Intensity Operations: Subversion, Insurgency, Peace-Keeping* (Hamden, CT: Archon Books, 1971;orig. London: Faber and Faber Ltd., 1971), to name two.

4. This was exactly the argument posed by France's leading colonial soldiers of the 19th century and no small number of American soldiers. See Douglas Porch's discussion of France's "colonial school" of soldiering in "Bugeaud, Galliene, Lyautey: The Development of French Colonial Warfare," *The Makers of Modern Strategy From Machiavelli to the Nuclear Age*, Peter Paret, ed. (Princeton, NJ: Princeton University Press, 1986), especially 403-404. See also Perry Jamieson, *Crossing the Deadly Ground: U. S. Army Tactics, 1865-1899* (Tuscaloosa, AL: University of Alabama Press, 1994), especially 36-53; Robert Wooster, *The Military and United States Indian Policy, 1865-1903* (New Haven, CT: Yale University Press, 1988), 136-41.

5. *Ibid.*, the phrase is Porch's.

6. Jamieson, 37.

7. Attack Indian villages in winter, kill the ponies and the buffalo, use converging columns, use Indian auxiliaries but do not ever trust them, use firepower as a substitute for ingenuity, and so on. See *ibid.*, p. 36 and following.

8. See Andrew Birtle, *US Army Counterinsurgency and Contingency Operations, 1860-1941*(Washington, DC: US Army Center of Military History [CMH], 1998), vii.

9. Add to the American experience that of the French, British, and Russian armies, to name only three of the most prominent modern expeditionary armies, and there is no reason for military theory and doctrine in this field to remain dormant.

10. Barry M. Blechman and Stephen S. Kaplan, *Force Without War: U. S. Armed Forces as a Political Instrument* (Washington, DC: Brookings Institution, 1978), 16.

11. Barry M. Blechman and Tamara Cofman Wittes, "Defining Moment: The Threat and Use of Force in American Foreign Policy," *Political Science Quarterly* (Spring 1999), 2. Accessed at <http://web8.epnet.com> 2 September 2003. The criteria used in this account appear to have been a good deal less rigorous than Blechman and Kaplan's earlier accounting. Here, Blechman would include very small-scale missions such as the Army's relatively well-known 55-man "mission training team" deployed to El Salvador in the 1980s.

12. See Major Jeffrey Stamp's essay in this volume, "Lost in the Snow: The US Intervention in Siberia During the Russian Revolution."

13. One may see this phenomenon in virtually every intervention mentioned in this volume.

14. Removing US forces following the "Black Hawk down" disaster in Mogadishu may be taken as a case of mission contraction, but this instance is more correctly seen as mission failure. The same may be said of another case not discussed in this volume, the bombing of the US Marine

barracks in Beirut in 1983. But, again, this tragedy seems to have come about because the marines' mission expanded in the eyes of their enemies. The US Marines' subsequent withdrawal from Lebanon, therefore, could also be seen as the result of mission expansion.

15. In this volume, see especially Irving Levinson, "Occupation and Stability Dilemmas of the Mexican War: Origins and Solutions"; J.G. Dawson, "Reconstruction as Nation Building: The US Army in the South"; Robert Wooster, "The Frontier Army and the Occupation of the West"; and Robert S. Cameron, "US Constabulary Activities in Postwar Germany."

16. See Brian Linn, "The US Army, Nation Building, and Pacification in the Philippines," in this volume. The reconstitution of the German army into pockets of guerrilla resistance was an important early concern in planning for the Allied occupation of Germany. See Robert S. Cameron, "US Constabulary Activities in Postwar Germany," in this volume.

17. The occupation of both Germany and Japan are important exceptions. However, these occupations accomplished something less than their promoters claimed at the time, and a distinct line was drawn between military government and "nation building" as the term is used presently.

18. Douglas Pike, "Conduct of the Vietnam War: Strategic Factors, 1965-1968," *The Second Indochina War: Proceedings of a Symposium Held at Arlie, Virginia, 7-9 November 1984* (Washington, DC: CMH, 1986), 99-116; see especially 110-11.

19. Ibid. Two classic works offer the depth and texture of modern organizational theory to Pike and Huxley's interpretation of "vincible ignorance." See Graham T. Allison, *The Essence of Decision: Explaining the Cuban Missile Crisis* (Boston: Little Brown, 1971); Irving L. Janis, *Victims of Groupthink* (Boston: Houghton Mifflin, 1982).

20. Diane Vaughan's study of the *Challenger* disaster is more forthright: "routine and taken-for-granted aspects of organizational life . . . created a way of seeing that was simultaneously a way of not seeing." See Diane Vaughan, *The Challenger Launch Decision: Risky Technology, Culture, and Deviance at NASA* (Chicago: University of Chicago Press, 1997), 394.

21. Ibid., 389 and following; *Columbia Accident Investigation Board Report,* vol. 1 (Washington, DC: Columbia Accident Investigation Board Limited First Printing, August 2003), especially 121-70, <www.caib.us/news/report/default.html> accessed 26 August 2003.

22. B.H. Liddell Hart, *Why Don't We Learn From History?* (New York: Hawthorne Books, Inc., 1971; orig. London: Allen & Unwin, 1944): 70.

23. The term is Diane Vaughan's.

About the Presenters

Bianka J. Adams was born and raised in Germany and received her master's degree in political science from the Christian-Albrechts University in Kiel, Germany. After emigrating to the United States, she attended the Catholic University of America in Washington, DC, and earned her Ph.D. in US diplomatic history. Dr. Adams is presently a historian with the US Army Center of Military (CMH), Fort McNair, Washington, DC.

Robert S. Cameron received a Ph.D. from Temple University. He is currently the Army's Armor Historian, Fort Knox, Kentucky. His focus lies in documenting developments related to the Stryker Brigade combat team and the unit of action/future combat system. His studies and publications have addressed historical trends in tank design, the related combat development processes, and urban warfare training at Fort Knox. He recently completed a staff ride handbook for the battle of Perryville, Kentucky, and has a forthcoming article, "Building on a Heritage of Success: The 4th Armored Division's Arracourt Legacy and Army Transformation" in *Military Review*. The presentation made during this conference is part of a larger, ongoing study focusing on the experience and effectiveness of the US constabulary in postwar Germany.

Donald B. Connelly, Ph.D. is a retired US Army military intelligence officer and former military history instructor with the Combat Studies Institute, US Army Command and General Staff College (CGSC), Fort Leavenworth, Kansas. He has recently completed his Ph.D. in history at the University of Houston. His dissertation, "Political Soldier: John M. Schofield and the Politics of Generalship," is undergoing revision for the University of North Carolina Press.

Joseph G. Dawson III, Ph.D., Professor of History, Texas A&M, was educated at Louisiana State University, earning his B.A. in history in 1967, his M.A. in 1970, and his Ph.D. in 1978. He served in the US Army in 1970-1971. He has been a faculty member at Louisiana State University at Eunice, Texas A&M University at Galveston, and Texas A&M University at College Station. In College Station, he was Director of the Military Studies Institute from 1986-2000 and promoted to professor in 2000. He is the author of *Army Generals and Reconstruction: Louisiana, 1862-1877* and *Doniphan's Epic March*. He has addressed aspects of the US military in the 19th century in an article in the *Journal of Military History* (1998) and in an essay dealing with post-Civil War developments in the *Encyclopedia of the American Military* (1994), John Jessup, ed.

Kevin W. Farrell, Lieutenant Colonel, US Army, holds an M.A. from Columbia University in modern European history, an M.Phil. from Columbia University, and a Ph.D. in modern European history from Columbia University. LTC Farrell graduated from the US Military Academy (USMA), West Point. He is a career armor officer currently slated to take command of 1-64 Armor, 3d Infantry Division, Fort Stewart, Georgia in 2004. His operational deployments include operations officer for Task Force 1-77 Armor, Kosovo, and adviser to the Afghan National Army, Kabul, Afghanistan. LTC Farrell currently serves as the chief, Research and Publication Team, CSI.

Richard L. Kiper earned his Ph.D. in history at the University of Kansas. He previously served as an officer in Special Forces, airborne, and infantry units stateside and overseas. He also served on the Army Staff and was an instructor at the USMA and at the

CGSC. He earned a Combat Infantryman Badge and Purple Heart in Vietnam, where he served as an infantry company commander and in the 5th Special Forces Group. He is the author of *Major General John Alexander McClernand: Politician in Uniform* that received the Fletcher Pratt Award for best nonfiction Civil War book in 1999. He also edited *Dear Catharine, Dear Taylor: The Civil War Letters of a Union Soldier and His Wife* published in 2002. He coauthored *Weapon of Choice: Army Special Operations in Afghanistan* to be published in 2004. Dr. Kiper teaches history at Kansas City Kansas Community College.

Irving Levinson received his Ph.D. in Latin American history from the University of Houston (2003). Other graduate degrees include an M.A. from the University of Houston (1997) and an M.B.A. from Temple University (1977). Before beginning his new career as a historian, he worked for 17 years in human resources management. Much of the research for this TRADOC presentation was funded by a Fulbright grant. In addition to his teaching duties, Dr. Levinson works as a consulting historian.

Brian McAllister Linn is a graduate of the University of Hawaii. He received his master's and doctorate degrees from the Ohio State University. He is currently Professor of History and Director of the Military Studies Institute at Texas A&M University. He is the author of *Guardians of Empire* and *The Philippine War, 1899-1902*, both of which were selected by the History Book Club and received the Society for Military History's Distinguished Book Award. His article, "The American War of War Revisited," *Journal of Military History*, was awarded a Moncado Prize in 2003. He has been an Olin Fellow at Yale University, a Hoover Fellow at Stanford University, and the Harold K. Johnson Visiting Professor of History at the US Army War College. He received a John Simon Guggenheim Memorial Foundation Fellowship for 2003-2004 to research a project titled "War in American Military Thought."

Katherine K. Reist is an associate professor of history and department head at the University of Pittsburgh, Johnstown, Pennsylvania. Specializing in East Asian history, her research focuses on the American military in China in the first half of the 20th century.

Roger J. Spiller served in the US Air Force from 1962 to 1965. He holds a B.A. in English literature and international relations and an M.A. in history from Southwest Texas State University. He received a Ph.D. in history at Louisiana State University. In 1978, he took a visiting associate professorship in military history at CGSC, where he became one of the founding members of CSI. He is currently the George C. Marshall Professor of History at CGSC. His most recent book is *Sharp Corners: Urban Operations at Century's End*. His first work of fiction, *In War Time*, will be published by Random House. Dr. Spiller is a contributing editor to *American Heritage* magazine and a member of the Board of Trustees of the Society for Military History.

Jeffrey W. Stamp, Major, US Air Force, received a B.S. from the US Air Force Academy in 1992 and an M.A. in military history from the University of Alabama in 1998. He has held a number of active duty postings around the world, from the wing level to the unified command staff. Major Stamp has taught history at the US Air Force Academy since 2001 and specializes in the history of unconventional warfare and the small wars of the late 19th and early 20th centuries.

Richard W. Stewart received a Ph.D. from Yale University. He was previously the command historian, US Army Special Operations Command, Fort Bragg, North Carolina, and historian, Center for Army Lessons Learned, Fort Leavenworth, Kansas. He is a retired colonel in military intelligence in the US Army Reserve with 30 years of commissioned service and a graduate of CGSC. He has deployed to theaters of operations as a combat historian during Operations DESERT STORM; UNOSOM II (Somalia), where he supported Task Force Ranger; MAINTAIN/RESTORE DEMOCRACY (Haiti); JOINT FORCE (Bosnia); and ENDURING FREEDOM (Afghanistan and Uzbekistan), where he was supporting special operations forces. He has conducted more than 600 oral history interviews in garrison and combat environments and has authored extensive publications on military history. Dr. Stewart is currently chief, Histories Division, CMH.

William Stivers earned a Ph.D. in international relations history from the Johns Hopkins University. He has held teaching posts at the University of California, Santa Cruz; the Colorado College; the University of Southern California's international relations graduate program in Germany; and the Martin Luther University in Halle, Sachsen-Anhalt. From 1986-1990, he worked as historian, G5, US Command, Berlin. He came to CMH in 1998 and has just returned from a three-year posting at the George C. Marshall Center in Garmisch, Germany. He has published books and articles dealing with Anglo-American relations in the 1920s, US Middle East policy, and postwar German history. He is currently working on a book dealing with the US occupation of Berlin during the military government period, 1945-1949.

Robert Wooster received his Ph.D. in 1985 from the University of Texas and joined the faculty at Texas A&M University, Corpus Christi the following year. He chaired the Department of Humanities from 1997-2000 and was named a Piper Professor for his distinguished teaching in 1998. His scholarly books on military history include *Soldiers, Sutlers, and Settlers: Garrison Life on the Texas Frontier*, *The Military and United States Indian Policy, 1865-1903*, *Nelson A. Miles and the Twilight of the Frontier Army*, and his forthcoming book *Soldier, Surgeon, Scholar, the Memoirs of William Henry Corbusier, 1844-1930*.

Appendix A. Program

Day 1

Tuesday, 5 August 2003

0630-0730   Breakfast at Conference Center

0745-0800   Opening Remarks

Session 1

0800-0945   *Mid 19th-Century Irregular Warfare, Stability Operations, and Nation Building (Mexican War, Civil War, and Reconstruction)*

"Occupation and Stability Dilemmas of the Mexico War: Origins and Solutions"
Dr. Irving W. Levinson
University of Houston

"General Order 11 and the Politics of War in the Department of the Missouri"
Dr. Donald B. Connelly
University of Houston

"Reconstruction as Nation Building: The U.S. Army in the South"
Prof. Joseph G. Dawson III
Texas A&M University, College Station

Panelist

Dr. James B. Martin
Friends University

Moderator

Dr. Curtis S. King
Combat Studies Institute

Session 2

1000-1145   *Late 19th-Century Irregular Warfare, Stability Operations, and Nation Building (American West and the Philippines)*

"The Frontier Army and the Occupation of the West"
Prof. Robert Wooster
Texas A&M University, Corpus Christi

"The U.S. Army and Nation Building and Pacification in the Philippines"
Prof. Brian McAllister Linn
Texas A&M University, College Station

Panelist

Mr. Richard E. Killblane
U.S. Army Transportation Corps

Moderator

Dr. Lawrence A. Yates
Combat Studies Institute

1200-1300 Lunch at Conference Center

Session 3

1300-1445 *Early 20th-Century Intervention (Russia and China)*

"Lost in the Snow: The U.S. Intervention in Siberia During the Russian Revolution"
MAJ Jeffrey Stamp, U.S. Air Force
U.S. Air Force Academy

"State Department Soldiers: Warlords, Nationalists, and Intervention"
Prof. Katherine K. Reist
University of Pittsburgh

Panelist

Dr. Andrew J. Birtle
U.S. Army Center of Military History

Moderator

Dr. Lawrence A. Yates
Combat Studies Institute

Session 4

1500-1645 *Occupation (Post-World War II Germany)*

"U.S. Constabulary Activities in Postwar Germany"
Dr. Robert S. Cameron
U.S. Army Armor School

"Reconstructing the Civil Administration of Bremen, U.S. Enclave"
Dr. Bianka J. Adams
U.S. Army Center of Military History

"Americans and Berliners in Germany's *Stunde Null*"
Dr. William Stivers
U.S. Army Center of Military History

Panelist

Dr. Boyd L. Dastrup
U.S. Army Field Artillery Center and Fort Sill

Moderator

Prof. Theodore A. Wilson
University of Kansas

Day 2

Wednesday, 6 August 2003

0645-0745   Breakfast at Conference Center

Session 1

0800-0945   *Modern Irregular Warfare (Korea, Vietnam, and Latin America)*

"Ps, Gs, and UW—Partisan Operations in the Korean War"
Dr. Richard L. Kiper
Kansas City Kansas Community College

"Special Forces: Counterinsurgency Era From Vietnam to El Salvador"
Prof. John Waghelstein
U.S. Naval War College

Panelist

Mr. Cecil Bailey
Consultant

Moderator

Prof. Geoff Babb
U.S. Army Command and General Staff College

Session 2

1000-1145 *Intervention and Peacekeeping (Panama and Bosnia)*

"The Transition From Combat to Nation Building in Panama"
Dr. Lawrence A. Yates
Combat Studies Institute

"The United States in Bosnia"
Dr. Robert F. Baumann
U.S. Army Command and General Staff College

Panelist

Dr. Curtis S. King
Combat Studies Institute

Moderator

LTC Kevin W. Farrell, U.S. Army
Combat Studies Institute

1200-1300 Lunch at Conference Center

Session 3

1300-1445 *Nation Building (Somalia)*

"UNOSOM II: Nation Building in Somalia"
LTG Thomas Montgomery
U.S. Army (Retired)

Panelists

Mr. Thomas Daze
U.S. Army Command and General Staff College

Mr. Brooks Lyles
Contractor

Moderator

Dr. Robert F. Baumann
U.S. Army Command and General Staff College

Session 4

1500-1645 *Historical Tour of Fort Leavenworth*

Tour Guide

Mr. Kelvin Crow
Combined Arms Center Command History Office

Day 3

Thursday, 7 August 2003

0645-0745   Breakfast at Conference Center

Session 1

0800-0945   *Afghanistan and the Global War on Terrorism*

"U.S. Army Special Forces in Afghanistan, October 2001-March 2002"
Dr. Richard W. Stewart
U.S. Army Center of Military History

"To Succeed Where Others Have Failed: Forming and Training the Afghan National Army"
LTC Kevin W. Farrell, U.S. Army
Combat Studies Institute

Panelist

Dr. Charles H. Briscoe
U.S. Army Special Operations Command

Moderator

Dr. Robert F. Baumann
U.S. Army Command and General Staff College

Session 2

1000-1145   *Operation IRAQI FREEDOM*

"Organization for Combat Historical Coverage of Operation IRAQI FREEDOM"
COL Donald W. Warner, U.S. Army
U.S. Army Center of Military History

"Military Operations During Operation IRAQI FREEDOM"
MAJ William Story, U.S. Army
Combined Forces Land Component Command History

"Logistics: Gulf War I and II"
Dr. Gary Trogdon
U.S. Army Center of Military History

"Occupations: Then and Now"
Dr. Richard W. Stewart
U.S. Army Center of Military History

Moderator

COL Donald W. Warner

1200-1300	Lunch at Conference Center

Session 3

1300-1445	*Overview and Closing Remarks*

Dr. Roger J. Spiller
U.S. Army Command and General Staff College

www.ingramcontent.com/pod-product-compliance
Lightning Source LLC
Chambersburg PA
CBHW080439170426
43195CB00017B/2818